Wales in England, 1914–1945

Wales in England, 1914–1945

A Social, Cultural, and Military History

WENDY UGOLINI

Great Clarendon Street, Oxford, OX2 6DP,
United Kingdom

Oxford University Press is a department of the University of Oxford.
It furthers the University's objective of excellence in research, scholarship,
and education by publishing worldwide. Oxford is a registered trade mark of
Oxford University Press in the UK and in certain other countries

© Wendy Ugolini 2024

The moral rights of the author have been asserted

All rights reserved. No part of this publication may be reproduced, stored in
a retrieval system, or transmitted, in any form or by any means, without the
prior permission in writing of Oxford University Press, or as expressly permitted
by law, by licence or under terms agreed with the appropriate reprographics
rights organization. Enquiries concerning reproduction outside the scope of the
above should be sent to the Rights Department, Oxford University Press, at the
address above

You must not circulate this work in any other form
and you must impose this same condition on any acquirer

Published in the United States of America by Oxford University Press
198 Madison Avenue, New York, NY 10016, United States of America

British Library Cataloguing in Publication Data
Data available

Library of Congress Control Number: 2023950909

ISBN 978–0–19–886327–4

DOI: 10.1093/oso/9780198863274.001.0001

Printed and bound in the UK by
Clays Ltd, Elcograf S.p.A.

Links to third party websites are provided by Oxford in good faith and
for information only. Oxford disclaims any responsibility for the materials
contained in any third party website referenced in this work.

In loving memory of my parents

Mike Herbertson (1940–2012) and Val Herbertson (1940–2020)

Acknowledgements

This book has been a labour of love, extended unexpectedly by the outbreak of the covid-19 pandemic, enriched by a wide range of archives, and sustained by the support of many people along the way. I am very grateful for the assistance and expertise of archivists and librarians at Bangor University Library, the Bodleian Library, BBC Written Archives Centre (WAC), the British Library, Cardiff University Special Collections and Archives (CUSCA), the Churchill Archives Centre, Cambridge (CAC), the Friends Library, London, the Gladstone Library, Hawarden, the Harry Ransom Center, University of Texas at Austin, the Imperial War Museum, John Rylands Special Collections, Manchester, King's College, Cambridge, the Liddell Hart Centre for Military Archives, King's College, London, Liverpool Record Office, the National Archives, the National Library of Wales (NLW), the UK Parliamentary Archives, the Rex Whistler Archive, Salisbury Museum, the Royal Artillery Museum, St John's College Library, Oxford (SJC), Suffolk Regiment Museum, the Tank Museum, the V & A's Theatre and Performance Archives, and the Welsh Guards Archive. Particular thanks and appreciation go to the late Sam Perry and the Archive Group at Shrewsbury House Youth Club—'The Shewsy'—in Everton, Liverpool. This youth and community centre, founded in 1903 as part of the philanthropic public school mission movement by Shrewsbury School, still flourishes and runs a full programme of activities for young people living locally. Its Archive Group, run by a group of volunteers, has done an amazing job in preserving and transcribing a significant archive of Second World War material relating to their 'Old Boys', making it accessible for external researchers. It was an absolute pleasure to work with them. I would also like to extend my thanks to John Hutchison for permission to cite this material.

For their helpful advice and guidance, I would especially like to thank Alison Harvey at CUSCA, Iwan ap Dafydd at NLW, Katharine Thomson at CAC, Radhika Jones at SJC, Louise North at WAC, and Mary Stewart, Cai Parry-Jones, and Rob Perks at the British Library Sound Archive. Numerous individuals kindly provided documents, images, and personal insights, including Andrew Fetherston, the Commonwealth War Graves Commission Archive, Owen Humphrys on behalf of the Wavell Estate, Kay Jones, at the Museum of Liverpool, James Maynard at the University of Buffalo Libraries, Gareth Sandham, National Trust Powis Castle, Dr Non Vaughan-O'Hagan, the former CEO at the London Welsh Centre, Stephen Walton, Imperial War Museum Duxford, Stuart Allan, James Ford, James Holland, Gemma Jones, Andy Merriman, David Owen, Keith

Roberts, Emma Smith, Guy Woodward, and Sgt E Maslen at the Welsh Guards Archive, who also gave me an impromptu tour of Rex Whistler's paintings at the Regimental HQ. I would also like to acknowledge the importance of two major online resources which I used for my research, *Cymru 1914—The Welsh Experience of First World War* and *Welsh Newspapers Online*.

I am indebted to the late Enid Martin-Jones and Emily Gwynne-Jones who generously agreed to be interviewed as part of this project. For permission to cite family papers and documents, I would like to thank David Clement-Davies, Mark Crawshay-Williams, Celia Denney, Lyn Jones and family, Mary-Lynne Jones, Jenny Kassman, Sue Llewellyn, the Estate of Selwyn Lloyd, Julia Maxted, Amanda Royde-Smith, Susanna Taylor, and the copyright holder of O. E. Roberts's Papers. Williams Graves has been incredibly supportive in allowing usage of material from the Robert Graves Papers held at St John's College; the Robert Graves Copyright Trust is currently undertaking the invaluable task of digitizing this material to make it more widely available. Thanks to the Estate of David Jones for permission to cite material held at the National Library of Wales. Finally, thanks to David Asprey for generously sharing his unpublished memoir of childhood, genealogical notes and, via email, his invaluable insights on his cousin, Richard Llewellyn's family history. It was a privilege to have these conversations.

Thanks to the Edinburgh Welsh Society for providing a translation of material from the OE Roberts's Undeb Cymru Fydd Papers held at Bangor University. I am also grateful to Tate Images, Bridgeman Images on behalf of the Estate of Augustus John, the National Archives, the National Library of Wales, and National Museums Liverpool for permission to reproduce images held in their collections, in addition to the generosity of David Asprey, the Estate of Selwyn Lloyd and the Robert Graves Copyright Trust for allowing me to publish family photographs. This book includes material which first appeared in Ugolini, W. (2019). The 'Welsh' Pimpernel: Richard Llewellyn and the Search for Authenticity in Second World War Britain. *Cultural & Social History*, 16(2) © The Social History Society, reprinted by permission of Taylor & Francis Ltd, http://www.tandfonline.com on behalf of The Social History Society. Thanks to Cambridge University Press for permission to reproduce material which appeared within: Ugolini, W. (2021). 'The Band of Brothers': The Mobilization of English Welsh Dual Identities in Second World War Britain. *Journal of British Studies*, 60(4), 822–847. © The Author(s), published by Cambridge University Press. I have been fortunate to work with wonderful colleagues at Oxford University Press and, in particular, would like to thank Stephanie Ireland, Cathryn Steele, and Imogene Haslam for their encouragement and advice. Every effort has been made to trace and contact all copyright owners; if there are any inadvertent omissions, the publishers will be pleased to correct these at the earliest opportunity.

When embarking on the initial research for this project I benefited from the advice and immense generosity of my former PhD supervisor at the University of

Edinburgh, Maggie Mackay. I am pleased to acknowledge the award of a Travelling Scholarship from Newnham College, Cambridge and the generous financial support of the School of History, Classics & Archaeology, University of Edinburgh. For the period 2021–2023, I co-managed the Second World War Network (Scotland), funded by the Royal Society of Edinburgh, with Professor Toby Kelly, which provided the opportunity to interact with inspiring Second World War scholars working across the globe.

Thanks and appreciation to Martin Johnes, University of Swansea, who was always willing to answer my queries, big and small, drawing upon his vast expertise in the history of Wales and the Welsh language. In producing the final work, thanks go to both Martin and Chris Williams, and the anonymous journal reviewers, for their insightful comments and supportive feedback on earlier draft journal articles. My gratitude extends to Stephen Bowd, Simon Brooks, Ewen Cameron, Trevor Griffiths, Charles Jenkins, Wendy Webster, and the anonymous readers at OUP for reading individual chapters and providing invaluable feedback. I also benefited from the thoughtful insights and expertise of Louise Jackson who provided feedback on Chapter 3. A particular acknowledgement goes to my brother-in-law, Charles Jenkins, for his thoughtful commentary and his willingness to answer my interminable queries on military and regimental matters. This book has also benefited significantly from feedback provided on invited talks and conference papers from colleagues at the Birmingham Centre for Modern and Contemporary History, the North American Association for the Study of Welsh Culture and History (NAASWCH), the Social History Society, the 'Formations and Representations of British National Identity' conference at Warwick, the 'Gendering Peace in Europe' conference at Sheffield, the Britain and the World conference at Exeter, the International Robert Graves Conference at Oxford, 'Redcoats, Tommies, and Dusty Warriors' at Leeds, the Celtic and Scottish Studies seminar, University of Edinburgh, and the reading group of the Second World War Research Group, North America.

I have been working on this book for a considerable amount of time and appreciate the friendship of wonderful colleagues at the University of Edinburgh during this period: Anna Groundwater (now at National Museums Scotland), Tereza Valny, Stephen Bowd, Angela Bartie, Martin Chick, Jeremy Crang, Rob Crowcroft, Gayle Davis, Kirsty Day, Trevor Griffiths, Lucy Grig, Megan Hunt, Louise Jackson, David Kaufman, Toby Kelly, Katey Lee, Stephen McDowall, Esther Mijers, Stana Nenadic, and Meha Priyadarshini. Undertaking fieldwork in Cambridge also enabled me to renew my acquaintanceship with Gill Sutherland, my former Director of Studies at Newnham College, which has been a personal highlight of this research.

My grandfather's late cousin, Pat Hughes, of Bryn-y-Maen, responded with grace and generosity to the teenager who appeared on her doorstep many decades ago asking questions about family history, and, over the intervening years, kindly shared genealogical notes, papers and photographs. Thanks and much love to my husband Paul for bearing the brunt of the childcare during my numerous archive trips over many years and for always being there when I need him. At the start of my fieldwork, our two children, Alex and Holly, were schoolchildren and they are now gorgeous adults out in the world. I am immensely proud of them both. Finally, this book began as a homage to my late grandfather, John Herbertson, who appears regularly within the following pages, and ends as a dedication to my late parents, Mike and Val, who both died whilst I was researching and writing this book. They set an example to me as parents—loving, generous, and supportive—which I can only hope to replicate in my own life.

Contents

List of Illustrations	xiii
List of Abbreviations	xv
Introduction	1

PART ONE INVENTING AND ENCOUNTERING

1. Elite Identities	33
2. Welshburbia: Welshness in the English Suburbs	59
3. Narrating and Encountering Wales	84

PART TWO REGIMENTING AND MOBILIZING

4. First World War Identities	117
5. Second World War Identities	140
6. Mourning and Memorializing	172

PART THREE CREATING AND FAKING

7. Imagining Wales from England	195
8. Constructing Wales as a Site of Solace	222
9. Welshness as Masquerade	245
Conclusion	272

Bibliography	281
Index	287

List of Illustrations

1.1 Selwyn Lloyd pictured directly at Lloyd George's right shoulder, Cambridge 1927. 44
Source: Churchill Archives Centre; SE11/20. Reproduced with permission of the Estate of Selwyn Lloyd.

3.1 John Herbertson, seated on the left of the picture, with his younger siblings and their Welsh mother, Annie, in front of their home at 138 Delamore Street, Liverpool, *c.* 1922. 94

5.1 Members of the 46th Battalion (Liverpool Welsh) Royal Tank Regiment, Everton, Liverpool. 149
Reproduced with permission of Shrewsbury House Archive, Liverpool.

5.2 Temporary wooden crosses marking the graves of Mary and Geraint Clement Davies, Meifod Parish Churchyard. 164
Source: National Library of Wales; S/5/82.

6.1 'The Recording Angel'. Houses of Parliament, The Memorial, pen, pencil and watercolour on paper by Charles Terry Pledge, *c.* 1921. 173
Source: The National Archives; WORK29/3364 (Detail).

6.2 Park Road Welsh Congregational Chapel font with names of chapel members killed during the Second World War. 190
Source: National Museums Liverpool; MOL.2011.37.1.

7.1 Augustus John, 'Lyric Fantasy', *c.* 1913–14. 198
Reproduced with permission of Tate Images and the Estate of Augustus John.

8.1 Portrait of David Graves taken during his service with the Royal Welch Fusiliers. 237
Reproduced with permission of William Graves and The Robert Graves Copyright Trust.

9.1 Childhood portrait of Richard Llewellyn, on the left of the picture, with his siblings Gladys, Lorna, and Trevor, London. 252
Reproduced with permission of David Asprey.

List of Abbreviations

AA	Anti-Aircraft
ATS	Auxiliary Territorial Service
GTAT	Goodbye To All That
HGWMY	How Green Was My Valley
ODNB	Oxford Dictionary of National Biography
RTR	Royal Tank Regiment
RWF	Royal Welch Fusiliers
SWB	South Wales Borderers
THGLM	The Happy-Go-Lucky Morgans

Introduction

In September 1939, a wood engraver turned land girl, Gwenda Morgan, strode out across the West Sussex hayfields in the company of her pet terrier. Morgan's art and life were immersed in, and sustained by, the 'rolling Sussex countryside'.[1] Yet, the dog who accompanied her on these early morning walks was named Cymru, a signal that even within this most English of landscapes, Wales and Welshness mattered.[2] Morgan was one of many cultural figures of the twentieth century who were born in England but had familial ties with Wales, in her case, through her paternal grandfather. This book unearths a vast array of English people with parental, ancestral, diasporic, affinity, affective, and elective connections with Wales in the first half of the twentieth century who interacted with and identified with Wales in a variety of ways and for whom a sense of 'Welshness' held *meaning*. It considers the ways in which Welshness was imagined, performed, and self-fashioned in England in the first half of the twentieth century and argues that this diasporic construction of Welshness held a wide urban appeal, which had significant implications for military enlistment, cultural production, suburban transculturality, and commemorative practices. In particular, it addresses the heightened expression of dual identifications with both England and Wales during the two world wars, making use of individual English Welsh case studies from the worlds of art, literature, politics, and soldiering to provide a wholly new perspective on the social, cultural, and military history of Britain at war.

Katie Gramich notes that an important dimension of British studies is to explore the influence of Wales on England.[3] This book will explore how ideas and understandings of Wales and Welshness informed social, cultural, military, and political life in England. Overall, it will recover and reconstruct Welshness as a significant 'constitutive' part of English identity amongst thousands of descendants of Welsh settlers in English cities in the first half of the twentieth century.[4] Whilst recognizing the historical willingness of the English to primarily avow an Anglo-British identity, this book will argue that, for English men and women of

---

[1] John Randle, 'Gwenda Morgan Obituary', *The Independent*, 12 January 1991.
[2] Gwenda Morgan, *The Diary of a Land Girl* (Risbury, 2002), p. 2.
[3] Katie Gramich, 'Cymru or Wales?: Explorations in a Divided Sensibility', in *Studying British Cultures. An Introduction*, edited by Susan Bassnett (London, 1997), p. 117.
[4] Mo Moulton, *Ireland and the Irish in Interwar England* (Cambridge, 2014), p. 7.

Welsh origin, the idea of being in some part 'Welsh' both informed and reaffirmed their own understanding of what it meant to 'be British'.[5]

Following Linda Colley's seminal work on the forging of Britishness in the long eighteenth century, historians of modern Britain have largely worked with the idea of 'concentric rings of territorial identities' to locality, nation, and imperial state.[6] However, there is comparatively little historical work exploring how dual national identities are 'complexly interwoven' across and within constructions of Britishness.[7] Avtar Brah highlights how, within the 'diaspora space,' there is often a requirement for an individual to 'name an identity,' which then renders invisible 'all the other identities' available to them. She detects a deep-seated resistance to the idea of being *'both'*.[8] Bronwen Walter, in her analysis of second-generation Irish identity in late twentieth-century Britain endorses this idea, calling for more recognition of 'the possibility of *both/and* identities, rather than the *either/or* choices which characterize ideologies of assimilation and integration.'[9] This book embraces the idea of 'both' and aims to illuminate the functioning of English Welsh dual identifications as an important strand of pluralistic Britishness in the first half of the twentieth century.

As part of this undertaking, *Wales in England 1914–1945* seeks to recover and map 'chains of connection': the intricate interactions, interpersonal relations, and social networks operating between English individuals with Welsh connections stretching across the spheres of class, politics, culture, and the military in the first half of the twentieth century.[10] In part, it aims to reconstruct an 'ego-centred' or 'partial' network whereby 'individuals are identified and their direct and indirect links to others are traced' and will illuminate 'political ties, kinship obligations, friendship, or work relations,' which often functioned in a reciprocal fashion.[11] In many ways, these partial but elaborate networks mirror the characters of Anthony Powell's twentieth-century fictional masterpiece and their *Dance to the Music of Time*.[12] Kevin Kenny notes how the idea of diaspora 'can illuminate particular aspects of the world migration creates, revealing a dynamic range of patterns, connections and interactions.'[13] Above all, it involves communication 'among

---

[5] Michael Kenny, 'The Return of "Englishness" in British Political Culture—The End of the Unions?', *Journal of Common Market Studies*, 53, 1 (2015), pp. 35–51. doi.org/10.1111/jcms.12203.

[6] Linda Colley, *Britons: Forging the Nation, 1707–1837* (New Haven, 1992); T. C. Smout, 'Perspectives on the Scottish Identity', *Scottish Affairs*, vi (1994), p. 102.

[7] Bronwen Walter, Sarah Morgan, Mary J. Hickman, and Joseph M. Bradley, 'Family Stories, Public Silence: Irish Identity Construction Amongst the Second-generation Irish in England', *Scottish Geographical Journal*, 118, 3 (2002), p. 202. doi.org/10.1080/00369220218737147.

[8] Avtar Brah, *Cartographies of Diaspora. Contesting Identities* (London, 1996), p. 3.

[9] Bronwen Walter, 'English/Irish Hybridity: Second-generation Diasporic Identities', *International Journal of Diversity in Organisations*, 5, 7 (2005/6), p. 18. doi:10.18848/1447-9532/CGP/v05i07/39196.

[10] John Scott, *Social Network Analysis* (London, 2013), p. 14.   [11] Scott, *Social*, pp. 32–3.

[12] Hilary Spurling, *Invitation to the Dance: A Handbook to Anthony Powell's A Dance to the Music of Time* (London, 2005).

[13] Kevin Kenny, *Diaspora. A Very Short Introduction* (Oxford, 2013), pp. 14–15.

various overseas communities of common origin, conceived as nodes in a network or web.'[14] Kenny emphasizes that migrants and their offspring often use the idea of diaspora 'to make sense of their experience, to build communities, to express themselves culturally, and to mobilize politically.'[15] Addressing the late nineteenth and early twentieth centuries, John S. Ellis acknowledges the value that Welshness, in particular, had 'within the personal and institutional networks that helped connect the British world.'[16] This monograph will examine this phenomenon in depth in the context of English society during the two world wars; essentially, it aims to recapture what Santanu Das terms 'the experiential texture' of English Welsh lives in the period from 1914 to 1945.[17]

In addition, this book highlights the porosity of the borders between Wales and England: 'the permeability and instability of the extensive borderlands' between the two nations.[18] It explores how the personal identity construction of second- and third-generation Welsh men and women was informed by the regularity with which they travelled back and forward across these boundaries, shaping their narrations of self and articulations of an emotional commitment to both nations. In practical terms, these journeys could encompass working-class English children being sent to relatives in Wales when their mothers were in confinement, middle-class children having holidays in Wales and upper-class boys educated in the English public school system returning to Welsh family estates in their vacations, the bodies of dead expatriates being returned by rail from England to Wales for burial, English service personnel being stationed in Wales for training during both world wars, and the process of evacuation, involving adults as well as children, from England to Wales in the Second World War. In the course of a lifetime English men and women of Welsh origin could access Wales as a site of holidays, honeymoons, funerals, and retirement, creating an intricate web of lifelong interconnections. Furthermore, a 'return' movement back to Wales, latent since the late Victorian period, was reinvigorated during the Second World War when many older and wealthier members of the community elite prematurely retired to Wales and relative safety from aerial bombardment in English conurbations.[19] In the first three years of the Second World War, around 200,000 people also moved to Wales from England seeking some form of 'refuge', including members of the diaspora.[20]

---

[14] Kenny, *Diaspora*, p. 13.   [15] Kenny, *Diaspora*, p. 14.
[16] John S. Ellis, 'Making Owen Rhoscomyl (1863–1919): Biography, Welsh Identity and the British World', *Welsh History Review*, 26, 3 (2013), p. 501.
[17] Santanu Das, *India, Empire, and First World War Culture. Writings, Images, and Songs* (Cambridge, 2018), p. 23.
[18] Kirsti Bohata, *Postcolonialism Revisited* (Cardiff, 2004), p. 7.
[19] Colin G. Pooley, 'Welsh Migration to England in the Mid-nineteenth Century', *Journal of Historical Geography*, 9, 3 (1983), p. 287. doi.org/10.1016/0305-7488(83)90184-6.
[20] Martin Johnes, *Wales Since 1939* (Manchester, 2012), p. 11.

The Historical Relationship between England and Wales

The close historical relationship between England and Wales has deep roots: Martin Johnes emphasizes how 'wars, religion and Empire created powerful common experiences and emotional bonds' between the two nations.[21] Since the time of incorporation, as Gwynfor Jones demonstrates, the Tudors and Stuarts used aspects of Welsh identity to confer a sense of antiquity and heritage on their rule and to foster a sense of common citizenship between England and Wales.[22] The Tudor Settlement (1536–43) emphasized existing interrelationships and interdependency and facilitated 'administrative and legal unity' between England and Wales.[23] Chris Williams confirms the 'level of interconnectedness' between the two nations following the Acts of Union: the English system of local government was extended to Wales, Wales sent Members of Parliament to Westminster and, with one exception, Welsh people acquired equal status with the English under English law.[24] After the Acts of Union all legislation that applied to England applied also to Wales and, thus, Williams notes, 'Wales became a junior partner in the expanding British state'.[25] From the mid-sixteenth to the late eighteenth centuries, 'A high degree of cultural dissimilarity coexisted equally'.[26] Indeed, Krishan Kumar cites Philip Jenkins's observation that whilst seventeenth- and eighteenth-century Wales was 'perhaps the most thoroughly "other" and "Celtic" society in the British Isles', it was also 'so assimilated in political terms as to be essentially indistinguishable from any English region'.[27] Donald M. MacRaild and Philip Payton note how, 'overwhelmingly, the Welsh subscribed to a Protestant identity, whether high-or-low church, Anglican or Dissenting, and their congruence with the religious tenets of British identity made the Welsh look, at face value at least, as the very epitome of Britishness'.[28] The work of Aled Jones and Bill Jones also makes clear the extent to which, by the nineteenth century, Wales was a willing participant in the British imperial project, both in terms of its industrial contribution and as part of a 'Welsh civilising mission'.[29] They note 'the increasingly close ties between Wales and the British Empire' from the

---

[21] Martin Johnes, *Wales: England's Colony?* (Cardigan, 2019), p. 4.
[22] Gwynfor Jones, *Early Modern Wales c. 1525–1640* (Basingstoke, 1994), pp. 75–90, 208–11.
[23] Jones, *Early*, p. 86.
[24] Chris Williams, 'Problematizing Wales: An Exploration in Historiography and Postcoloniality', in *Postcolonial Wales*, edited by Jane Aaron and Chris Williams (Cardiff, 2005), pp. 4–6.
[25] Williams, 'Problematizing', p. 5.
[26] Krishan Kumar, *The Making of English National Identity* (Cambridge, 2006), p. 138.
[27] Kumar, *Making*, p. 138.
[28] Donald M. MacRaild and Philip Payton, 'The Welsh Diaspora', in *British and Irish Diasporas. Societies, Cultures and Ideologies*, edited by Donald M. MacRaild, Tanja Bueltmann, and J. C. D. Clark (Manchester, 2019), p. 248.
[29] Aled Jones and Bill Jones, 'The Welsh World and the British Empire, c. 1851–1939: An Exploration', *Journal of Imperial & Commonwealth History*, 31, 2 (2003), p. 64. doi.org/10.1080/03086530310001705606. See also Williams, 'Problematizing', pp. 9, 11.

mid-nineteenth century onwards, which contributed to its representation as 'part of the metropolitan core of empire rather than a colonial dependency':

> During that period Wales's growing economic importance created by its dominant coal export sector, its greater political assertiveness, the founding of its own 'national' institutions such as the University of Wales, National Library and National Museum, the growth in the number of Welsh speakers, and the 'cultural renaissance' of Welsh-language literature, education, publishing and music took place within an accepted British Imperial framework.[30]

Daniel G. Williams agrees that, in the nineteenth century, the increasing emphasis on 'Britishness' was 'broadly welcomed by the Welsh who considered themselves to be lineal descendants of the ancient Britons'. At the same time, he suggests that the Welsh 'sought to take advantage of the British context to construct a highly respectable Welsh identity that could nevertheless be contrasted to Englishness.'[31] Matthew Cragoe concurs that from the 1850s onwards, amongst radical MPs representing Wales at Westminster, there was a growing conviction that 'Wales was a "nation of nonconformists" and, as such, morally superior to England'.[32]

A significant part of historiographical enquiry is dedicated to the question of whether Wales can be viewed as 'England's first colony'.[33] The medievalist, R. R. Davies, characterized Wales as displaying 'most of the well-recognized features of a colonial society'—military conquest and the establishment of alien political rule—from the period 1282 to 1400, ranging from Edward I's conquest of Gwynedd to the outbreak of the revolt of Owain Glyndŵr.[34] Chris Williams accepts that it is plausible to argue that before 1536, 'Wales stood in something of a colonial relationship to England', but not afterwards.[35] As well as the willing involvement by the Welsh in the British Empire, Williams points to 'the admiration of many Welsh people for England, English culture and the English language'[36] and underscores the need to 'locate Wales historically, in relation to the power exercised over it (primarily politically and economically but also culturally) by England, and in relation to other societies that were unambiguously "colonies" and part of the British Empire'.[37] In the most recent attempt at wrestling with this question, Johnes concludes that 'Medieval Wales was a colony through

---

[30] Jones and Jones, 'Welsh World', p. 57.
[31] Daniel G. Williams, *Ethnicity and Cultural Authority. From Arnold to Du Bois* (Edinburgh, 2006), p. 17.
[32] Matthew Cragoe, *Culture, Politics and National Identity in Wales 1832–1886* (Oxford, 2004), pp. 38–41.
[33] Jones and Jones, 'Welsh World', p. 57.
[34] R. R. Davies, 'Colonial Wales', *Past & Present*, 65 (1974), p. 3.
[35] Williams, 'Problematizing', p. 4. [36] Williams, 'Problematizing', p. 13.
[37] Williams, 'Problematizing', p. 4.

conquest, but modern Wales was British through choice rather than coercion.'[38] At the same time, Williams emphasizes that accepting that Wales has not been a colony of England since 1536 does not deny the 'lopsided nature' of the relationship between the two societies and some of the inequalities inherent within it.[39] One notorious moment of tension occurred in 1847 when the Royal Commission into the state of education in Wales not only commented on 'the backwardness and immorality of the people (especially the women)' but also attributed this to the influence of dissent and the Welsh language, arousing strong protest.[40] Whilst, the sense of outrage triggered by the 'Treason of the Blue Books' helped 'to assert and defend Welsh nationality and culture', it also underscored that points of divergence between the two nations remained.[41]

Thus, as Paul Ward acknowledges, by the early twentieth century, Wales 'was more culturally distinct and yet more politically integrated into the United Kingdom than Scotland', with the existence of two languages—in 1901, a recorded 50 per cent of the population could speak Welsh[42]—inherently making the idea of 'dual identities' more 'palpable'.[43] The closeness of the relationship between England and Wales was still being politically endorsed from Westminster by the time of the Second World War. For example, in a radio broadcast entitled 'St David's Day' on 28 February 1943, Welsh-born Gwilym Lloyd George, the then Minister of Fuel and Power, stated that 'the great strength of the British race' lay in its mixture of the characteristics of different races, 'Roman, Norman, Saxon, Scandinavian and Celt'. Lloyd George ruminated on how, after many generations, the 'bitterness' of past conflicts between Wales and England was now largely expressed via the medium of rugby played at Cardiff Arms Park or Twickenham, concluding that, 'we have proved that it is possible for nations to live in harmony without sacrificing their inheritance.'[44] These sentiments were reiterated in the 1944 film *The Halfway House*, set in a small hotel in Wales, where Mervyn Johns's character, Rhys, the landlord, articulates the closeness of the relationship to one of his wartime guests:

> No nation is conquered, sir, if it keeps its soul and its language as we've done. The English are our friends and our neighbours; we live at peace with them. Their enemies are our enemies and their war is our war. I'm proud of being a

---

[38] Johnes, *Wales: England's Colony?*, p. 4.   [39] Williams, 'Problematizing', p. 8.
[40] Prys Morgan, 'From a Death to a View: The Hunt for the Welsh Past in the Romantic Period', in *The Invention of Tradition*, edited by Eric Hobsbawm and Terence Ranger (Cambridge, 1992), p. 92.
[41] Williams, 'Problematizing', pp. 5–6.
[42] John Davies, *A History of Wales* (London, 1993), p. 496.
[43] Paul Ward, *Unionism in the United Kingdom, 1918–1974* (Basingstoke, 2005), p. 72. Ward also suggests that the experience of the Second World War and the establishment of the welfare state afterwards further confirmed the benefits of Britishness for Wales, p. 79.
[44] Parliamentary Archives; Lloyd George Papers; LG/I/3/2/36.

Welshman, sir, but I wouldn't put the betterment of Wales before the betterment of humanity.[45]

However, Jane Aaron and Chris Williams suggest that the idea of 'the creation of "transcultural" forms in the contact zone' between England and Wales may raise 'many awkward questions for Wales and the people of Wales'.[46] With increasingly powerful cultural and institutional assertions of Welsh nationhood in the latter half of the twentieth century, including the enactment of 'its first ever degree of democratic national self-government' in the shape of the National Assembly for Wales (now the Senedd) in 1999, there may be some ambivalence about acknowledging the once close alignment of Wales and England.[47] In an attempt to counter this cultural blind spot, this book aims to recover and reconstruct the functioning of English Welsh dual identities and subjectivities and the intimate socio-cultural interaction of English and Welsh identities in the first half of the twentieth century.

War as a Site of Identity Formation

Wales in England 1914–1945 sits at the intersection of three key historiographical areas: war studies, British studies, and diaspora studies. It is the first cultural history written about English Welsh duality as a lived identity in wartime. Judy Giles and Tim Middleton note how wars are 'obvious occasions when ideas about national identity become particularly visible'.[48] In the twentieth century, war forced people to think about what they were fighting for, thus reinforcing ideas of Britishness defined against enemies both abroad and at home.[49] Paul O' Leary points out that perceived external threats around the time of the Crimean War led to the emergence of a Volunteer Movement which, in turn, 'encouraged a closer

---

[45] *The Halfway House*, dir. Basil Dearden, 1944. This presented an inversion of the Welsh Nationalist Party's position which encouraged wide-scale resistance to military conscription on the grounds of resisting 'the demands of English militarism'. D. Hwyel Davies, *The Welsh Nationalist Party 1925–1945* (Cardiff, 1983), pp. 223–4.

[46] Jane Aaron and Chris Williams, 'Preface', in *Postcolonial Wales*, edited by Aaron and Williams, p. xvi.

[47] Johnes, *Wales: England's Colony?*, pp. 162–4; Johnes, *Wales Since*, p. 3; James Ford, 'The Art of Union and Disunion in the Houses of Parliament 1834–1928' (PhD dissertation, University of Nottingham, 2016), p. 63; Daniel G. Williams, *Wales Unchained. Literature, Politics and Identity in the American Century* (Cardiff, 2015).

[48] Judy Giles and Tim Middleton, *Writing Englishness: An Introductory Sourcebook* (London, 1995), p. 110.

[49] Max Jones, 'War and National Identity Since 1914', in *20th Century Britain: Economic, Cultural and Social Change*, edited by Francesca Carnevali and Julie-Marie Strange (London, 2007), p. 81.

bonding together of the different peoples of Britain'.[50] By the early twentieth century, as Ward points out, Britishness was an identity accepted, put together and lived by the majority of the people within the United Kingdom.[51] Kumar identifies the fundamental importance of the British Empire, a tightly knit British economy and industrial system, trade unionism and the Labour Party, and the BBC as buttressing a sense of Britishness within and across the borders of the United Kingdom.[52] In particular, the two world wars contributed to 'a sense of a shared fate that came to characterize the Welsh-English relationship'.[53] There is a consensus that the experience of fighting in the First World War had a cohesive effect on members of the constituent territories of Britain. Keith Robbins believes that, despite internal differences and rivalries, the Great War demonstrated that 'the "British nation" did exist'.[54] In relation to Wales, John Davies memorably suggests that 'By suffering alongside Geordies and Brummies, Cockneys and Scousers, Micks, Jocks and Aussies, the Taffs became part of a new brotherhood; to become a soldier was to assume a new nationality'.[55] Catriona Pennell's study, examining the response of the populations of England, Wales, Scotland, and Ireland to the outbreak of the First World War, confirms that men of military age from all four nations united behind the British war effort, arguing that 'the threat from Germany provoked a shift in national symbols and rites, and people became "United Kingdomers"'.[56] Angela Gaffney's analysis of First World War commemoration confirms that local memorialization in post-war Wales consistently situated loss within a wider British and imperial identity, providing evidence of 'a nation at ease with its own position within the British state and the empire'.[57] Johnes views the Second World War as a period which both promoted a heightened 'sense of Welshness' and reaffirmed the interconnectedness between Welsh and British identities.[58] However, whilst wartime exigencies created 'a new sense of a socially cohesive British identity', Sonya O. Rose argues that the drive for unity was also 'haunted by the spectre of division and difference', including

---

[50] Paul O'Leary, 'Arming the Citizens: the Volunteer Force in Nineteenth-century Wales', in *Wales and War. Society, Politics and Religion in the Nineteenth and Twentieth Centuries*, edited by Matthew Cragoe and Chris Williams (Cardiff, 2007), pp. 65–6.

[51] Paul Ward, *Britishness Since 1870* (London, 2004), p. 7. [52] Kumar, *Making*, pp. 235–7.

[53] 'English migration', BBC Wales History website (2008), http://www.bbc.co.uk/wales/history/sites/themes/society/migration_england.shtml, accessed 1 May 2019.

[54] Keith Robbins, *Nineteenth-Century Britain. England, Scotland, and Wales. The Making of a Nation* (Oxford, 1989), p. 174.

[55] Davies, *History*, p. 514.

[56] Catriona Pennell, *A Kingdom United: Popular Responses to the Outbreak of the First World War in Britain and Ireland* (Oxford, 2012), p. 228.

[57] Angela Gaffney, *Aftermath. Remembering the Great War in Wales* (Cardiff, 1998), p. 168. Gaffney argues that this trend continued after the Second World War where an individual who 'may have fought and died as a Welsh man or women' was commemorated 'as a British citizen'. Angela Gaffney, '"The Second Armageddon": Remembering the Second World War in Wales', in *Wales and War*, p. 195.

[58] Johnes, *Wales Since*, pp. 3, 29.

competing geographic identities.[59] She notes how, whilst it was necessary to depict Britain 'as a cultural, if not political "multi-nation" composed of four distinctive "national" cultures: Northern Ireland, Wales, Scotland, and England', there were inherent tensions within these official constructions.[60]

Against this historiographical backdrop, surprisingly little attention has been paid to the plurality of British identity in wartime or to how the existence of 'hybrid "dual identities"' within the constituent countries informed the functioning of Britishness during both world wars.[61] Whilst these major studies acknowledge plural identities, in the sense of a Welsh/British identification or an English/British identification, they do not take into consideration the range of dual identifications *across* two nations, for example a sense of *both* Welshness and Englishness. This book attempts to remedy this by reconstructing and recovering the lived wartime experience of the descended Welsh in England and highlighting the importance of dual identifications in their response to war. It presents case studies of men such as Liverpool-born John Herbertson, who, when he enrolled in the Home Guard in 1943, identified his mother as 'Welsh', his father as 'English', and himself as 'British', thus demonstrating how a sense of dual inheritances confirmed his own British status.[62] In particular, this book will focus on the raising of three 'hybrid' army regiments, exploring how both world wars provided a moment of galvanization for diasporic Welsh patriotism in both London and Liverpool which, in turn, illuminated the willingness of some English men to enlist on the basis of their Welsh antecedents. In the First World War this was expressed through the formation of the 15th (1st London Welsh) Battalion of the Royal Welch Fusiliers (RWF), which will be addressed in Chapter 4. In the Second World War this duality was performed via the establishment of two territorial units, the 99th (London Welsh) Heavy Anti-Aircraft Regiment and the 46th (Liverpool Welsh) Royal Tank Regiment, which will be analysed in Chapter 5. Daniel Travers and Ward have highlighted the need to adopt a 'four nations and more' approach to the history of the Second World War suggesting that the dominance of the reductive 'Churchillian paradigm' within public understanding of the conflicts risks masking 'the assertion of local, regional and national identities in wartime,' the diversity of the British Isles and its 'distinct subcultures'.[63] In this book, I demonstrate that English Welsh duality forms one of these overlooked 'subcultures'.

---

[59] Ward, *Britishness*, p. 124; Sonya O. Rose, *Which Peoples War? National Identity and Citizenship in Wartime Britain 1939–1945* (Oxford, 2006), p. 286.
[60] Rose, *Which?*, pp. 197–8.
[61] Thomas Hajkowski, *The BBC and National Identity in Britain, 1922–53* (Manchester, 2010), p. 2.
[62] Form of Enrolment in the Home Guard, 9 September 1943. In author's hands.
[63] Daniel Travers and Paul Ward, 'Narrating Britain's War: A "Four Nations and More" Approach to the People's War', in *The Long Aftermath. Cultural Legacies of Europe at War (1936–2016)*, edited by Manuel Braganca and Peter Tame (Oxford, 2016), p. 85.

The Welsh Diasporic Space in England

By the beginning of the twentieth century, 265,000 Welsh-born inhabitants lived in England, of whom 35,000 resided in London and 87,000 in the North West counties of Lancashire and Cheshire.[64] Their families and descendants contributed to the urban cosmopolitanism of major cities such as London and Liverpool.[65] Welsh migration to England had been steady throughout the nineteenth century and was significantly reinvigorated during the interwar Depression.[66] Davies notes that there was 'a huge outflow' of migrants from Wales to England in this period, with many settling in Oxford.[67] However, as most of these migrants came from the more 'anglicized' industrial regions of the south they 'were not as eager as their predecessors to create microcosms of Wales'.[68] It is worth noting that Welsh migration into England in the nineteenth century occurred against the backdrop of widely understood 'social hierarchies' which, as Steve Garner notes, 'created and maintained internal borders between the more and the less white'.[69] Whilst in Britain, migrant groups such as the Irish, Jews, and Italians could often be racialized as internal 'others', it could be argued that Welsh migrants, with their 'Protestant work ethic' and claims to respectability were perceived as 'more securely white'.[70] In particular, the Welsh were able to utilize prevailing 'constructions of whiteness' to position themselves favourably in comparison with the Irish who, in turn, were more vulnerable to racialized understandings of 'who' fitted 'where' in social hierarchies.[71] In areas of settlement such as Liverpool, this would often rest on the Welsh community's sense of their religious, political, and cultural 'superiority' to the more 'turbulent' Irish Catholic population.[72]

---

[64] Davies, *History*, p. 443.

[65] John Belchem and Donald M. MacRaild, 'Cosmopolitan Liverpool', in *Liverpool 800. Culture, Character & History*, edited by John Belchem (Liverpool, 2006).

[66] Davies, *History*, pp. 578–9. See a journalist's contemporary observation, 'Now the men of Glamorgan, thrown out of work by the industrial depression there, migrate in great hordes, to try their hand at building, or singing, or what you will...' Glyn Roberts, *I Take This City* (London, 1933), p. 105.

[67] Davies, *History*, pp. 578–9.

[68] Davies, *History*, p. 579. See also J. Mervyn Williams, 'The New London Welsh', *Welsh Outlook*, 17, 7 (1930); Mari A. Williams, '"The New London Welsh": Domestic Servants 1918–1939', *Transactions of the Honourable Society of Cymmrodorion*, 9 (2003).

[69] Steve Garner, *Whiteness. An Introduction* (London, 2007), p. 63.

[70] Anne McClintock, *Imperial Leather. Race, Gender and Sexuality in the Colonial Contest* (Abingdon, 1995), pp. 52–3; Wendy Ugolini, *Experiencing War as the 'Enemy Other'. Italian Scottish Experience in World War II* (Manchester, 2011), pp. 26–8; Mike Benbough-Jackson, 'Negotiating National Identity during St David's Day Celebrations on Merseyside, 1880–1900', in *Merseyside. Culture and Place*, edited by Mike Benbough-Jackson and Sam Davies (Newcastle, 2011), p. 265; Richard Dyer, *White* (Abingdon, 1997), p. 4.

[71] Garner, *Whiteness*, p. 68.

[72] R. Merfyn Jones, 'The Liverpool Welsh', in *Liverpool Welsh & Their Religion*, edited by R. Merfyn Jones and D. Ben Rees (Liverpool, 1984), p. 28; M. Wynn Thomas, *The Nations of Wales 1890–1914* (Cardiff, 2016), p. xiii.

MacRaild and Payton pinpoint the late nineteenth and early twentieth centuries as the period when 'Welsh transnationality had its greatest force as both a demographic and an ideological phenomenon'.[73] However, there is surprisingly little published work addressing the Welsh dimension of the diaspora space of England. Colin Pooley has published articles on Welsh settlement patterns in mid-nineteenth century England and more recently, Mike Benbough-Jackson has examined nineteenth-century Welsh associational culture in Merseyside.[74] D Ben Rees and Emrys Jones have provided broad overviews of the Welsh diaspora in Liverpool and London, respectively, with Merfyn Jones focusing more critically on second-generation experience.[75] Work has also been undertaken on the substantial Welsh presence in cities such as Manchester, Middlesbrough, and Oxford.[76] Pooley notes that spatial proximity and the size of urban centres were the main factors controlling movement from Wales to England: although whilst London attracted migrants from all parts of Wales, in Liverpool, over 60 per cent of the Welsh came from the four northern counties of Wales.[77] The Welsh community in Liverpool was constantly replenished by fresh immigration from Wales: between 1851 and 1911, Liverpool attracted at least 20,000 Welsh people in every decade. As a consequence, at the first meeting of the Liverpool Welsh National Society in 1885, Lord Mostyn christened the city 'the metropolis of Wales'.[78] Writing in the 1930s, the Welsh journalist Glyn Roberts articulates an expansive view of Welshness, downplaying any sense of borders between the two nations. He points to the commonplace view amongst his compatriots that it 'is easier to get from most Welsh villages to London than it is to get from any Welsh village to any other Welsh village.' He also references Cardiff and Liverpool as 'the only other great Welsh cities' besides London.[79]

---

[73] MacRaild and Payton, 'Welsh Diaspora', Abstract, https://www.manchesterhive.com/abstract/9781526127860/9781526127860.00012.xml, accessed 1 May 2019.

[74] Colin G. Pooley, 'The Residential Segregation of Migrant Communities in Mid-Victorian Liverpool', *Transactions of the Institute of British Geographers*, 2, 3 (1977); Pooley, 'Welsh Migration'; Colin G. Pooley and John C. Doherty, 'The Longitudinal Study of Migration. Welsh Migration to English Towns in the Nineteenth Century', in *Migrants, Emigrants and Immigrants. A Social History of Migration*, edited by Colin G. Pooley and Ian D. Whyte (London, 1991); Benbough-Jackson, 'Negotiating'.

[75] D. Ben Rees, *The Welsh of Merseyside in the Twentieth Century* (Liverpool, 2001); *The Welsh in London 1500–2000*, edited by Emrys Jones (Cardiff, 2001); Merfyn Jones, 'Welsh Immigrants in the Cities of North West England. 1890–1930: Some Oral Testimony', *Oral History*, 9, 2 (1981); Jones, 'Liverpool Welsh'.

[76] Jones, 'Welsh Immigrants'; Richard Lewis and David Ward, 'Culture, Politics and Assimilation: The Welsh on Teesside, c. 1850–1940', *Welsh History Review*, 17, 4 (1995); R. C. Whiting, *The View from Cowley: Impact of Industrialization Upon Oxford, 1918–39* (Oxford, 1983); R. J. W. Evans, 'Wales and Oxford: Historical Aspects, National and International', in *Wales and the Wider World: Welsh History in International Perspective*, edited by T. M. Charles-Edwards and R. J. W. Evans (Donington, 2010).

[77] Pooley, 'Welsh Migration', p. 293.   [78] Jones, 'Liverpool Welsh', p. 20.

[79] Roberts, *I Take*, p. 254.

Pooley suggests that the first generation of Welsh settlers 'managed to live in two culture worlds' by maintaining a distinct identity through chapel attendance, language preservation, and Welsh language newspapers.[80] The fact that the Welsh in England maintained their cultural and ethnic distinctiveness leads MacRaild and Payton to define them as a 'near diaspora'.[81] Making use of the networks emerging from chain migration from Wales, chapels performed an important function for the first settlers within diasporic Welsh civic society, acting as 'a labour exchange as well as a source of friendship, culture and discipline'.[82] Nonconformist chapels in English cities with significant Welsh settlements initially served as key vehicles for Welsh language preservation. At the same time, John Belchem and MacRaild note how 'In preserving Welsh while encouraging English', the chapels also helped migrants 'adjust to a broader British identity and loyalty'.[83] As the Welsh community progressed into its second and third generation of settlement, it also became less anchored in institutionalized forms of Welshness, taking on a more fully anglophone complexion with less commitment to chapel attendance. In Liverpool, the Welsh community came to dominate the building industry although in a visible form of 'upward social mobility' they also extended out into 'large-scale speculatory building, and then into the related fields of estate agency and building finance.'[84] By the mid-nineteenth century, Welsh migrants in London, especially those from Ceredigion, were closely associated with the dairy trade: they 'cornered the milk rounds, in the suburbs and in the city, where they sold their pints and pats of butter along Fleet Street'.[85] By the end of the century, Welsh settlers were also dominant in the drapery business with names such as Peter Jones, D. H. Evans, and William Owen becoming visible parts of the retail landscape.[86] Both London and Liverpool are acknowledged as historically important sites of Welsh nation-building. In the former, the second half of the eighteenth century saw 'a flowering of Welsh societies which would have a radical effect not only on the lives and activities of the Welsh in London but on Wales and Welsh culture generally.'[87] Prys Morgan confirms that the earliest of the societies 'specifically devoted to things Welsh' was the Society of Ancient Britons set up in 1715. This in turn 'spawned' the Honourable Society of Cymmrodorion in 1751, which hosted 'all kinds of literary gatherings, concerning itself with history and antiquities and present-day questions.'[88] Johnes points

---

[80] Pooley, 'Welsh Migration', p. 302; Davies, *History*, p. 443.
[81] MacRaild and Payton, 'Welsh Diaspora', p. 247. [82] Davies, *History*, p. 443.
[83] Belchem and MacRaild, 'Cosmopolitan', p. 347. [84] Jones, 'Welsh Immigrants', p. 35.
[85] Emrys Jones, 'The Early Nineteenth Century', in *Welsh in London*, p. 101; Davies, *History*, p. 443; John Harris, '*Afterword*' in Caradoc Evans, *My Neighbours* (Aberystwyth, 2005), p. 185..
[86] Emrys Jones, 'Victorian Heyday', in *Welsh in London*, p. 110.
[87] Emrys Jones, 'The Age of Societies', in *Welsh in London*, p. 66.
[88] Prys Morgan, 'From a Death', pp. 58–9. Since its establishment, the society has habitually reformed, playing an important role in the maintenance of cultural links with Wales. See Emrys Jones and Dewi Watkin Powell, *The Honourable Society of Cymmrodorion. A Concise History 1751–2001* (Aberystwyth, 2002).

out that modern Wales, with its history of immigration, has always been an 'imagined community' and, for its inhabitants, Welshness has 'a plethora of different meanings for the people who possess and make it'.[89] Williams agrees that, with significant levels of English immigration into Wales, there were competing versions of Welshness grounded in religious, class, linguistic, and other 'ethnic' differences. He illuminates the points of convergence between liberal-Cambrianists and *Plaid Genedlaethol Cymru* in the interwar period in promoting essentialist ideas of a racial Welsh identity based on 'blood' ties.[90] These different ideas about Welshness, based on language skills and chapel attendance, could also be circulated, filtered, and refracted within the diaspora space of England. Johnes acknowledges that, in nineteenth-century Wales, the Welsh language functioned as 'the most important reason for the survival of a sense of Welsh cultural identity'.[91] However, the 1911 census—which recorded 43.5 per cent of the Welsh population as Welsh-speaking—was the first where English monoglots outnumbered those able to speak Welsh, revealing Welsh as a minority linguistic culture within Wales. The early twentieth century, therefore, witnessed the gradual emergence of a sense of Welshness that was not primarily defined by language.[92] As Davies summarizes, since the beginning of the twentieth century, 'the concept that the non-Welsh-speaking Welsh are integral members of the Welsh community has been central to the viability of Welsh nationality'.[93] This linguistic backdrop opened up opportunities for English individuals of Welsh background to access Welsh identity without speaking the Welsh language. Indeed, many of those who appear in the following pages, who were capable only of reproducing the odd Welsh phrase or endearment, could still imagine themselves as 'Welsh'.

In terms of the diaspora, Tomos Owen highlights 'the performative character' of Welshness in London.[94] In his analysis of the late nineteenth-century bilingual newspaper, the *London Kelt*, Owen notes how the Welsh community in the metropolis came 'to position itself in relation to its current London location and real-and-imagined Wales left behind' which, he argues, testifies to 'the bifurcated nature of the London-Welsh condition'.[95] Fundamentally, this well-connected diasporic elite was engaged in 'a conscious self-fashioning', an exiles' version of Wales in which Welshness was being 'constructed and asserted in the very act of

---

[89] Martin Johnes, *A History of Sport in Wales* (Cardiff, 2005), p. 109.
[90] Chris Williams, 'The Dilemmas of Nation and Class in Wales, 1914-45', in *Debating Nationhood and Governance in Britain 1885–1945. Perspectives from the 'Four Nations'*, edited by Duncan Tanner, Chris Williams, Wil Griffith, and Andrew Edwards (Manchester, 2006), pp. 156–7.
[91] Johnes, *Wales: England's Colony?*, p. 115.
[92] Janet Davies, *The Welsh Language: A History* (Cardiff, 2014), p. 87; Thanks to Martin Johnes for sharing his expert knowledge.
[93] Davies, *Welsh Language*, p. 87.
[94] Tomos Owen, 'The London Kelt 1895–1914: Performing Welshness, Imagining Wales', *Almanac: Yearbook of Welsh Writing in English*, vol. 13, edited by Katie Gramich (Cardigan, 2009), p. 122.
[95] Owen, 'London', p. 111.

its performance and articulation.[96] This supports the argument of R. Merfyn Jones that the act of migration made the Welsh more conscious of their national identity: 'To be Welsh in Wales was unremarkable, to be Welsh in Liverpool was to be visible and to be conscious of that position.'[97] Jones sees the Liverpool Welsh as 'amongst the most efficient promulgators of a "Welsh identity" consisting of religiosity, respectability, conscientiousness and democracy.'[98] As a Welsh writer based in London, Caradoc Evans, contemporaneously sought to puncture aspects of this constructed diasporic identity. In his iconoclastic depiction of London Welsh society set during the First World War, *My Neighbours* (1919), he targeted the perceived religious hypocrisy, false piety and money worship of the 'drapers, milkmen, ministers and politicians' who made up the diasporic elite.[99]

Second-Generation Identities: Duality, Hybridity, and Borderlands

The functioning of dual English Welsh identities articulates a form of Britishness which arises from both the considerable length of Wales' border with England and migratory patterns of the late nineteenth and early twentieth centuries, with MacRaild and Payton noting how 'migration across Offa's Dyke went both ways and were clearly manifestations of interregional economic exchange'.[100] In the nineteenth century, the development of travel and communication links, tourism, and increasingly standardized forms of consumerism forged new communities of mobile British citizens. Robbins writes that 'Mobility between one part of Britain and another, and intermarriage, diluted the "purity" of the Englishman, the Scot or the Welshman. It is an over-simplification, in other words, to take borders and frontiers too seriously. They existed to be crossed—in both directions'.[101] Hazel Easthope concurs that, by the close of the nineteenth century, there was a shift from 'relatively stable identities rooted in place to hybrid identities characterized by mobility and flux'.[102] Neil Evans suggests that levels of mixing of the populations of the United Kingdom were so high in the wake of nineteenth century urbanization, that it is more helpful to acknowledge that 'we are dealing with multiple regional and religiously based cultures rather than four nations'.[103]

---

[96] Owen, 'London', pp. 122, 110.   [97] Jones, 'Liverpool Welsh', p. 34.
[98] Jones, 'Liverpool Welsh', p. 33.
[99] Harris, 'Afterword', pp. 183–200; John Harris, '"Gazing at an Inferno": An Afterword', in Caradoc Evans, *Nothing to Pay* (London, 1990), p. 223. See also Glyn Roberts's observation, 'In the law and in medicine they have distinguished themselves, and in business', *I Take*, p. 121.
[100] MacRaild and Payton, 'Welsh Diaspora', p. 247.   [101] Robbins, *Nineteenth-Century*, p. 6.
[102] Hazel Easthope, 'Fixed Identities in a Mobile World? The Relationship between Mobility, Place and Identity', *Identities: Global Studies in Culture and Power*, xvi (2009), p. 65.
[103] Neil Evans, '"A World Empire, Sea-Girt": The British Empire, State and Nations, 1780–1914', in *Nationalizing Empires*, edited by Stefan Berger and Alexei Miller (Budapest, 2015), p. 67.

I use the unhyphenated term *English Welsh duality* here to reflect the neglected diasporic phenomenon of dual identification both in England and Wales among the second- and third-generation Welsh and also to acknowledge that the descended Welsh in twentieth-century England did not themselves adopt a hyphenated identity.[104] In her study of diasporic identity, Walter emphasizes the ways in which second-generation migrants born in Britain can express a sense of dual identity by identifying on the basis of 'cultural background rather than simply birthplace'.[105] The phenomenon of duality or dual identifications is often overlooked when we talk about early twentieth-century constructions of Britishness or the existence of 'white' diasporic identities. Marc Scully underlines the importance of 'localised hybrid identities', pointing out that for second-generation immigrants, adopting a hybridized label creates a 'conceptual space' for a different type of identity to be imagined, one that emphasizes the 'localised specificity' of their identities.[106] His work points to the potential for the creation of a specific form of Welshness 'rooted' in English cities and localities.[107] Walter suggests that placename labels, such as the 'London Irish' or the 'London Welsh', allow ' "both/and" identities to be expressed in an uncontroversial way'. For second-generation Irish migrants, for example, such names acknowledge 'the duality of their placement in the city or town of their birth... but enabled them to retain and express a particular brand of Irishness'.[108] Dual identification with Wales and England could also move beyond these localized placename identities. The vast majority of case studies examined in this book often disregarded or moved away from the more structured Welsh associational life of clubs and chapels: the Brockley-born poet David Jones, for example, was keen to point out that his Welsh father 'was not one of these Cymry Llundain' who 'cultivate their Welshness'.[109] In his landmark publication, *The Location of Culture,* Homi K. Bhabha signals the importance of the space 'in-between the designations of identity', writing that, 'this interstitial passage between fixed identifications opens up the possibility of a cultural hybridity that entertains difference without an assumed or imposed hierarchy'.[110] Mary J. Hickman et al. characterize hybridity as the site where two hegemonic domains—in their case, Ireland and England—'intersect' in the lives of second-generation migrant children. They view hybridity as reflecting 'the

---

[104] See Tanya Golash-Boza, 'Dropping the Hyphen? Becoming Latino(a)-American through Racialized Assimilation', *Social Forces*, 85, 1 (2006).

[105] Walter, 'English/Irish Hybridity', p. 19.

[106] Marc Scully, ' "Plastic and Proud"?: Discourses of Authenticity Among the Second-generation Irish in England', *Psychology & Society*, 2, 2 (2009), pp. 133, 131.

[107] Marc Scully, 'Discourses of Authenticity and National Identity among the Irish Diaspora in England' (PhD dissertation, The Open University, 2010), p. 15.

[108] Walter, 'English/Irish Hybridity', p. 20.

[109] National Library of Wales (NLW); CF1/9; David Jones Papers; Draft Letters 1929–1982; letter to National Museum Wales, Cardiff, c.1954.

[110] Homi K. Bhabha, *The Location of Culture* (2nd edn, London, 2004), p. 5.

complexity of the identifications and positionings' of children of Irish origin in England as well as allowing for 'the conceptualisation of new forms of identities which arise out of the experience of "dwelling-in-displacement".'[111] At the same time, as Brah emphasizes, the 'multi-placedness of "home" in the diasporic imaginary does not mean that diasporian subjectivity is "rootless"'; second-generation migrants often feel securely anchored and 'at home' in the place of settlement.[112] Historically, therefore, the idea of being 'London Welsh' or 'Liverpool Welsh', for example, has worked to acknowledge not just the presence of first-generation Welsh settlers in England but also the expression of dual identifications amongst their descendants 'varying contextually in time and space', foregrounded or concealed at different times.[113] When discussing the borderlands writer, Nigel Heseltine, M. Wynn Thomas suggests that the 'meeting, mingling and cross fertilisation' of English Welsh identities highlight the potential significance of hybridity within Welsh diasporic experience as the space 'where cultural differences "contingently" and conflictually touch.'[114] Uxbridge-born Margiad Evans, discussed in Chapter 7, is another writer whose creativity emerged from her proximity to the borderlands between England and Wales: the 'historically constructed spatial entities' which formed 'the basis of cultural interactions, exchanges and admixtures.'[115] Focusing on the internal borderlands of the United Kingdom after 1707, Paul Readman, Cynthia Radding, and Chad Bryant note how the Welsh and Scots borderlands with England were 'independent of state boundaries, being contained within in a union of multiple national identities' but at the same time were important sites for the 'negotiation and expression' of the accommodation of 'an ideology of Unionism'.[116] They argue that borderlands can best be understood as 'ecumenes', areas of persistent cultural exchange where 'ideas, goods, and people move among various contact zones' and 'key sites of intercultural contact, conflict, exchange, and identity formation'.[117]

For the second generation born and raised in England, Jones writes, being Welsh was very often a matter of choice or identification.[118] Increasingly, Welsh language speaking became associated with the religious domain of the chapel and less with their day-to-day lives. Whilst acknowledging that some suffered an 'identity crisis', Jones points to the existence of a cohort of second-generation

---

[111] Mary J. Hickman, Sarah Morgan, Bronwen Walter, and Joseph Bradley, 'The Limitations of Whiteness and the Boundaries of Englishness', *Ethnicities*, 5, 2 (2005), pp. 177–8; Walter et al., 'Family Stories', p. 202.

[112] Brah, *Cartographies*, p. 194.   [113] Walter et al., 'Family Stories', p. 202.

[114] M. Wynn Thomas, '"A Grand Harlequinade": The Border Writing of Nigel Heseltine', *Welsh Writing in English*, vol. 11, edited by Tony Brown (2006–7), p. 52; Bhabha, *Location*, p. 296.

[115] Paul Readman, Cynthia Radding, and Chad Bryant, 'Introduction: Borderlands in a Global Perspective', in *Borderlands in World History, 1700–1914*, edited by Paul Readman, Cynthia Radding, and Chad Bryant (Basingstoke, 2014), p. 2.

[116] Readman, Radding, and Bryant, 'Introduction', p. 12.

[117] Readman, Radding, and Bryant, 'Introduction', pp. 3–4.

[118] Jones, 'Liverpool Welsh', p. 29.

Welsh men and women who found little difficulty in living in 'two worlds' and for whom a sense of duality was the norm.[119] At a basic level, this could mean hearing and understanding the Welsh language when spoken at chapel but speaking English at school and in the wider world. Chapter 3 will show how, for many second-generation anglophone children, Welsh was often experienced as the conveyer of 'secrets' within the family home, the language adults would switch to when they didn't want to be overheard. Thus, as Jones concludes, 'Those born into this community were obliged to live with dual identities, they were conscious of their Welshness but they could not avoid being English at the same time.'[120] To paraphrase John Herson, descendants of Welsh migrants, 'even those from ethnically "mixed" marriages, might still have a proud heritage of family connections and identify with their place (or places) of origin.' This did not mean, however, that they necessarily expressed 'Welshness' in terms of adherence to nationalist causes, social activities, or even religion.[121] The ways in which the descended Welsh in England connected with the Welsh language, if at all, also depended on which part of Wales their family originated from and visited. Whilst this book cannot capture the experiences of English people of Welsh origin who felt themselves to be wholly English, it is my contention that for those with dual English Welsh heritage growing up in England there was always likely to be some sense of connection with Wales, however understated or inconsequential. Essentially, this book will illuminate the complex 'range of identifications' across Englishness and Welshness amongst the descended Welsh, reflecting class, gender, and generational differences.[122] It follows Emma Jinhua Teng, whose study of Eurasian identities in the United States, China, and Hong Kong acknowledges the importance of 'privilege' within the construction of life story narratives and the fact that those with 'cultural capital' experienced their dual identities in different ways than those lower down the social scale, as well as being more likely to deposit their recollections in public archives and repositories for posterity.[123]

English Welsh Subjectivities

An analysis of Welsh diasporic experience can help to recover and reconstruct the 'hidden Welsh world' which ran throughout English culture and society in the first half of the twentieth century.[124] The politician Enoch Powell, the son of a

---

[119] Jones, 'Liverpool Welsh', p. 35.   [120] Jones, 'Liverpool Welsh', p. 35.
[121] John Herson, *Divergent Paths: Family Histories of Irish Emigrants in Britain 1820-1920* (Manchester, 2015), p. 15.
[122] Walter, 'English/Irish Hybridity', p. 20.
[123] Emma Jinhua Teng, *Eurasian. Mixed Identities in the United States, China, and Hong Kong, 1842-1943* (Berkeley, 2013), p. 9.
[124] Jones and Jones, 'Welsh World', p. 76.

fourth-generation descendant of Welsh emigrants to the Black Country, acknowledged that 'there is a Welshman hidden in many an Englishman, a Wales hidden in England'.[125] Referring to the poets Edward Thomas and David Jones, Robbins notes that, around the time of the First World War, it appeared 'as though literary England was full of *secret Welshmen*' (my italics).[126] This book focuses on the subjectivities and narratives of the descendants of Welsh migrants and the articulation of their sense of duality within English society. The second- and third-generation Welsh did not share the 'oppositional connotations' which were attached to the identity formation of racialized migrant groups such as the Catholic Irish and Italians in Britain (a hostility which was reinforced for the latter group during the Second World War due to their 'enemy' status). Rather, they could benefit from their access to 'a romantic cultural association which was not available to the "non-ethnic" English'.[127] Robbins believes that the second- and third-generation Welsh could often express a connection with Wales based upon '*hiraeth* (nostalgia/longing) for the land of their fathers which they had never known'.[128] Thus, the willingness of this generation of English men and women to signal some level of connectedness to Wales could also reflect what Raphael Samuel defines as 'the romance of otherness' conferred by the idea of a genealogical 'second identity' or, indeed, a desire for authenticity.[129]

This book will examine several key English figures who chose to assert a range of Welsh attachments and identities. Malcolm Ballin has argued that 'notions of Welshness' reverberated in the 'epi-centre' of twentieth century British political and cultural life. His biography of the cultural mandarin and director of the Army Bureau of Current Affairs, William Emrys Williams, examines how a man born and part-raised in Manchester came to embody the idea of 'Welshness' during the Second World War.[130] Famously, two iconic Welsh political actors were both born in North West England: David Lloyd George, the towering figure of Welsh Liberalism, in Manchester whilst one of the founders of modern Welsh nationalism, Saunders Lewis, was born, brought up, and educated on Merseyside.[131] The politician Selwyn Lloyd, from a family of Welsh extraction living on the Wirral in the interwar period, had a lifelong attachment to the idea of Wales, visiting

---

[125] Simon Heffer, *Like the Roman. The Life of Enoch Powell* (London, 1998), p. 2; Roger Thomas, *The Welsh Quotation Book* (London, 1994), p. 70.

[126] Robbins, *Nineteenth-Century Britain*, p. 37.

[127] Ugolini, *Experiencing War*, p. 3; Walter, 'English/Irish Hybridity', pp. 20, 21.

[128] Robbins, *Nineteenth-Century*, p. 36.

[129] Raphael Samuel, *Theatres of Memory. Vol 1: Past and Present in Contemporary Culture* (London, 1994), p. 247; Wendy Ugolini, 'The "Welsh" Pimpernel: Richard Llewellyn and the Search for Authenticity in Second World War Britain', *Journal of Cultural and Social History*, 16, 2 (2019), pp. 185–203, doi: 10.1080/14780038.2019.1585315.

[130] Malcolm Ballin, 'The Welshness of William Emrys Williams: Strands from a Biography', in *Almanac: Yearbook of Welsh Writing in English*, vol. 13, edited by Katie Gramich (Cardigan, 2009), pp. 81–2, 98.

[131] Bruce Griffiths, *Saunders Lewis* (Cardiff, 1989), pp. 2–3.

regularly. Individuals such as Lloyd typically viewed Britain through the dual lens of England and Wales. For example, as an ambitious undergraduate in 1925, he wrote to his father about his involvement in a Cambridge Union debate:

> I made quite a good speech, and towards the end was comparing English oratory with Welsh oratory and, as a specimen of the latter, I was in the middle of a most eloquent passage re: Welsh mountains, when instead of 'crags' I said 'crabs', which completely spoilt the rhetorical effect of the passage, but had the merit of making the House laugh.[132]

Numerous cultural figures of the twentieth century displayed varying manifestations of English Welsh duality. The Hampshire-born architect, Patrick Gwynne was able to build his modernist masterpiece, The Homewood, in Esher, on the proceeds of his father's sale of the family inheritance, the Welsh-planned town, Aberaeron, in 1936.[133] Born in Shropshire and raised in the 'bath-chair seaside town' of Bournemouth, the film critic Dilys Powell asserts that her childhood environment was 'almost pure Welsh'.[134] Her contemporary, the stage actress, Gwen Ffrangcon-Davies was matter of fact in referencing her own sense of duality, describing herself as: 'Ethereal from the waist up and all Welsh pony down below.'[135] In his wartime novel, *Blitz Hero* (1942), the Liverpool writer Frank Elias—using the pen name John Owen—used his personal insights to capture the experience of the Liverpool Welsh being evacuated back to the fictional 'Llanfair-on-Sea' in North Wales and encountering the 'real' Welsh.[136] During the Second World War, when Enfield-born writer Norman Lewis was assigned to the Intelligence Corps, he felt able to rely on his 'Celtic intuition'[137] whilst Londoner J R Davies, serving as a gunner in the 88th Heavy Anti-Aircraft Regiment, wrote of his 'Celtic blood' inspiring him to feats of athleticism.[138] At the same time— and perhaps as a result of this duality—this research cohort of English men and women often self-identified as 'outsiders', occupying liminal spaces. This book will explore the ways in which many English cultural figures of Welsh origin, responsible for some of the most significant literary and artistic works of the twentieth century, often felt that they did not quite 'fit' in with their childhood

---

[132] Churchill Archives Centre, Cambridge; The Papers of Selwyn Lloyd; GBR/0014/SELO 1/27; Letter from Lloyd to father, June 1925.
[133] British Library Sound Archive; C467/36; Interview with Patrick Gwynne by Neil Bingham, 12 October 1997, Architects' Lives, copyright British Library Board.
[134] British Library Manuscripts (BLM). Add. MS 87684, Memoir by Dilys Powell covering the years from her childhood to her time at Somerville College, Oxford; n.d., p. 2.
[135] Helen Grime, *Gwen Ffrangcon-Davies, Twentieth-Century Actress* (London, 2016), p. 183. Ffrangcon-Davies was born in Hampstead in 1891, the daughter of Welsh opera singer, David Thomas Ffrangcon-Davies.
[136] John Owen, *Blitz Hero* (London, 1942), p. 11.
[137] Norman Lewis, *Jackdaw Cake* (London, 1985), p. 203.
[138] Imperial War Museum (IWM); 13167; Private Papers of J. R. Davies, Letter 1 March 1943.

milieu. Ballin notes the 'ambivalence' and personal contradictions at the root of William Emrys Williams's self-construction as 'a Welshman' and argues that these contributed to 'the perceptions of Williams as an outsider, "on the edge" perhaps, someone not always wholly comfortable in the centres of metropolitan power.'[139] The second-generation Welsh in England could also feel marked out due to physical signifiers of their 'difference': Norman Lewis was accepted as 'Welsh by derivation' due to his 'feverish black eyes, hair and mustache' whilst Willesden-born Richard Llewellyn was described by contemporaries as 'a small neat dark Celt'.[140] The daughter of artist, Allan Gwynne-Jones, born in Richmond in 1892, recalled that, 'He had very dark eyes and very dark hair as a young man and wasn't very tall and looked Welsh.'[141] The descended Welsh could therefore both be externally identified and have an internal sense of themselves, as the 'Celtic' other.

As well as addressing second-generation men and women who grew up in England with either one or two Welsh parents, this book will also address those with a sense of ancestral Welshness, as encapsulated in the title of writer, Berta Ruck's memoir, *A Trickle of Welsh Blood*.[142] Many English families clung to the idea of descent from an ancient Welsh family. Jeremy Hooker notes how the novelist John Cowper Powys, 'feeling himself to be a misfit in English society', acquired 'a passion for "everything Welsh"', his imagination having been fired by his father's tales of ancestral Wales.[143] Evelyn Waugh's first volume of autobiography parades his ancestral ties with the 'Morgans of Tylyrcoh [sic]' whilst in his memoir, author Anthony Powell asserts, 'Like many Welsh families, my father's has been documented from an early period, a line settling in what was to become Radnorshire in the twelfth century.'[144] In a review of a Powell biography, Ian Sansom remarks that 'The Welsh thing obviously appealed to a wild, romantic longing in Powell's otherwise rather tight-buttoned upbringing.'[145] The ability of English novelist Richard Hughes to trace his family's ancestry through Elystan Glodrydd (*c*.940–1010) to Beli Mawr, king of the Britons during the time of Julius Caesar, meant he 'considered himself a Welshman'.[146] In a short memoir published in 1931 Hughes made the significance of these ancestral links explicit:

---

[139] Ballin, 'Welshness', p. 86.
[140] Julian Evans, *Semi Invisible Man. The Life of Norman Lewis* (London, 2009), pp. 417–18; Peter Quennell, *The Wanton Chase* (New York, 1980), p. 28.
[141] Author interview with Emily Gwynne-Jones by Wendy Ugolini, 2 August 2016.
[142] Berta Ruck, *A Trickle of Welsh Blood* (London, 1967).
[143] Jeremy Hooker, *Imagining Wales. A View of Modern Welsh Writing in English* (Cardiff, 2001), p. 16.
[144] Evelyn Waugh, *A Little Learning: The First Volume of an Autobiography* (London, 1990), p. 15; Anthony Powell, *To Keep the Ball Rolling* (London, 1983), p. 11.
[145] Ian Sansom, ' "Every Rusty Hint". Anthony Powell: A Life by Michael Barber', *London Review of Books*, 26, 20 (2004), pp. 10–11.
[146] Meic Stephens, 'Hughes, Richard Arthur Warren (1900–1976)', *Oxford Dictionary of National Biography* (*ODNB*) (2011), https://doi-org.ezproxy.is.ed.ac.uk/10.1093/ref:odnb/31260.

I am of Welsh descent, although it is now remote, seeing that my family emigrated to England, like so many Welshmen, in the time of the Tudors...My own family—known till then by the curious name of The Fourteenth Royal Tribe—adopted the patronymic of Hughes, and settled down to being English country gentlemen, and for the most part, Admirals in the British Navy; and yet, so strong is the racial type, that after three hundred years both my grandfather and my father would have been taken for Welshmen anywhere; and I myself, from the first time I visited Wales, at the age of eleven, felt a homesickness to go back there that I never felt for the south country where I was born and bred.[147]

The importance of these distant patrilineal attachments can also be seen in the desire of Powell in 1939 to follow his English father into The Welch Regiment, an act immortalized in his 1964 book *The Valley of Bones* where his literary alter ego Nick Jenkins also signals his Welsh heritage, and Cambridge undergraduate Christopher Williams-Ellis who claimed direct descent from Owain Gwynedd and followed his English father, the architect, Clough Williams-Ellis, into the Welsh Guards, being killed in 1944. These narratives of filiation will be examined more closely in Chapter 5 which argues that patrilineal ties often prompted romanticized constructions of Wales which compelled some men to serve on behalf of 'the Land of My Fathers'.

When interviewed by the cultural magazine, *Wales*, in 1946, the artist David Jones defined himself as being 'a person of mixed English and Welsh blood and affinities'.[148] Although Jones himself was of paternal Welsh origin, this book expands the concept of 'affinity Welsh' to include Englishmen with no Welsh heritage, most famously Robert Graves, author of the First World War text, *Goodbye to All That*.[149] John Betjeman, whose foreign-sounding surname meant that he was bullied at school for being 'a German spy' during the First World War, often felt like an outsider within British society.[150] To overcome this, argues his biographer, Philip Payton, Betjeman constructed a 'Celtic' identity for himself, 'clutching at a Welsh twig in his family tree' to bolster his claims.[151] He was so attached to the idea of Wales that he took Welsh lessons at Oxford as an undergraduate. In the nostalgic poem, 'Myfanwy at Oxford', he also fetishizes his friend, Myfanwy Piper née Evans, the daughter of a Welsh chemist in London, positioning her at the heart of a quintessentially English locale:

---

[147] Richard Hughes 'Autobiographical Introduction', *Richard Hughes. An Omnibus* (New York, 1931), pp. xvi–xvii.
[148] David Jones, ' "Wales" Questionnaire', *Wales*, vi, 2 (1946), p. 84.
[149] Robert Graves, *Goodbye To All That* (London, 1929).
[150] A. N. Wilson, *Betjeman* (London, 2007), p. 26.
[151] Philip Payton, *John Betjeman and Cornwall. 'The Celebrated Cornish Nationalist'* (Exeter, 2010), p. xviii.

> Pink may, double may, dead laburnum
> Shedding an Anglo-Jackson Shade,
> Shall we ever, my staunch Myfanwy,
> Bicycle down to North Parade?
> Kant on the handle-bars, Marx in the saddlebag,
> Light my touch on your shoulder-blade.[152]

Here, Betjeman is attracted to the idea of English Welsh duality as embodied by Piper, using a romanticized attachment to the idea of Welshness as a gateway, or entry, into 'belonging'. This book will also investigate examples of elective Welshness addressing the life stories of the novelists Richard Llewellyn and Naomi Royde-Smith, William Emrys Williams, and the soldier-writer, Owen Rhoscomyl (Lt. Col. Arthur Vaughan) who all engaged in performances of Welshness which masked their English roots.

In the first half of the twentieth century, particularly the interwar period, there was a glut of cultural commentators, including H. V. Morton and J. B. Priestley, seeking to identify and elucidate English national traits and values or what Robert Colls defines as 'the idea of a national identity based on the structural properties of the people'.[153] Kumar, however, argues that Englishness 'cannot be understood from the inside out but more from the outside in' pointing to the fundamental significance of England's relationship with its 'near neighbours', Wales, Scotland and Ireland, and its formative role in British imperialism.[154] This book adopts a fresh perspective, highlighting the ways in which, in the first half of the twentieth century, Englishness could be porous, fluid, and accommodating of difference. Brah suggests that the presence and intersection of minority groups, such as the Welsh, in the diaspora space called 'England' could in itself reinscribe 'the entity constructed as "Englishness"'.[155] Giles and Middleton agree that for a writer such as Edward Thomas, born in Lambeth to Welsh parents, having different national origins impacted upon his 'perception of Englishness'.[156] They note how much of Thomas's output is 'a celebration of a mythic English pastoralism' and argue that, due to his Welsh origins, he 'not only contributed to the construction of a mythology of England but often modified an existing set of myths to allow a place for that which had been previously excluded.'[157] *Wales in England 1914–1945* looks at the ways in which Welshness became 'complexly imbricated' in English culture

---

[152] 'Myfanwy at Oxford' in John Betjeman, *Old Lights for New Chancels* (London, 1940), pp. 49–50. Betjeman wrote another poem about Piper in the same volume simply entitled 'Myfanwy'. For more on Betjeman, see Chapter 8 'Affinity Welsh'.
[153] Robert Colls, *Identity of England* (Oxford, 2002), p. 304; H. V. Morton, *In Search of England* (London, 1927); J. B. Priestley, *English Journey* (London, 1934).
[154] Kumar, *Making*, p. xii.   [155] Brah, *Cartographies*, pp. 205–6.
[156] Giles and Middleton, *Writing*, p. 22.   [157] Giles and Middleton, *Writing*, pp. 75, 23.

and society.[158] It complements Mo Moulton's work on the Irish presence in interwar England by suggesting that Welshness comprised a 'constitutive' element of Englishness for some of the descended Welsh living in England in the first half of the twentieth century.[159]

Narrating the Self—'The Roberts is important'

The uneven nature of the documentation I have uncovered during ten years of archival fieldwork—reflecting the subterranean aspects of English Welsh duality as a lived identity—means that I follow Das in attempting 'to weave together a narrative of fugitive fragments'.[160] As well as more traditional sources such as letters, diaries, memoirs, and archived oral testimonies, this book analyses art, memorials, BBC radio broadcasts, war diaries, in-house regimental newsletters, and fictional representations of English Welsh experience in order to reconstruct the overlooked world of Welshness in early twentieth-century England. It addresses notions of individual subjectivities, narrations of self, and the self-fashioning of English Welsh individuals. Ellis acknowledges the historical turn towards the genre of biographical writing and need to study individual lives in order to explore 'the construction and interactions of imperial, national and personal identities' and, in this case, to better present England as 'a plurality of experiences, cultures and identities'.[161]

The nascent idea for this study began in the 1980s when, as a teenager, I would be driven by my grandfather, John Herbertson, in his white mini, around the streets of Liverpool, revisiting his childhood haunts: the terraced house in Kirkdale where he grew up with his Welsh grandparents, Welsh mother, and English father, the houses in the nearby streets where his Welsh aunts lived with his cousins and the site of the Welsh chapel where his grandfather, Taid, acted as a sidesman. I made contemporaneous notes of these journeys and my grandfather's reminiscences of his childhood in a 1983 Waterlow diary. When, many decades later, as a university history lecturer undertaking archival research, I encountered the Second World War letters of the London gunner, J. R. Davies, the son of a Welsh father and English mother, in the Imperial War Museum, Davies's articulation of a deep connection with Wales reminded me of my grandfather's sense of dual inheritance and inspired me to attempt to capture and reconstruct this once relevant and *meaningful* form of identity.

This monograph will consider why, in their life-writing and cultural imprints, so many English men and women chose to foreground their identification with

---

[158] Paul Readman, 'Living a British Borderland: Northumberland and the Scottish Borders in the Long Nineteenth Century', in *Borderlands*, p. 187.
[159] Moulton, *Ireland*, p. 7.   [160] Das, *India*, p. 9.   [161] Ellis, 'Making', p. 484.

Wales. It examines the ways in which English men and women identified with Wales, how they understood and narrated their own sense of Welshness, and why, for them, Welshness held *meaning*. For example, in one archived oral history interview held at the British Library, ostensibly undertaken to focus on the professional teaching career of the informant Margaret Roberts, the latter insists at the outset, 'The Roberts is important. I'll tell you about that later.'[162] For a substantial part of the interview, Roberts reflects upon and returns to the significance of having a Welsh father, discussing the ways in which he influenced both her childhood growing up in North Finchley after the First World War *and* the military choices her male siblings made on the outbreak of the Second World War, including the decision by one brother to conscientiously object. Personal narratives such as these demonstrate the importance of recovering subjective accounts of lived experience. As Penny Summerfield writes, 'every individual is a social being, whose life, however exceptional, however unique, is indicative of the vast social processes stretching over time that we call "history".' In particular, personal narratives give the historian access 'to the processes by which a subject constitutes him or herself in relation to the social world and its public discourses, at any point in the past.'[163] In his exploration of Anzac veteran narratives, Alistair Thomson concludes that, 'Our identity (or "identities", a more appropriate term to suggest the multi-faceted and contradictory nature of subjectivity) is the sense of self that we construct by comparisons with other people and with our own life over time.'[164] This study uncovers a significant number of English individuals who often interweaved a sense of 'Welshness' within their life-writing narratives and illuminates the 'varying degrees of ethnic distinctiveness and allegiance' which exists amongst the descended Welsh in England. In his analysis of second-generation Irish memoirs, Tony Murray points out that second-generation migrants can be 'remarkably adroit at adapting their cultural identities to differing circumstances' taking an active part in two cultures.[165]

Although I have previously worked extensively with oral history as a research methodology, I only undertook one oral history interview for this book, not just because my target age group had largely died, but also because I felt that an interview which alerted English respondents to my interest in Welsh identity would by its very nature influence the outcome of the collected material, thus limiting its narrative value. Instead, I accessed existing archived oral testimonies which had

---

[162] British Library Sound Archive (BLSA); C464/68; Margaret [Peggy] Roberts, interviewed by Mary Stewart, 17 October 2008, copyright British Library Board.

[163] Penny Summerfield, 'Subjectivity, the Self and Historical Practice', in *New Directions in Social and Cultural History*, edited by Sasha Handley, Rohan McWilliam, and Lucy Noakes (London, 2018), p. 37.

[164] Alistair Thomson, *Anzac Memories. Living with the Legend* (Oxford, 1994), p. 9.

[165] Tony Murray, 'A Diasporic Vernacular? The Narrativisation of Identity in Second-Generation Irish Memoir', *The Irish Review*, 44 (2012), p. 76.

often been undertaken to focus on different topics (education, conscientious objection, and military service to name a few) but which incidentally included reflections on Welsh heritage or connections. By adopting this 'cultural memory approach', I was able to examine the complex ways in which people recall their life histories, construct their personal identities, and convey meaning through the structure of their narratives.[166] Although difficult to locate, I eventually found a substantial body of oral history interview transcripts, primarily located at the Sound Archives of the British Library and the Imperial War Museum, which proved to be fruitful sources. Joanna Bornat and Gail Wilson have written on the merits of reusing archived oral material originally undertaken for another academic purpose, pointing out how the reworking of archived oral history interviews 'opens up possibilities for new theories, concepts and data to be created'.[167]

Overall, I identified material relating to over one hundred individual case studies, including documentation held in national and local archives in England and Wales and the Harry Ransom Center at the University of Austin, Texas. I accessed both published and unpublished autobiographical and life writing material including memoir manuscripts held at the British Library and the Bodleian Library, letters at Gladstone Library, the National Library of Wales, the Parliamentary Archives, the Churchill Archives Centre, Kings College, Cambridge, the Liddell Hart Centre for Military Archives, St John's College, Oxford, and John Rylands Library, diaries at the Imperial War Museum and Cardiff University Special Collections and Archives, radio scripts at BBC Written Archives, press cuttings at Liverpool Record Office and the Friends Library London, and war diaries and intelligence reports at the National Archives. Following Teng, this book unavoidably 'gives more space to the stories of literate, and necessarily more privileged' and acknowledges the difficulties in recovering working-class experience.[168] However, it does make use of some significant and original datasets of Second World War letters, including a unique series of 'news sheets' drawing upon the correspondence of a group of working-class Liverpudlians serving in the 46th (Liverpool Welsh) Royal Tank Regiment, in addition to a set of 128 letters written by an Eighth Army gunner to his Welsh father and English mother living in London.

---

[166] Penny Summerfield and Corinna Peniston-Bird, *Contesting Home Defence. Men, Women and the Home Guard in the Second World War* (Manchester, 2007), pp. 207–8; Kate Fisher, *Birth Control, Sex and Marriage in Britain 1918–1960* (2nd edn, Oxford, 2008), p. 25.

[167] Joanna Bornat and Gail Wilson, 'Recycling the Evidence: Different Approaches to the Reanalysis of Elite Life Histories', in *Researching Families and Communities: Social and Generational Change*, edited by Rosalind Edwards (London, 2008), p. 95.

[168] Teng, *Eurasian*, p. 9.

Outline of Chapters

Tracing Welsh dominance and influence within British political life, Chapter 1 illuminates the dynamic parliamentary interplay between Welsh and English identities in the run-up to, and during, the First World War. It includes a case study of Lloyd George, addressing his totemic, almost talismanic, role in the performance of 'Welshness' within political and public arenas as well as his family's wider engagement in Welsh cultural and military affairs in England. This chapter will also briefly address the lives of female political campaigners and social reformers such as Edith Picton-Turbervill. Following Angela V John, it notes the tendency of a group of influential English-born women to 'romanticise Wales partly because they did not live there'.[169] This chapter also delineates another distinctive strand of English Welsh identity in this period: well-connected aristocratic or landed families with stately homes in both England and Wales, who, through their 'transnational land ownership', were enmeshed in the higher echelons of British political and cultural society.[170] It will map out the border crossings of younger family members, who were born in England and shaped through the English public school system, whose lives straddled both metropolitan society and Welsh family estates. This chapter also reviews the work of lesser-known English war poets, contemporaneously termed 'the nightingales of Wales', namely Eliot Crawshay-Williams, Colwyn Philipps, and Evan Morgan. Whilst serving in the armed forces during the First World War they produced poetry which addressed England but also articulated a form of *hiraeth*, a nostalgic longing for Wales.

Chapter 2 introduces the concept of 'Welshburbia', drawing upon the idea of the English suburbs as the site of a self-consciously Welsh middle-class identity in the first half of the twentieth century.[171] For second-generation Welsh men and women, the experience of living on the margins in English suburbs could reinforce their own sense of difference or 'outsider' status. In light of Kenny's observation that the diaspora 'opens up new cultural spaces beyond the boundaries of homeland and hostland', this chapter also argues for recognition of the influential role of the English suburbs in shaping the artistic and creative imagination of second-generation Welsh transcultural subjects.[172] It follows the work of Charles Burdett, Loredana Polezzi, and Barbara Spadaro in addressing 'the

---

[169] Angela V. John, *Rocking the Boat. Welsh Women Who Championed Equality 1840–1990* (Cardigan, 2018), p. 111.

[170] Annie Tindley, 'The Big House in Four Nations—new directions for the study of landed and aristocratic elites?' *Four Nations Blog*, https://fournationshistory.wordpress.com/2017/02/06/the-big-house-in-four-nations-new-directions-for-the-study-of-landed-and-aristocratic-elites/, accessed 23 February 2017.

[171] 'A Personal View: Gareth Miles', in *Presenting Saunders Lewis*, edited by Alun R. Jones and Gwyn Thomas (Cardiff, 1983), p. 17.

[172] Kenny, *Diaspora*, p. 12.

dynamic and plural nature of processes of identification' and 'multimodal links' to ideas of home and citizenship.[173] In particular, this chapter provides a case study of the poet, Edward Thomas, who defined himself as 'five eighths Welsh'. For Thomas, who immortalized his London Welsh childhood in *The Happy-Go-Lucky Morgans* (1913), the edges where English suburbia touched rural hinterlands could deepen a sense of connection with his idealized vision of 'wild Wales'.[174] Yet, despite this clear affection for Wales, when faced with the prospect of military service in 1914, Thomas became increasingly preoccupied with his own sense of 'Englishness', which ultimately compelled him to enlist. This chapter explores Thomas's display of dual allegiance during the First World War and, overall, addresses how a sense of mixed heritage amongst second-generation writers potentially fed into multifaceted cultural representations of British identities.

Chapter 3 addresses the ways in which English men and women narrate memories of their childhood selves and their familial connections with Wales in the first half of the twentieth century. Focusing on the interwar period, it analyses the shared motifs of these childhood narratives, including Welsh-naming patterns, language, social isolation, Gothic themes of death and mortality, and a sense of dual identifications. Second-generation Welsh men and women in England could grow up experiencing a sense of 'difference' and outsider status, reflected in their culturally distinctive narratives of childhood. Their encounters with Wales also served to heighten a sense of belonging to two nations at once. This chapter explores views of Wales from England, including the persistence of national and racial stereotyping and considers how these prejudices were absorbed, navigated, or challenged by those of Welsh heritage. It makes use of a range of original accounts including the unpublished life-writing of cultural figures such as Dilys Powell, Myfanwy Piper, and Naomi Royde-Smith as well as the memoirs of the writers Norman Lewis, Mervyn Jones, and John Osborne. The chapter also addresses how second-generation men and women encountered Wales as children, including those who were evacuated from England to Wales during the Second World War.

As discussed above, this book will examine the extent to which a sense of English Welsh dual identifications was effectively mobilized in both world wars. Chapter 4 focuses on the organization of English men with Welsh antecedents into active military units during the First World War. In particular, it addresses the establishment of the 15th (1st London Welsh), RWF, one of the battalions of the Welsh Army Corps which aimed to recruit Welshmen and those of Welsh

---

[173] Charles Burdett, Loredana Polezzi, and Barbara Spadaro, 'Introduction: Transcultural Italies', in *Transcultural Italies. Memory, Mobility and Translation*, edited by Charles Burdett, Loredana Polezzi, and Barbara Spadaro (Liverpool, 2020), p. 4.
[174] See Lynne Hapgood, *Margins of Desire. The Suburbs in Fiction and Culture 1880–1925* (Manchester, 2009).

origin living in London. It analyses Lloyd George's wartime relationship with the London Welsh soldier, William Pugh Hinds, the son of his parliamentary colleague, John Hinds MP, to illuminate the ways in which politicized displays of Welsh patriotism in the metropolis were implicated in the military voluntarism of a cohort of English soldiers. Chapter 5 moves on to address the Second World War, focusing on the formation of two territorial units, the 99th (London Welsh) Heavy Anti-Aircraft Regiment and the 46th (Liverpool Welsh) Royal Tank Regiment and addressing how the war provided the opportunity for a cohort of male English volunteers to express an identification with Welshness at the point of enlistment. Following Brah, this chapter examines the tensions between English Welsh servicemen's subjective wartime constructions of 'home' as 'a mythic place of desire' (Wales) and 'home' as the 'lived experience of a locality' and 'everyday social relations' (England).[175] Acknowledging Ellis's argument that there are competing traditions of militarism and pacifism within traditional understandings of Welsh identity, this chapter also analyses the life writing of a number of English men and women with Welsh ties who registered as conscientious objectors, reflecting upon the ways in which individuals made use of their Welsh antecedents and affinities when formulating their opposition to war.[176]

Chapter 6 focuses on the mourning and commemorative practices surrounding the English Welsh war dead including the appearance of Welsh epitaphs on the tombstones of English-born soldiers, officially commissioned memorial artwork which acknowledged dualities, and the involvement of English Welsh sculptors and artists, such as Alice Meredith Williams, in British memorialization activity. It then goes on to address the shift in English Welsh memorialization activity between the two world wars. This chapter also discusses the funerals of two well-connected First World War soldiers which took place across national borders: the Squire of Hawarden, Lt William Gladstone MP and Viscount Clive of the Powis family, showing how the multinational symbolism of the mourning processes surrounding these two men entrenched the patrician expression of the bonds between Wales and England.

Chapter 7 addresses the literary, artistic, and dramatic works which emerged from the functioning of English Welsh duality in the first half of the twentieth century. Following Hooker, it investigates how various English writers constructed 'imaginative versions of Wales' and creatively made use of their Welsh diasporic links.[177] It analyses the life-writing and literary output of authors such as Richard Hughes, John Owen, Charles Morgan, and the border novelist Margiad Evans. Engaging with painterly representations of national identity, this chapter

---

[175] Brah, *Cartographies*, pp. 188–9.
[176] John S. Ellis, 'A Pacific People – A Martial Race: Pacifism, Militarism and Welsh National Identity', in *Wales and War*.
[177] Hooker, *Imagining*, p. 4.

highlights the willingness of the Welsh cultural establishment in the first decades of the twentieth century to promote a fluid conception of Welshness which accommodated English painters, sculptors, and dramatists of Welsh extraction. Chapter 8 addresses the ways in which Wales was often conceived as a site of wartime refuge and depicted within twentieth century life-writing as a site of healing or rejuvenation. This chapter will discuss the Royal Welch Fusiliers poet, Robert Graves, who plotted to live in a cottage in Harlech after the First World War, viewing this as a restorative site of solace where he could recover from his combat experiences. In addition, it looks at how Graves's affinity with Wales, and pride in his Welsh regimental identity, had implications for his eldest son David, who died in 1943 whilst serving with the RWF. It will also examine the experiences of Royal Engineer Alex Cordell, the self-styled 'quarter' Welshman, whose military convalescence in Harlech during the Second World War served to reignite an authorial connection with his ancestral 'homeland', informing his post-war literary output which focused on Welsh history. This chapter introduces the idea of the 'affinity' Welsh: English cultural figures with no ancestral connection with Wales but who expressed a strong affinity with the nation, such as the artist and conscientious objector, John Petts.

The final chapter addresses the notion of masquerade, or the use of Welshness to mask Englishness, with the life story of the author, Richard Llewellyn providing the primary case study. Llewellyn achieved worldwide fame in 1939 with his novel, *How Green Was My Valley*, a story of the South Wales coalfield. The book was a wartime bestseller both in Britain and America and in 1941 was made into an Academy award-winning film, linking Llewellyn indelibly in the public mind with a particular vision of Wales and Welshness. Yet, after his death in 1983, it emerged that Llewellyn was not born in Pembrokeshire, as he had claimed, but rather in London to Welsh parents, a revelation which attracted accusations of fakery. Mapping Llewellyn's military service in the Welsh Guards and wartime work with the BBC, this chapter traces the author's complex negotiation of selfhood during the Second World War and highlights how Llewellyn was ultimately embraced as a cultural representative of transnational Welshness within a wider British and imperial nation. This chapter will also address other examples of elective Welshness such as Owen Rhoscomyl, Naomi Royde-Smith, and William Emrys Williams who all engaged in performances of Welshness which masked their English roots.

In reviewing the 'mixing' between Welsh and English identities, which emerged from the Welsh diasporic presence in twentieth century England, *Wales in England 1914–1945* aims to highlight both the multistranded and fluid nature of Englishness and culturally accommodating aspects of Welsh national identity construction, complicate the notion of fixed singular national identities within the constituent countries of the United Kingdom, and underscore the importance of dual identifications *across and within* the borders of England and Wales in advancing our historical understanding of British society in wartime. Through an analytical focus on second-generation diasporic identity in particular, *Wales in England 1914–1945* provides a useful model for exploring the variegated and interweaved strands of national identities functioning across *all* the internal borders of the United Kingdom in the twentieth and twenty-first centuries.

PART ONE
INVENTING AND ENCOUNTERING

1
Elite Identities

Writing during the Second World War, the poet Idris Davies said of the Welsh in England, 'We have carried our accents into Westminster|As soldiers carry rifles into the wars.'[1] This chapter examines the parliamentary aspect of English Welsh identities in the early twentieth century and its implications for wider national identity formation amongst the descended Welsh in England. Tomos Owen points to London as an important space for the 'collective imagining and re-imagining of Wales' in the late nineteenth century with Westminster as a site which crystallized the connections between Wales and England.[2] Pointing to Welsh dominance and influence within British political life from the late nineteenth century onwards, this chapter illuminates the dynamic parliamentary interplay between Welsh and English identities in the run-up to, during, and beyond the First World War. In particular, it explores the influence of dynastic political families such as the Gladstones and Lloyd Georges in contributing to the public visibility of English Welsh affiliations. The second half of the chapter addresses a number of case studies representing transnational landed families with estates or homes in Wales and England whose existence demanded that they perform split lives. For this privileged grouping, the First World War provided a specific moment in which they were able to demonstrate their duality through the expression of Welsh-hued martial patriotism.

Matthew Cragoe argues that, in the context of British politics, '"Wales" itself only came into being during the mid-Victorian period.'[3] He points out that from the 1850s onwards, Welsh radicals 'represented Wales as a "nation", defined by its adherence to nonconformity, characterized by its peculiar culture, and ambitious for equal representation with the other nations of Britain in the Imperial parliament.'[4] Thus, from the 1868 election onwards, 'it became a commonplace...that the job of Welsh MPs was to fight for the interests of "Wales" at Westminster as stoutly as Members from Scotland and Ireland battled on behalf of their nations.'[5] The emergence of the *Cymru Fydd* movement, associated with Thomas E Ellis MP and Lloyd George, was also significant in consolidating ideas

---

[1] Idris Davies, 'London Welsh', *Wales*, Vol III, 3 (1944), p. 7.   [2] Owen, 'London', p. 109.
[3] Cragoe, *Culture*, p. 2.   [4] Cragoe, *Culture*, p. 38.
[5] Cragoe, *Culture*, p. 2. Cragoe thus qualifies the traditional historiographical emphasis on the 1880s as the beginning of Wales's national renaissance. See Kenneth O' Morgan, *Rebirth of a Nation. A History of Modern Wales* (Oxford, 1998).

of Welsh cultural difference.[6] Founded in London in 1886, *Cymru Fydd* was a nationalist movement within Welsh Liberalism[7] which called for Welsh Home Rule and Welsh disestablishment.[8] From the 1880s onwards, therefore, new institutions, legal changes and increasingly vocal Welsh Liberal MPs brought Welsh issues to the fore, helping to 'establish a distinctly Welsh presence in Westminster'.[9] In Chris Williams's view, any separatist spirit in Wales was increasingly 'killed by Kindness', the passage of the Welsh Sunday Closing Act in 1881, for example, being 'a recognition of the legitimacy of Welsh cultural and religious identities, in an era which saw the creation of key Welsh civic institutions such as a university, national library and national museum'.[10]

Whilst Lloyd George provides the focal point of any discussion of Wales's imprint on British parliamentary affairs, the connections between an earlier prime minister, William Ewart Gladstone, and Wales were also significant. Gladstone, whose final term as prime minister ended in 1894, had married Catherine Glynne whose family owned a large ancestral estate, Hawarden, in Flintshire. From the 1850s onwards, the couple spent up to half a year at Hawarden Castle, only a few miles from the border with the English county of Cheshire.[11] Although Gladstone himself was born in Liverpool of Scots ancestry, as a result of his marriage, argues Ronald Quinault, his changing perception of the borderlands between England and Wales 'helped to refashion national attitudes'.[12] Quinault notes that whilst Gladstone's gradual emergence as a champion of distinctive Welsh culture owed much to his wider commitment to Irish Home Rule, his residence at Hawarden 'did affect both his attitude to Wales and his sense of family identity' and had a political importance that should not be underestimated.[13] In 1873, Gladstone spoke to the Welsh National Eisteddfod at Mold, stating that his 'connexion [sic] with Wales' was 'very dear' to him.[14] In an 1888 Eisteddfod speech, Gladstone referred to 'his Welsh wife' and his hope that their children 'will not forget that they are in part Welsh people'. However, he also acknowledged that because Hawarden was close to the border with England it had not 'come so absolutely under Welsh influence'.[15] Cragoe notes that in the post-1867 period, 'the enthusiasm of Welsh liberals for Gladstone was

---

[6] Wynn Thomas, *Nations*, pp. 6–13.   [7] See Williams, 'Problematizing', p. 7.

[8] Morgan, *Rebirth*, 114; Wynn Thomas, *Nations of Wales*, p. 9. When the movement effectively folded, in 1896, Lloyd George decided that 'it was as a British Liberal not a Welsh nationalist that his future was to lie'. From this point onwards, his Welshness 'was always connected to a wider Britishness'. See Morgan, *Rebirth*, p. 118; Ward, *Unionism*, p. 74.

[9] Benbough-Jackson, 'Negotiating', pp. 263–90, 267.   [10] Williams, 'Problematizing', p. 6.

[11] Ronald Quinault, 'Unofficial Frontiers: Welsh-English Borderlands in the Victorian Period', in *Borderlands*, edited by Readman, Radding, and Bryant, p. 286.

[12] Quinault, 'Unofficial', p. 286.

[13] Quinault, 'Unofficial', p. 288. For more on the Gladstones, see Chapter 6, 'A Veray Parfit Gentil Knyghte'.

[14] Quinault, 'Unofficial', p. 287.   [15] Quinault, 'Unofficial', p. 288.

extraordinary' suggesting a level of reciprocated affection.[16] The arrival of Lloyd George in the political firmament, who became the first Welsh-speaking prime minister, further consolidated the parliamentary bond between the two nations.

Elected to Parliament in 1890 as the MP for Caernarfon Boroughs, Lloyd George was appointed President of the Board of Trade in the 1906 Liberal administration, then Chancellor of the Exchequer in 1908 where he introduced an ambitious programme of social reform. He became a wartime prime minister in 1916.[17] Commemorating his fifty years in Westminster in 1940, the London Welsh Association referred to him as 'the most renowned Welshman in the World's history'.[18] Ward notes how Lloyd George utilized his Welshness to strengthen his position within British Liberalism and then, as prime minister, 'played upon a story of his life that portrayed a rise from humble beginnings to Downing Street, in which he rode democratic Welsh society to a path of respectability and self-discipline.'[19] However, Lloyd George himself emerged from the Welsh diaspora in England; his Welsh parents were living in Manchester when he was born in 1863, an 'accident of birth which made him officially English'.[20] In a 1960 memoir, his eldest son, Richard Lloyd George, relates how he once challenged his father on this fact: '"You're a Mancunian by birth. Don't you ever identify yourself with Manchester and the English?" He laughed. "National feeling has nothing to do with geography, Dick. It's a state of mind".'[21] Lloyd George's family, the 'First Family of Wales', was also complicit in the wider performance of Welshness in England.[22] Richard recalls how, from the time of their move from Criccieth to London, his parents mixed with 'an elect colony' of Welshmen, including bankers, insurance underwriters, and 'drapers in Oxford Street, who had founded famous firms' such as D. H. Evans.[23] During these early years, the Lloyd Georges stayed with the retailer R. O. Davies in Acton and also with one of Lloyd George's mistresses, 'Mrs Tim', Elizabeth Davies, the wife of a draper who lived in Putney.[24] The Lloyd George family spoke Welsh in their London homes and had staff recruited from Criccieth.[25] In his memoir, Richard recalls:

---

[16] Cragoe, *Culture*, p. 36.
[17] Kenneth O. Morgan, 'George, David Lloyd, first Earl Lloyd-George of Dwyfor', *ODNB* (2018), https://doi-org.ezproxy.is.ed.ac.uk/10.1093/ref:odnb/34570.
[18] *Y Ddolen*, Mehefin 1940, p. 4.   [19] Ward, *Unionism*, p. 97.
[20] Roy Jenkins, *David Lloyd George: The Great Outsider* (London, 2010), p. 1.
[21] Richard Lloyd George, *Lloyd George* (London, 1960), p. 17. Lloyd George received the freedom of the city of Manchester in September 1918; he boasted that he was 'a Mancunian by birth and a Welshman by blood—and proud of both'. 'Mr Lloyd George on Manchester', *The Guardian*, 26 April 1938, p. 14.
[22] Ward, *Unionism*, p. 82.   [23] Lloyd George, *Lloyd George*, p. 48.
[24] David Wyn Davies, *A Welshman in Mesopotamia* (Aberystwyth, 1986), p. 2; Ffion Hague, *The Pain and Privilege. The Women in Lloyd George's Life* (London, 2009), p. 135.
[25] Ward, *Unionism*, p. 83; Owen Lloyd George, *A Tale of Two Grandfathers* (London, 1999), p. 17.

All our [London] homes were comfortable, very well run and invariably staffed by Welsh servants. There was a rather strange contrast in our lives as a result: as soon as we stepped outside the house we were in a foreign land with a different language, customs and mental climate.[26]

Richard transmits an awareness of his own 'otherness' in the metropolis, returning to this point later in his memoir and suggesting that his parents' Downing Street home 'must have presented a weird spectacle to their English friends and visitors: the wild clansmen from foreign parts picnicking in the heart of Westminster.'[27] The family also maintained their Welsh links through their visible chapel attendance in London. Lloyd George had a particularly close association with the Welsh Baptist Chapel in East Castle Street; his daughter Olwen married Thomas Carey Evans there in June 1917 in a ceremony conducted 'almost entirely in Welsh.'[28] Its significance was summarized by a contemporary Welsh journalist: 'Here was the prime minister of Great Britain, a world leader, a war leader, attending a Baptist chapel to give away his beautiful daughter to be married to one of Wales's best sons, and doing so in the Welsh language, without a shadow of shame about their culture, their language, their religion, their nation.'[29] Lloyd George's wife, Margaret, attended the Welsh Presbyterian Chapel, Clapham Junction, with her daughters Mair and Megan and son Gwilym; when Mair died in 1907, the family commissioned the artist Thomas Figgis Curtis to design a stained glass memorial window.[30] Within media representations, the female members of the family were constructed in terms of their philanthropy, often attached to ideas of Welshness. Mair's obituary noted, 'She had latterly been interested, like her mother, in temperance and mission work, and only a couple of Sundays before her death she had been with some of her young girl friends from the chapel to a Welsh Mission in the East End.'[31] During the First World War, Margaret was positioned at the forefront of gendered diasporic initiatives in support of the Welsh. She sat on the Ladies' Committee of the 15th Battalion Royal Welch Fusiliers and, on St David's Day 1916, helped organize the London Welsh 'Flag and Postcard Day': a street collection by three thousand women in Welsh costume aiming to provide 'comforts' for Welsh regiments. As part of this initiative, 'two giant leeks hung from a centre lamp' at 11 Downing Street.[32] A First World War press cutting of Margaret with her daughter, Olwen Carey Evans, at the opening of a canteen for war workers at Shepherd's Bush, is entitled 'Wales at the White City', embodying

---

[26] Lloyd George, *Lloyd George*, p. 49.   [27] Lloyd George, *Lloyd George*, p. 92.
[28] 'Marriage of Miss Olwen Lloyd George', *North Wales Chronicle*, 22 June 1917, p. 5; Olwen Carey Evans, *Lloyd George Was My Father* (Llandysul, 1985), p. 94.
[29] Cited in Huw Edwards, *City Mission: The Story of London's Welsh Chapels* (Talybont, 2014), p. 215.
[30] Hywel Thomas, 'Mair Memorial' *The Times*, 4 March 2009, p. 27.
[31] *Evening Express*, 6 December 1907, p. 3.
[32] 'Welsh Flag Day in London', *North Wales Chronicle*, 3 March 1916, p. 5.

the women as the Welsh nation. As Paul Ward comments, Margaret provided 'a feminine symbol of patriotism to Welsh women as the two sons of the Lloyd George family, Gwilym and Richard, provided masculine symbols in their enlistment to the army.'[33] A couple of months before the outbreak of the Second World War, Margaret, in her role as president of the Young Women's Christian Association in Wales, 'went to Liverpool to try to interest Liverpool-Welsh women in the work.'[34] During the war, Olwen was appointed chair of the Ladies' Committee of the Welsh Troops' Service Club in London.[35] Even in the late 1930s, the official representatives of the London Welsh community continued to find relevance via their association with the family. On the occasion of Lloyd George's golden wedding anniversary in 1938, celebrated in Antibes, the London Welsh newsletter, *Y Ddolen,* recounts: 'a large number of the congratulatory telegrams… came from their compatriots in the Metropolis. It was in London that the future Prime Minster and his young bride from Mynydd Ednyfed spent their honeymoon and shortly afterwards they came here to live.'[36] In 1940, the London Welsh Association announced the Lloyd George 'Shilling Fund' in recognition of the politician's fifty years as a member of parliament and 'long association with London Welsh life' and, significantly, his physical embodiment of the link ('*y ddolen*') between the two nations: 'Attention was called to his great services for our nation, which he "put on the map" in more ways than one, and to his energy, foresight and great driving power during the last war, which secured the safety of Wales and England.'[37]

Lloyd George as Talisman

Lloyd George makes an appearance in many of the diasporic life writing sources explored in this book, taking on a talismanic significance as the supreme representative of Welshness in England. For example, poet Edward Thomas's civil servant father was said to converse with Lloyd George, 'as they took their daily morning walk "across the park" from the underground station at Westminster'.[38] The politician could also be spotted like an exotic bird. Eliot Crawshay-Williams, his one-time parliamentary private secretary, writes of a 1912 motoring holiday to the Wrexham Eisteddfod where he caught glimpses of Lloyd George 'picnicking up mountain streams with little Megan'.[39] The Wirral dentist, Jack Lloyd, whilst on holiday in Criccieth in 1919, wrote back home, 'Lloyd George was on

---

[33] Ward, *Unionism*, p. 79.
[34] 'Dame Margaret', *Nottingham Evening Post*, 21 January 1941, p. 4.
[35] Carey Evans, *Lloyd*, p. 165.   [36] *Y Ddolen*, Chwefror, 1938, p. 14.
[37] *Y Ddolen*, Mehefin, 1940, p. 4.
[38] R. George Thomas, *Edward Thomas. A Portrait* (Oxford, 1997), p. 17.
[39] Eliot Crawshay-Williams, *Simple Story. An Accidental Autobiography* (London, 1935), p. 121.

the shore during the week and it was interesting to see the little children go up to him, he kissed some of them.'[40] In the early months of the First World War, for the fathers of English sons considering service in Welsh regiments, Lloyd George was their first port of call. In August 1914, Alfred Graves, a fortnight after his son Robert's enlistment in the Royal Welch Fusiliers at Wrexham, wrote to Lloyd George 'asking him to speak out on the subject of the Welsh volunteering'.[41] When the idea of the London Welsh battalion was first mooted, the poet David Jones's father contacted Lloyd George directly, and in reply received a badge for his son.[42] For second-generation Welshmen in England, eligible for enlistment, the idea of Lloyd George was there to be engaged with, either positively or negatively. David Jones went to hear Lloyd George speak in public three times, including his infamous address at Queen's Hall in September 1914.[43] Thomas Dilworth even suggests that Lloyd George's 'oratorical panache' on this occasion may have informed the 'great, rhetorically heightened boast' by Dai Greatcoat which appears in Jones's 1937 modernist text, *In Parenthesis*.[44] Conversely, Battersea-born civil servant Julian Thomas railed against Lloyd George in his diary, writing in October 1915 of 'the invidious attempts of the grinning Lloyd-George-Northcliffe demons to terrorise the simple-hearted common people'.[45] By February 1918, he viewed the Prime Minister as someone who had, 'half a million broken lives on his conscience already'.[46] Similarly, in a 1917 letter to his mother, Susan, from France, poet Wilfred Owen spoke of the dreadful battle conditions his regiment were enduring and concluded bitterly, 'if there is any power whom the Soldiery execrate more than another it is that of our distinguished countryman. You may pass it on via Owen, Owen.'[47] This was an allusion both to Owen's own Welsh ancestry and Lloyd George's association with the owner of Liverpool's flagship retail store, Owen. Guy Cuthbertson confirms that Wilfred Owen's father was a great admirer of the prime minister, 'partly because Lloyd George was Welsh'.[48] Cuthbertson also suggests that Owen's famous poem, 'Anthem for Doomed Youth' which 'asks for bells, orisons, choirs, prayers, candles and flowers' in honour of the war dead, mirrors an argument Lloyd George had made a year earlier, in 1917, at the Aberystwyth National Eisteddfod: 'Why should we not sing during war? Why, especially, should we not sing at this stage of the War? The blinds of Britain are not down yet, nor are they likely to be.' This latter sentiment

---

[40] SELO 1/6, Letters to SL's parents from their children and each other 1914–22, 13 July 1919.
[41] Alfred Perceval Graves, *To Return To All That. An Autobiography* (London, 1930), p. 297.
[42] Thomas Dilworth, *David Jones in the Great War* (London, 2012), pp. 35–6.
[43] Dilworth, *David Jones*, pp. 36–7.   [44] Dilworth, *David Jones*, p. 37.
[45] Cardiff University Special Collections and Archives (CUSCA) 424/5/5/1/3, Julian Thomas diary, p. 51.
[46] CUSCA 424/5/5/1/3, Julian Thomas diary, p. 68.
[47] 'Letter 480, 16 January 1917', in *Wilfred Owen. Collected Letters*, edited by Harold Owen and John Bell (London, 1967), p. 428. For more on Owen Owen see Davies, *Welshman in Mesopotamia*.
[48] Guy Cuthbertson, *Wilfred Owen* (New Haven, 2015), p. 202.

is captured in the poem's last line, 'And each slow dusk a drawing-down of blinds.'[49]

Concentric Political Circles

Such was the political magnetism of Lloyd George that he also influenced subsequent generations of English Welsh politicians, such as Eliot Crawshay-Williams and Selwyn Lloyd. Crawshay-Williams was an MP for Leicester from 1910–13 and for many years a star in the Liberal firmament at Westminster, before scandal destroyed his career.[50] The English-born son of Welsh MP Arthur John Williams, Crawshay-Williams provides a quintessential example of a dual identifying dynastic politician. His mother, Rose, was the daughter of Robert Thompson Crawshay of Cyfarthna Castle near Merthyr Tydfil in South Wales, heir to the 'Iron King'. Crawshay-Williams was born in London in 1879 and experienced the classic upbringing for a Welsh parliamentarian's son: childhood homes in both England and Wales, and an education in England combined with a strong sense of Welsh identification instilled through familial and political ties. In his 1935 autobiography, *Simple Story*, Crawshay-Williams records that he was born at 'Ynyslas', a house in South Kensington, but that until the age of ten he lived almost entirely in Eastbourne. He reminisces fondly of his childhood home at 7 South Cliff, 'looking out over the sea, so that I could build light-houses of bricks in front of the nursery window, with a nightlight a-top to bring the ships that went down the Channel safe to port.'[51] Crawshay-Williams states that the 'pivot' of his life shifted when his family moved to the country house his father had built near Bridgend, Plas Coed y Mwstwr: 'Between the ages of ten and twelve my brother and I vegetated in Wales.'[52] He depicts his new life as 'uneventful', consisting of walks up country lanes looking at 'the fauna, flora, and other ingredients of the countryside'. For him and his brother Leslie, this did not compare favourably with the 'seaside watering place' they had left behind.[53] Crawshay-Williams also points to their struggle to conform to the ideal of 'a country gentleman', writing that 'the genuine local article never really took us to their hearts. They looked upon us, indeed, more or less as aliens, if not as interlopers; this attitude being intensified by the fact that my father did not hunt or shoot, and was a Liberal MP.'[54] Crawshay-Williams was educated at Eton and Trinity College, Oxford.[55] Following graduation, he was commissioned into the Royal Field Artillery and

---

[49] Cuthbertson, *Wilfred*, pp. 200–2.
[50] He was named as co-respondent in a divorce case brought by his fellow Liberal MP, Hubert Carr-Gomm. Crawshay-Williams, *Simple*, p. 123.
[51] Crawshay-Williams, *Simple*, p. 23.   [52] Crawshay-Williams, *Simple*, pp. 27, 30.
[53] Crawshay-Williams, *Simple*, p. 28.   [54] Crawshay-Williams, *Simple*, p. 28.
[55] Crawshay-Williams, *Simple*, pp. 30–43.

posted to India.[56] Ultimately, however, he decided to pursue a political career and was nominated as the Liberal candidate for Chorley. In 1904 he became preoccupied with a campaign around 'Tests for Teachers' which drew him into Lloyd George's orbit. The campaign, he wrote, served to 'divide my attention between Wales and Lancashire…Wales, as always in such a matter, was to the fore; and Lloyd George, with equal inevitability, took the lead for Wales.' As part of this process, Crawshay-Williams was appointed Honorary Secretary to the Campaign Committee of the Welsh National Liberal Council, an organizational responsibility which involved him visiting what he calls 'my native land'.[57] When Crawshay-Williams failed to get elected in 1906, he became employed in the Colonial Office, an appointment heralded in the Welsh press as 'Welshman's Success'.[58] J Graham Jones notes that whilst interested in a candidacy at Pembrokeshire, Crawshay-Williams delivered lectures to Liberal associations across South Wales and, in 1907, was appointed a JP for the county of Glamorgan.[59] In 1912, he supported the campaign to disestablish and disendow the Welsh Church, and after being elected MP for Leicester in 1910, Crawshay-Williams became Lloyd George's parliamentary private secretary.[60] During this period, Crawshay-Williams lived at 28 Langham Mansions in Earl's Court Square and married Alice Gay Roberts in Westminster in 1908.[61] However, their daughter, Olwen, born in London in 1909, was christened at a ceremony in Coychurch, 'our Welsh village'.[62] Thus, whilst Crawshay-Williams was born and based in England, Wales remained hugely important to his own sense of selfhood. In 1911, Eliot started an acquaintance-ship with a young Welsh composer, Morfydd Llwyn Owen, which heightened his enthrallment with Wales.[63] In a 1912 letter Morfydd alludes to '"Nancy" (the girl who's going to teach you Harmony in Welsh).'[64] The following month, she writes from Maida Vale: 'you must learn Welsh. You'd love to write Welsh poetry—the words are so much more expressive than English ones they seem to mean so much more.'[65] Owen died prematurely in 1918 and in a short memoir, written four decades later, Crawshay-Williams reproduces this letter, lamenting, 'But alas! I never learnt Welsh.'[66]

[56] Crawshay-Williams, *Simple*, pp. 46–7. [57] Crawshay-Williams, *Simple*, p. 53.
[58] *Evening Express,* 5 March 1906, p. 4.
[59] J. Graham Jones, 'Champion of Liberalism: Eliot Crawshay-Williams', *Journal of Liberal History* 59 (2008), pp. 4–15, 7–8.
[60] Graham Jones, 'Champion', p. 11; Crawshay-Williams, *Simple*, pp. 96, 103.
[61] Crawshay-Williams, *Simple*, pp. 65, 78. [62] Crawshay-Williams, *Simple*, p. 92.
[63] NLW; GB 0210 ELICRAAMS; Eliot Crawshay-Williams Papers (ECW); G29/6, Letter from William Owen, 6 May 1911.
[64] NLW; ECW; G26/40, Letter from Morfydd Owen, 17 October 1912.
[65] NLW; ECW; G26/49, Letter from Morfydd Owen, 20 November 1912.
[66] NLW; ECW; G26/49; Eliot Crawshay-Williams, 'The Tragedy of Morfydd', in *Ddwias* (Mar 1959), pp. 17–18.

Throughout his parliamentary career, Crawshay-Williams was firmly based in England but made regular sojourns into Wales.[67] For example, he says of 1912, 'We spent the autumn between Wales and London, with political jaunts, for me, both to my constituency and to other parts of the Kingdom.'[68] Crawshay-Williams's affair with Kathleen Carr-Gomm, the wife of a parliamentary colleague, had its roots in Wales. He refers to the decision of the two married couples in 1911 to have a 'joint camping enterprise near my home in Wales...we four roughed it rather luxuriously in tents in a field.'[69] On hearing that he was cited as the Carr-Gomm divorce co-respondent, Crawshay-Williams recognized it as 'the death blow of my career'.[70] In the midst of the scandal he was involved in a defensive correspondence with his Welsh mother. In a letter of 27 January, marked 'not sent', he indicates that their falling out constitutes a breach with Wales, concluding: 'it will never come to pass that Alice or I or the children will ever ask to come to our home again .... Well, I shall have to come to Bridgend on magisterial matters, and I shall stay at the Dunraven Arms.'[71] However, by March 1913 their correspondence had reverted back to polite discourse about the South Wales Horse Show Society and in June Crawshay-Williams thanked his mother for her parcel of asparagus and artichokes: 'they are so much nicer than the London ones'.[72] In 1914, he and Kathleen moved into 16 Embankment Residences, London, a city for which he displays an equal affection:

> The view of the Thames, with its ceaseless change of colour and scene; the Whistlerian hazes of mist and cloud at evening and in the early morning; the faint outlines, in summer, of Epsom Downs to the south...all have come to be a part of my life which would leave a sad gap if wrenched away.[73]

Around this time, Crawshay-Williams also purchased a land plot in Deal, Kent and built a new home, named 'Tybryn'—'the Welsh compression of "House on the Hill"'.[74] He informs the reader: 'Tybryn (of which name, lest it suffer cruel mispronunciation, or even be perverted to "Tyburn", let me say each "y" is short).'[75] His duality continued to be performed throughout the First World War. In May 1914, Crawshay-Williams took over the command of the Leicestershire Royal Horse Artillery (TF) Battery and, on the declaration of war, characterized his sentiments as 'less ardently bloodthirsty than those of the average patriotic Englishman of the moment'.[76] In 1917, he published a volume of poetry, *Songs on*

---

[67] Crawshay-Williams, *Simple*, p. 91.   [68] Crawshay-Williams, *Simple*, p. 108.
[69] Crawshay-Williams, *Simple*, pp. 118, 120.   [70] Crawshay-Williams, *Simple*, p. 123.
[71] NLW; ECW; D3/1, [Draft] Letter to mother, 27 January 1913. He sends a briefer version of this letter on 29 January.
[72] NLW; ECW; D3/1, Letter to mother, 17 June 1913.   [73] Crawshay-Williams, *Simple*, p. 146.
[74] Crawshay-Williams, *Simple*, pp. 145–6.   [75] Crawshay-Williams, *Simple*, p. 162.
[76] Crawshay-Williams, *Simple*, pp. 147, 151.

Service which was picked up by the Welsh press on the grounds of Crawshay-Williams being a 'member of a well-known Glamorganshire family'.[77] The collection included these lines from the poem, 'September in Egypt': 'Ever in my ears are the home names ringing: Kénfig, Llysworney, Tresilian, Tondu|In my deep heart are my Welsh folk singing|Rich as the sunset, strong as the sea.'[78] Here, Crawshay-Williams cites Welsh place names in the Vale of Glamorgan as a form of incantation whilst expressing a possessive claim with 'my Welsh folk'. He underscores his avowed sense of Welshness by dedicating the anthology to Lloyd George, pointing to their shared affection for 'our own dear mountain land'. However the collection also includes a poem about England, where Crawshay Williams actually lived.[79] In his wartime journal, *Leaves from an Officer's Notebook*, published in 1918, Crawshay-Williams consistently refers to his home nation as England, rather than Britain, and uses English mores as a continual point of reference.[80] However there is one illuminating scene where he mentions the presence of a Welsh Infantry Division (Transport) on a 1916 voyage to Alexandria and their impromptu choral session on the ship's forepart:

> The Welshmen sat in a little group in the sunshine, the sergeant who was conducting them in their midst. For a moment there was silence while they watched him. Then he motioned with his hand, and there arose the wailing minor strains of 'Aberystwith' [sic]. It was a strange effect, that little group of men out on the sea…with those wonderful rich voices that are their natural right. I heard song after song full of the mournful beauty of my lovely land, and, despite myself, my eyes filled with tears.[81]

During the same voyage, Crawshay-Williams represents Wales versus 'the World' at deck quoits.[82] He also mentions that he is accompanied by his pet dog, Tynton, whose name is 'really Welsh, but it sounds Pekinese'.[83] Thus, through his various forms of life writing, Crawshay-Williams consistently signals his emotional ties with Wales, whilst his more formal parliamentary or military personas remain attached to England.

In 1917, Crawshay-Williams lost his military command.[84] He returned to England 'in a state of spiritual misery' and was posted to the Honourable Artillery

---

[77] *The Cambria Daily Leader*, 26 April 1917, p. 2.
[78] Eliot Crawshay-Williams, *Songs on Service* (Oxford, 1917), pp. 52–3.
[79] 'One Night at Okehampton', in Crawshay-Williams, *Songs*, p. 9.
[80] Gaffney has noted that some memorialization events in post–First World War Wales referred to sacrifices made specifically for 'England' demonstrating 'no contradiction in the use and interchangeability' of the terms 'Britain' and 'England'. Gaffney, *Aftermath*, pp. 159–60.
[81] Eliot Crawshay-Williams, *Leaves from An Officer's Notebook* (London, 1918), p. 115.
[82] Crawshay-Williams, *Leaves*, p. 118.   [83] Crawshay-Williams, *Leaves*, p. 16.
[84] Crawshay-Williams, *Simple*, pp. 199–203.

Company at Leeds.[85] The following year, he was indicted at Leeds Assizes for 'a serious offence' against the ten year-old daughter of the couple with whom he was lodging. The *Glamorgan Gazette* refers to the 'grave charge' against Captain Eliot Crawshay-Williams 'of the Army Quartering Department, Park Square, Leeds, and of Coedymwstwr, Bridgend' that he had 'tampered with the child' whilst her parents were absent.[86] After being acquitted on all charges, Crawshay-Williams spent more time at the family mansion in Bridgend, re-establishing himself, in the interwar period, as an author and tennis player, representing Wales.[87]

The politician John Selwyn Brooke Lloyd was born in West Kirby on 28 July 1904, the son of surgeon-dentist Jack Lloyd and Mary Warhurst, and the great grandson of Rev. John Lloyd of Llanidloes.[88] When Lloyd stood as a Liberal Party candidate for the Macclesfield constituency in 1929, his party literature defined him as 'a Cheshire man for a Cheshire constituency'.[89] However, his ease with the idea of Welshness, born of his ancestral links and reinforced by regular family holidays in Wales, meant Lloyd was able to comfortably fit in with the influential Welsh Liberal political elite. Lloyd was raised in a solidly middle class environment in 25 Banks Road, West Kirby with his father attending Welsh dinners on St David's Day at the Adelphi Hotel.[90] After being privately educated at Fettes College, Edinburgh, Lloyd read law at Magdalene College, Cambridge. Once at university, in 1923, Lloyd sought to cultivate a relationship with Lloyd George as a way of furthering his own political ambitions, firstly gaining access as an undergraduate member of Cambridge University's Liberal Club and, secondly, through a friendship with Lloyd George's daughter, Megan, forged whilst holidaying in Criccieth. Lloyd's letters to his family from Cambridge reveal how, in October 1926, he had tea with Lloyd George's elder daughter, Olwen Carey Evans, when she came to open the Liberal Bazaar.[91] In 1927 he spotted Lloyd George and Megan at the Summer School Garden party at King's and, as shown in Figure 1.1, had his photograph taken alongside the former.[92]

The following year Lloyd got closer to his political hero when he had tea with Lloyd George 'in a private sitting-room at the Varsity Arms'.[93] Lloyd also wrote to his mother about a Liberal reception, 'Gwilym Lloyd George and his wife were there with Lloyd George. I had a word with Lloyd George himself later in a room

---

[85] Crawshay-Williams, *Simple*, p. 205; NLW; ECW; D3/1, Letter to mother, 17 April 1917.
[86] 'Grave Charge Against Capt. Eliot Crawshay Williams', *The Glamorgan Gazette*, 29 November 1918, p. 3.
[87] Crawshay-Williams, *Simple*, pp. 260, 282.
[88] SELO 12/162; Funeral cards, notes from Parish registers and correspondence.
[89] SELO 1/1, Letters from family and colleagues 1910–1971; Letter from father, 24 May 1929; SELO 6/12; Correspondence on Liberal Party activities 1927–34; 'The Prospective Candidate', *Macclesfield Times*.
[90] SELO 12/20, Letters to family and friends 1869–1911; 1913 pocket diary of J. W. Lloyd.
[91] SELO 1/27, Letters from Lloyd at Magdalene 1925–27.
[92] SELO 1/15, Letters from Lloyd while at Cambridge 1922–27; July 1927.
[93] SELO 1/36, Letters from Lloyd 1928–29, Letter to father, March 1928.

Figure 1.1 Selwyn Lloyd pictured directly at Lloyd George's right shoulder, Cambridge 1927.
Source: Churchill Archives Centre; SE11/20. Reproduced with permission of the Estate of Selwyn Lloyd.

downstairs. He asked after Macclesfield, and said he remembered seeing me down at Criccieth.'[94] Lloyd's family regularly holidayed in Criccieth where the Lloyd Georges had a family home, Brynawelon, and this secured another vantage point for the aspiring politician. In the late 1920s, Lloyd wrote from Henfaes Private Hotel:

> Criccieth is much the same as usual. On Monday I went up to tea at the Lloyd Georges' after golf in the morning. On Tuesday I took Megan to an agricultural show in Anglesey & dined with the Lloyd Georges... [on Thursday] spent some time on the shore with Megan in the morning and watched the cinema with her in the afternoon and went out to tea with her and Miss Cazalet... so you can see that I am losing no opportunity with her!![95]

---

[94] SELO 1/37, Letters from Selwyn Lloyd and Rachel Lloyd to their parents 1928–38; Letter to mother from 122 Victoria Road.
[95] SELO 1/32, Letters from Lloyd to his mother and sisters 1927–29 & undated; Letter to mother and Rachel, n.d.

In this period, Lloyd was keen to make links with those who were 'useful' to his career, particularly via his Welsh ties:

> I met on Tuesday a man called Captain Crawshay whom I have long wanted to meet: he is a great friend of Megan Lloyd George's, an Arch-Druid or Arch-bard or something important in the Eisteddfod, on the Welsh Rugger Union, President of the London Welsh and incidentally Liberal candidate for Pontypool. He was a captain in the Welsh Guards—only about 35, and an interesting and useful man to know.[96]

Lloyd was called to the Bar in 1930, establishing a legal practice in Liverpool. By this time, he appears to have solidified his network of English Welsh acquaintances. His foray into the Welsh Liberal political establishment also involved the Gladstone dynasty. Following his unsuccessful electoral attempt in 1929, the Gladstone family invited him to parties, to play tennis at Hawarden, and to take part in village cricket matches. In 1930, Lady Maud Gladstone wrote, 'I think you must now consent to be considered a member of our very large family, and do feel able to come over whenever you can.'[97] In a letter to his mother from this period, Lloyd writes from Hawarden Castle, 'I spent the morning talking politics to H N G [Henry Neville Gladstone] and the afternoon playing games about the house.'[98] Whilst working as a barrister in Liverpool in 1932 he wrote to his father:

> Sunday 240 miles—to Criccieth via Ruthin, Betws etc, lunch with the Lloyd Georges, on to Portmeirion after lunch, back by Festiniog-Betws [sic] and the Denbigh moors, home for late tea, dinner at Hawarden.[99]

In the mid-1930s, Lloyd was also befriended by the Mostyn family of Flintshire. Based in Liverpool, he was invited by various female members of the family to events such as 'the Welsh Dragon Ball' and the Denbigh Tournament.[100] It seems clear that once Lloyd had stood as a Liberal candidate, he was embraced by the elite Welsh Liberal establishment, and used his Welsh associations to his advantage.[101] Indeed, Lloyd was also caught up in rumours of a supposed intimacy with Megan. He wrote to his mother in January 1928, 'I have just written giving an unqualified denial to the Megan Lloyd George rumour!! Everyone is very much

---

[96] SELO 1/15, Letter to father, 24 November 1927.
[97] SELO 1/17, Letters from Lady Gladstone 1928–33; 16 August 1929; 6 August 1930.
[98] SELO 1/37, Letter from Lloyd to his mother, n.d.
[99] SELO 1/46, Letters from Lloyd to his parents 1931–32, 17 May 1932.
[100] SELO 1/24, Letters from family and friends to Lloyd 1925–37; Letters from members of the Mostyn family, 28 April 1935, 28 June 1935.
[101] Lloyd broke with the Liberals in 1931 and eventually switched his allegiance to the Conservatives. See D. R. Thorpe, *Selwyn Lloyd* (London, 1989), pp. 55–9.

amused about it and wants to know whether it is really true. I think that they suspect something beneath the surface!'[102] And four days later:

> I wrote to the *Macclesfield Times* about the Megan affair. To my horror I find in this week's *Times* (Macclesfield) the paragraphs from the People plus a section from my letter. Mr Lloyd, interviewed, said:
> 'I do not know whether I am the gentleman referred to but, if so, the rumour is utterly without foundation, and I give it an unqualified denial.' There is a small headline describing this as an 'emphatic statement'!!! ... I will send you the thing about Megan.[103]

In spite of this, Lloyd's friendship with the Lloyd Georges persisted through the 1930s. In 1934 Megan invited him to Criccieth, 'Father wants to have a political discussion tomorrow night...and he would like you to come.'[104] Following the outbreak of the Second World War, when he was based at the Staff College, Camberley, Lloyd writes to his father in Criccieth, asking to be remembered 'to Megan if you see her, and thank her for her kind messages'.[105] In March 1941, on leave at Criccieth, from his home posting with the 43rd Wessex Division, Lloyd revisits Brynawelon:

> It is not the same place without Dame Margaret. Megan and Olwyn [sic] and Tom Carey Evans are here for a week—strange how they always seems to come the same week as I do...Megan looks fairly well. She is very busy planning a corner of their garden as a sort of memorial garden to her Mother.[106]

Whilst serving in the Army during the war Lloyd received a letter from a friend who was on sick leave in Denbigh, 'your native country',[107] highlighting the extent to which Lloyd was perceived to be Welsh by his peers. Yet, at Christmas 1941, sending festive greetings to his parents, he remarked, 'On the whole there are very few countries where people will be able to be as happy as we in England, and on the whole very few places with less cause for unhappiness than Hoylake.'[108] Overall, over the course of decades, Lloyd seems not to have been unduly preoccupied with his Welshness within his personal correspondence, but his letters do illuminate the ways in which he used this ancestral connection, combined with knowledge acquired through holidays in Criccieth, to assert a sense of Welsh

---

[102] SELO 1/37; 11 January 1928.   [103] SELO 1/37, Letter to mother, 15 January 1928.
[104] SELO 6/12, Letter from Megan Lloyd George, September 1934.
[105] SELO 1/55, Letters from parents and sisters to Lloyd during his time at Camberley, September–November 1939; 9 November 1939.
[106] SELO 1/72, Letters from Lloyd to his parents, April 1941; 25 March 1941.
[107] SELO 1/61, Letters from family and friends to Lloyd during his military service, January–March 1940; Letter from Gordon Clover, n.d.
[108] SELO 1/68, Letters from Lloyd to his parents, December 1941–May 1943; 20 December 1941.

identification, foregrounding this when he was pursuing political ambitions within the world of Welsh Liberalism in England.

Gendering Dualities

Another expression of English Welsh identities within the political world came from a group of female political campaigners and social reformers who included Margaret Haig Thomas, Margaret Wynne Nevinson, and Edith Picton-Turbervill. In her biography of Nevinson, Angela V. John notes the tendency of this metropolitan group of English Welsh women to 'romanticise Wales partly because they did not live there'.[109] In her discussion of the London-born Welsh suffragette, Margaret Haig Thomas, John alludes to 'the multiple identities that an individual can hold in tension at any one time'.[110] This analysis is also pertinent for their contemporary, Picton-Turbervill, who was born in Hereford in 1872 and educated in Bath, before her father inherited Ewenny Priory Estate, in the Vale of Glamorgan, in the 1890s.[111] In the opening page of her autobiography, Picton-Turbervill goes straight to the heart of her historical dual inheritance, staking out a claim for Welsh affinity:

> The Turbervills invaded Glamorgan late in the eleventh century and the founder of the family, Payn Turbervill, was one of the twelve knights who followed Fitzhammon down to Glamorgan.... Having married frequently into leading Welsh families the Turbervills became more Welsh in their sympathies than the Welsh.[112]

Although neither of her parents was born in Wales, Picton-Turbervill is insistent in her Welsh identity claim throughout her memoir, asserting that 'it would be affectation to call ourselves anything but Welsh'.[113] Overall, she presents a romanticized relationship with Wales and her Welsh lineage, recalling how, whilst at Ewenny Priory:

> Many an afternoon I spent alone on the top of the portcullis tower, Bible in hand. Here I looked away to the Welsh hills from whence in days gone by Owen Glyndwyr and other Welshmen again and again attacked the fortified walls of the monastery.[114]

---

[109] John, *Rocking the Boat*, p. 111.
[110] Angela V. John, 'Lifers: Modern Welsh History and the Writing of Biography', *Welsh History Review*, 25, 2 (2010), p. 267.
[111] Edith Picton-Turbervill, *Life is Good. An Autobiography* (London, 1939), p. 29.
[112] Picton-Turbervill, *Life*, p. 9.   [113] Picton-Turbervill, *Life*, p. 57.
[114] Picton-Turbervill, *Life*, p. 84.

During the First World War, Picton-Turbervill worked with the YWCA to provide hostels, canteens, and club-rooms for women workers in munition factories.[115] Her commitment to Welsh affairs, from a distance, continued into her parliamentary career. Elected Labour MP for Wrekin in 1929, her maiden speech was on the 1929 Coal Bill: 'My home for many years, indeed, until recently, was in the Vale of Glamorgan, and no one living there within ten or fifteen miles of one of the largest coal-fields in the world, could be indifferent to, or ignorant of the great problems of the coal-fields, unless he was indifferent to human affairs.'[116] In July 1939, Picton-Turbervill attended a Foyles Welsh Luncheon at Grosvenor House for the launch of her autobiography, *Life is Good*. At the event she noted the presence of the visiting Welsh playwright, Jack Jones, urging everyone to see his play *Rhondda Roundabout* 'if they wished to know something of the life of such a depressed area as the Rhondda.'[117]

In her memoir, Picton-Turbervill refers to another female philanthropist with a similar English Welsh background, Violet Douglas-Pennant, and alludes to the latter's abrupt dismissal as Commandant of the Women's Royal Air Force in August 1918.[118] Douglas-Pennant was born in London in 1869, the sixth daughter of the Welsh peer, second Baron Penrhyn, himself born in Yorkshire of Scottish descent. Her philanthropic work typically crossed the borders between Wales and England: she sat on the London county council education committee, was a governor of the University College of South Wales, and in 1911, was appointed national health insurance commissioner for South Wales.[119] The reasons behind her dismissal from the WRAF, touching obliquely upon suggestions of 'sexual impropriety' became a national *cause célèbre* with Douglas-Pennant utilizing her high-level contacts to resist the decision.[120] Laura Doan notes that, 'This sense of herself as a lady from a prominent family explains why... she did not retire quietly.'[121] Indeed, propelled by the personal intersection between her class, gender, and national identities, Douglas-Pennant displayed a keenness to draw specifically upon her family's ancient Welsh heritage in order to confer authority upon her 'private crusade.'[122] In a confidential report commissioned by Lloyd George in 1918, his secretary Cecil Harmsworth wrote, 'The old Penrhyn spirit is there and I do not think there is any chance of dissuading [her]'

---

[115] Picton-Turbervill, *Life*, p. 117.   [116] Picton-Turbervill, *Life*, p. 175.
[117] *Y Ddolen*, Awst, 1939, p. 6. For a contested version of this occasion, see Jack Jones, *Me and Mine* (London, 1946), p. 108.
[118] Picton-Turbervill, *Life*, pp. 136–7.
[119] Beryl E. Escott, 'Pennant, Violet Blanche Douglas (1869–1945)', *ODNB* (2005), https://doi-org.ezproxy.is.ed.ac.uk/10.1093/ref:odnb/67667.
[120] Douglas-Pennant was, essentially, 'the victim of a whispering campaign intimating that young women under her command were deemed unsafe with an alleged sapphist'. See Laura Doan, *Disturbing Practices. History, Sexuality and Women's Experiences of Modern War* (Chicago, 2013), pp. vii, 140, 147–63.
[121] Doan, *Disturbing*, p. 149.   [122] Escott, 'Pennant'.

from fighting to clear her name.[123] As if to underscore this point, the frontispiece of Douglas-Pennant's own 1922 account of the case, *Under the Search-Light*, includes a Welsh quotation: 'Y gwir yn erbyn y byd' (The truth against the world).[124]

Landed Elites

Another distinctive strand of English Welsh identity in this period was composed of well-connected, aristocratic, or industrial families with stately homes in both England and Wales, who, through their 'transnational land ownership' were enmeshed in the higher echelons of British political and cultural society.[125] Following the Tudor incorporation, Krishan Kumar notes 'the rise of an anglicized Welsh gentry with extensive connections to England'.[126] A demographic crisis in the first half of the eighteenth century meant that, increasingly, economic interests, political ambitions, and the status aspirations of the landed classes coalesced and Welsh landowners 'found themselves tied to their English cousins by marriage and connection'.[127] David Cannadine points to 'the interlocking, interrelated, and interacting élites of England, Ireland, Scotland, and Wales' as a 'supra-national territorial entity' which came into existence from the 1780s to the 1830s.[128] A significant consequence of this extended 'truly British' territorial class was mapped out by the border crossings of younger family members, who were born in England and shaped through the English public school system, whose lives straddled both metropolitan society and Welsh family estates.[129] By the late 1870s, land ownership was concentrated amongst 250 territorial magnates; 'educated at public schools and sometimes at Oxbridge; they lived in country mansions and town houses.... In the localities, they made up county society, and in London they were the foundation of high society.'[130] In his study of Victorian Carmarthenshire, Cragoe points to the functioning of an ethos of paternalism amongst the aristocracy which 'found powerful and practical expression in the

---

[123] Doan, *Disturbing*, p. 149.
[124] Violet Douglas-Pennant, *Under the Search-light. A Record of a Great Scandal* (London, 1922). As a result of Douglas-Pennant's campaigning, there was a House of Lords committee inquiry, as well as high-profile libel suits.
[125] Annie Tindley, 'The Big House in Four Nations – New Directions for the Study of Landed and Aristocratic Elites?' *Four Nations Blog*, https://fournationshistory.wordpress.com/2017/02/06/the-big-house-in-four-nations-new-directions-for-the-study-of-landed-and-aristocratic-elites/, accessed 23 February 2017.
[126] Kumar, *Making*, p. 74.
[127] David Cannadine, *Aspects of Aristocracy. Grandeur and Decline in Modern Britain* (New Haven & London, 1994), pp. 11, 33, 34.
[128] David Cannadine, *The Decline and Fall of the British Aristocracy* (New Haven & London, 1990), p. 5.
[129] Cannadine, *Decline*, p. 5.   [130] Cannadine, *Decline*, pp. 10, 13.

'moral economy" of the landed estate' with its community of landowners and tenants.[131] Furthermore, their local leadership roles as justices of the peace, patrons of local churches, and 'father figures' at local eisteddfodau, 'effectively knit the aristocracy closely into the historic life of the communities they led'.[132] However, the decade of the 1880s marked a watershed when a worldwide collapse in agricultural prices meant that estate rentals fell dramatically, and land values plummeted.[133] In Wales, disendowment and disestablishment of the Church, as well as tensions surrounding the Welsh land question, also served to undermine 'the social ascendancy' of the landowning elite.[134]

The rhetoric of Welsh political radicalism in the second half of the nineteenth century had underpinned constructions of 'Wales' as Welsh-speaking, nonconformist and Liberal in opposition to 'an alienated English-speaking, Anglican, Tory-voting aristocracy'.[135] Lloyd George, in particular, showed a willingness to partially base his political crusade 'on a mass hostility towards the domination of the landlords'.[136] A series of policies, such as the People's Budget of 1909 which demanded 'new exactions on land' and the 1911 National Insurance Act, heightened a sense amongst 'the landed rich' that they were the deliberate target of Lloyd George's proposals.[137] In response, those who felt under attack displayed a willingness to racially denigrate the Chancellor: his son records that when, in 1911, Lloyd George's legislative reforms provoked aristocratic outrage, thousands of 'Conservative ladies' packed the Albert Hall 'singing Taffy was a Welshman, Taffy was a Thief'.[138]

By 1914, many landowners had decided to sell off parts of their holdings, a process accelerated by the First World War.[139] At the same time, the war presented a final chance of glory: 'Fighting was the aristocratic profession par excellence' and the landed elites stepped up to play a pan-British role in recruiting for the military.[140] Cannadine argues that, in 1914, many elite men volunteered to fight in order to justify their existence: to become a 'patriotic class of knightly crusaders and chivalric heroes'.[141] English Welsh elites were not immune to the pull of the dominant construction of the imperial 'soldier hero' spawned in the British public school system and buttressed by popular adventure stories and

---

[131] Matthew Cragoe, *An Anglican Aristocracy: The Moral Economy of the Landed Estate in Carmarthenshire 1832–1895* (Oxford, 1996), p. 9.
[132] Morgan, *Rebirth*, p. 10; Cragoe, *Anglican*, pp. 3, 5–6.   [133] Cannadine, *Decline*, p. 27.
[134] Morgan, *Rebirth*, p. 172; David W. Howell, 'The Land Question in Nineteenth-century Wales, Ireland and Scotland: A Comparative Study', *Agricultural History Review*, 61, 1 (2013), pp. 83–110.
[135] Cragoe, *Culture*, p. 44; Morgan, *Rebirth*, pp. 10–11.
[136] Morgan, *Rebirth*, p. 10.   [137] Cannadine, *Decline*, p. 48.
[138] Lloyd George, *Lloyd George*, p. 121. See also John Campbell, *If Love Were All… The Story of Frances Stevenson and David Lloyd George* (London, 2007), p. 16.
[139] Cannadine, *Decline*, p. 71.   [140] Cannadine, *Aspects*, p. 22.
[141] Cannadine, *Decline*, pp. 73–4.

comics.[142] They included among their number English scions of landed dynasties, who embodied this English Welsh transnational landed tradition. Pyers George Joseph Mostyn was the grandson of Sir Pyers Mostyn, eighth Baronet of Talacre, Flintshire, the family seat since the sixteenth century. On the death of his cousin in 1917, Mostyn succeeded as eleventh Baronet, inheriting the extensive estate.[143] Mostyn himself was born at Perry Crofts, Staffordshire in 1893, to George Mostyn and an English mother, Augusta Walmesley, who died that same year.[144] He was educated at Stonyhurst College and Sandhurst, his headmaster at the former remarking that Mostyn demonstrated 'superior' intelligence.[145] When Mostyn applied for a Commission with the Royal Welch Fusiliers (RWF) in November 1912, he staked his claim to the regiment on the grounds that he was 'descended from an old Welsh family'. He burnished this with the additional information that he was 'a distant relation of Major General Hon Sir S Mostyn KCB (Col of Regiment)', a reference to Sir Savage Lloyd Mostyn.[146] Mostyn also stated that he desired to wait for the RWF, in the event of a vacancy not being available, although he was living with his father at Clifton Hill in Lancashire.[147]

Mostyn was appointed second lieutenant in the RWF in January 1913 and was promoted to Captain by 1915. During the First World War, he served both in France and Mesopotamia, was wounded three times, and awarded the Military Cross.[148] When invalided to England in 1917, his return to the RWF base at Litherland was heralded by Robert Graves in a letter to fellow poet Siegfried Sassoon: 'Pyers Mostyn is back here with three gold stripes from Messpots.'[149] Mostyn can be glimpsed as a fearless character in memoirs collated from the First World War, appearing as one of 'the most indefatigable and adventurous of patrollers' in no-man's land. As his battalion's history records:

> Mostyn was always aggressive; the policy of "crossing to the other side of the road" on sighting someone whose looks were not liked was not his. He was so much at home against the German wire that on a cold night he took a blanket with him to be quite comfortable.[150]

---

[142] Graham Dawson, *Soldier Heroes. British Adventure, Empire and the Imagining of Masculinities* (London, 1994).
[143] 'Sir Pyers Mostyn', *The Tablet*, 6 March 1937, p. 27.
[144] The National Archives (TNA); War Office (WO) 339/8852, Captain Pyers George Joseph Mostyn, The Royal Welsh Fusiliers.
[145] TNA; WO 339/8852; Form of recommendation, 17 July 1911.   [146] TNA; WO 339/8852.
[147] TNA; WO 339/8852.   [148] 'Sir Pyers Mostyn', p. 27.
[149] Paul O' Prey, ed., *Broken Images. Selected Letters of Robert Graves 1914–1946* (London, 1982), p. 83.
[150] *The War the Infantry Knew 1914–1919. A Chronicle of Service in France and Belgium* (London: P S King & Son Ltd, 1938), p. 120.

Categorized as 'permanently unfit GS', in April 1918, Mostyn continued to signal his dual existence during his post-war recuperation.[151] After residence in a Chelsea nursing home, in 1919 he wrote to the War Office from the Royal Thames Yacht Club, Piccadilly, requesting retirement from the Army. A month before this was actioned, in January 1920, he wrote from Talacre advising the War Office that he was moving to the Hotel Beau Site, Cannes for his health.[152] Mostyn embodies what Cannadine defines as the aristocratic 'warrior class' who, 'by tradition, by training, and by temperament' knew how to lead and to command.[153] But Mostyn also represented the British supra-national formation, an Englishman who was determined to enact his military duty via service with a Welsh regiment, whilst remaining anchored in two elite worlds.

The son of the earl of Powis was another highly visible representative of the English Welsh landed class who opted to serve in a Welsh regiment. Born in London in 1892, Viscount Clive was christened Percy Robert, after two notable ancestors, his grandfather, General Sir Percy Herbert, of Crimean fame, and Lord Robert Clive, an army officer in the East India Company and one-time governor of Bengal. As the son of the 4th earl of Powis and Violet Herbert, the daughter of the 15th Baron Darcy de Knayth, he was heir to large cross-border estates in the counties of Shropshire and Powys. His legitimacy regarding his Welsh credentials was readily established in contemporary newspaper reports by reference to his 'distinguished and ancient lineage':

> Viscount Clive was twenty sixth in descent from Bleddyn ap Cynfyn, who was Prince of Powis and sovereign paramount of all Wales at the time of the Norman conquest. It was Bleddyn's son, Cadogan, who built Powis Castle in the 13th century.[154]

It was reported that there were 'great rejoicings' on the family lands at the time of Clive's birth and when his father brought him to Powis Castle the following year, 'a great ball for the townspeople and tenantry' was held.[155] At his coming of age, celebrations were held at the family's Shropshire estates at Montford, Styche, and Walcot.[156] Clive had joined the army in October 1913, being gazetted to the Scots Guards, and receiving the order to join his battalion in July 1914. He served three months in France before being invalided home just before Christmas, suffering from frostbitten feet.[157] The *Llangollen Advertiser* records that, on his recovery,

---

[151] TNA; WO 339/8852.
[152] TNA; WO 339/8852; Trevor Mostyn, 'Letter', *The Independent*, 27 April 1993, http://www.independent.co.uk/voices/letter-the-family-cursed-by-a-witch-from-prestatyn-1457907.html, accessed 26 May 2016.
[153] Cannadine, *Decline*, p. 73.
[154] 'Death of Viscount Clive', *Llangollen Advertiser*, 20 October 1916, p. 3.
[155] 'Death of Viscount Clive', p. 3.   [156] 'Death of Viscount Clive', p. 3.
[157] 'Death of Viscount Clive', p. 3.

Clive 'manifested his associations with Wales' by transferring to the newly formed Welsh Guards.[158] Clive was also involved in recruitment activity in Powys encouraging men in the local area to enlist, including those from the family estate. The *Llangollen Advertiser* acknowledges this role, stating that Clive was 'a much photographed figure' in charge of the Welsh Guards 'who marched singing through the streets of London and made a recruiting tour to Cardiff and South Wales'.[159] Indeed, in July 1915, Clive led eighty Welsh Guards—comprising a 'glee party' due to perform in Cardiff—in a march through the streets of London to Paddington station, singing Welsh anthems:

> There were great scenes of enthusiasm, crowds lining every street en route, loudly applauding the singing and cheering and waving handkerchiefs and hats.... There was a great gathering of Welshmen at Paddington, the platforms being crowded. Mr Ellis Griffiths, M.P., was one of those who welcomed the party. A miniature Eisteddfod was then held. The National Anthem of Cymro was given in conclusion and the crowd bared their heads. The music could not be restrained, however, and in their compartment the men still sang on. And so the Celts left London with the music of their native country on their lips.[160]

This piece of reportage highlights the public visibility surrounding patrician figures such as Clive and the obligations placed upon them in galvanizing and promoting Welsh martial spirit in London. This performance of English Welsh interconnections eerily foretold the choreography of the public rituals surrounding Clive's funeral the following year, discussed in Chapter 6.

The English magnate, John Wynford Philipps, Ist Viscount St Davids, lost his two sons in the conflict. St Davids had served as a Liberal MP for Pembrokeshire from 1898–1908 and was made Lord Lieutenant of the county in 1911. He owned residential properties in both England and Wales: Queen Anne's Gate, Westminster and 3 Richmond Terrace in London, and Roch Castle and West Lodge, Lydstep in Pembrokeshire. A wealthy businessman with close ties to Lloyd George, St Davids had amassed a fortune through investments in Argentinian

---

[158] 'Death of Viscount Clive', p. 3. Family papers loaned to National Trust Powis Castle for a 2016 exhibition record that Clive felt an obligation to transfer to the Welsh Guards. See also 'Percy's letters bring home horror of war at Powis Castle', *Shropshire Star*, 15 April 2016, https://www.shropshirestar.com/entertainment/2016/04/15/percys-letters-bring-home-horror-of-war-at-powis-castle/, accessed 25 April 2016. The official regimental history trumpeted the importance of 'the historic name of Clive' amongst the Welsh Guardsmen. See C. H. Dudley-Ward, *History of the Welsh Guards* (London, 1920), p. vi.
[159] 'Death of Viscount Clive', p. 3.
[160] '"Cymru Am Byth"', *Llangollen Advertiser*, 30 July 1915, p. 6.

railways and was 'known in the City as £.s.d.'.[161] In 1914, St Davids became an active recruiter in the county for the Welsh Army Corps.[162] His English wife, Leonora Gerstenberg, a campaigner for women's suffrage, was also said to have 'a deep and abiding love' for Wales. She was president of the Welsh Union of Women's Liberal Associations from 1892 and took a leading part in the 1909 national pageant at Cardiff.[163] Wynn Thomas suggests that the fact that Philipps was the English-born daughter of European Jewish parents 'may possibly have predisposed her to sympathise with marginalised peoples like the Welsh'.[164] As a well-known hostess within London society, Philipps undertook philanthropic duties 'both in the East End of London and in the villages of South Wales'.[165] This affection towards Wales was transmitted to her two English sons and was enacted via the mediums of altruism and poetry, respectively. The younger son, Roland, was born in Westminster in 1890. Educated at Winchester College, Oxford, he began his career in Liverpool at his father's Pacific Steam Navigation Company. However, in 1912, having encountered a local scout troop whilst out walking, he decided to seek employment within the Scouting movement.[166] Recounting Roland's meeting with the founder, Robert Baden-Powell, his biographer depicts him as a 'young talkative Welshman with burning brown eyes' despite his English upbringing.[167] From the beginning, Roland's role in the Scouts reflected this duality. By November 1913, Roland was the Commissioner for Stepney, Poplar and Bethnal Green as well as Assistant Commissioner for Wales. Having given up his business career, 'Scouting filled the sparse years of his manhood to the exclusion of all else.'[168] Indeed, Roland's biographer presents a level of sacrifice and public duty—he gave up 'money, company, fame, love'—which anticipates the military sacrifice Roland would ultimately make. Roland was gazetted to the 9th Battalion Royal Fusiliers, departing for France in March 1915. In a letter to his mother, he mentions a pre-departure Royal visit to his regiment where he sat next to George V at dinner: 'the King spoke amongst other things about the Welsh Guards (which he jokingly told me I ought to join).'[169] Here, we see an external identification of Roland as Welsh and, as with Clive, an assumption that he was obliged to join the Welsh Guards as the representative of an English Welsh landed family. By the time Roland left for France both his mother and brother were dead, the latter 'leading the Blues in a bayonet charge against the German trenches'.[170] In a letter dated 31 March 1915 to Baden-Powell, Roland expressed how scouting 'means

---

[161] Wynn Thomas, *Nations*, fn. 20, p. 293; D. H. Barber, *The House on the Green* (London, 1960), p. 23.
[162] NLW; GB 0210 WELARMRPS Welsh Army Corps Records, 1914–1925 (WAC); AS/60; Letter, 24 November 1914; Letter, 7 December 1914.
[163] Linda Walker, 'Philipps, Leonora, Lady St Davids (1862–1915)', *ODNB* (2015), https://doi-org.ezproxy.is.ed.ac.uk/10.1093/ref:odnb/57852.
[164] Wynn Thomas, *Nations*, fn. 20, p. 293.   [165] Barber, *House*, p. 19.
[166] Barber, *House*, pp. 21–7.   [167] Barber, *House*, p. 28.   [168] Barber, *House*, p. 47.
[169] 3 March 1915. Cited in Barber, *House*, pp. 53–4.   [170] Barber, *House*, p. 56.

more to me than anything else in the world' and stated that in his will he had left 'about £15,000 for the future benefit of Scouts in East and North-East London, in Wales, in Manchester, in Colchester, and for my own Special Troop in Lydstep.' He also gifted Stepney House, off the Mile End Road, which became known as 'Roland House'.[171] This bequest reflected a cross-border expression of Roland's devotion to scouting in both nations; a vision which he retained for the remainder of his life. From France in October 1915, he wrote to Lady Baden-Powell:

> The great thing out here seems to be to *want* to live, but to be absolutely *ready* to die. Personally it will be the most wildly happy moment of my life if, when the war is over in about a hundred years' time, I can go back, with a Scout smile, to continue work amongst the boys of East London and Wales.[172]

In another letter to Lady Baden-Powell, written from the Western Front whilst wounded, Roland self-defined as Welsh:

> How tremendously bucked up I was today in hospital to feel that I would have had such a very kindly welcome awaiting me at Ewhurst [home of Baden Powell]. My only reason for not reporting myself at once was that I heard the Chief was having a proper rest, and you know how impossible the society of a wild, fanatical Welshman is when one is resting![173]

This motif of martial Welsh masculinity was replicated in a letter from Roland's Battalion Commander to his father following Roland's death on 7 July 1916 during the Battle of the Somme: 'His courage and dash and enthusiasm would have appeared fanatical were it not for the coolness and sane decision he displayed when his objective was attained.'[174] Yet the post-war legacy of Philipps was largely cherished and nurtured in England. In 1925, the Quiet Room of Roland House was converted into a chapel. During the construction, the Warden collected Roland's battle cross from the War Cemetery at Aveluy and his sword was mounted in the chapel with his medals.[175] Significantly, present-day websites still celebrate Roland's place in the scouting movement, but the Welsh dimension of his mission, which reflected his own dual identifications, is no longer foregrounded.[176]

Roland's older brother, Colwyn, who was born in London in 1888, pursued an army career after Eton and was serving as a Captain in the Horse Guards when

---

[171] Barber, *House*, pp. 55–6.   [172] 29 October 1915. Cited in Barber, *House*, p. 58.
[173] 6 March 1916. Cited in Barber, *House*, p. 62.
[174] August 1916. Cited in Barber, *House*, p. 68.   [175] Barber, *House*, pp. 140–1.
[176] Gateways to the First World War website, https://www.gatewaysfww.org.uk/events/roland-philipps-scout-soldier-somme, accessed 9 June 2021; Scout Guide Historical Society website, http://scoutguidehistoricalsociety.com/roland.htm, accessed 3 March 2018.

the war broke out. He was killed in action near Ypres in May 1915. An anthology of his poetry appeared almost contemporaneously with his death, in the form of a memorial volume with the eponymous title *Colwyn Erasmus Arnold Phillips*. The text, which likely appeared as a result of his family's wealth and status, also incorporated letters written to his mother from the front and tributes from fellow officers on his death. The immediate rush to print served to forge an important memorial image of Philipps, with his passionate love of Wales being repeatedly rehearsed. Although Colwyn's death was briefly mentioned in the *Times* it was largely the Welsh press which took an interest in and carried reviews of his posthumous book of poetry. The *Welsh Outlook* described the poems as 'a memorial to a very gallant gentleman' whilst the *Brecon & Radnor Express* noted his 'passionate love of his Welsh home' and alluded to the 'fascination of his native Pembrokeshire' as a source of inspiration.[177] The *Cambria Daily Leader* observed, 'Colwyn Philipps, the eldest of two sons Lord St. Davids gave to his country, looked over his trench, and beyond the desolation of No Man's Land saw peace and beauty.'[178] As Jo Gill and Melanie Waters note, the language contained within the lyric mode of poetry can be read as 'referential and as expressive of the poet's own intimate—if veiled—experience or emotion'. As with other forms of autobiographical life writing, poetry can be considered as 'a site rich with historical and geographical resonance'. Furthermore, because of its 'explicit and (self-)conscious linguistic licence' poetry may be precisely the place where questions of autobiography are 'crystallised and explored'.[179] Colwyn's poem 'Lydstep' refers to his family's home in Pembrokeshire, ending with the lines: 'There, there liveth the Angel of Peace, And *only there* may I find release.'[180] But whilst Philipps's poetry speaks to Wales, 'home' is also England, where his parents were largely based. Indeed, Philipps's lived reality of dual existence is captured in his poem 'Two Houses', which refers to both Lydstep and Exning Hall in Suffolk which St. Davids had acquired just before the war: 'Exning is all that is bright and gay|Lydstep alone is the place I love.'[181] His poems, by flagging up two inheritances which were not oppositional but rather coexisted, encapsulate the dual associations upon which the assumed power, influence, and authority of the landed elite rested.

Another English Welsh soldier poet who was published around this time was Evan Morgan. Morgan, the only son of Baron Tredegar, who owned estates in Newport and London, was described by contemporaries as a 'descendant of Welsh Royalty'.[182] He was also immortalized in Ronald Firbanks's 1923 novel *The Flower*

---

[177] *Welsh Outlook,* May 1916; *Brecon & Radnor Express,* 13 January 1916, p. 6.
[178] 'Welsh Singers', *The Cambria Daily Leader,* 29 November 1917, p. 3.
[179] Jo Gill and Melanie Waters, 'Poetry and Autobiography', *Life Writing,* 6, 1 (2009), pp. 3, 5. doi: 10.1080/14484520802550262.
[180] *Colwyn Erasmus Arnold Phillips* (London, 1915), p. 4.
[181] *Colwyn Erasmus Arnold Phillips,* p. 9.
[182] 'Welsh Societies', *The Cambria Daily Leader,* 4 September 1917, p. 3.

beneath the Foot as an 'eccentric Englishman from Wales'.[183] Reluctantly following the martial tradition of his family—Steffan Ellis remarks that 'this was most likely to have been his father's idea than his own'—Morgan was commissioned into the Welsh Guards in June 1915.[184] However, by 1917 Morgan was working in Whitehall as personal private secretary to William Bridgeman MP. When Morgan's second poetry collection, *Gold and Ochre*, was published in 1917, it was promoted in the *Cambria Daily Leader* as 'the work of a Welshman who takes a keen interest in national life' and as representative of 'a house better known in Wales for action than for the poetic muse', possibly a dig here at the unmartial nature of Morgan's wartime career.[185] Whilst for Morgan there were clearly tensions between his expected masculine role as heir to a Welsh military dynasty and his own personal preferences, in his third collection of poetry, *Psyche*, he chose to underscore his Welsh martial connection by dedicating the volume to the Welsh Guards.[186] In 1917, the *Cambria Daily Leader* praised the poetry of Colwyn Philipps, Crawshay-Williams, and Morgan collectively, describing them as 'the nightingales of Wales:

> Her poets raise their heads from the red mire of Flanders, and look into the blue beyond the barrage. There is clear sky above! The wrath of earth has wrecked our little day. But it has not crushed the soul of our singers.[187]

This review highlights how their poetry was received and mediated through the Welsh press and was part of a reciprocal shaping of their self-identification as Welsh. Whilst it should be recognized that the press often functioned to buttress the position of these elite English Welsh families, these soldier poets were contemporaneously claimed as Welsh. It could also be argued that whilst these lesser-known war poets addressed England in their work, they also articulated nostalgic longing, or *hiraeth*, whilst on military service, constructing 'Wales' from a rarefied perspective as a desired place of belonging.

Conclusion

This chapter highlights the significance of elite social networks underpinning English Welsh political, aristocratic, and military interactions in the run-up to and during the First World War. It has recovered and reconstructed the dual

---

[183] Ronald Firbank, *The Flower Beneath the Foot* (London, 1923) p. 92. See also Alan Pryce-Jones, *The Bonus of Laughter* (London, 1987), pp. 30–1.
[184] Steffan Ellis, 'Evan Morgan and the First World War', Tredegarhouse website, https://tredegarhouse.wordpress.com/tag/evan-morgan/, accessed 29 August 2022.
[185] 'Welsh Singers'. [186] Evan Morgan, *Psyche: an Unfinished Fragment* (London, 1920).
[187] 'Welsh Singers'.

identifications of a number of significant political figures who operated in both Wales and England. Addressing the period 1834–1928, James Ford argues that 'Anglo-Britishness' most aptly describes the sense of national identity embodied in the Palace of Westminster. He views this as an inclusive form of identity, in the sense that it 'gives some recognition to the UK nations other than England'.[188] As Wynn Thomas notes, at Westminster in the late nineteenth century, 'new forms of Welsh social identity were in process of being formed by being "performed" there.'[189] He characterizes the rise of Lloyd George as the 'most spectacularly successful of all attempts to form a new kind of Welsh identity through performance on the grandest of political stages.'[190] Increasingly, Welsh MPs at Westminster formed an elite representation of wider settlement patterns amongst the Welsh diaspora in cities across England; residing in London, many raised and educated their offspring within English society, reinforcing ties between the two countries. In addition, Lloyd George played an important talismanic role for members of the Welsh diaspora in England and acted as an inspiration for upcoming generations of English Welsh politicians. Another powerful expression of English Welsh dual identifications at the turn of the twentieth century emerged from the presence of landed elites with transnational ownership of extensive estates in both Wales and England. As 'supra-national' territorial entities embedded in the higher echelons of British political and cultural society, these landed families identified with Welshness largely through the lens of a traditional Anglican landowner identity. However, their sense of dual attachments to both nations was also an important part of their social cachet within the wider British world. At the outbreak of the First World War, men of military age from privileged English Welsh landed families felt compelled both to recruit for the British military and to volunteer to serve, often in a Welsh regiment. For this war generation, their long-nurtured sense of dual identifications could be expressed through acts of military heroism and sacrifice, philanthropic endeavours, or via nostalgic wartime poetry.

[188] Ford, 'Art of Union', Abstract.
[189] Wynn Thomas, *Nations*, p. 47.
[190] Wynn Thomas, *Nations*, p. 68.

2
Welshburbia
Welshness in the English Suburbs

The English suburbs have been acknowledged as the site of 'a self-consciously Welsh middle-class identity' in the first half of the twentieth century, highlighting the existence of something which I term the imagined transcultural space of 'Welshburbia'.[1] Saunders Lewis, one of the founders of the Welsh nationalist party Plaid Cymru, is viewed as a product of this 'Welsh bourgeoisie' in England whilst the First World War conscientious objector, George Maitland Lloyd Davies, from a similar background in Liverpool, felt so negatively about his middle-class upbringing that he believed 'the devil created the suburb'.[2] This chapter explores how some diasporic twentieth-century artists, now prominently celebrated in Wales, were influenced and conditioned by their upbringing in the English suburbs. It touches upon the ways in which, for English artists and writers of Welsh parentage such as David Jones, Norman Lewis, and John Osborne, their childhood experience of suburbia informed their creative development. In particular, this chapter provides a case study of Lambeth-born poet Edward Thomas, who defined himself as 'mainly Welsh'. For Thomas, the edges where English suburbia touched rural hinterlands could deepen a sense of connection with his idealized imagining of Wales.[3] In this sense, Lynne Hapgood argues, his work can be viewed as 'a site of cultural reconciliation' between evoked rural landscapes—often associated with Welshness—and the English suburban realities of his own existence.[4] Yet, despite his clear affection for Wales, when faced with the prospect of military service in 1914, Thomas became increasingly preoccupied with his own sense of 'Englishness', which ultimately compelled him to enlist. This chapter explores Thomas's display of dual allegiances around the outbreak of the First World War and those of the wider Thomas sibling group.

---

[1] 'A Personal View: Gareth Miles', in *Presenting Saunders Lewis*, edited by Alun R. Jones and Gwyn Thomas (Cardiff, 1983), p. 17.
[2] 'Personal View', p. 17; Jen Llywelyn, *Pilgrim of Peace. A Life of George M Ll Davies* (Talybont, 2016), p. 28.
[3] Hapgood, *Margins*, pp. 7–8.   [4] Hapgood, *Margins*, p. 71.

'The Rustle of Silk'

The first wave of suburbanization started in early nineteenth-century Britain but it was not until the 1880s and 1890s that the suburb 'became a positive social fact'.[5] According to Simon Gunn and Rachel Bell, the 'move towards the suburbs' was part of a great social movement, a conscious decision to create living spaces away from the smoke, disease, and overcrowding attached to the centres of the industrial cities.[6] F. M. L. Thompson points out that 'it was becoming the ambition of all those who could afford it to live as close to the edge of the country as possible', including the lower middle classes.[7] He points to the importance of 'rural pre-development features in influencing the shape, form, character, and timing of suburbanization' as well as the mixed social character of suburban districts. Thus, the world of suburbia was one which exhibited 'the marks and scars of its rural antecedents', and where 'field paths and boundaries, ancient tracks, and property boundaries' remained visible.[8] Roger Silverstone depicts the experience of suburbia as one of inhabiting 'spaces on the edge', viewing the modern suburb as 'a social as well as a cultural hybrid'.[9] As a place which represents 'an in-betweenness' of country and city, suburbia, therefore, should be interpreted around ideas of 'ambiguity, double-sidedness and fragmented experience'.[10] This chapter maps the ways in which members of the Welsh diaspora growing up in English suburbs reflected this sense of liminality and duality in their own life writing and remembered experiences.

The works of both David Gilbert and Rebecca Preston and Gunn and Bell stress the strong association between the suburb and notions of Englishness.[11] The latter point to the emergence of associational life, shopping parades, and entertainments in the suburbs, which facilitated middle-class sociability and came to stand for '"middle England", the hard-working, home-owning and respectable backbone of the nation'.[12] However, Gilbert and Preston also insist on the conceptualization of suburban sites 'as specific points in wider flows and connections' including those of human migration.[13] An example of this are the

---

[5] Simon Gunn and Rachel Bell, *Middle Classes. Their Rise and Sprawl* (London, 2003), p. 17; Hapgood, *Margins*, p. 1.

[6] Gunn and Bell, *Middle Classes*, pp. 28–9.

[7] F. M. L. Thompson, 'Introduction: The Rise of Suburbia', in *The Rise of Suburbia*, edited by F. M. L. Thompson (Leicester, 1982), pp. 16–17.

[8] Thompson, 'Introduction', p. 17.

[9] Roger Silverstone, 'Preface', in *Visions of Suburbia*, edited by Roger Silverstone (London, 1997), p. ix.

[10] Hapgood, *Margins*, p. 7; David Gilbert and Rebecca Preston, "Stop Being So English': Suburban Modernity and National Identity in the Twentieth Century', in *Geographies of British Modernity. Space and Society in the Twentieth Century*, edited by David Gilbert, David Matless, and Brian Short (Oxford, 2003), p. 188.

[11] Gilbert and Preston, 'Stop Being', p. 190; Gunn and Bell, *Middle*, pp. 79–80.

[12] Gunn and Bell, *Middle*, pp. 79–80.   [13] Gilbert and Preston, 'Stop Being', p. 189.

significant areas of Welsh settlement in the English suburbs from the mid-Victorian era onwards. This was such a recognized social phenomenon that fears were expressed that members of the Welsh diaspora would become subsumed into the English suburban landscape. An 1896 *Young Wales* editorial recited Londoner Ernest Rhys's opinion that 'the Cockney is a more dangerous enemy than ever was Saxon or Norman. We have to encounter all kinds of smug cosmopolitanism, and resist all kinds of cheap commercial bribes—all those things in short that seek to destroy the national sentiment, and make Wales into a London suburb.'[14] In a series of lectures undertaken in the 1920s, reflecting on his own childhood in late Victorian Liverpool, university professor J. Glyn Davies stated that for Welsh immigrants arriving in Liverpool in the early nineteenth century, 'The suburbs were the Promised Land'.[15] In the Victorian era, terraces and villas for the professional classes were found in Everton and West Derby in Liverpool which were also recognized as sites of Welsh settlement.[16] In the interwar period, journalist Glyn Roberts remarked that in the 'inner Cockney suburbs' of Walham Green, Camden Town, Stratford, and Islington, 'you may often see a surprisingly extensive store dominating the scene, with a Welsh name across the building and hear many Welsh accents behind the counters.'[17] Davies identifies the implications of suburban living for the second-generation Welsh:

> Unlike their parents, the Liverpool-born generation knew nothing of mean dwelling places and dirty neighbours. They were born in the suburbs. Those with well-to-do parents lived in good and roomy houses, and their neighbours were of their own standing in income. The new generation went to English day schools, and in school were indistinguishable from English boys.[18]

In the interwar era, this suburban Welsh presence was buoyed by a local press which hired columnists to monitor and praise their social activities such as Harold Tudor, who wrote 'Cymric Causerie' columns in the *Liverpool Echo* under the pseudonym 'Talwrn' and 'A Welsh Causerie' in the *Liverpolitan* magazine.[19]

Merfyn Jones characterizes many members of the Welsh diaspora in North West England at the start of the twentieth century as 'rapidly upwardly socially mobile'.[20] The leaders of the Welsh community in Liverpool were merchants, financiers, and wealthy industrialists.[21] This mobility is evident in the oral testimony of one of Jones's respondents, Mr C.T.J., born in Liverpool in 1906, to Welsh parents:

---

[14] Cited in Wynn Thomas, *Nations*, p. 13.
[15] J. Glyn Davies, *Nationalism as a Social Phenomenon* (Liverpool, 1965), p. 24.
[16] Gunn and Bell, *Middle*, p. 59.   [17] Roberts, *I Take*, p. 264.
[18] Davies, *Nationalism*, p. 25.
[19] Liverpool Record Office (LRO); *Liverpolitan*, February 1935–July 1936.
[20] Merfyn Jones, 'Welsh Immigrants', p. 33.   [21] 'A Personal View', p. 17.

The second generation people had had the advantage of decent schooling. It was the ambition of Welsh parents to try and get them into the Collegiate or the Institute, particularly the boys… and once they were there, they found it fairly easy, through Welsh connections, to get into the banks, particularly the Midland, and into the insurance offices.[22]

Although Benbough-Jackson points out that the Liverpool Welsh could be found in a range of occupational groups, from the building trade to domestic service, 'the middle classes, particularly those who attended places of worship, came to represent the Welsh on Merseyside'.[23] Discussing the London Welsh in 1933, Glyn Roberts refers to 'the successful men, the politicians, business men and barristers, who meet every so often at Cymmrodorion Dinners, St David's Day Dinners, Cardiganshire Dinners, and so forth, and doubtless have a grand time in boiled shirts and unnatural splendour'.[24] Third generation Welshman, J. Glyn Davies, depicts a class-ridden Welsh diasporic society in Liverpool, inflected with social snobbery. Davies's father, John, born in Liverpool in 1823, was a successful tea and coffee merchant.[25] Davies observed that many of his father's generation would have abandoned the markers of their Welsh identity but for one deterrent:

> These people had by reasons of financial standing a certain prestige in Welsh polite society, and they contributed generously to Welsh causes. They counted as somebody in Welsh society, in particular in their chapel circles. If they went English they would be nobody. Snobbery was rampant amongst them.[26]

Jones agrees that whilst many Welsh immigrants succeeded in their ambition of being 'indistinguishable from the English families in the surrounding villas' there was still a significant element of the elite Welsh diaspora who 'were conscious of a historic responsibility towards their homeland'.[27] In Liverpool, therefore, there was a Welsh middle class 'which was conscious not only of its Welshness but also of itself as a class'.[28] Jones suggests that the Welsh often had 'a high opinion of themselves' looking down on the Irish immigrant population in Liverpool above whom they rested on the social hierarchy, as well as feeling superior to the people back home in Wales.[29] Jones remarks that despite the allegiance of Welsh migrants to Gladstonian Liberalism and 'talk of "Home Rule all round"', 'it was part of the Welsh definition of themselves that they were superior in every way to the Catholics'—in terms of religion, morals, politics, and their way of life.[30] The wealthier diasporic families often had second homes in Wales such as Davies's tea

---

[22] Jones, 'Welsh Immigrants', p. 36.   [23] Benbough-Jackson, 'Negotiating', p. 265.
[24] Roberts, *I Take*, p. 267.   [25] Llywelyn, *Pilgrim*, p. 23.   [26] Davies, *Nationalism*, p. 27.
[27] Jones, 'Liverpool Welsh', p. 31.   [28] Jones, 'Liverpool Welsh', p. 25.
[29] Jones, 'Welsh Immigrants', p. 40.   [30] Jones, 'Liverpool Welsh', p. 28.

merchant father, who owned a house in Abergele.[31] The Liverpool Welsh, says Jones, impressed their compatriots on visits back home: they became ever associated in Welsh minds with the 'rustle of silk'.[32] In the city itself, Mr C.T.J. recalls:

> The people who went to Princes' Road (chapel) and paraded the Princes Boulevard on a Sunday morning, you know there were streams of them...these people paraded the Boulevard...dressed for the occasion...they really did fancy themselves.[33]

Being Welsh added nonconformist chapel attendance and social values—such as an adherence to temperance—to pre-existing layers of English suburban norms of respectability. Roberts captures chapel attendance on Sundays in 'the Welsh chapels and churches' across 'a dozen London suburbs':

> In a congregation you will see scores of those red shining fat faces crowned with well-brushed black hair, so common in the hills, in the back seats and in the galleries, and in the front seats many pompous and severe gentlemen, "the Big Heads", with the Mussolini expression of Vigour with Virtue stamped on their faces.... After the services there is a long and animated conference in the road, where perched black bowlers and puce overcoats and kid gloves are much in evidence.[34]

Jones characterizes the chapel as 'the public presence of the Welsh community' in England which organized the lives of the first settlers and 'promised friends, cultural security, discipline and employment'. On Merseyside there were over fifty Welsh nonconformist chapels at the beginning of the twentieth century, populated by the 'pious and the affluent'.[35] Whilst these chapels provided an umbrella of social support as protective cover for Welsh immigrants, they could also function as oppressive spaces. Glyn Davies's brother, George Maitland Lloyd, was born and raised near Sefton Park in Liverpool. Jen Llywelyn underlines the significance of his birth into the affluent Liverpool Welsh middle class: 'the attitudes and values of this close-knit group, and the oppressiveness of the Welsh-built suburbs they lived in, were George Davies' foundation in life, and he never completely escaped their influence.'[36] Shortly before his suicide in 1949, aged sixty-nine, George wrote: 'God created the countryside, man created the town, but the devil created the suburb.'[37] He stated that there was no 'good neighbourliness' in a suburb, a fact which his biographer links to his lifetime resentment at how his

---

[31] Jones, 'Liverpool Welsh', p. 24.
[32] Jones, 'Liverpool Welsh', p. 24.
[33] Jones, 'Welsh Immigrants', p. 35.
[34] Roberts, *I Take*, p. 265.
[35] Jones, 'Liverpool Welsh', pp. 22–3.
[36] Llywelyn, *Pilgrim*, p. 15.
[37] Llywelyn, *Pilgrim*, p. 28.

family were shunned by fellow chapel goers at Princes Road when his father went bankrupt in 1891.[38]

The contemporaneous short stories of Caradoc Evans illuminate the social pretensions of Welshburbia, furiously lampooning the middle-class diasporic Welsh as hypocritical snobs who conformed to norms of respectability through chapel attendance and the performance of temperance. As Daniel G. Williams notes, 'literature often embodies the multiple possibilities, the residual and emergent social forces, and the diverse range of possible social identities that characterize ideas of nationhood and ethnicity.'[39] John Harris suggests that, having worked in the drapery trade in London, Evans had 'peculiar access to the London Welsh, the one or two who placed their names above a West End store and the rest who made their way to the suburbs.'[40] Evans captures the typical suburban dweller, for example, in the 1919 story 'Love and Hate':

> By living frugally—setting aside a portion of his Civil Service pay and holding all that he got from two butchers whose trade books he kept in proper order—Adam Powell became possessed of Cartref in which he dwelt and which is in Barnes, and two houses in Thornton East; and one of the houses in Thornton East he let to his widowed daughter, Olwen, who carried on a dressmaking business.[41]

In *My Neighbours*, notes Harris, the Welsh despise the 'ungodly' English but also ape their social ways: 'They puff up their surnames ("the hyphen is the mark of our ambition"), regally christen their houses, forsake their native language for "classier" English.'[42]

Jones notes that the Welsh chapels faced many challenges in their effort to retain the allegiances of the descended Welsh, 'who had no difficulty with the English language, nor with English ways.'[43] Indeed, most of the case studies examined in this book were anglophone, rather than Welsh, speakers. Within life writing sources, second-generation children often rail against what Edward Thomas described as 'deathly solemnity' of obligatory chapel attendance. Thomas recalls being dragged with his brothers to various different chapels in London with his Welsh father: 'in our stiff Sunday clothes and our Sunday hats'. As a result of this ritual, he says he developed 'a profound quiet detestation of Sunday.... I think I began learning to hate crowds and societies, and grown-up people, and black

---

[38] Llywelyn, *Pilgrim*, p. 27.
[39] Daniel G. Williams, *Black Skin, Blue Books. African Americans and Wales 1845–1945* (Cardiff, 2012), p. 17.
[40] Harris, '"Gazing"', p. 223. [41] Caradoc Evans, *My Neighbours* (London, 1919), p. 91.
[42] Harris, 'Afterword', p. 188. [43] Jones, 'Welsh Immigrants', p. 38.

clothes, and silk hats and neatly folded umbrellas.'[44] Ifanwy Williams, born in Liverpool in 1922, the youngest of ten, refers to the compulsory chapel attendance in her family: 'It was sort of three times a day, Sunday, and then during the week we would go as well. I think that the boys particularly fought very hard against all this. But they were obliged, or went, anyway, till a certain age.'[45] By 1930, J. Mervyn Williams acknowledged that 'more than one-half of the Cymric legions of London never frequent a Welsh place of worship.'[46] This non-attendance would have been most pronounced amongst the children of Welsh immigrants who were more likely to eschew institutionalized forms of Welsh identity based around ideas of nonconformity and language, and instead carve out new identities. Jones says that many second-generation children faced pressures from their parents to attend chapel and to speak Welsh within that context but, ultimately, the vast majority, moved increasingly towards what he terms 'the comforts of Englishness'.[47]

However, the pull towards the communal respectability of Welsh suburban settlement continued in the first decades of the twentieth century. In 1933, Roberts commented on the number of migrants from South Wales settling in the West and North of London: 'They now have a "Harrow Welsh" Rugby Club as the population of that town is quite largely Cymric.'[48] Barrister Malcom Pill, born in 1938, recalls his parents setting up home at Worcester Park, Surrey in the late 1930s, buying a newly built house on the Manor Estate. His father was a Welsh barrister's clerk, working with Owen Temple-Morris MP for Cardiff East. Pill remarks: 'They cannot have had noticeably Welsh accents because they were canvassed by a milkman who complained to them about the number of Welsh people buying houses on the Estate.'[49] In acknowledgement of the sizeable Welsh presence in England's capital city, the London Welsh Centre was established in Mecklenburgh Square in 1930. Largely bankrolled by the building contractor and London County Council member, Howell J. Williams, the long-term objective was to establish a 'Welsh National Centre' which would act as a 'rallying point for the whole of Wales', positioned within the wider idea of imperial British identity.[50] At the opening ceremony, Williams stated:

---

[44] Edward Thomas, *The Childhood of Edward Thomas. A Fragment of Autobiography with a Preface by Julian Thomas* (London, 1938), pp. 32–3.
[45] BLSA; C880/21; Ifanwy Williams interviewed by Rena Feld, Women Conscientious Objectors, 19 May 1998, copyright British Library Board.
[46] Williams, 'The New London Welsh', p. 193. This ties in with John Davies's observation that, 'the irreligious are a lost element in Welsh historiography', Davies, *History*, p. 427. See also Williams, *Black Skin*, pp. 11–12.
[47] Jones, 'Welsh Immigrants', p. 39.   [48] Roberts, *I Take*, p. 105.
[49] Malcolm Pill, *A Cardiff Family in the Forties* (Frome, 1999), p. 19.
[50] *Y Ddolen*, Gorffennaf, 1940, p. 4; London Welsh Centre Archive (LWCA); *The Young Wales Association Brochure*, 29 November 1930 (London, 1930), p. 3.

> The Celtic influence has been an enormous one in the building of Britain. It can still give its quota and also retain its valuable traditions for the Welsh people. Here in the ancient capital of our race we again unfurl our flag, bound rightly to the Union Jack for the mutual advantage of the British people.[51]

As Moulton writes about Irish associational culture in interwar England, many Welsh settlers 'lived their personal lives in largely ethnically specific but also politically neutral social spaces' which were 'based on personal religious observance and leisure activities'.[52] Writing five years after the foundation of the Welsh nationalist party, Plaid Cymru, J. Mervyn Williams, remarked that 'the majority of the London Welsh are not so easily attracted by national movements as it is sometimes imagined. Many find their interests running on vertical lines that cut across racial frontiers, while not a few are in a hurry to get absorbed in English life.'[53] However, the centre did feel compelled to confront anxieties around the perceived negative impact of English suburban living on Welsh identities. In 1934, the editor of the *London Welsh Year Book* attempted to counter accusations that those who participated in the club's activities were simply masquerading as 'imitation English', and made 'A Plea for Tolerance':

> There is no use railing at tennis and bridge and dancing…They are a part of our life not only in London but also in Wales, a feature of that world-wide 'standardisation' which is the penalty of easy communication and a popular press.[54]

The centre essentially promoted itself as a social and cultural society, highlighting whist drives, dances, a tennis club, a music club, and a historical research association.[55] In this way, the club created a social space which more closely reflected the suburban modernity of the descended Welsh. For example, the 1940 wedding of J. Tudor Williams, the only son of Mr and Mrs J. R. Williams of Ealing, to Tina Gray of Acton at the Welsh Presbyterian Church, notes that 'Both bride and bridegroom are well known in London Welsh circles as members of Ealing Cymric Lawn Tennis Club.'[56]

---

[51] LWCA; *London Welsh Yearbook 1938–39*, p. 24. [52] Moulton, *Ireland*, p. 271.
[53] Williams, 'New London Welsh', p. 193. See William Hywel Davies, *The Welsh Nationalist Party 1924–1945* (Cardiff, 1983).
[54] LWCA; *London Welsh Year Book for 1933–34*, p. 72.
[55] LWCA; *Young Wales Association*, pp. 4–5. [56] *Y Ddolen*, Medi-Hydref, 1940, p. 6.

Croquet, Tennis, and the Welsh 'help'

In life story narratives, Welshburbia emerges as a land of croquet, tennis, and well-ordered domesticity. Dilys Powell was born in Bridgnorth in 1901 but her Welsh banker father moved his family from Shropshire to Bournemouth for health reasons:

> I must have been five or six years old when, trailing reminiscences of Shropshire and Wales, we settled in what was then a new house, a detached house with a garden, near one of the town's golf-courses... we all, my mother included, played croquet on the lawn at the back of the house.[57]

Peggy Roberts, the daughter of a Welsh draper in Finchley, recalled her childhood home, 58 Woodside Park as a double-fronted, five-bedroomed house with a drawing room with French windows to the garden where her family played croquet.[58] Ifanwy Williams, who grew up with nine siblings in a house with grounds five miles out of Liverpool city centre, remembers, 'We had a tennis court, we had a croquet lawn, we had a lot of people coming in.'[59]

Welshburbia often rested upon the service of working-class Welsh domestic servants; a commonplace figure within diasporic narratives is the Welsh 'help'. In Liverpool, Welsh female migrants were often recruited into domestic service by wealthy Welsh chapel members. In the nearby seaside resort of Southport, 'an area with a high demand for domestic servants', there were 876 Welsh-born women in 1921.[60] Writing of the London Welsh and their exploitation of Welsh domestic servants, J. Mervyn Williams commented in 1930: 'Small Welsh employers are too prone to retain the semi-feudal conditions of nineteenth-century farming in Wales. Mr and Mrs Jones, we agree, are nothing if not modern, but they *do* like to have a little dash of rural serfdom in the kitchen.'[61] Writer Norman Lewis, who grew up in Enfield, noted the interwar practice of 'young Welsh girls imported from some wretched village in Wales, who suffered the normal degree of exploitation that was the lot of so many of the daughters of that martyred country.'[62] But the presence of Welsh servants could also reinforce a familial identification with Wales, especially among the children in a household. At Edward Thomas's family home near Wandsworth Common, 'Welsh servants and mother's helps came and went.'[63] Thomas's daughter Myfanwy, born in 1910, recalls her

---

[57] BLM; Add. MS 87684; Dilys Powell, Memoir, pp. 2, 4.
[58] BLSA; C464/68; Margaret [Peggy] Roberts.   [59] BLSA, C880/21, Ifanwy Williams.
[60] Jones, 'Liverpool Welsh', p. 27.   [61] Williams, 'New London Welsh', p. 193.
[62] Lewis, *Jackdaw Cake*, p. 83.
[63] R. G. Thomas, *Edward Thomas. A Portrait* (Oxford, 1985), pp. 5, 8.

visits to her grandparents' home in Balham where 'there was a fierce Welsh cook named Emma, who lived most of the time in the basement and wore a very long, white, starched apron.'[64] Peggy Roberts's family in Finchley had a 'mum's help', a washer lady and gardener. After a much-loved nursemaid left, Roberts recalls: 'There was a Mrs Wedlake who lived in Lodge Lane and she had an Agency for these girls—some of them from Wales—and they used to come and they would live in and they would have their own bedroom.'[65] Saunders Lewis associates the presence of Welsh retainers in the family home with the forging of his own links to Wales:

> girls would come to our house—and to my aunt's house in Liverpool—as maids from Anglesey and Caernarfonshire [sic] and they would be monoglot Welsh-speakers. They would attend chapel with us for a few years, then get married, and return to Wales, with as little English as they had had when they came to England. There was a monoglot Welsh-speaking community in Liverpool in my time, just as in a village somewhere in Anglesey.[66]

For the writer Naomi Royde-Smith, growing up in Victorian Halifax, there were three Welsh cousins working as domestic maids. Writing in 1958, she recalls how in the kitchen within their substantial family villa, Craven Edge, 'Sarah, the cook, Ellen, the housemaid, and Margaret, the parlourmaid, took their ease and drank tea of an afternoon.'[67] The latter, a 'little black-eyed Welsh housemaid', also helped in the nursery, bringing in hot water for the infant's bath.[68]

Transcultural Subjects

Arguing that suburbia exerts a cultural influence, Todd Kuchta calls for more attention to be paid to 'the suburb's relevance to literary and cultural production in the late nineteenth and early twentieth centuries.'[69] Charles Burdett, Loredana Polezzi, and Barbara Spadaro point, in particular, to the importance of diasporic experience and the 'multimodal nature of creative practices of cultural production in migrant contexts'.[70] A transcultural perspective recognizes that an author's subjectivity is not 'related to one particular "national literary space"' but connects

---

[64] Helen Thomas with Myfanwy Thomas, 'Myfanwy's Childhood Memories', *Under Storm's Wing* (London, 1988), p. 262.
[65] BLSA; C464/68; Margaret [Peggy] Roberts.   [66] Cited in 'A Personal', p. 17.
[67] V & A Theatre and Performance Archives (VATPA), Ernest Milton Collection, Naomi Royde-Smith unpublished autobiography 'Nine Lives in My Own', p. 17.
[68] VATPA; 'Nine Lives in My Own', p. 34.
[69] Todd Kuchta, *Semi-Detached Empire. Suburbia and the Colonization of Britain, 1880 to the Present* (Charlottesville, 2010), p. 11.
[70] Burdett, Polezzi, and Spadaro, 'Introduction', p. 3.

their work to both 'local or regional modernities with their specific social, linguistic, and cultural constellations' and to a wider field of 'communicative interaction'.[71] For the poets David Jones and Edward Thomas, who served in the First World War, their upbringing in the London suburbs with Welsh fathers added to their sense of dual inheritances and informed their creative processes. Both Jones and Thomas can be viewed as transcultural subjects who navigated different cultural options, illuminating 'the dynamic and plural nature of processes of identification'.[72] They embraced ideas of Wales whilst distancing themselves from more formal elite constructions of Welshness within the diaspora, carving out their own sense of dual identities.[73] Ultimately, they filtered their understandings of Wales through their own lived experience of an English 'suburban imaginary'.[74] Edna Longley notes how in his autobiographical prose, Thomas consistently 'salutes his urban—and perhaps creative—origins'.[75] Writing to a correspondent in later life, David Jones also indicated the importance of the suburban landscape of his childhood, a time when Brockley:

was still within easy walking reach of the country, but fast becoming built up. Brockley Road had along its main stretch...a line of elm trees on both sides of the road and as far as I can remember the area beyond the public house called The Brockley Jack (and more or less opposite it, a largish house in ground called Brockley Hall) there were extensive open fields but with the beginning of extending suburb.

To organizers of a retrospective art exhibition in Cardiff he defined his birthplace as 'quasi-urban quasi-rural...the sprawl of outer-suburbia was still in process'.[76] We see the importance of the suburban in Jones's paintings from the 1920s such as *Hampstead Garden Suburb*, 1924, *Brockley Gardens (Summer)*, 1925, *Suburban Order*, 1926, and *The Maid at No. 37*, 1926.[77] René Hague notes how this series of English suburban paintings express a sense of duality, with Jones providing the perspective of 'an outsider' although 'native to the scene'.[78] Ariane Bankes agrees, stressing how, for Jones, the family home in Brockley continued to be 'the calm domestic centre from which he ventured out to Wales, Caldy, France, or wherever his painterly instinct and friendships led him.'[79]

---

[71] Frank Schulze-Engler, 'Introduction', in *Transcultural English Studies: Theories, Fictions, Realities*, edited by Frank Schulze-Engler and Sissy Helff (Amsterdam, 2009), p. xvi.
[72] Burdett, Polezzi, and Spadaro, 'Introduction', p. 4.
[73] For more on Jones, see Chapter 4 'Welsh Enough'.
[74] Hapgood, *Margins*, p. 4.
[75] Edna Longley, *Edward Thomas. The Annotated Collected Poems* (Tarset, 2008), p. 201.
[76] NLW; CF1/9; David Jones Papers; Draft letters 1929–1982; Draft letter to Mr Rank; Letter to National Museum Wales, Cardiff, c. 1954.
[77] See Ariane Bankes and Paul Hills, *The Art of David Jones. Vision and Memory* (Farnham, 2015).
[78] René Hague, ed., *Dai Greatcoat. A Self-portrait of David Jones in His Letters* (London, 1980), p. 24.
[79] Ariane Bankes, 'Artist in the City', in Bankes and Hills, *Art*, p. 69.

'A Fused Centre'

Edward Thomas was said to have rebelled 'against the smug suburbanism of his home'.[80] Born in 1878 at 10 Upper Lansdowne Road North, Lambeth, Thomas was the eldest son of the Welsh civil servant, Philip Henry Thomas and his Yorkshire-born wife Elizabeth Townsend who also had Welsh ancestry.[81] One lifelong friend defined Thomas as 'a Welshman of pure blood, born in a London suburb'.[82] This idea of dual personal identity forged through blood inheritance was also present in Thomas's father's reminiscences of his son:

> On his father's side his blood was mainly Welsh, but with a dash of Devonshire derived from the family of Eastaway whose name he took when he came out as a poet. They were mariners who plied up and down and across the Bristol Channel, and so came to mingle their blood with the Welsh blood of Glamorgan. This was on my father's side. On my mother's side his blood was that of the men of Gwent. Through his mother's family his blood was partly Welsh and partly English.[83]

Thomas's family moved to 61 Shelgate Road, Wandsworth, when he was ten.[84] Yet, although he lived in England all his life, Thomas once defined himself as 'mainly Welsh' with only an 'accidentally Cockney nativity'.[85] Thomas is increasingly claimed as a poet for Wales, a core argument of Andrew Webb who seeks to firmly 'reposition Thomas as a Welsh writer'.[86] Webb characterizes Thomas as 'a Wales-identified, but London-born, writer', arguing that Thomas's 'consciousness of a Welsh identity informed his aesthetic'.[87] He points to the centrality of many aspects of Welsh cultural tradition—folklore and popular poetry, ancient Welsh historiography, the *barddas* tradition, the *Mabinogion*, and classic medieval poetry—to Thomas's work.[88] This view was certainly endorsed by some contemporaries. In the 1939 foreword to a collection of Thomas's letters, Lloyd George wrote that he was attracted by Thomas's work 'because he was a Welshman'.[89]

---

[80] CUSCA 424/6/4/2/1/3, Typescripts by Myfanwy Thomas of some of the memories collected by Rowland Watson 1940s. Letter from Rev. B. H. Davies, 12 February 1947.
[81] Jean Moorcroft Wilson, *Edward Thomas. From Adlestrop to Arras* (London, 2015), pp. 12–13.
[82] Sir Ian MacAlister, 'I Knew Edward Thomas', *Listener*, 5 January 1939, p. 32.
[83] CUSCA 424/6/4/2/1/1, Memories of Edward Thomas Collected by Rowland Watson; Julian Thomas, 'Philip Thomas. Notes on the Life and Ancestry of Edward Thomas', n.d.
[84] Thomas, *Edward*, p. 5.
[85] Edward Thomas, *The South Country* (London, 1909), p. 7; Hazel W. Davies, 'Edward Thomas: Twelve Unpublished Letters to O. M. Edwards', *National Library of Wales Journal*, 28, 3 (1994), p. 340.
[86] Andrew Webb, *Edward Thomas and Wales, Anglocentrism and English* (Cardiff, 2013), p. 138. See also Jeff Towns, *Edward Thomas & Wales* (Cardigan, 2018).
[87] Webb, *Edward*, pp. 21, 25.   [88] Webb, *Edward*, p. 138.
[89] David Lloyd George, 'Foreword', in *The Life and Letters of Edward Thomas*, edited by John Moore (London, 1939), p. xv.

However other commentators acknowledge the importance of Thomas's English sensibilities. In the immediate aftermath of the First World War, Walter de la Mare said of Thomas's death: 'a mirror of England was shattered of so pure and true a crystal that a clearer and tenderer reflection of it can be found no other where than in [his] poems.'[90] De La Mare viewed Thomas as an 'ardent lover of England and Englishness', writing that 'The word "England" meant for him its loveliness and oldness, its centuries of quiet labour, its homes and solitudes.'[91] Fundamentally, therefore, 'Thomas's biography enshrines a double story.'[92] Analysing *The Childhood of Edward Thomas*, Thomas's posthumously published memoir, Cuthbertson notes how, 'Wales is especially potent as a name and an idea as well as a place; but in much the same way, England was a powerful place too.'[93] Jean Moorcroft Wilson insists that Thomas 'saw no contradiction in his dual allegiance' to both nations.[94] Indeed, his sense of duality was neatly encapsulated in his 1915 poem, *Words* which references both 'sweetness from Wales' alongside Wiltshire, Kent, and Herefordshire.[95]

An early biographer, R. George Thomas, believed that Thomas's dual heritage 'sharpened the sense of himself as a fused centre between the dream world of a long-vanished civilisation and the natural world he observed scientifically.'[96] Thomas's sense of duality was forged in the suburban landscape of his youth; in his memoir, *Childhood*, he describes himself as 'a citizen's son of London'.[97] Hapgood points out how Thomas's writing 'remarks on the strange contrast between the human-scale functionality of the suburb and its suggestion of a hinterland of inaccessible meanings.'[98] From Thomas's perspective:

> the suburbs become a kind of shadowy borderland of ambiguous meaning or a parallel universe of appearances, beyond or behind which something else, wilder, deeper and truer, can be found by those who desire to discover it. This 'wild space' is a site of masculinity, where adventures, boyish pranks and carefree wanderings can be imagined.[99]

For the poet, Wandsworth Common was 'his earliest scene of nature'.[100] In his memoir, Thomas writes, 'I lay in the tall grass and buttercups of a narrow field at

---

[90] Cited in Jacek Wisniewski, *Edward Thomas: A Mirror of England* (Newcastle, 2009), p. 9.
[91] CUSCA 424/6/4/2/1/1, Letter from Walter de la Mare to The Clerk of the Council, Lambeth, 24 November 1945; CUSCA 424/6/4/2/1/1, 'Memories', p. 67.
[92] Stan Smith, *Edward Thomas* (London, 1986), p. 17.
[93] Guy Cuthbertson, ed., *Edward Thomas. Prose Writings. A Selected Edition. Volume 1 Autobiographies* (Oxford, 2011), p. xx.
[94] Moorcroft Wilson, *Edward*, p. 13.
[95] Edna Longley, *Edward Thomas. The Annotated Collected Poems* (Tarset, 2008), pp. 91–3.
[96] Thomas, *Edward*, p. 17.   [97] Thomas, *Childhood*, p. 56.
[98] Hapgood, *Margins*, p. 1.   [99] Hapgood, *Margins*, p. 61.
[100] Henry W. Nevinson, 'A Poet as Boy', *The Spectator*, 22 April 1938, p. 720.

the edge of London and saw the sky and nothing but the sky.'[101] His younger brother Theodore later recalled how they would go 'for long walks in search of butterflies, birds' eggs, or nothing in particular other than isolation from mankind coupled with a complete disregard for the laws of trespass.... I well remember walking with Edward from Clapham to Richmond Park late one afternoon to ground bait a selected part of one of the Penn ponds.'[102] Another brother, Julian, remembers Thomas as a 'savage youngster' devoting his time to 'fishing, fighting, paperchasing, bird's nesting'.[103] Thomas's autobiographical writing, which often 'straddles the rural and urban', consistently reflects the suburban motif of urban encroachment upon older rural communities.[104] In 1913, Thomas immortalized his London Welsh childhood in *The Happy-Go-Lucky Morgans* (THGLM), a semi-fictional account of a Welsh family living in Abercorran House in Balham. Cuthbertson notes how, suffering from depression, Thomas began 'journeying into his own youth', mining his suburban upbringing for inspiration.[105] He aimed 'to understand the nature of the spreading disease of suburbia that was obliterating the London he had once known with its ready access to the life of nature.'[106] The real life model for the fictional Morgans was supposedly the Jones family mentioned in *Childhood* 'intermingled with anecdotal family memories of the once popular London Welsh poet Lewis Morris'.[107] Hapgood sees the text as 'a remarkable apprehension of the suburb as a site of cultural reconciliation'.[108] She notes how, 'Abercorran House, which at the opening of the book already holds the histories of Wales and of the Morgans in its name, absorbs all the stories and, by the end of the novel, is the sum of what has been shared inside its walls. It is also part of Balham.'[109] R. George Thomas agrees that whilst *THGLM* 'is a curious mixture of autobiography, fantasy, speculation about poetry, and Welsh legends' it is also 'firmly placed within the suburban London life between Clapham Junction and Richmond Park.'[110] Capturing the essence of Thomas's duality, the book:

> remains too finely balanced—like Thomas himself—between Abercorran House on the edge of Hammersmith and Abercorran hamlet in Carmarthenshire. The actions of the characters are in suburbia; the stories and recollections that form the book's staple events are mythical, fanciful, Welsh, or wayfaring and idyllically rural from an England half-way between Cobbett and Jefferies.[111]

---

[101] Thomas, *Childhood*, p. 14.   [102] CUSCA 424/6/4/2/1/1, 'Memories', p. 8.
[103] Julian Thomas, 'Preface', in *The Childhood of Edward Thomas. A Fragment of Autobiography*, edited by Edward Thomas (London, 1938), p. 8.
[104] Hapgood, *Margins*, p. 85; Gunn and Bell, *Middle*, p. 75.   [105] Cuthbertson, *Edward*, p. xiii.
[106] Thomas, *Edward*, p. 208.   [107] Thomas, *Edward*, p. 11.
[108] Hapgood, *Margins*, p. 71.   [109] Hapgood, *Margins*, p. 84.
[110] Thomas, *Edward Thomas*, pp. 11–12.   [111] Thomas, *Edward Thomas*, p. 206.

THGLM includes a set piece deliberating on the nature of Englishness in a speech by the character Mr Stodham from Hampshire, which illuminates the sense of dualism informing Thomas's work: 'Someone with a precocious sneer asked if England was now anything more than a geographical expression and Mr Stodham preached a sermon straight away.... "England made you, and of you is England made".'[112] In the text, Stodham continues: 'The more you love and know England the more deeply you can love the Wilderness and Wales. I am sure of it.'[113] Stodham's speech, in making rhetorical connections between London, Wiltshire, Surrey, and Hampshire mirrors Thomas's affectionate 1909 travelogue, *The South Country* and highlights the ways in which Thomas imaginatively connected with Wales through an appreciation of his English environs: the edges where suburbia touched rural hinterlands reminded Thomas of 'wild Wales.'[114] In *THGLM*, Thomas further explored this notion:

> Our own neighbourhood was by no means unproductive, and the only part of it which was sacred was the Wilderness....Private shrubberies became romantic at night to the trespasser...The scene was a region of meadows, waiting to be built on and in the meantime occupied by a few horses and cows, and a football and a lawn-tennis club.[115]

Thus, Thomas's sense of living on the boundaries was bolstered by his own dual identifications. Lucy Newlyn notes how, in his writings about English places, 'a combination of "insider" and "outsider" perspectives can be observed' and a 'biographical, temperamental, economic' marginality.[116] At the same time, his daughter Myfanwy points to the complexity behind Thomas's construction of personal identity, admitting:

> I am sure that my father's feeling of searching for something, of not belonging, came from a yearning—hiraeth (a beautiful, untranslatable Welsh word)—to belong to Wales but that he could not honestly ease his way in, as it were, without being born and reared there.[117]

---

[112] Edward Thomas, *The Happy-Go-Lucky Morgans* (London, 1913), pp. 220–2.
[113] Thomas, *Happy*, p. 224.
[114] Cuthbertson, *Edward*, p. 129, fn. 240. See also Hapgood, *Margins*, pp. 80–6.
[115] Thomas, *Happy*, pp. 73–4.
[116] Lucy Newlyn, 'Introduction', in *Oxford. Introduction and Notes by Lucy Newlyn*, edited by Edward Thomas (Oxford, 2005), p. xxxv.
[117] Myfanwy Thomas, 'Foreword', in *Letters to Helen. Edward Thomas*, edited by R. G. Thomas (Manchester, 2000), p. vii.

'Thou Hadst Sought Thy Mother Wales'

Jeremy Hooker identifies a number of twentieth-century English writers who, missing something in their English surroundings, 'chose Wales as their imaginative matrix'.[118] In his short story, 'Home', published in 1911, Thomas characterizes Wales as a country where 'they spoke a different language, had queer names, different food, different ways and...a kind of common life as of one big family'.[119] For Thomas, childhood holidays in Wales, a friendship with the Welsh bard, Gwili, the influence of his Welsh history tutor at Oxford and time spent as a travel writer undoubtedly heightened his self-styled 'passion' for Wales.[120] In a 1908 letter, Thomas defined himself as '5/8 Welsh' yet admitted to the recipient, A. D. Williams, that his relationship with Wales was 'flimsily connected' by 'birth, a few acquaintances, love of the country and a useless sentiment'.[121] To his Oxford tutor, O. M. Edwards, in 1901, he had been more categorical, writing, 'I am Welsh', although at the time, he was seeking paid work to help 'the Welsh cause'.[122]

In his life writing, Thomas emphasizes the significance of a 'long holiday' he took with his mother, travelling around Wales to visit his mother's friends and relatives, stopping at Caerleon upon Usk.[123] He recalls an 'abiding memory' of a childhood visit to Abertillery and comments 'a nucleus had been formed, to which I gradually added fact and legend'.[124] In the summer of 1898, Edward and his brother Reggie spent six weeks with cousins in Pontarddulais. Around this time, Thomas befriended John Jenkins, better known as 'the preacher-bard', Gwili who was a tutor at Watcyn Wyn's private academy at Ammanford, which some of the younger Thomas brothers attended.[125] They would go walking together in South Wales and Thomas would consult Gwili 'about Iolo, Borrow, the Mabinogion, and the Welsh metrical system'.[126] In 1920, Gwili wrote an elegy, 'Edward Eastaway' which records their walks whilst acknowledging Thomas's duality:

> Thither we sauntered in the after-years,
> When London cares had made thy Celtic blood
> Run slow, and thou hadst sought thy mother Wales
> Full suddenly—for all too brief a stay.[127]

---

[118] Hooker, *Imagining*, pp. 197–8.
[119] Edward Thomas, *Light and Twilight* (London, 1911), p. 27.
[120] Davies, 'Edward Thomas', p. 336; Thomas, *Edward*, p. 80.
[121] Moore, *The Life and Letters*, p. 306.   [122] Davies, 'Edward Thomas', p. 343.
[123] Thomas, *Childhood*, pp. 21–2. His mother, who was born in Headingley, was raised in Newport from age four. Moorcroft Wilson, *Edward Thomas*, p. 13.
[124] Thomas, *Childhood*, pp. 54–5.   [125] Thomas, *Edward*, pp. 65–6.
[126] CUSCA 424/6/4/2/1/1, 'Memories', p. 51.   [127] Cited in Towns, *Edward*, p. 267.

However, within the testimonies that Gwili's nephew, Elis Jenkins, later gathered from Gwili's sisters about these walks, there is a hint that Thomas's sense of Welshness remained unstable and could be contested:

> There was the occasion when, after tramping over the Black Mountains to Dryslwyn, the two called at a farm for refreshment: Edward attempted a conversation with the Welsh dairymaid, who turned to Gwili and asked in Welsh, "What's this Cockney trying to say?"[128]

Hazel Davies points out that Thomas made 'connection to the Welsh tradition in the unlikely ground of an Oxford relationship' when, as an undergraduate at Lincoln College, from 1897–1900, the Welsh scholar, O. M. Edwards, acted as his History tutor.[129] She believes that, at university, Thomas retained a sense of '"Welsh" outsiderness' and views his post-graduation correspondence with Edwards, when Thomas was asking his tutor's guidance on 'Welsh studies', as reflecting a time when Thomas was 're-inheriting' his Welsh links.[130] According to R. George Thomas, a holiday in Pontarddulais with his wife immediately after his Oxford days, consolidated Thomas's 'adult love of Wales', providing memories that 'filtered through into most of his narrative-descriptive sketches as well as the first half of his book, *Beautiful Wales*'.[131] In this 1905 publication, Thomas 'employs a series of anecdotes and cultural allusions to inform English readers of the otherness of Wales'.[132] Thomas's professed love of Wiltshire was also connected with his feelings for Wales. He was heavily influenced by the Wiltshire writer, Richard Jefferies, about whom he wrote a biography in 1909.[133] Wiltshire often acted as a 'substitute' for Wales; in January 1917, Thomas wrote, 'Some day I hope we shall live on Salisbury Plain, if it can't be Wales.'[134] In a 1909 travelogue, *The South Country*, paying tribute to the counties of Wiltshire, Kent, Surrey, and Hampshire, Thomas asks, 'is this country, though I am mainly Welsh, a kind of home, as I think it is more than any other to those modern people who belong nowhere.'[135] Newlyn sees this passage as both underscoring Thomas's position as a 'semi-outsider' and intensifying 'his attachment to England' through a recognition of the south of England as 'home'.[136] The latter sentiment was to become increasingly foregrounded on the outbreak of the First World War.

---

[128] CUSCA 424/6/4/2/1/1, 'Memories', p. 49. [129] Davies, 'Edward Thomas', p. 339.
[130] Davies, 'Edward Thomas', pp. 339, 343, 338. [131] Thomas, *Edward*, p. 81.
[132] Webb, *Edward*, p. 113. [133] Longley, *Edward*, p. 22.
[134] Cuthbertson, *Edward*, p. xxxiii. [135] Thomas, *South Country*, p. 7.
[136] Newlyn, 'Introduction', pp. x–xi.

Embracing Englishness

The First World War is acknowledged as a watershed in Thomas's creative development and his emergence as a poet: between December 1914 and his death in 1917 he wrote over 140 poems. Having joined the Artists' Rifles in July 1915, the following year, Thomas 'applied for some kind of "Welsh Army job"'. When nothing came of it, he was appointed Second Lieutenant with 244 Siege Battery, Royal Garrison Artillery.[137] In December 1916, he volunteered for service overseas and embarked for France in the New Year. He was killed by the blast of a shell as the Arras 'offensive' began on 9 April 1917 and was buried in the military cemetery in Agny.[138] Thomas's decision to enlist threw a spotlight on his affection for England and the English countryside. His friend, Eleanor Farjeon, recalled that when she had asked Thomas, ' "Do you know what you are fighting for?", he had stopped, picked up a pinch of earth and said, ' "Literally for this".'[139] Writing contemporaneously about Thomas's death, Thomas Seccombe observed, 'The praise of what we love is sweeter when we are beginning to fear that we might lose it.'[140] Thomas had already attempted to capture 'Englishness' in prose works like *The Heart of England* (1906) and *In Pursuit of Spring* (1914), and in poems such as 'Adelstrop'.[141] In Philip Larkin's view, military service did not so much give Thomas a subject 'as bring his proper subject, England, into focus'. He sees Thomas's response to the war as intimately tied up with his sense of Englishness: 'the England of 1915, of farms and men "going out", of flowers still growing because there were no boys to pick them for their girls.'[142] Paul Nash's widow, Margaret, also believed that Thomas shared with her husband, 'a personal attitude towards the poetic inspiration of the English countryside and the English scene'.[143] In August 1914, Thomas was commissioned by the *English Review* to produce a series of essays, including 'England' and 'This England' in which he mediated on 'the antiquity and sweetness of England' and 'flowers, childhood, Shakespeare, women, England, the war', respectively.[144] In the latter essay, he used the memory of a stay in Herefordshire in August 1914, to articulate his reasons for joining up:

> it seemed to me that either I had never loved England, or I had loved it foolishly, aesthetically, like a slave, not having realised that it was not mine unless I were willing and prepared to die rather than leave it as Belgian women and old men

---

[137] Thomas, *Edward*, p. 268.   [138] Longley, *Edward*, p. 324.
[139] Eleanor Farjeon, *Edward Thomas. The Last Four Years* (2nd edn, Oxford, 1979), p. 154.
[140] Thomas Seccombe, 'Edward Thomas', *Times Literary Supplement*, 19 April 1917, p. 189.
[141] Moorcroft Wilson, *Edward Thomas*, pp. 12–13.
[142] Philip Larkin, 'Grub Village', in *Required Writing. Miscellaneous Pieces 1955–1982* (London, 1983), pp. 188–90.
[143] CUSCA 424/6/4/2/1/1, 'Memories', p. 4.
[144] Longley, *Edward*, p. 264; *The Last Sheaf. Essays by Edward Thomas. With a Foreword by Thomas Seccombe* (London, 1928), pp. 109, 218.

and children had left their country.... Something, I felt, had to be done before I could look again composedly at English landscape.[145]

In 1915, Thomas published the anthology, *This England*, including extracts from writers such as Milton, Wordsworth, Chaucer, Keats, and Dickens, stating, 'I wished to make a book as full of English character and country as an egg is of meat'.[146] He also composed his epic poem, 'Lob'—a paean to the English countryside—while compiling the anthology.[147] Ultimately, however, the war further illuminates Thomas's sense of duality. Longley demonstrates how the 'poetic landscapes' produced by Thomas in France distil his experience of both the English and Welsh countryside.[148] She argues that his wartime poetry both explores and complicates 'identity politics':

> in representing 'England' with an inwardness partly learned from Irish, Welsh and American sources.... Thomas does not fix new boundaries, just as he does not ring-fence a national canon. His Welsh horizons, which make 'home' itself ever unstable, prompt many kinds of poetic border-crossing.[149]

R. G. Thomas emphasizes how Thomas's understanding of 'England' always incorporated 'an earlier "Britain" where his own mixed ethnic inheritance from Devon and Dyfed could feel at home'.[150] Giles and Middleton agree that for Thomas, having different national origins impacted upon his perception of Englishness.[151] They argue that, due to his Welsh heritage, Thomas 'not only contributed to the construction of a mythology of England but often modified an existing set of myths to allow a place for that which had been previously excluded.'[152] Thus by the time of the First World War, Thomas's verse 'provided an encoding of what was being fought for'.[153] This pluralistic outlook is visible in his 1916 poem, 'Home' ("Fair was the morning") about the shared experiences between military comrades: 'Between three counties far apart that lay|We were divided and looked strangely each|At the other, and we knew we were not friends|But fellows in a union that ends|With the necessity for it, as it ought.'[154] In the poem, Longley notes, the army recruits are from diverse backgrounds but the idea of 'England' also connects Thomas and his fellow soldiers.[155] In a February 1916 letter to Gordon Bottomley from his Romford barracks, Thomas wrote,

---

[145] *The Last Sheaf*, p. 221.
[146] Edward Thomas, *This England. An Anthology From Her Writers* (London, 1915), Note.
[147] Moorcroft Wilson, *Edward*, p. 13. For 'Lob' see Edward Thomas, 'Lob', in *Poems* ("Edward Eastaway") (London, 1917), pp. 30–5.
[148] Longley, *Edward*, p. 18.   [149] Longley, *Edward*, pp. 21–2.
[150] Thomas, *Edward*, pp. 239–40.   [151] Giles and Middleton, *Writing*, p. 22.
[152] Giles and Middleton, *Writing*, p. 23.   [153] Giles and Middleton, *Writing*, p. 74.
[154] Longley, *Edward*, pp. 113–14.   [155] Longley, *Edward*, p. 283.

'I furbish up my knowledge of England by finding some place that each man knows & I know & getting him to talk. There isn't a man I don't share some part with.'[156] This sentiment could also incorporate his deep knowledge of Wales.

Longley states that Thomas favoured 'Home Rule all round' and notes how his 1911 short story 'Home' problematized rigid ideas of home and nation. Here a soldier from London dreams, as he dies in the South African war, of a childhood trip to Wales.[157] Thomas's bereaved father, Philip, later made links between this story and their own relationship, underscoring the significance of their shared Welshness:

> In view of his falling in battle, away in France, on an April morning, it is curious to notice that in an essay called Home, written several years ago...he depicted a London Welsh boy, taken to Wales by his father, and having a vision of death as a soldier in a foreign land. I give a passage from pp 36 and 37: ' "My country", muttered the dreamer lying still and blinked his eyes as the tent flapped, and he saw outside the sun of another country blazing and terrible as a lion above the tawny hills. The country that he had been fighting for was not this solitude of the marsh, the mountains beyond, the farms nestling in the beards of the mountains, the brooks and the great water, the land of his father and of his father's fathers, of those who sang the same songs, the young men and the old, and the women who had looked kindly on him. Where were these young men scattered? Where had their war march on that April morning led them?' Is not that passage strangely suggestive of his own fate?[158]

The Thomas Siblings

It is recorded that Edward shared a meal with all his five brothers during his last visit to the parental home in Rusham Road, Balham, before leaving for France.[159] His brothers, all sharing the same background, were physically rooted in England, although they also stayed on holidays with Welsh relatives in Swindon and Wales, and Reggie, Julian, and Oscar briefly attended Gwynfryn School, Ammanford.[160] Evidence of their lived experiences can be gleaned from family papers held at Cardiff University Special Collections and Archives and the life writing of

---

[156] R. George Thomas, ed., *Letters from Edward Thomas to Gordon Bottomley* (London, 1968), p. 259.
[157] Longley, *Edward*, p. 283.
[158] CUSCA 424/6/4/2/1/1, Julian Thomas, 'Philip Thomas', n.d. Julia Maxted suggests these ruminations may have been dictated to Julian, perhaps as background to the production of the anthology *Valour and Vision* (1920).
[159] Edward Eastaway Thomas, 'Julian Thomas', *The Edward Thomas Fellowship Newsletter*, 33 (1995), p. 11.
[160] CUSCA 424/6/4/2/1/1, 'Memories', p. 48.

Thomas's daughter, Myfanwy. The latter remembers her tall, dark, and 'handsome' uncles who visited her grandmother's house: Ernest, an artist, was married to a 'cockney girl', Florrie Witts, and lived in Sheen. He earned his living by designing posters and 'decorating chocolate box lids with paintings of roses and gorgeous ladies.'[161] He had also once won a prize 'at the national Eisteddfod' for illustrations to the Welsh language novel, *Rhys Lewis*.[162] There was also Oscar, connected to the theatre, and Theodore, who achieved high status as General Manager of London Passenger Transport Board, and was his father's 'pride and joy'.[163] Myfanwy recalls how, 'Uncle Reggie, dark and handsome, with curly hair, was my favourite. He could play and sing at the piano…concert parties and music hall. I only saw him once or twice at Granny's house, looking very fine in his uniform…. I remember being entranced by his singing sentimental ballads, with tears in his eyes.'[164] Reggie, a one-time parliamentary agent's clerk with a 'consuming passion for Shakespeare and the stage', joined the Artists' Rifles in October 1915 but was not posted overseas.[165] In November 1918, he was placed in Warley Military Hospital, Brentwood suffering from double pneumonia and bronchitis caused by the 'pestilence' of Spanish influenza.[166] His brother Julian records his protracted demise, surrounded by his family, over the course of a few days: 'To see Reggie so changed was an inexpressible shock. He breathed in quick, short gasps; his face was dark, his lips cracked, dry & blackening.' Whilst the overworked doctor had given up hope his mother continued to nurse him. Two brothers, Oscar and Ernest, arrived with a London specialist, Sir Maurice Anderson, who had procured a cylinder of oxygen: 'Oscar had brought champagne & this with brandy, he has every two hours. So he still lives, struggling for breath.'[167] Reggie died on 8 November 1918. A military funeral was held at Morden Cemetery a few days later, poignantly coinciding with local Armistice celebrations. Representatives and friends from the Artists Rifles were present and after the Positivist burial service, a firing party fired three rounds blank into the air and the Last Post was played. Julian records in his diary:

> It was all over. He who was perfectly well, singing & playing, two short weeks ago, was gone from us for ever, to join his elder brother. What would we not have given to have had his company these days, now that the Germans have surrendered & signed an armistice & the people are merry making, crowding

---

[161] 'Myfanwy's Childhood Memories', p. 262; Thomas, 'Julian Thomas', p. 11.
[162] Davies, 'Edward Thomas', p. 344.
[163] In 1939 he was responsible for the transport arrangements for the evacuation of London children, and later received a knighthood. See Thomas, 'Julian Thomas', p. 11; 'Myfanwy's Childhood Memories', p. 264.
[164] 'Myfanwy's Childhood Memories', pp. 265–6.
[165] Thomas, *Edward*, p. 65; CUSCA 424/5/5/2/1, Julian Thomas diary, p. 53.
[166] CUSCA 424/5/5/2/1, Julian Thomas diary, p. 72.   [167] CUSCA 424/5/5/2/1, p. 73.

Whitehall, Trafalgar Square, The Strand, as though there has been no sorrow, no four years of blankest misery. No merry-making for us. The distant sounds of shouting, fireworks, & the rest are an empty mockery just now; the final blow.[168]

At Morden Cemetery, the two Thomas brothers who died were locked in an egalitarian commemorative mirroring with the epitaph 'Poet-Soldier | Actor-Soldier | And Those That Fall Shall Rise in Victory' inscribed on their joint tombstone.[169]

The youngest brother, Julian, was 'a minor civil servant' in the Exchequer & Audit Department whose job 'consisted mainly of going to military and naval depots to sort of clear up the financial muddle of World War One'.[170] His wartime diary presents a very English perspective, immersed in the suburban world of Tooting and the civil service. He refers to Britain as 'our'—for example British troops are 'our men'—and refers to 'England' frequently. However in later life, his son Edward Eastaway Thomas, born in 1918, described Julian as a 'Welshman' viewing his occasional bursts of temper as a Welsh characteristic.[171] He also characterized his father as 'totally Welsh in appearance' although he 'spoke no more than a few phrases of the language'.[172] It was Julian who acknowledged the Thomas siblings' shared sense of duality in a memorial poem for Edward, 'To E.T.':

> Never again shall Welsh roads feel your tread,
> Or children hail you from that Hampshire hill.
> Your body lies at Agny, sightless, dead:
> Your sad-sweet English voice is singing still.[173]

Whilst the Thomas siblings have inevitably left a less rich evidential trace than Thomas in relation to the ability to reconstruct their own sense of selfhood, they all carry the patina of suburban Englishness whilst presenting varying degrees of personal connections with Wales.

Suburbia in English Welsh Life Writing

The idea of being an 'outsider' visible in Thomas's output is also a common trope within the life writing of those with Welsh ancestry in a subsequent generation

---

[168] CUSCA 424/5/5/2/1, pp. 75–7.
[169] Memorial inscription and grave of Reginald Thomas. Morden Cemetery London. Plot: K. 897.
[170] BLSA; C464/37; David Traherne Thomas interviewed by Linda Sandino, 14 February 2003, copyright British Library Board.
[171] Thomas, 'Julian Thomas', p. 12.   [172] Thomas, 'Julian Thomas', p. 15.
[173] NLW; Ex 2879; Edward Thomas Family Papers; Papers, 1913–2011. A different version of this poem, 'In Memoriam: Edward Thomas', was published in Jacqueline T. Trotter, ed., *Valour and Vision. Poems of the War* (London, 1920). This included the line, 'Never to die whilst English names are dear/ And England breeds the men you charactered', p. 103.

who grew up in London's suburbs and who could also be viewed as transcultural subjects. The writer Norman Lewis, who produced the war classic, *Naples '44*, was born on 28 June 1908 in Forty Hill, Enfield which he defines as a 'remote and run-down outer suburb'.[174] In his autobiographical writing, Lewis registers an adolescent sense of *ennui* growing up in Enfield: 'we faced the matter-of-fact nothingness of present times from which the imagination offered no escape'.[175] He recalls that Forty Hill:

> was on the borders of Enfield Chase, a landscape covered with ancient oaks.... The land and its hamlets were owned and ruled by Colonel Sir Henry Ferryman Bowles, a sporadically benevolent tyrant who would not have been out of place in Tsarist Russia.... The village possessed a few small shops, giving tick to impoverished customers, a bookmaker, an alcoholic doctor, and two pubs in which sorrows were drowned in sourish ale at fourpence a pint.[176]

Lewis's unease was magnified by a sense of marginality based on an acute awareness of his father's Welshness, his increasingly idiosyncratic behaviour, and the family's insecure class status.[177] Although his father was the local pharmacist, Lewis writes that 'the social complexities of Forty Hill were wholly foreign to rural Wales', so that his parents 'found themselves among people they could only study and seek to emulate with, at best, partial success'.[178] Lewis's biographer, Julian Evans, cites an unpublished essay in which Lewis describes his father, Richard Lewis, from Carmarthen, as 'a stranger in a foreign land':

> Everything about England and the English mystified him, and he was handicapped in his contacts by a poor English vocabulary.... Father found his surroundings alien and uncomfortable. Carmarthen was set among the green hills, littered with ruined castles and abandoned chapels.... From my father's bedroom window he saw a flat landscape without surprises.[179]

Evans uses the term 'outsider' repeatedly when referring to Lewis, highlighting the bullying Lewis endured at school in Enfield.[180] He also links Lewis's narrated sense of childhood marginality to his suburban upbringing, noting how his life 'began in edges and oppositions: the edge of the capital, the edge of a wilderness; he was the explorer who returned nightly to the protection of his suburban home'.[181] What Evans says of Lewis is equally applicable to English Welsh writers

---

[174] Lewis, *Jackdaw*, p. 30.   [175] Lewis, *Jackdaw*, p. 57.
[176] Norman Lewis, *The Happy Ant Heap* (London, 1999), pp. 1, 3.
[177] Julian Evans, *Semi Invisible Man. The life of Norman Lewis* (London, 2009), p. 10.
[178] Lewis, *Happy*, p. 5.   [179] Evans, *Semi Invisible*, p. 5.
[180] Evans, *Semi Invisible*, p. 20.   [181] Evans, *Semi Invisible*, p. xxiii.

across the generations, including Edward Thomas and the younger John Osborne. Osborne, born in Crookham Road in 1929, recalls how one of his ex-wives used to refer to him pejoratively as 'a Welsh Fulham upstart': 'I must say that I didn't mind the description at all. For one thing, it seemed accurate enough even if meant unkindly.'[182] Osborne's Welsh grandparents had moved from Newport at the turn of the century to 'a pointless green circle of suburban grass' in London.[183] In 1936, his parents moved to Stoneleigh, a 'Byzantium of pre-war mediocrity', where his paternal Welsh grandmother was also based: 'Grandma Osborne's house was at the end of Clandon Close, a long cul-de-sac of pebble-dash counter clerk's Tudor with a back garden leading on to a large field encircled by exactly similar houses.' Like Thomas before him, Osborne notes how for a seven-year-old boy, 'the rolling acres of suburbia' could hold out 'promises of freedoms and discoveries that were not to be found in the streets of Fulham'.[184] Similarly, when Osborne's family moved to Epsom, he recalls:

> In between the new houses and beyond there were still steamy woods, thick with nesting birds and ponds full of frogs. Only ten yards or so from Conway Drive or Edith Way I might pass in a few steps from suburbia into thick, silent copses, from civilization into the jungle, like passing from the palms and greenery of a florist's shop into a backroom of great primeval forests. The glimpse and plunge from trim pavement to untrodden undergrowth was startling. For me, at least, Ewell had its scattered White Rabbit holes for the imagination, popping up all over the place, to follow obediently and headlong behind the stockade of fences and garden sheds.[185]

Osborne's childhood experience in the suburbs, and marginal status, was a spur for creativity. At eighteen, he wrote his first play, 'The Devil Inside Him', which was set in an upmarket boarding house in South Wales with the dim-witted Huw as the main protagonist. Reviewing the National Theatre Wales 2010 revival of the play, Michael Billington notes 'the fledgling Osborne's instinctive sympathy with the outsider'.[186]

Conclusion

This chapter highlights the significance of aspects of diasporic Welsh identifications permeating through England's suburban imaginary in the early twentieth

---

[182] John Osborne, *Looking Back. Never Explain, Never Apologise* (London, 2004), p. 8.
[183] Osborne, *Looking Back*, pp. 39, 43.   [184] Osborne, *Looking Back*, pp. 30–1.
[185] Osborne, *Looking Back*, p. 52.
[186] Michael Billington, 'The Devil Inside Him', 12 May 2010, *Guardian,* http://www.theguardian.com/stage/2010/may/12/the-devil-inside-him-review, accessed 12 October 2015.

century. The existence of a successful middle-class stratum of diasporic Welsh settlers encouraged a sense of pride and conformity to norms of public respectability but this could also prove stifling to younger generations who sought imaginative escape. Whilst those of Welsh heritage who were raised in England could often experience a sense of liminality, the 'inbetween' nature of emerging suburbia, with its intimate sightings of rurality, amplified their dual sensibilities—in some cases, by reminding them of Wales—and could act as a creative spur to those who forged 'a distinctive suburban literary mode of genre hybridity'.[187] Adopting a transcultural perspective illuminates how ideas of belonging were constantly being mediated in the narratives of English-born subjects who identified with Wales 'whose material, affective and emotional trajectories' transcended national boundaries.[188] The fluidity of diasporic subjectivities, visible in life writing sources, points to the multiple ways of Welsh belonging in the English suburbs: the imaginative realm of Welshburbia.

---

[187] Hapgood, *Margins*, p. 6.   [188] Burdett, Polezzi, and Spadaro, 'Introduction', p. 4.

3
Narrating and Encountering Wales

This chapter addresses the ways in which English men and women narrate memories of their childhood selves and their familial connections with Wales in the first half of the twentieth century. It analyses the shared motifs of these childhood narratives, including Welsh naming patterns, language, isolation, Gothic themes of death and mortality, duality, and a sense of difference. It also explores views of Wales from England, including the persistence of national stereotyping and considers how these prejudices were absorbed and navigated by those of Welsh heritage. It makes use of a range of original accounts including the life writing of cultural figures such as Dilys Powell, Myfanwy Piper, and Patrick Gwynne as well as the memoirs of the writers Norman Lewis, Mervyn Jones, and John Osborne. The chapter also addresses how second-generation men and women encountered Wales as children via family holidays and visits, as well as wartime evacuation. It will use the unpublished memoir of the designer Jill Greenwood, formerly Gillian Crawshay-Williams, as its primary case study, analysing her retrospective reflections on her annual visits in the 1920s to her grandmother's home at Plas Coed-y-Mwstwr near Bridgend.

Childhood Narratives

As the research of David McCrone et al. demonstrates, 'a person's national identity, as presented to others, is not only socially constructed but sensitive to context'; individuals make identity claims, 'be they explicit or very tentative, in differing contexts over time, and these claims are received in different ways, and in turn modified according to their reception.'[1] This chapter demonstrates the ways in which a sense of Welshness could be foregrounded or played down at particular points in the life cycle of second- and third-generation Welsh migrants in England. In the early 2000s, Bronwen Walter undertook a series of interviews with people of immediate Irish descent in England. Walter found that for British-born participants with one or two Irish-born parents, their choice of how they

---

[1] D. McCrone, R. Stewart, R. Kiely, and F. Bechhofer, 'Who are We? Problematising National Identity', *Sociological Review*, 46, 4 (1998), p. 651, https://doi.org/10.1111/1467-954X.00134; F. Bechhofer, D. McCrone, R. Kiely, and R. Stewart, 'Constructing National Identity: Arts and Landed Elites in Scotland', *Sociology*, 33 (1999), p. 527.

identified themselves rested upon a range of explanations, including 'upbringing, childhood associations, closeness to a particular parent' and sometimes, 'simply preference'. Furthermore, interviewees 'often reported that their siblings held quite different views, and also reported changes in their own and others' identifications over their lifecycle.'[2] Having an English Welsh dual identity in early twentieth-century England can refer to being born to Welsh parents or being the offspring of mixed marriages between Welsh and English partners. The latter, in particular, could contribute to the sense of having a split identity, of being 'half' something, and Lucy Thomas refers to potential internal tensions caused by the 'dual influences of the maternal and paternal cultures'.[3] Addressing identity formation amongst second-generation immigrants, Herson emphasizes the crucial role played by family. He writes that the values and norms present in the diasporic family unit 'would carry major messages about desirable identity that would influence the individual ... the family was the repository of its own cultural heritage transmitted through memories, myths and naming practices as well as by more concrete traditions such as religion or political affiliation.' At the same time, there was an awareness amongst second-generation children that there had to be a 'workable accommodation with the world in which they were actually growing up'.[4] For those narrators who had one parent from England and one from Wales, there was a tendency to highlight the idea of duality when discussing their constructed sense of personal identity. Peggy Roberts, born in Finchley in 1916, reports that her father was 'an English-speaking Welshman from North Wales' who met her English mother when he was working in a London drapery store: 'so I am partly, 50 per cent Welsh, you see'.[5] London-born Mervyn Jones remarks: 'I entered the world defined as a Welshman by patrilineal law and a Jew by matrilineal law. I am grateful to my parents for endowing me with this double identity.'[6] Born in Clevedon in 1926 to an English mother and Welsh father, the transgender pioneer Jan Morris experienced their sense of duality as enabling a wider outlook on the world and its possibilities. Writing in later life, Morris foregrounds a childhood memory of using a telescope to look out over the Bristol Channel:

> If I looked to the east I could see the line of the Mendip Hills, in whose lee my mother's people ... flourished. ... If I looked to the west I could see the blue mass of the Welsh mountains, far more exciting to me, beneath whose flanks my father's people had always lived. ... Both prospects, I used to feel, were mine, and

---

[2] Walter, 'English/Irish Hybridity', p. 21.
[3] Lucy Thomas, '"Born to a Million Dismemberments": Female Hybridity in the Border Writing of Margiad Evans, Hilda Vaughan and Mary Webb', in *Rediscovering Margiad Evans. Marginality, Gender and Illness*, edited by Kirsti Bohata and Katie Gramich (Cardiff, 2013), pp. 40, 45.
[4] Herson, *Divergent Paths*, pp. 14–15.   [5] BLSA, C464/68, Margaret [Peggy] Roberts.
[6] Mervyn Jones, *Chances. An Autobiography* (London, 1987), p. 2.

this sense of double possession sometimes gave me a heady sense of universality.[7]

Morris refers to looking 'Janus-like to my double childhood view' and reflects on how a sense of 'dual affinities', experienced in terms of gender, was also present in their national identifications.[8]

Those with two Welsh parents who were born in England also expressed a capacity for moving between two worlds. Bridgnorth-born Dilys Powell recalls her first trip to her uncle's residence in Newtown on 4 August 1914. Here, her sense of dual identifications becomes entangled within her memory of the outbreak of the First World War:

> As my father and I rattled north through beaming English countryside the roar of war came south. I am not sure where we passed the first troop-train; perhaps standing at a station, for the words we heard were clear, not blown away in the wind of transit: "Are we down-hearted?" Faces glistening with heat, in their clumsy Khaki the soldiers leaned out of the carriage windows waving and shouting. "Are we down-hearted?" And the answer roared back: "No-o-o!"....In memory it seems to me that the excited cry echoes all the way to Shrewsbury, that the whole of England was full of it—until towards evening we slanted towards the quiet fields and rounded hills of the Wales which I thought of as my own country.[9]

As already noted in Chapter 2, the idea of being an 'outsider' is a common trope within the autobiographical writing of English people with Welsh ancestry. A related motif emerging from the narratives of descended Welsh children born and raised in England is an accentuated sense of difference. In addition to religious affiliation, this could revolve around language and appearance. Anna Davin, in her study of poor London 1870–1914 points out that the children of immigrants often felt 'different': 'on the one hand in their sense of identity, created in home, community and perhaps religion and on the other in being perceived and treated as different by some of their peers.'[10] It would appear that Welsh diasporic families in England were not immune to these discourses. For Saunders Lewis, the racial prejudice he encountered against the Welsh within English society heightened his own sense of alienation and personal identification with Wales. Writing to his future wife, Margaret Gilcriest, in 1916, he states:

---

[7] Jan Morris, *Conundrum* (2nd edn, London, 2002), p. 3. [8] Morris, *Conundrum*, p. 114.
[9] BLM; Add. MS 87684; Memoir by Dilys Powell, p. 12.
[10] Anna Davin, *Growing Up Poor: Home, School and Street in London 1870–1914* (London, 1996), p. 200.

when even the fellows I best like put their hands up in horror at any taint of Welsh, I always feel a barrier between me and them, and then I feel alien and one of a people not understood. So that I long to be back among them and home again—and home for me means then the other side of Offa's Dyke.[11]

As discussed in the Introduction, the Welsh diaspora felt relatively secure in its whiteness as a migrant group in England yet it remained vulnerable to expressions of anti-Welsh prejudice. By the first half of the twentieth century, stereotyping of the Welsh people had long been present within English society. Gillian E. Brennan notes how in Shakespeare's *The Merry Wives of Windsor* (1602) '"Welshness" was put to comic effect' through the character of Sir Hugh Evans, arguing that he was made Welsh 'so that his long windedness could be exaggerated'.[12] In his study of early modern satirical prints published in England, Michael Duffy points out that the Welsh were often treated as 'domestic foreigners': the Welshman 'usually symbolised with a leek in his cap and a lump of cheese about his person to indicate his poor origins and simple domestic fare'. There were also accusations that 'Taffy was a thief' with Duffy identifying a cartoon from 1781 which represented Saint David as a highway thief.[13] Although negative images of Wales diminished during the eighteenth century with the revival of middle-class interest in Welsh history, literature, language, and customs, traces of this superior attitude towards the Welsh in England endured through the decades.[14] A significant moment which crystallized the notion of English superiority was the 1847 Royal Commission into the state of education in Wales which reported its findings in its 'Blue Books'. As Morgan summarizes, these reports 'presented a damning picture of the Welsh common people...a people retarded and benighted by their lack of English, fickle, laggardly, unreliable, dishonest, dirty, unresourceful and lacking any methodicality, their womenfolk little better than slatterns'.[15] Absorbing prevailing stereotypes, in his 1905 text, *Beautiful Wales*, Edward Thomas suggests that those who had not visited the country were most likely to condemn the Welsh as 'thieving, lying, religious, and rebellious knaves'.[16] The Welsh Prime Minister, Lloyd George, seen to embody these characteristics, was often portrayed as a 'crafty little schemer'.[17] He appeared dismissively as 'Davy Bach' in T. W. H. Crosland's satirical tome, *Taffy Was a Welshman*

---

[11] Mair Saunders Jones, Ned Thomas, and Harri Pritchard Jones, ed. *Saunders Lewis. Letters to Margaret Gilcriest* (Cardiff, 1993), p. 191.
[12] Gillian E. Brennan, 'The Cheese and the Welsh: Foreigners in Elizabethan Literature', *Renaissance Studies*, 8, 1 (1994), p. 53.
[13] Michael Duffy, *The Englishman and the Foreigner. The English Satirical Print 1600–1832* (Cambridge, 1986), pp. 18, 258.
[14] Duffy, *Englishman*, p. 18; Prys Morgan, 'Early Victorian Wales and Its Crisis of Identity', in *A Union of Multiple Identities. The British Isles, c.1750–c.1850*, edited by Laurence Brockliss and David Eastwood (Manchester, 1997), p. 94.
[15] Morgan, 'Early', pp. 99–100.   [16] Edward Thomas, *Wales* (Oxford, 1983), p. 2.
[17] Alun Arthur Gwynne Jones, 'Taffy Is Not Like You Think', *TLS*, 18, August (1972), p. 965.

(1912).[18] In George Bernard Shaw's 1912 play, *Pygmalion*, the character of Alfred Doolittle, from Hounslow, is said to have a Welsh mother with his 'Welsh strain' held responsible for his 'mendacity and dishonesty'.[19] In Margiad Evans's *Country Dance* (1932), the main protagonist Ann Goodman, who lives in the borderlands, employs this stereotype to insist upon her allegiance to England: '"I was with English folk in Wales, and I hate the Welsh and all their shifty ways of dealing."'[20] Journalist H. V. Morton, in his 1932 travelogue, *In Search of Wales*, identifies the Welsh language as the source of his prejudice: 'It must be admitted that a touch of sinister is imparted to the thousands of apparently English Joneses and Williamses when they suddenly speak in a strange and difficult tongue. The Englishman, who hates the unfamiliar and the unexpected, begins to feel that there is something queer and uncomfortable about Taffy. There is something unnecessary, and— yes—sly, about this second language, almost as if Taffy belonged to a secret society!'[21] A 1940 review of Welsh actor, Emlyn Williams by William E. Williams, himself of Welsh origin, notes the former's 'candid admission of the dexterity with which a Welshman can turn black into white'.[22]

Writing of the influx of unemployed Welsh industrial workers into 1930s London, J. Mervyn Williams notes that, in some parts of the city, 'an unusual degree of racial feeling has been aroused. The Welshman, in common with other incomers, is charged with stealing the Londoner's job.'[23] Similarly, some magistrates were 'vociferous' in their criticism of female Welsh migrants who appeared in court on petty theft or larceny charges. The declaration by a Marylebone magistrate, in 1928, that 'Welsh girls were particularly prone to thieving' caused a public outcry in Wales, whilst plugging into wider cultural understandings.[24] Writing in 1933, Glyn Roberts identified a 'deep-rooted conviction' for every London Welshman that there is a 'relentless and unreasoning prejudice against him and his race'.[25] These residual prejudices persisted into the Second World War. Dominic Hibberd notes that in the 1940s, Wilfred Owen's brother, Harold, was unwilling to acknowledge their shared Welsh ancestry, only becoming reconciled to it later in life.[26] Indeed, when Wilfred was described as a 'Welsh poet' in a 1944 radio broadcast, their sister, M. M. Owen, wrote to *The Listener* to state that 'Wilfred was born in Oswestry, Salop, and would, I feel sure, have mildly resented the suggestion that he was Welsh.'[27] The circulation of these negative caricatures within wider public discourse impacted across all social classes within the Welsh

---

[18] T. W. H. Crosland, *Taffy Was a Welshman* (London, 1912), p. 178.
[19] George Bernard Shaw, *Pygmalion: A Romance in Five Acts* (London, 1929), pp. 134–5.
[20] Margiad Evans, *Country Dance* (Cardigan, 2006), p. 30. See Chapter 7 'Borderlands'.
[21] H. V. Morton, *In Search of Wales* (London, 1932), p. 4.
[22] William E. Williams, 'Critic on the Hearth', *The Listener*, 24, 612 (3 October 1940), p. 496.
[23] Williams, 'New London Welsh', p. 193.
[24] Williams, '"The New London Welsh": Domestic Servants', p. 145.
[25] Roberts, *I Take*, p. 254. [26] Dominic Hibberd, *Wilfred Owen* (London, 2003), p. 8.
[27] 'Wilfred Owen', *The Listener*, 32, 811, 27 July 1944, p. 101.

diaspora in England. Selwyn Lloyd, as an undergraduate at Magdalene College, Cambridge in 1925, wrote to his father, 'There is a debate next week on the Celt v. the Saxon. I think I must go and say something in defence of Taffy was a Welshman, Taffy was a thief.'[28] Peggy Roberts states 'when I was young the Welsh weren't thought very highly of'. She elaborates:

> We didn't learn to speak Welsh because at that time the Welsh weren't very popular and there was a saying: 'Taffy's a Welshman, Taffy is a thief, Taffy came to my house and stole a leg of beef'. Well, that wasn't very promising. So Mum who was a Londoner, wasn't keen for us to learn Welsh.[29]

For second-generation Welsh children living in England, language could operate on two distinct levels, either accentuating a sense of difference or as a cloak for family secrets. In the *London Welsh Year* book for 1933–34, the editor, G.O.J., linked the propensity amongst its membership to speak English to contested ideas over what it meant to 'be' Welsh in a diasporic context:

> there are many sections of the London Welsh community who do not readily speak or fully understand the Welsh language.... There are various explanations—or excuses—for this ignorance of Welsh. Some of us have been brought up and educated in London or other English towns.... Others come from counties which are largely English-speaking, such as parts of Pembrokeshire, Flintshire or Montgomery. But all are imbued with some portion of the national spirit, and would strongly resent any attempt to exclude them from the London Welsh community. Language is important but it is not everything.[30]

The 1921 census showed that just 39 per cent of the population in Wales spoke Welsh, with the native language remaining strong mainly in the predominately rural counties of North, Central, and West Wales.[31] The ways in which the descended Welsh in England connected with the Welsh language could therefore depend on which part of Wales their family originated from and visited. Overall, however, there was a significant loss of Welsh language skills amongst the diaspora by the close of the nineteenth century, bemoaned by J. Glyn Davies. He argued in the 1920s that the reasons for the public demise of Welsh speaking were social embarrassment and fear of ridicule, relating an anecdote from his home city:

---

[28] SELO 1/27; Letters from Lloyd at Magdalene 1925–27, 10 May 1925.
[29] BLSA, C464/68, Margaret [Peggy] Roberts.
[30] LWCA; *London Welsh Year Book for 1933–34*, pp. 70–1.   [31] Morgan, *Rebirth*, pp. 242–3.

> A country minister was taken by his son, a clerk in a Liverpool office, to a café for lunch. Before eating, the old man asked grace in a very loud voice. When he sat down again, he found his son had bolted. He could not face the ridicule, and he had to change his café. Making a rule of always speaking Welsh to a countryman would have invited banter from English friends, a deadly deterrent.[32]

Davies states that the reluctance amongst 'the well-to-do' to speak Welsh in the street meant that their second-generation children came to feel like they were 'living in dual worlds', with the use of the Welsh language largely restricted to home or chapel.[33] Enid Martin-Jones, born to Welsh parents in Birkenhead in 1915, testifies to a sense of split identity engendered through language. She spoke Welsh at home until she started school where, 'I was a bit of a joke really. With the other children, girls. Half-Welsh and half-English.'[34] When discussing playing with other children at school or in the street Jones repeats the refrain, 'I was a bit of a joke' three times. Over time, a linguistic distance developed between the original Welsh settlers and their offspring. Born in Poplar in 1895, barrister and judge Hildreth Glyn-Jones recalls that his pharmacist father, 'a monoglot', was brought up in Aberdare where the speaking of Welsh was discouraged. Glyn-Jones's mother, from the Carmarthenshire–Cardiganshire border, was Welsh-speaking, but her children, growing up in four rooms above their Poplar medicine shop, spoke English only. In a 1959 speech, he recalls the poignancy of his mother's death: 'As mother lay dying, she reverted to the language of her youth, and spoke to us in Welsh, to which we, her children, could make no answer.'[35]

Welsh was also the language of secrets in England. Growing up in the central Kirkdale district of Liverpool, John Herbertson was born in 1913, within a Welsh family. He recalls how, in his terraced home, his Welsh aunts would congregate in the kitchen with his mother, conversing in Welsh but switching back to English when he entered the room.[36] Owen Lloyd George, born in Chelmsford in 1924, recalls a similar phenomenon when his family elders were discussing his grandfather's adulterous affairs:

> As a child one had not of course the slightest inkling of anything 'going on'; if the adults' conversation turned to anything interesting of that sort, which looking back it clearly did fairly often, they switched to Welsh, which, as none of us grandchildren had ever learnt the language, was perfectly maddening.[37]

---

[32] Davies, *Nationalism*, p. 41.
[33] Davies, *Nationalism*, p. 29; Jones, 'Welsh Immigrants', p. 38.
[34] School of Scottish Studies Archive (SSSA); SA2013.019; Enid Martin-Jones interviewed by Wendy Ugolini, 11 April 2013.
[35] Margot James, 'LWA Honours "Eight Just Men of Wales" at Savoy Dinner', *Y Ddinas*, May (1959), pp. 14–15.
[36] Personal Conversation, 1983.   [37] Lloyd George, *Tale*, p. 21.

In an earlier generation, Thomas writes of being taken to church by his paternal Welsh grandmother in Victorian Swindon where he would be put on display and discussed:

> My grandmother took me to several old Welshwomen, and they all said, 'He's a regular....' They used to remark how well my father was doing, my grandfather who had long been dead having only been a fitter. To hide something from me, they spoke in Welsh.[38]

Another trope which emerges in the life writing of English Welsh individuals is the idea of physical appearance as a marker of difference. Male writers, in particular, associate their physical attributes with being Celtic, in particular having dark hair and eyes. Norman Lewis refers to his features of 'aquiline nose and dark eyes' and compares his younger self to an 'Arab child'.[39] Indeed, as a teenager in Enfield, he 'claimed to be of Arab origin through his mother (who was from Carmarthen).'[40] Others would also ascribe Celtic traits to them. A letter from S. J. Perlman in 1953 describes Lewis as 'Welsh by derivation...feverish black eyes, hair and mustache'.[41] Similarly, the critic Peter Quennell described the Willesden-born writer, Richard Llewellyn, as 'a Welshman of the dark Iberian strain'.[42]

Naming patterns acted as an important indicator of Welshness within English society with second- and third-generation children being bequeathed Welsh first names to mark out their heritage. Pablo Mateos, Paul A. Longley, and David O'Sullivan suggest that parental naming practices provide important information about social structure by conveying ethno-cultural attachments. Indeed, 'distinctive naming practices in cultural and ethnic groups' can persist 'long after immigration to different social contexts'.[43] Edward Thomas named his three English-born children Mervyn, Bronwen, and Myfanwy. The latter, born in 1910, recites the selection process of her father, 'after much thought and consulting the Mabinogion, pondering on Olwen, discarding Blodwen as being too much like Bronwen, their second child's name, he chose Myfanwy.'[44] The English Welsh sculptor Ivor Roberts-Jones also opted for Mervyn as the name of his first child,

---

[38] Thomas, *Childhood*, p. 48.   [39] Lewis, *Jackdaw*, pp. 3, 134.
[40] Evans, *Semi Invisible*, p. 4. The 1911 census records his mother's birthplace as Shoreditch, London, but she was likely raised in Carmarthen.
[41] Cited in Evans, *Semi*, pp. 417–18.
[42] Peter Quennell, 'Ever Thought of Writing a Novel?', *Daily Mail*, 9, October (1943), p. 2.
[43] Pablo Mateos, Paul A. Longley, and David O' Sullivan, 'Ethnicity and Population Structure in Personal Naming Networks', *PLoS ONE*, 6, 9 (2011), p. 2, https://doi.org/10.1371/journal.pone.0022943.
[44] 'Myfanwy's Childhood Memories', p. 249.

born in Northern Ireland in 1941.[45] Richard Hughes christened his first son, born in London in 1932, Robert Elistan Glodrydd.[46] In her unpublished childhood memoir, Dilys Powell reimagines her siblings 'frozen by memory into an eternal present' and then incants each name to establish the specificity of their English Welsh upbringing in Bournemouth:

> Ioan, my eldest brother, the long dark-eyed face reflective, a musician's face; my sister Gwynedd with her pale shy look and a musical gift not quite strong enough to make her a true professional; and Ivor, the brother who played with me, who unconsciously taught me a kind of childish stoicism.[47]

Father, 'Mam', and Welsh Relatives

Although the idea of the 'Welsh Mam' looms large in cultural constructions of Welsh family life, the diasporic narratives recovered for this book demonstrate the power, presence, and pull of the Welsh father in reconstructing Welsh identity and second-generation identifications with Welshness.[48] Many narrations of self seem heavily influenced by patrilineal ties to Wales. Clearly, where a child was half Welsh and had an English mother, the father with a Welsh surname was the carrier of identity. A number of respondents highlighted the importance of their father when constructing their sense of personal identity. Mervyn Jones, born in London in 1922, son of the Welsh psychoanalyst, Ernest Jones, writes that his father 'was infinitely the most important person in my life throughout my childhood and youth...he was honourable, high-principled, and generous—so much as that he possessed abilities far beyond my reach.... He was emphatically proud of being Welsh, and more so as he grew older.'[49] Peggy Roberts says her father was her 'main influence' in childhood and recalls 'seeing him in his Welsh tradition' when they were on holidays in North Wales:

> He would take us walking in the mountains and he could always go to any farm and say he was William Roberts and they always produced a glass of milk for us. But they said they only did it because he was a Welshman. They didn't do it for the English they said. So, I'm very proud of my Welsh heritage really because

---

[45] Jonathan Black, 'Ivor Roberts-Jones', in Jonathan Black and Sara Ayres, *Abstraction and Reality. The Sculpture of Ivor Roberts-Jones* (London, 2013), p. 17.
[46] Richard Perceval Graves, *Richard Hughes* (London, 1994), p. 221.
[47] BLM; Add. MS 87684; Dilys Powell, Memoir, p. 5.
[48] For more on the Welsh 'mam' see Deirdre Beddoe, 'Images of Welsh Women', in *Wales: The Imagined Nation. Essays in Cultural & National Identity*, edited by Tony Curtis (Bridgend, 1986).
[49] Jones, *Chances*, pp. 9–12.

I do think they're a very imaginative people and they are a very independent people as well, and I think I've inherited that trait.

Roberts says of her father: 'he had his roots very deeply in the Welsh mountains'.[50] Here, Roberts draws upon imaginative tropes associated with Wales: a sense of pastorality which incorporates the idea of 'mountains' as emblematic of Wales, which in turn encourages a sense of belonging and connection. In his published autobiography, John Osborne, born in Fulham in 1929, expresses a tension between his fondness for his Welsh father and a sense of social embarrassment. His father, Thomas Godfrey Osborne, born in Newport in 1900, worked as an advertising copywriter in London. Osborne describes his appearance—'white hair, pale hands, unpressed suit but smart collar and cuffs…a rather greasy bowler hat and a mac'—and concludes, 'In all, he must have seemed a little like a Welsh-sounding, prurient, reticent investigator of sorts from a small provincial town.'[51] In John Heilpern's view, Osborne both romanticized his father and identified with him, believing that he was 'the only adult throughout his childhood who cared about him'.[52] According to Luc Gilleman, following his father's premature death in 1940, Osborne cherished his memory to such a degree that he came to locate authenticity in his father's remembered Welshness.[53]

Deirdre Beddoe writes of the nineteenth-century construct of the 'the stereotypical "Welsh Mam", the cherished image of womanhood which prevailed in south-east Wales' who was 'the moral custodian of the home'. She argues that whilst this image was a mixture of reality and myth, the 'Mam' remained 'an icon' into the interwar period, 'venerated like the Angel-Mother'.[54] Affection for 'Mam' was also present in diasporic life writing. Edward Thomas writes of his Welsh-raised mother, 'Her singing at fall of night, especially if we were alone together, soothed and fascinated me, as though it had been divine, at once the mightiest and the softest sound in the world.'[55] In an 1899 notebook he associates the notion of Welshness with the mother, writing whilst on holiday in Pontardulais of his 'passion' for Wales:

It is like a homesickness, but stronger than any homesickness I ever felt—stronger than any passion. Wales indeed, is my soul's native land, if the soul can be said to have a *patria*—or rather, a *matria*, a home with the warm sweetness of a mother's love, and with her influence too.[56]

---

[50] BLSA; C464/68; Margaret [Peggy] Roberts.   [51] Osborne, *Looking Back*, pp. 5–6.
[52] John Heilpern, *John Osborne. The Many Lives of the Angry Young Man* (London, 2008), p. 46.
[53] Luc Gilleman, *John Osborne: Vituperative Artist* (London, 2002), p. 19.
[54] Deirdre Beddoe, 'Munitionettes, Maids and Mams: Women in Wales, 1914–1939', in *Our Mother's Land. Chapters in Welsh Women's History 1830–1939*, edited by Angela V. John (Cardiff, 2011), pp. 202–3.
[55] Thomas, *Childhood*, p. 19.   [56] Thomas, *Edward*, p. 80.

Throughout her unpublished autobiography, Naomi Royde-Smith builds up a similarly idealized picture of her Welsh mother: 'My mother's skin was very soft and smooth and like new ivory. She had eyes the colour of mountain pools.'[57] As a schoolgirl in Victorian London, Royde Smith suffered what she terms a 'nervous breakdown' and returned home to be nursed by her mother for six weeks. She recalls her convalescence in 'the gas-lit nursey' sitting in a rocking-chair while her mother read to her, 'the cadences of her soft Welsh voice broken by an occasional sleepy word.'[58] A noteworthy element amongst narrators with a pronounced attachment to Wales is the loss of a mother. Richard Llewellyn pointed to the influence of his Welsh mother whose relatively early death in 1928, when he was twenty-one, is of potential significance in nurturing his emotional identification with Wales.[59] John Herbertson's father was an English meat importer's clerk, whilst his mother, Annie, had migrated from Ruthin to Liverpool with the rest of her Welsh family at the turn of the twentieth century. Herbertson grew up with his Welsh grandparents, Taid and Nain, and his parents sharing the same home and with two Welsh aunts living nearby (see Figure 3.1). Raised as an English speaker, an enduring memory of his childhood was his mother's nightly salutation, '*Nos da, cariad bach*' ('Goodnight, little love').[60] In 1933, when Herbertson

Figure 3.1 John Herbertson, seated on the left of the picture, with his younger siblings and their Welsh mother, Annie, in front of their home at 138 Delamore Street, Liverpool, *c.* 1922.

[57] VATPA, 'Nine Lives', p. 28. [58] VATPA, 'Nine Lives', p. 52.
[59] See Chapter 9 'The Welsh "Pimpernel"'. [60] Personal Conversation with author, 1983.

was twenty, his mother died prematurely and the family dispersed shortly afterwards with his Taid retiring to Wales and his widowed father undertaking moonlight flits between rented properties, and marrying a further two times. Herbertson was left with an abiding connection with Wales which translated into holidays to North Wales throughout his life, including his honeymoon in 1939. Whilst Herbertson continued to treasure memories of his mother into later life, these were filtered retrospectively through the prism of his father's subsequent two marriages. Indeed, it could be argued that he came to associate his mother's Welshness with the togetherness of a childhood which had fragmented in his late adolescence.

Another significant element for the descended Welsh in England was the presence of Welsh relatives in their childhood homes and environs. Edward Thomas's daughter, Myfanwy, recalls how they would go to visit their Thomas grandparents in Balham:

> The family circle—grandparents, aunts, uncles and cousins—was an important part of our lives.... Like the rest of us, Bronwen was a little in awe of Gappa, and remembered especially being taken by him to a service at the Positivist Chapel off Lambs Conduit Street, Bloomsbury, and being patted on the head by large, bearded gentlemen in frock coats.[61]

Dilys Powell, born in Bridgnorth in 1901, was raised by Welsh parents in Shropshire, then Bournemouth and describes her family as 'almost pure Welsh'.[62] Powell shared her home with her widowed Nain, who had been left penniless by a spendthrift husband:

> She shared in the cares of the household, she looked after the children. We took her for granted.... I can recall only one note of discord. My grandmother, coming from a generation and a society less puritanical in talk than my parents, was reflecting on the marvels of natural equipment. "And the old sow", she announced with relish, "has a teat for each little pig, exactly the right number". There was silence at the table. Then, "Nain", said my father, "is sometimes very coarse".[63]

John Osborne's grandparents had moved from Newport to London at the turn of the century.[64] In his autobiography, Osborne remembers his paternal grandmother as an 'excessively Welsh' person 'with her feet-tapping and meticulous hymn singing'. Grandma Osborne, a Welsh Anglican, listened to religious

---

[61] 'Myfanwy's Childhood Memories', pp. 258, 261.
[62] BLM; Add. MS 87684, p. 2.
[63] BLM; Add. MS 87684; Dilys Powell, Memoir, p. 3.
[64] Osborne, *Looking*, p. 39.

broadcasts on Sundays: 'She was an incomparably lazy woman, as comfort-loving and selfish as a cat. Her husband did all her shopping for her and the wireless did her churchgoing'.[65] Her connection with Wales was assiduously maintained through the *South Wales and Newport Argus*, 'the only paper she ever read at length, mostly the names of those in the Births, Marriages and Deaths columns'.[66] After her husband's death, Osborne's grandmother moved into a small flat above Tesco's in Ewell with her two Welsh sisters, 'Auntie Bessie…was kindly in a twinkling sort of way with a streak of Welsh deceit and petty vindictiveness which were harmless enough'.[67]

The Thomas family had Welsh relatives in nearby Swindon, including their paternal grandmother. According to R. George Thomas, she 'carried the Welsh language with her, later in life, to the clannish Welsh community that developed around the Great Western Railway works.'[68] Theodore Thomas confirms, 'We used to spend holidays together at Swindon where our grandmother lived. There in the early morning we would start the fire, sole means of boiling a kettle, cooking a meal and heating the cottage.'[69] However, Edward Thomas's recollections also connect some of his grandmother's less attractive traits with her Welsh background:

> She was marvellously kind and necessary but we were never close together; and, when there was any quarrel, contempt mingled with my hate of her inheritance from semi-rural Wales of George the Fourth's time. She was bigoted, worldly, crafty, narrow-minded, and ungenerous, as I very early began to feel. She read her Bible and sang hymns to herself, sometimes in Welsh.[70]

It is interesting to note that both Osborne and Thomas, though two generations apart, occasionally write in unflattering terms about their Welsh relatives, linking Welshness to ideas of religious hypocrisy, deviousness, and deceit and indulging in national stereotyping.

Keshav Nath points out that themes often expressed in transcultural writing include nostalgia, belonging, exile, and the desire to develop connections.[71] It is striking how many of the life writing sources analysed for this chapter point to the narrator experiencing a sense of isolation within their wider neighbourhoods. Powell's memoir emphasizes her Welsh family's social detachment, growing up in an English seaside town:

---

[65] Osborne, *Looking*, p. 36.   [66] Osborne, *Looking*, p. 39.   [67] Osborne, *Looking*, p. 104.
[68] Thomas, *Edward Thomas*, p. 3.   [69] CUSCA 424/6/4/2/1/1, 'Memories', p. 8.
[70] Thomas, *Childhood*, p. 47.
[71] Keshav Nath, 'Transcultural Literature, Nationalism and its Adequacy in World Literatures: Pedagogical Requirements', *postScriptum: An Interdisciplinary Journal of Literary Studies* (2019), p. 4. doi.org/10.5281/zenodo.2564101.

My parents had acquaintances but no friends. An uncle, one of my father's brothers, came with his wife and daughter to settle in Bournemouth, but their presence, though amiable, never warmed our lives.... Sometimes an attempt would be made to find friends for the younger members of the family. It was always a dead failure.[72]

This sense of family seclusion is present in an oral testimony by Myfanwy Piper, née Evans, born in London in 1911, who, when reflecting upon her 'pretty solitary' childhood in Maida Vale, repeats the refrain, 'We didn't really entertain much'.[73] In second-generation narratives a sense of outsider status and social unease is implicitly linked to the idea of having Welsh migrant parents. In Powell's recollections, she is aware that her family's behaviour could be perceived as 'eccentric': 'I myself must have looked odd. I had no idea how to get on with children of my own age; I hid from their ridicule even while I pined to belong to their company.'[74] This echoes Edward Thomas's childhood memoir of late Victorian London, where he notes how, 'Except relatives I think there were few visitors to the house... I was not much at other boys' houses except for Christmas or birthday parties.... Most of them lived in the same street, but their parents and mine were not as a rule on terms of more than distant acquaintanceship.'[75] Thomas lays the reason for his siblings' social inhibitions at his parents' door: 'Our boy friends seldom came to the house. Nor were we very anxious that they should, knowing that we should be constrained by the presence of father or mother. For we had one way at home, another abroad.'[76] As indicated in the above testimonies, any social deficit experienced by Welsh diasporic families could be ameliorated by Welsh relatives living nearby or visiting. Ifanwy Williams, born in Liverpool in 1922, confirms, 'everybody who came from North Wales, all the relatives seemed to gather in our home'.[77] J. R. Davies, born in Wandsworth in 1906, also recalls that his Welsh father 'was a great man for the relations: second cousins, third cousins. There was a lot of visiting—as a matter of interest, I wrote down on a piece of paper over Christmas, the names of a number of family, and friends, and close relations we were in touch with: more than fifty!'[78]

The material culture of the Welsh diasporic home in England could also subtly inform the formation of personal identity. In Herbertson's Liverpool terrace, the Welsh family bible recording births, deaths, and marriages was a significant domestic artefact. Another allusion to Welsh ties was paintings on the walls of the family home. For example, the Morgans in Thomas's semi-autobiographical novel

[72] BLM; Add. MS 87684, p. 4.
[73] BLSA; C466/25; Myfanwy Piper, interview by Margaret Garlake, Artists' Lives, 21 November 1994, copyright British Library Board.
[74] BLM; Add. MS 87684, p. 8.   [75] Thomas, *Childhood*, pp. 24–7.
[76] Thomas, *Childhood*, p. 108.   [77] BLSA; C880/21; Ifanwy Williams.
[78] IWM 26841; Sound Archive, John Rhys 'Jack' Davies, interviewed by Peter M. Hart, March 2003.

have a painting of the 'Owen Glendower' on their wall.[79] In his own childhood home, Thomas recalls a photograph of Tintern Abbey.[80] In his 1942 novel, *Blitz Hero*, John Owen mentions that the Liverpool office of the English Welsh protagonist, Morrow Charlton-Davies, contains 'a single etching—one of D. Y. Cameron's few Welsh landscapes'.[81] When Enid Martin-Jones was in high school, her family moved to a three-bedroom detached house in Bebington in a street built by her father named 'Ffrancon Drive'. Enid had suggested the street name in honour of the picture they had on their wall of Nant Ffrancon in Snowdonia.[82] The architect Patrick Gwynne recalls how his childhood home in Esher contained his father's 'two Welsh chests which were rather sought after pieces, quite nice rustic, thick, not carved but faceted drawer faces, all of which worked frightfully badly' and a set of 'family portraits which were painted in Wales' of his ancestors, Thomas Jones Gwynne and Mariah Susannah Jones.[83] There were also more direct links with Wales. Powell remembers how, 'an aunt in Wales would regularly send us a Christmas goose. For a week beforehand we lived in anxiety, and the cry "Has the goose come?" echoed through the house.'[84] Jill Greenwood, born in London in 1910, was a boarder at Chantry Mount School, Bishop's Stortford, from the age of seven but retained strong links with her Welsh family. She says she won the school gardening prize every year, 'because my grandmother sent me a sack full of good Welsh earth with lobelia and begonias from the Coed-y-Mwstwr gardens'.[85] For Welsh families in Liverpool there was also a sense of geographical proximity to North Wales. Dorice Lloyd, born in 1897, and living in West Kirkby, wrote to her father during the First World War, 'Baby and I went out between the showers and she enjoyed it very much. The sun seemed to be shining over in Wales every time I looked that way.'[86] During the next conflict, her mother comments on how friends who had moved into West Kirkby, 'can see Wales from the windows'.[87]

Memories of the Dead

To a notable degree, the personal narratives of English Welsh individuals within my research sample are often tinged with gloom, with the morbid topics of dead

---

[79] Thomas, *Happy*, p. 19.   [80] Thomas, *Childhood*, p. 55.   [81] Owen, *Blitz Hero*, p. 107.
[82] SSSA; SA2013.019; Enid Martin-Jones.
[83] BLSA; C467/36; Patrick Gwynne interviewed by Neil Bingham, 12 October 1997, Architects' Lives, copyright British Library Board.
[84] BLM; Add. MS 87684, p. 4.
[85] Bodleian Library, Oxford, MS.Eng. C6365, Papers of Lady Greenwood, unpublished manuscript, p. 20.
[86] SELO 1/6 Letters to Lloyd's parents from their children and each other 1914–22; Letter from Dorice, 18 August.
[87] SELO 1/61 Letters from family and friends to Lloyd during his military service Jan–Mar 1940; Letter from mother, 14 January 1940.

siblings, cemeteries, and séances recurring frequently. Cannadine suggests that falling rates of infant mortality by the first decade of the twentieth century may have increasingly made the death of young ones 'the hardest form of bereavement to bear'.[88] He also suggests that the high death toll of the First World War meant that an 'all-pervasive pall of death' hung over Britain in the interwar years.[89] There certainly appears to be an emphasis on the gothic themes of death and mortality in Welsh diasporic life writing. Sara Wasson defines gothic as less a genre than a *mode* of writing, providing 'a particular emotional colouring of the narrative filter'.[90] Jane Aaron points to the emergence, in the second half of the eighteenth century, of writers who sought to create a Gothic literature 'capable of arousing strong effect, be it sentimental, sublime or terror-ridden'.[91] She argues for Welsh Gothic as a specific branch of this genre, with the presence of dark themes linked to historical ideas of conquest and 'ethnic annihilation', as well as to the sprawling industrial landscapes of modern Wales with the 'omnipresent possibility of sudden death'.[92] Many of the memoirists under review, when addressing their childhood, focus on the haunting death of a sibling. Indeed, with this consistent narrative emphasis, there is a sense that this group was 'marked for life' by these deaths.[93] Dilys Powell, the youngest in a family of four, writes:

> There had been another child, a first son. But he died before I was born; I suspect that I was intended as a replacement.... After Sunday lunch... I was allowed to take a book from a bookcase at other times kept locked. It was the library of that dead, much-mourned first-born son; he had jacketed each volume with smooth pale paper on which he had written the title.[94]

Powell recalls how her mother would rest on a Sunday afternoon and then reappear wearing 'a gold locket with two coloured photographs, one of me, one of my dead brother'.[95] Richard Hughes—born in Weybridge in 1900—had an early childhood similarly overshadowed by the death of two older siblings and his father in quick succession before he was six. Within eight days of his birth, Richard's thirteen-month-old brother, Arthur, died followed by the death of his sister Gracie in 1902. Although he was very young at the time of Gracie's death, Hughes eulogizes this sibling in an autobiographical note from 1931:

---

[88] David Cannadine, 'War and Death, Grief and Mourning in Modern Britain', in *Mirrors of Mortality. Social Studies in the History of Death*, edited by Joachim Whaley (Routledge, 1981), p. 217.
[89] Cannadine, 'War and Death', p. 230.
[90] Sara Wasson, *Urban Gothic of the Second World War: Dark London* (Basingstoke, 2010), p. 2.
[91] Jane Aaron, *Welsh Gothic* (Cardiff, 2013), p. 2.   [92] Aaron, *Welsh*, pp. 2, 6.
[93] Geoffrey Goodman, 'Obituary: Mervyn Jones', *Guardian*, 25 February 2010.
[94] BLM; Add. MS 87684; p. 6.   [95] BLM; Add. MS 87684, p. 5.

I think those who knew us felt that Death had chosen selfishly in taking my sister rather than me. Everyone liked her. She used to sit perfectly still for hours till the pigeons came and ate crumbs from her hand; but I would hide in the bushes till the birds were within a foot of her, and then roll out with a loud "boo" to scare them. This I thought very funny; but nobody else did.[96]

In Richard Perceval Graves's opinion, the 'devastating' sense of loss caused by this familial trilogy of deaths 'ran deep into the bedrock of Hughes's personality, creating a series of minute fissures'.[97] Death became a recurring theme in his writing, with his first stage play, *The Sisters' Tragedy* (1922), including fratricide and his radio play, *Danger* (1924), ending with the death of an Englishman, Mr Bax, in a Welsh coal mine accident.[98] Decades later Hughes's novel *The Fox in the Attic* (1961) opens with the 'Anglo-Welsh' protagonist, Augustine Penry-Herbert, carrying a drowned child across the Welsh sea marshes: 'The younger man was springy and tall and well-built and carried over his shoulder the body of a dead child. Her thin muddy legs dangled against his chest, her head and arms hung down his back; and at his heels walked a black dog.'[99] In D. S. Savage's view, this scene suggests that the 'Hughes-like Augustine' still carries 'the inert burden of an unassimilated childhood'.[100] When writer Naomi Royde-Smith was fourteen, in 1899, her mother had a stillbirth at home. Her biographer suggests that 'This traumatic experience would inform an obsession in her fiction with the dangers of parturition and the imagery of dead foetuses.'[101] Mervyn Jones refers to three childhood memories which 'stand out with unmistakeable accuracy, and are so vivid that they come back to me at unlikely moments with undiminished force.... They are all memories of death':

By far the most significant of these memories is the death of my sister Gwenith, who was eighteen months older than me. There was something strange about Gwenith—"the word would be fey", my mother said to me years later. She was sweet and affectionate, and certainly she was much loved, but she lived in a contented present that envisaged no future.[102]

Gwenith died of pneumonia in 1928 when Jones was six. Even the iconic 'First Family of Wales' suffered the loss of a child: Mair Eluned Lloyd George.[103] In November 1907, aged seventeen, Mair was taken ill whilst at Clapham High

---

[96] Hughes, 'Autobiographical', pp. viii.   [97] Graves, *Richard Hughes*, p. 8.
[98] 'Danger', in *Richard Hughes. An Omnibus*, p. 221. See also Chapter 7 'Richard Hughes'.
[99] Richard Hughes, *The Fox in the Attic* (London, 2011), p. 4; D. S. Savage, 'Richard Hughes, Solipsist', *The Sewanee Review*, 94, 4 (1986), p. 605.
[100] Savage, 'Richard Hughes', pp. 608, 610.
[101] Jill Benton, *Avenging Muse. Naomi Royde-Smith 1875–1964* (Xlibris, 2015), pp. 19–20.
[102] Jones, *Chances*, p. 3.   [103] Ward, *Unionism*, p. 82.

School and died of peritonitis four days later at the family home in Routh Road, Wandsworth.[104] Her sister Olwen, though absent at school in Dolgellau, rehearses the deathbed scene in her memoir, 'She just slipped away, and her last words were: "The Lord is merciful and wise."'[105] Similarly, their brother Richard records: 'Mair alone was sweetness and light'.[106] In all these narratives, the deceased child is presented as more revered than those left behind, an object of lost perfection. John Osborne's older sister Fay, who died of tuberculosis, was 'Like a fairy on top of the Christmas Tree'.[107] Jones writes of his sister:

> Throughout my childhood, I was convinced that my parents...regarded me as a bad and difficult child. Life would have been much easier for them, surely, if I had died instead of Gwenith. But of course, if Gwenith was too good to live—a thought that, although they wouldn't have expressed it in the sentimental language of the Victorian age, must have occurred to them—I wasn't good enough to take my departure.[108]

Another common motif within English Welsh narratives is cemeteries. In a 1933 travelogue, when referring to which Welsh words she knows, Naomi Royde-Smith mentions 'graveyard' in a list of seven, introducing a note of existential gloom.[109] In Owen's 1942 novel, *Blitz Hero*, set in a fictionalized Liverpool, 'Weftport', a Welsh timberman ruminates on how his father, 'knew every Welshman in Weftport and his age and what he had to leave and which was on his parents' stone in Anfield cemetery'. The novel centres on the character of Geoffrey Charlton Davies whose 'favourite walk' is through Anfield cemetery and who decides to fake his own funeral.[110] By the time he was eight, all three of Norman Lewis's older brothers had died. It has been suggested that Lewis's 'emotional life froze' with the death, in 1916, of his final surviving brother, Monty.[111] In his 1985 autobiography, Lewis connects Monty to earlier family deaths:

> There had been two other brothers I had never known. The first also had sickened and died, also at the age of seventeen, in a matter of days, and the second, dropped as an infant by a girl who was looking after him, was carried off by meningitis.[112]

---

[104] Carey Evans, *Lloyd*, pp. 29–30. [105] Carey Evans, *Lloyd*, p. 30.
[106] Lloyd George, *Lloyd George*, p. 92. [107] Osborne, *Looking*, p. 29.
[108] Jones, *Chances*, pp. 3–4.
[109] Naomi Royde-Smith, *Pilgrim from Paddington. The Record of an Experiment in Travel* (London, 1933), p. 216.
[110] Owen, *Blitz*, p. 31.
[111] Nicholas Shakespeare, 'Norman Lewis: A Master of Evasion', *The Telegraph*, 20 June 2008, https://www.telegraph.co.uk/culture/books/non_fictionreviews/3554328/Norman-Lewis-a-master-of-evasion.html, accessed 2 January 2014.
[112] Lewis, *Jackdaw*, p. 29.

He remarks that his brothers 'had left their earthly bodies in the cemetery at the top of the Lavender Hill'.[113] Following the death of his older sister, Osborne recalls sombre walks on Fulham Palace Road:

> On the left there is a huge cemetery (containing first my sister and then my father), a stonemason's scrapyard of broken tombstones and dead daffodils in milk bottles. It stretches as far as Fulham Broadway, where my mother would walk past my sister's grave on her way to pay the bill at the Gas, Light and Coke Company.[114]

In the 1930s, Powell received letters from her widowed mother in which she often mentions her visits to a cemetery in Bournemouth 'to put the first flowers' on her son's grave. When her daughter Gwenydd dies in 1937, she writes to Dilys: 'Another dear grave to watch over now'.[115] The Sussex artist Gwenda Morgan's older brother Owen died aged twenty-three in a motorcycling accident on Bury Hill, just a few miles from Petworth in December 1929, 'a death from which she never fully recovered'.[116] In her otherwise impersonal wartime diary, Morgan annually records the ritual of visits to the local Petworth church on the anniversary of her brother's death:

> 3 Dec 1939. To cemetery with Owen's flowers before church.
> 3 Dec 1940. To cemetery in car with flowers for Owen.
> 3 Dec 1941. Took lovely chrysanths down for Owen at dinner time.[117]

As a child, Lewis moved temporarily to Wales, following his older brother's death. When he returned to Enfield, Lewis discovered that his father had become a Spiritualist medium, compelled by grief to attempt communication with Lewis's dead brothers: 'their astral and imperishable bodies were with us, and now that we were on the verge of communication, the last of their sorrows had been overcome.'[118] When Lewis himself is reluctantly persuaded to try his hand at mediumship, his first spiritual guide is 'a Methodist minister in a Welsh coal-mining town in this life', a neat signal to his dual identities.[119]

---

[113] Lewis, *Jackdaw*, p. 29. [114] Osborne, *Looking*, p. 8.
[115] BLM; Add MS 87624, Letter from Dilys Powell's mother, M. J. Powell, 2 July 1937.
[116] Peter Jerome, 'Petworth Personalities of the Twentieth Century, Gwenda Morgan', *The Petworth Society Magazine*, 133 (2008), p. 42; John Randle, 'Gwenda Morgan Obituary', *The Independent*, 12 January 1991.
[117] Gwenda Morgan, *The Diary of a Land Girl* (Risbury, 2002), pp. 19, 55, 81.
[118] Lewis, *Jackdaw*, p. 29. [119] Lewis, *Jackdaw*, p. 42.

Encountering Wales

Another significant dimension of these childhood narratives is the idea of crossing borders, a notion which includes remembered burial practices. Emrys Jones notes how, in mid-twentieth century London, 'the funeral service on Platform One in Paddington was not an infrequent sight' due to the desire of Welsh migrants to be buried in Wales.[120] One of the earliest memories of Herbertson was the sight of his Welsh Nain laid out in the front parlour in Delamore Street, Liverpool before her final interment back in Ruthin, North Wales.[121] Caradoc Evans also picks up on this phenomenon of diasporic bodies being transported on trains back to Wales in his 1919 short story 'Joseph's House': 'Moreover, people, look you at John Lewis. Study his marble gravestone in the burial ground of Capel Sion: "His name is John Newton-Lewis; Paris House, London, his address. From his big shop in Putney, Home they brought him by railway".'[122]

John Davies notes that the diasporic Welsh in England made 'frequent visits to the places from which they had sprung'.[123] Another common narrated experience was being sent to Wales for varying periods of time and for varying reasons. In 1918, at the age of ten, Lewis was sent to stay with his father's family in Wellfield Road, Carmarthen, due to experiencing intense bullying at school.[124] His Welsh grandfather, David Warren Lewis, a successful tea merchant, appears as a forceful character:

> It was my grandfather's ambition to make a Welshman of me, so my mother had brought me to this vast house, with little preparation, telling me that I was to live among these strangers for whom I was to show respect, even love, for an unspecified period of time.[125]

In his memoir, Lewis presents his childhood self as traumatized by his experience in Carmarthen, describing himself at one point as a 'captive'.[126] He paints his memories of Carmarthen in gloomy hues:

> This was Welsh Wales, full of ugly chapels, of hidden money, psalm-singing and rain. The hills all round were striped and patched with small bleak fields, with the sheep seen from our house—as small as lice—cropping the coarse grass, and seas of bracken pouring down the slopes to hurl themselves against the walls of the town.[127]

---

[120] Emrys Jones, 'Flow—and Ebb', in *Welsh in London*, p. 130.
[121] Personal Conversation with author, 1983.   [122] Evans, *My Neighbours*, pp. 151–2.
[123] Davies, *History*, p. 443.   [124] Evans, *Semi-Invisible*, p. 19.   [125] Lewis, *Jackdaw*, p. 3.
[126] Lewis, *Jackdaw*, p. 96.   [127] Lewis, *Jackdaw*, p. 5.

Lewis was mortified by the habit of one aunt of dressing up in bizarre outfits and discomfited by his cousin, Dai, who had pronounced learning difficulties.[128] Attending Pentrepoeth School, where some lessons were conducted in Welsh, Lewis was nicknamed 'Dickie Dwl' (stupid Dick) by his teacher and classmates.[129] He says that he was disciplined for his inability to understand Welsh, 'not only to cure me of idiocy, but to punish what was suspected as stubborn muteness or malice'.[130] Lewis returned to Enfield after the failed suicide attempt of his epileptic aunt Polly who had been accused of writing poison pen letters.[131] He concludes that, following this set of unsettling experiences in Carmarthen, he adopted 'a posture of non-commitment like a personal camouflage'.[132] Thus by the time he was a teenager, Lewis appeared to be positioned in a liminal space—failing to belong to either nation. However, as the distance from his childhood increased, Lewis began to consciously cultivate his ties with Wales. Having paid only two 'duty visits' to Carmarthen since his 'disastrous' childhood sojourn there, once he got married in 1931, he travelled back with his wife Ernestina, staying at the Ivy Bush Hotel in Carmarthen and calling in 'on a number of distant relatives'.[133] In the immediate aftermath of the Second World War, Lewis briefly moved to Tenby in West Wales and took over the tenancy of St Catherine's Fort.[134] His biographer Evans notes that, ultimately, Lewis's childhood immersion in Wales: 'strongly affected his idea of himself: he saw himself afterwards as Welsh, not English.'[135] It is significant that Lewis chose to open his 1985 memoir, *Jackdaw Cake*, with two chapters on his short time in Carmarthen, thus introducing himself to readers in a firmly Welsh context.

Second-generation children could be sent 'out of the way' to Wales when their mothers were in confinement. Herbertson recalls being sent to stay with his butcher uncle in St Asaph during the First World War and reluctantly watching him working in his abattoir, whilst his mother in Liverpool gave birth to his younger brother. Naomi Royde-Smith, born in Halifax in 1875, recalls how she was sent to Wales for three weeks with her two younger sisters when their fourth sister was born.[136] She also confirms that they would be sent to stay with their grandmother in Merionethshire if one of them was ill or infectious.[137] For diasporic families, Wales was also a popular holiday location and, for descended Welsh children, these trips offered a moment of reconnection with their Welsh roots. Enid Martin-Jones would go with an English cousin to visit their grandparents in Chwilog, Gwynedd.[138] Third-generation Merfyn Thomas, born in Battersea in 1900, recalls how his father, Edward Thomas:

---

[128] Lewis, *Jackdaw*, pp. 17–19. [129] Lewis, *Jackdaw*, p. 13. [130] Lewis, *Jackdaw*, p. 12.
[131] Lewis, *Jackdaw*, pp. 24–5. [132] Lewis, *Jackdaw*, p. 42.
[133] Lewis, *Jackdaw*, pp. 94, 96. [134] Lewis, *Jackdaw*, p. 211.
[135] Evans, *Semi-Invisible*, p. 35. [136] VATPA, 'Nine Lives', p. 11.
[137] VATPA, 'Nine Lives', p. 7. [138] SSSA; SA2013.019; Enid Martin-Jones.

took me with him several times to South Wales to see friends and relations and from him I learnt to be proud of our Welsh ancestry. I well remember how, when I was resting before catching a night excursion train to Swansea, he had me woken by the playing of 'Men of Harlech' on a piano which pleased me enormously.[139]

Myfanwy Piper was the daughter of a Welsh father, a pharmaceutical chemist, and an English mother who worked as a secretary. Although the family lived in Maida Vale and Myfanwy attended the fee-paying North London Collegiate School, she says that their 'straitened' circumstances meant she had to spend every summer with her paternal grandparents in Tenby, Pembrokeshire: 'I used to be put on a train from the age of about three, in charge of the guard, and sent down for the whole of August and a little bit of September.' Her grandfather, a Baptist minister, was 'very literate' and indulged her passion for word play and games.[140] Defining herself as 'a very solitary child' both in Wales and England, in the former Myfanwy befriended the local milkman and would take long rides on the milk float.[141] Peggy Roberts makes link between annual holidays at her paternal aunt's home in Barmouth, North Wales and language acquisition:

> Although my father was very busy running the business, he always made a week for us in Barmouth. And he used to take us into the mountains and that's where we got to know the mountains around North Wales, including Snowden and Cadair Idris.... So, we had a good knowledge of North Wales and one of the things I learned to do was to say the longest word in Wales—Llanfairpwllgwyng yllgogerychwyrndrobwllllantysiliogogogoch—which is the name of a place about a church near a river. I also learnt *bara menyn* for bread and butter, and *nos da* for goodnight.[142]

The son of painter Augustus John and Dorelia McNeill, Romilly John, born in France in 1906, records how his father would take them on holidays to Wales, on one occasion renting a small house in 'a wide and desolate valley near Snowdon' where the children would be sent every morning to a farm at the foot of Arenig to fetch milk.[143] Selwyn Lloyd's family would go on day trips to Llangollen, spend weekends in Llandudno and take annual holidays to North Wales.[144] Well into his thirties, Selwyn Lloyd spent his holidays in Pwllheli or at the Henfaes Hotel, Criccieth, run by Miss Dilys Williams, reflecting generational continuity within his family. When his sister Dorice was staying at the Pen-y-Gwryd Hotel,

---

[139] CUSCA 424/6/4/2/1/1, 'Memories', p. 16.   [140] BLSA, C466/25, Myfanwy Piper.
[141] BLSA, C466/25, Myfanwy Piper.   [142] BLSA; C464/68; Margaret [Peggy] Roberts.
[143] Romilly John, *The Seventh Child: A Retrospect* (London, 1932), p. 78.
[144] SELO 1/6, Letters to Lloyd's parents from their children and each other, 1914–22.

Snowdonia, in 1927, she reports back to Selwyn that in the visitors' book, 'there is an entry for Sep 1867 J. W. Lloyd of Liverpool. I am sure it is Grandpa's signature'.[145]

In some remembrances of childhood, Wales was depicted as offering temporary access to elevated material conditions. Dilys Powell's family would be invited annually to stay with her 'well-to-do' uncle Edward, the chairman of Humber's, who lived at Plas-y-Bryn near Newtown, Powys.[146] Her memories of these visits hang on a sense of munificence from her Welsh relatives and distinct class difference:

> My brothers and my sister came back from their first visit with tales of mingled horror and grandeur. There were family prayers, attended each morning by the staff. There was a butler who unpacked the boys' clothes and waited at the table. My sister in particular was frozen by fear of committing, in these august surroundings, some fearful social error. But there were compensations. All three visitors brought home a bicycle, apiece.[147]

When Powell herself begins to visit Plas-y-Bryn, she values the immediacy of the countryside most: 'from my bedroom window I listened to the rasp of the corncrakes and smelled the sweetness of the air and the scent of grass and meadows'.[148] Third-generation John Casson, born in Pimlico in 1909, recalls family holidays at his great aunt's home at Bron-y-Garth, Porthmadog, an estate which his father ultimately inherited. Casson's father was the actor, Lewis Casson, born in Birkenhead in 1875, though educated at Ruthin School, North Wales. When Lewis's uncle, the solicitor, Randal Casson, died in 1914, his extensive estate was left to his widow, 'Aunt Lucy'. She was recalled by her great nephew as 'a rather terrifying old lady who...constituted herself as the keeper of the morals, class awareness and general social behaviour of the entire Casson family'.[149] Aunt Lucy held court in the West Room, a large drawing room looking out over the terrace 'to the mountains of Cnicht and the Arennigs'. In his autobiography, Casson repeatedly underlines his father's deep sense of connection with this place:

> This is where Lewis was always happy, looking at the ever-changing patterns of light over beyond Penryndaedrath. And it was he who took me out on the terrace to show me his beloved Wales before we all went upstairs to put on our best bibs and tuckers for dinner.... We came back to London knowing something of

---

[145] SELO 1/26, Letters from parents and sisters to Lloyd 1925–31; Letter from Dorice, 28 July 1927.
[146] BLM; Add. MS 87684, p. 13.   [147] BLM; Add. MS 87684, p. 12.
[148] BLM; Add. MS 87684, p. 13.
[149] 'Will of Mr Randall Casson', *North Wales Chronicle*, 11 September 1914, p. 6; John Casson, *Lewis & Sybil. A Memoir* (London, 1972), p. 73.

Lewis's home country, how to behave better as ladies and gentlemen and the joys of a large and adequately staffed country house.[150]

When his father inherited the house in 1934, Casson collected him at a London theatre at 11.30 p.m. and drove to Bron y Garth:

> This was the first of the famous night drives that I went on, leaving London after the show and reaching Portmadoc at about six in the morning to be met by Sarah, who always had a fine breakfast waiting for us directly we arrived.... On this particular morning it was completely clear and we watched the light of the dawn slowly spreading itself down the mountainsides and into the valleys. Lewis stood beside me with a look of breathless, smiling ecstasy on his face. "What a lovely welcome for you", he said as we got back into the car for the final fifteen miles to Bron y Garth.[151]

Overall, within life writing and recorded life stories, common narrative tropes include the appeal of the Welsh countryside, the mountains, a sense of rejuvenation, and familial connections. For those from wealthier middle-class families, the material comfort and splendid living afforded by access to these Welsh family homes was also a recurring theme.

Paradise Lost

> At Coed-y-Mwstwr there was a lovely lobby in the porch which had two stained glass windows leading into a very large hall where there were so many things cluttering it up. I loved the hall and its many treasures. On a table, which had a dark brown thick table cover with bobbles round the edge, there was a huge bound book of Dante's *Inferno* illustrated by Doré with horribly realistic pictures of people in hell. I used to frighten myself when I was a little girl by looking at these pictures. In the same volume was Milton's *Paradise Lost*. Part of the garden was called 'Paradise Lost' because in some extraordinary way the fact that Granny had lost her parasol in that part of the garden got linked with Milton. 'Paradise Lost' was to us a 'Paradise Found' but it kept its name.[152]

This is one of the earlier passages in an unpublished memoir by Jill Greenwood, an artist and designer with Jaeger, deposited at the Bodleian Library, Oxford.

---

[150] Casson, *Lewis*, pp. 140–1.   [151] Casson, *Lewis*, p. 184.
[152] Bodleian Library; MS.Eng. C6365, p. 233.

Formerly known as Gillian Crawshay-Williams, Greenwood was immersed in a strong English Welsh tradition. She was born in London in 1910 to Leslie Crawshay-Williams, a motor car dealer, the English-born son of Welsh MP Arthur John Williams, and brother of MP Eliot Crawshay-Williams, as discussed in Chapter 1. In 1984, Greenwood produced her unpublished memoir about her childhood, focusing particularly on her holidays spent in Wales. The manuscript provides a fascinating insight into her formative experiences; presented in several drafts, it continually reworks the same set of anecdotes and gradually opens out into a disclosure of harassment. Greenwood maps out the usual narrative themes cited above, of an English child's journey into a rejuvenating Welsh landscape: an upper middle-class world of servants, croquet lawns, beach picnics, and tennis, but gradually the tone alters, and Greenwood's text returns repeatedly to a discussion of her 'wicked uncle' Eliot.

Greenwood's manuscript self-consciously makes the decision to begin, on page one, 'with memories of glorious summer holidays' and outlines her visits to Plas Coed-y-Mwstwr, a twelve-bedroomed Victorian mansion built for her grandparents near Bridgend, South Wales.[153] She recalls the extended family of five children—herself and her brother Rupert, their two cousins, Olwen and Jon Crawshay-Williams, and her guardian's son, Gerard—travelling from London on the Great Western train:

> We all rushed to the window of the train so that we could catch the first glimpse of Coed-y-Mwstwr, a red Victorian brick building. We screamed with delight as it came into view.... At Bridgend station our grandmother was standing waiting for us—she was dressed in a long grey silk dress with a pink parasol. Our uncle Elliot [sic] was there too in kaki [sic] shirt and shorts. (He was Lt Colonel Crawshay-Williams in the first war).[154]

Initially, Greenwood constructs an image of her grandmother's Welsh home as a form of 'paradise': she speaks of it as 'a magic place' and of coming 'under its spell'.[155] She rhapsodizes, mirroring traditional romanticized accounts of holidays with a Welsh grandparent: 'I loved sitting with my grandmother in the porch where she spent a lot of time watching the bees flying from one flower to another. The scent of snapdragons will always remind me of a hot summer's day at Coed-y-Mwstwr.'[156] Greenwood touches upon her complicated domestic set-up in London, living with her father's mistress, and tends to present her holidays as stepping across a boundary from darkness into the light and sunshine of South

---

[153] Bodleian Library; MS.Eng. C6365, p. 1.
[154] Bodleian Library; MS.Eng. C6365, p. 1. Greenwood misspells Eliot's name throughout as Elliot. See Chapter 1 'Concentric Political Circles'.
[155] Bodleian Library; MS.Eng. C6365, p. 36. [156] Bodleian Library; MS.Eng. C6365, p. 3.

Wales. However, the figure of her Uncle Eliot intrudes from the earliest pages of the manuscript. For example, on the second page she discusses her father's mistress, her guardian, making arrangements:

> We always had a governess for this holiday in Wales who would be interviewed in London by "Mim". Rupert and I used to listen at the door and according to the would-be-governess's reaction to Mim's warnings about our Uncle Elliot, we gave her 24 hours if she said, "I am capable of looking after myself". If she said, "Oh dear" and seemed nervous we gave her 48 hours before she fell under Uncle Elliot's spell.[157]

Greenwood explains that following his 'public disgrace', Eliot Crawshay-Williams would spend his vacation at Coed-y-Mwstwr where he would write his books and 'organize our summer'. She comments that 'He was a very attractive man, good looking and a fascinating personality':[158]

> Elliot had such a bad reputation with the ladies that we were ostracized by the neighbouring families, so that we had to make our own amusements. As children we didn't know anything about the notorious side of Elliot's character, except what we overheard—even there of course we didn't know what it was all about. I think Elliot seduced all our governesses, except one.[159]

Later in the manuscript, Greenwood returns to this topic under the heading 'Coed-y-Mwstwr—Elliot', adding 'He even tried it on a school friend of mine aged fourteen without success I hope but I'm not too sure.'[160] Greenwood's intermittent discussion of Crawshay-Williams's seduction techniques within the memoir, and a heightened awareness of his notoriety, segues into a discussion of her own experiences at Coed-y-Mwstwr in the late 1920s:

> Elliot even had a go at seducing me. I was staying for a week or two with granny on my own when I was seventeen and very insecure and innocent. Elliot took me to the sand dune at the mouth of the river Ogmore to bathe and have a picnic. It was a lonely spot. After the bathe and before I had dried and while I was walking towards my clothes Elliot put his arms round me and tried to kiss me—I just laughed but he persisted I got frightened and tried to beat him off and of all things his little cairn terrier dog flew at me and tried to bite me. At that Elliot gave up and we went back home, but all the way he argued with me saying that I was certain to have a lover one day so why not let him be my teacher. That was the basis of his argument but as I was so innocent I didn't understand.[161]

---

[157] Bodleian Library; MS.Eng. C6365, p. 2. [158] Bodleian Library; MS.Eng. C6365, p. 39.
[159] Bodleian Library; MS.Eng. C6365, p. 23. [160] Bodleian Library; MS.Eng. C6365, p. 38.
[161] Bodleian Library; MS.Eng. C6365, p. 25. Greenwood returns to this incident again on p. 216.

Throughout the manuscript, Greenwood adopts a detached, almost droll tone on this subject matter. At one point, she states that she had considered entitling her memoir, 'My wicked Uncle'.[162] Whilst Greenwood presents a clear-sighted view of Crawshay-Williams's behaviour she depicts her adolescent self as remaining in thrall: 'Elliot, whatever his faults were to the outside world, was a very attractive personality and as our summer uncle he was greatly admired by all of us.' In the latter half of manuscript, Greenwood repeats the thwarted scene of seduction in the sand dune and takes the narrative forward:

> That same night at dinner we were just the three of us, Granny, Elliot and me. Elliot tried to make me drink some wine; but luckily for me I had already decided that I would never drink alcohol. I'm sure he was hoping to get me a bit drunk and therefore unable to resist his advances.
>
> Elliot asked me to go for a walk in the garden after dinner; but I knew I shouldn't even though I didn't know really why not; instinct, I suppose. I said, "Thank you but I would prefer to play cards with Granny" but Granny let me down and said, "Go with your uncle dear." Did she know? The walk was a fiasco—I lost a shoe and although there was a full moon it was difficult to see in the wood where Elliot had taken me. He tried again to kiss me and kept on talking, trying to persuade me to go to his tent in the garden. I fled back to the house having taken off the other shoe and ran barefoot to safety. Later when we had all gone to bed except Elliot I locked my door and threw the key out of the window. I had turned my light out and was trying to get to sleep when I heard Elliot whispering outside my door and I could see a beam of light from his torch; so I was thankful I had got rid of the key but I don't believe I would have gone with him because at that moment I found him extremely unattractive.[163]

Greenwood's manuscript is a complex piece of narrative. It acknowledges that her grandmother's home in Wales was a place of security, in contrast to her unhappy home life with divorced parents. It also contains lots of affectionate anecdotes about life at Coed-y-Mwstwr: fits of giggles in the house and at church, tennis matches, long walks, and organized games with Crawshay-Williams but it also focuses on more unsettling aspects of her time in Wales. In the memoir, Greenwood mentions that she and her husband, Tony Greenwood, returned to Coed-y-Mwstwr during the Second World War when it was being used as a home for delinquent girls:

---

[162] Bodleian Library; MS.Eng. C6365, p. 214.   [163] Bodleian Library; MS.Eng. C6365, p. 217.

There was a very good portrait of Elliot at his best hanging over the fireplace in the hall of the house. The Matron said 'My girls will never behave themselves until Colonel Crawshay Williams' face is turned to the wall.'[164]

Throughout the memoir, Greenwood demonstrates a capacity to treat the subject of her uncle Eliot with a sense of wry detachment. This conclusion transmits a sense of sophistication from the adult Greenwood, a pride that she went on to achieve so much in her life. And yet, there are also glimpses throughout the manuscript of a solitary child, abandoned by her mother, with a depressed brother, absent father, and predatory male kin that hints, perhaps, at a paradise lost.

Evacuation

In addition to peacetime holidays, the outbreak of the Second World War created a different type of opportunity for English children of Welsh origin to reconnect with a sense of Welshness. In the first three years of the conflict, around 200,000 people moved to Wales from England seeking some form of 'refuge', including around 110,000 evacuated children.[165] John Davies notes that all the evacuees billeted in Welsh homes came from England, including the children of the Welsh diaspora: 'The offspring of London milk retailers were sent to the homes of their ancestors in Cardiganshire, and the children of the Welsh of Dagenham and Slough returned to the valleys of the coalfield.'[166] The experience of evacuation could improve Welsh language skills and heighten an identification with Wales. In the obituary of Marilyn Butler, born in 1937 in Kingston upon Thames, it was mentioned that her family's wartime return to Wales shaped her 'internal Celt'. The daughter of the Welsh *Daily Express* journalist Trevor Evans, Marilyn's family moved to South West Wales on the outbreak of war in 1939. By the end of the war, writes her obituarist, 'Welsh was her shared first language, and Wales always mattered to her.'[167] Johnes suggests that, ultimately, evacuation made both English and Welsh people 'aware of the traditions, standards and way of life of the other and reinforced not just a sense of shared Britishness but also of the cultural diversity that existed within that Britishness.'[168] In September 1939, the Clement Davies family opened their Meifod home at Montgomery to evacuees from Liverpool.[169] Richard Hughes volunteered to help with the billeting of eight hundred children from Birkenhead who arrived in the area around Penrhyndeudraeth, taking

---

[164] Bodleian Library; MS.Eng. C6365, p. 36.
[165] Johnes, *Wales Since*, p. 11.   [166] Davies, *History*, p. 600.
[167] Dennis Kavanagh, 'Obituary: Marilyn Butler', *The Independent*, 20 March 2014.
[168] Johnes, *Wales Since*, p. 16.
[169] NLW; Clement Davies Papers (CDP); R/2/78; Typed out script for eulogy.

six girls into his home at Parc.[170] Nearby, Clough Williams-Ellis home at Brondanw took in seventeen children 'from Birkenhead's dockland'.[171] This phenomenon was captured in diasporic literature: in *The Beauty of the Ships* (1940), the main character's father, Ethelred Jones, recently returned to Anglesey, reluctantly takes charge of 'some evacuated children' from the city of Weftport (Liverpool).[172] For evacuee Diana Wynne Jones, born in London in 1934, the war 'caused complete disruption in what promised to be a peaceful suburban childhood' in Hadley Wood.[173] In August 1939, Jones's father deposited her and her younger sister in Pontarddulais, where her paternal grandfather was a chapel Minister:

> We were left in the austere company of Mam and Dad (as we were told to call them). Dad, who was a moderator of the Welsh Nonconformist Chapels, was a stately patriarch; Mam was a small browbeaten lady who seemed to us to have no character at all… Wales could not have been more different from our new house in Hadley Wood on the outskirts of London. It was all grey or very green and the houses were close together and dun-coloured. The river ran black with coal…. Above all, everybody spoke a foreign language. Sometimes we were taken up the hill into suddenly primitive country to meet wild-looking raw-faced old people who spoke no English, for whom our shy remarks had to be translated. Everyone spoke English to us, and would switch abruptly to Welsh when they wanted to say important things to one another. They were kind to us, but not loving. We were Aneurin's English daughters and not quite part of their culture.[174]

In her life writing, Jones constantly transmits the 'otherness' of Wales. She recalls that life with her grandparents revolved around 'Chapel', where they would sit sedately with their cousin Gwyn 'through hours of solid Welsh and full-throated singing.'[175] She also notes that at the local school 'everyone was taught in Welsh except me.'[176] However, although attaching a sense of strangeness to her inherited culture, Jones also acknowledges the long-term creative impact of her evacuation, linking this to memories of her grandfather:

> My grandfather went into the pulpit. At home he was majestic enough: preaching, he was like the prophet Isaiah. He spread his arms and language rolled from him, sonorous, magnificent, and rhythmic. I had no idea then that he was a

[170] Graves, *Richard*, p. 276.
[171] Clough Williams-Ellis, *Architect Errant* (Gwynedd, 1991), p. 229.
[172] John Owen, *The Beauty of Ships. A Story of the Present War* (London, 1940), p. 119.
[173] Diana Wynne Jones, *Reflections on the Magic of Writing* (Oxford, 2012), p. 181.
[174] Jones, *Reflections*, pp. 210–12.   [175] Jones, *Reflections*, p. 212.
[176] Jones, *Reflections*, p. 213.

famous preacher, nor that people came from forty miles away to hear him because he had an almost bardic tendency to speak a kind of blank verse—*hwyl*, it is called, much valued in a preacher—but the splendour and the rigour of it nevertheless went into the core of my being. Though I never understood one word, I grasped the essence of a dour, exacting, and curiously magnificent religion. His voice shot me full of terrors. For years after that, I used to dream regularly that a piece of my bedroom wall slid aside revealing my grandfather declaiming in Welsh, and I knew he was declaiming about my sins. I still sometimes dream in Welsh, without understanding a word.[177]

The arrival of Jones's mother and her anger at her daughter having acquired 'a strong Welsh accent' led to an abrupt return home to London by Christmas 1939. Jones thus identifies this period of evacuation as the beginning of an emotional estrangement from her mother, observing, 'When she arrived in Wales, she had seen me as something other, which she rather disliked'.[178]

In terms of adult migration from wartime England to Wales, Davies notes that this cohort would also have included the diasporic Welsh: 'wealthy exiles from south-east England settled into hotels on the Welsh coast with the intention of sitting out the war drinking gin, reading novels and playing cards'.[179] Furthermore, advertisements regularly appeared in the London Welsh Association newsletter, *Y Ddolen,* for guest houses in England run by Welsh people, which gained frequency during the run-up to the Blitz as if trying to entice readers to these so-called 'funk holes'. For example, Mrs Llewelyn invited readers to 'Spend your Spring in Peace and Comfort' at Wyncourt, Bournemouth, whilst Miss Wenna Hughes promoted 'Arvon' 19 Victoria Road, Worthing: 'Twixt Sea and Downs…Every comfort: Good Table: Moderate Terms'.[180]

Conclusion

This chapter has analysed the 'subjectivities and processes of identification' of those with Welsh origins living in England in the first half of the twentieth century, touching upon the importance of language, naming, material culture, and Welsh relatives, in both England and Wales, in retaining links with Wales.[181] At the same time, childhood experiences occurred within a wider public discourse of national stereotyping where the circulation of anti-Welsh prejudices needed to be navigated by those of Welsh heritage. In their biographical life writing, adult

---

[177] Jones, *Reflections*, p. 212.   [178] Jones, *Reflections*, p. 214.
[179] Davies, *History*, p. 600.   [180] *Y Ddolen*, Ebrill, 1940, p. 8.
[181] Burdett, Polezzi, and Spadaro, 'Introduction', p. 13.

narrators expressed a sense of childhood duality, at times introducing dark undertones which drew upon themes of social isolation and mortality. Collectively, these life story narratives tell us both how those of Welsh heritage often experienced a sense of 'othering' in England and how they cultivated important connections with Wales. The latter was reinforced by different types of border crossings relating to burial traditions, recuperation, holidays, and evacuation. Overall, these socio-cultural and familial exchanges backwards and forwards across the borders between England and Wales illuminate the complex construction, and interplay, of national identities, which, in turn, operated as an important strand of pluralistic Britishness in the early decades of the twentieth century.

PART TWO
REGIMENTING AND MOBILIZING

4
First World War Identities

In the Dantzig Alley British Cemetery at Mametz, the body of James Venmore, a lieutenant with the 14th Battalion Royal Welch Fusiliers (RWF), lies beneath a headstone inscribed in Welsh: *Cariad Mwy Na Hwn|Nid Oes Gan Neb* (Greater love hath no man than this). A few months before his death, Venmore had been singled out by a representative of the Welsh Army Corps (WAC) as being one of the 'young Welshmen' performing acts of bravery on the Western Front, having saved the lives of two men near the German lines.[1] Yet Venmore was from Liverpool, the descendant of a well-established Welsh family of builders who came to Liverpool from Llannerch-y-medd, Anglesey in the mid-Victorian era.[2] Born in West Derby in 1888, Venmore was studying architecture at Liverpool University when he enlisted, receiving his commission in the RWF in December 1914. On returning from a visit to the troops in France in February 1916, the Welsh Army Corps Secretary, Owen W. Owen, felt compelled to write to Venmore's father in Anfield, 'I heard very glowing accounts of brave deeds performed by your son. My informant told me that your son had, within a period of forty-eight hours, been instrumental in personally saving the lives of two men, who had been stranded between the British and the German lines.... I congratulate both him and you on his splendid conduct.'[3] This act of heroism was recorded in the *Times*.[4] When Venmore died on 11 July 1916 during the Battle of the Somme, he was an English soldier venerated and claimed, by both his family and the military, as Welsh.

This chapter focuses on the military phenomenon of the organization and enlistment of English men with Welsh antecedents into active service units during the First World War and their cultural representations. In particular, it addresses the establishment of the 15th (1st London Welsh) Battalion, RWF, which, as one of the four battalions of the First Brigade of the nascent Welsh Army Corps, existed to recruit Welshmen and those of Welsh origin living in London. Within this, it examines the relationship of Lloyd George with the English-born soldier William Pugh Hinds, the son of his Welsh parliamentary colleague, MP John Hinds, and provides a case study of David Jones, who

---

[1] NLW; WAC; AD/46, Letter from Owen W. Owen to Davies J. P., 22 February 1916.
[2] J. R. Jones, *The Welsh Builder on Merseyside. Annals and Lives* (Liverpool, 1946), pp. 128–9; Ben Rees, *Vehicles of Grace and Hope: Welsh Missionaries in India, 1800–1970* (Liverpool, 2002), p. 228.
[3] NLW; WAC; AV/8, Letter 23 February 1916.
[4] 'Gallant Deeds Rewarded', *The Times*, 15 April 1916, p. 7.

immortalized his military service in the 15th Battalion in the epic modernist poem, *In Parenthesis* (1937). This chapter also addresses English Welsh men serving in other Welsh regiments, including the London-based Welsh Guards, raised in 1915. It will touch upon Saunders Lewis's epiphany whilst serving in the trenches with the South Wales Borderers that he needed to return to his Welsh roots to 'build' himself. It will consider how even those with a distant ancestral connection to Wales such as the poet Wilfred Owen, fighting with the 2nd Battalion of the Manchester Regiment, could draw martial inspiration from 'my forefathers the agile Welshmen of the Mountains'.[5] Finally, it will address the case study of Captain Geraint Davies, who served with the 9th Battalion Northumberland Fusiliers and died in April 1918. Davies, as the son of the high-profile London Welsh doctor Morgan Davies was lavishly obituarized in both the Welsh and English press, serving to underscore the significance of the war as a publicly acknowledged 'moment' of dual identifications and mixed affiliations.

15th (1st London Welsh) Battalion

By the time of the outbreak of the First World War, in August 1914, an identity constructed around dual identification with Wales and England was highly visible and functioned on different class levels within British society. As seen in Chapter 1, scions of Welsh families, educated in English public schools, such as Pyers Mostyn, were inculcated with a sense of British imperial military tradition yet also made decisions based on a sense of dual allegiances. When applying for appointment to Commissions in the Army, successful candidates were requested to state a preference for regiments in which they wished to serve: 'Officers wishing for Scottish, Irish or Welsh Regiments should state their connection, if any, with the country in question' with the request that family or territorial claims be fully stated.[6] Iorwerth Glyndwr John, the Middlesbrough-born son of the Welsh MP for East Denbighshire, Edward T. John, applied for a temporary commission in March 1915, his order of regimental preference clearly indicating his commitment to Wales: 'Royal Welch Fusiliers, South Wales Borderers, Any Welsh Infantry Battalion'.[7] At the other end of the social scale, this sense of dual identification was evident in the request of a Northampton boy whose ambition was to be a boy mascot to the 5th Battalion RWF. In 1915, he wrote to the commanding officer, Colonel Basil Philips, explaining, 'I am half English boy and half Welsh. I know a lot of the Welsh drill because I camped out with the RWF for seven days

---

[5] Hibberd, *Wilfred*, p. 442.   [6] TNA; WO 339/8852; Captain Pyers George Joseph Mostyn.
[7] TNA; WO 339/43155; 2/Lieutenant Iorwerth Glyndwr John The South Wales Borderers. Application for Appointment to a Temporary Commission.

under canvas on the racecourse.'[8] In the 1970s, the reissue of RWF veteran Robert Graves's war memoir, *Goodbye To All That*, triggered a series of correspondence from fellow RWF soldiers, providing some rare insight into the origins of those who served in the other ranks. One letter to Graves declares, 'Because my great Grandmother was Welsh, I joined the Royal Welch Fusiliers.'[9] Another provided a more detailed reminiscence, recalling how he had once been in a lift with Graves and Siegfried Sassoon at the North British Hotel, Edinburgh, when one of them remarked to him: ' "You are a long way from Wrexham Taff".' The correspondent concluded, 'In fact, Sir, I am a Cockney London Welsh—my father was a Welshman.'[10]

This sense of dual identification found its fullest expression in the formation of the 15th (1st London Welsh) Battalion of the RWF. Since being raised in 1689, the two battalions of the Regiment 'had participated in nearly every major British land engagement and colonial war'.[11] By 1914, the RWF had acquired important customs and traditions important for ésprit de corps, imbued with notions of Welshness: 'In the officers' mess, the sergeants' mess and the soldiers' canteens, the latest joined officer, NCO or soldier eats a leek and then toasts St David.'[12] Yet, as Keith Simpson notes, 'although ostensibly a Welsh Regiment, before 1914, it was nicknamed the "Birmingham Fusiliers" on account of the very high proportion of recruits from that city.' Medical Officer for the RWF, Captain J. C. Dunn, calculated that in 1914 only 10 per cent of the 2nd Battalion were Welsh, although this was to change during the war, so that by 1917, after conscription, the Welsh made up 50 per cent of the other ranks. Before the war, the officers were middle-class professionals or landed gentry by background, many of them living in North Wales.[13]

Influential members of the London Welsh community campaigned to establish the 15th Battalion which ultimately became incorporated into the First Brigade of the Welsh Army Corps.[14] The London Welsh Battalion Committee was formed in September 1914 with Lord Plymouth as Chairman.[15] Lord Plymouth's family seat was based in Worcestershire but as Viscount Windsor of St Fagans, Mayor of Cardiff, and Lord Lieutenant of Glamorganshire, he and his family also spent part of every summer at St Fagan's Castle, near Cardiff and retained a high level of

---

[8] 'Boy's Ambition', *Flintshire Observer*, 22 April 1915, p. 8.
[9] Robert Graves Collection (RGC) St John's College, Oxford; GB 473; RG/K/WW1, Correspondence from former comrades and other materials concerning the First World War; Letter from Bill Warren, Christmas 1971.
[10] RGC; GB 473 RG/K/WW1, Letter from Charles E. Griffiths, 14 February 1977.
[11] Keith Simpson, 'Introduction', in *The War The Infantry Knew 1914–1919*, edited by Captain J. C. Dunn (London, 2004), pp. xxxvi–xxxvii.
[12] Simpson, 'Introduction', p. xxxvii.   [13] Simpson, 'Introduction', p. xxxviii.
[14] 'First Welsh Brigade', *Llangollen Advertiser*, 5 March 1915, p. 7.
[15] 'London-Welsh Movement', *Cambria Daily Leader*, 17 September 1914, p. 5; *Llais Llafur*, 26 September 1914, p. 6.

involvement in Welsh affairs.[16] Making use of their social and political networks, the battalion committee appointed Lloyd George, then Chancellor of the Exchequer, as their Honorary President, and were instrumental in organizing his landmark speech at Queen's Hall, London, on 19 September 1914 in which he signalled his support for the war and carved out the idea of a specifically Welsh martial contribution:

> I should like to see a Welsh Army in the field. I should like to see the race that faced the Norman for hundreds of years in a struggle for freedom, the race that helped to win Crecy, the race that fought for a generation under Glendower against the greatest captain in Europe—I should like to see that race give a good taste of its quality in this struggle in Europe; and they are going to do it.[17]

A London barrister present at the event, N. H. Thomas, noted 'the Cymric element in the air'. He also recorded how 'a resonant chord' was struck when Lord Plymouth, 'with manifest tears in his voice touched the heart of his audience with a repetition of Kipling's question, "Who dies, if England live?".'[18] This was a reference to the death of Plymouth's son, Archer Windsor-Clive, during the retreat from Mons the previous month. Born in Worcestershire in 1890, Windsor-Clive had played cricket for Glamorgan whilst still at Eton, underlining his split existence.[19] At the end of his speech Lloyd George acknowledged Plymouth's personal loss, turning to him and stating, 'Some have given more than their own lives—they have given the lives of those who are dear to them.'[20] Wynn Thomas depicts Lloyd George as 'the ultimate Recruiting Sergeant for the British Army' whilst Ward sees his public advocacy as both 'crucial' in the establishment of a Welsh Division of the British Army and in recognizing Welsh national distinctiveness.[21] On the announced intention to raise a London Welsh battalion, *The Times* reported, 'There should be no difficulty in raising it, judging by the enthusiasm of the young men eligible for the regiment, who filled the floor of the hall; and not less by the spirited and vivid singing of the fighting anthem of the Welsh nation [Men of Harlech].'[22] However, Lloyd George's secretary, Frances Stevenson, contemporaneously recorded the occasion in her diary, striking a more discordant note: 'There is no doubt that it was a tremendous success, but C was very depressed after it. He

---

[16] 'St Fagan's Castle', National Museum Wales website, https://museum.wales/stfagans/buildings/castle/, accessed 29 September 2016.

[17] A. J. P. Taylor, ed., *Lloyd George. A Diary by Frances Stevenson* (London, 1971), p. 2; *The Great War. Speech Delivered by The Rt. Hon. David Lloyd George, MP* (London, 1914), p. 13.

[18] 'London Welsh and the War', *Amman Valley Chronicle*, 1 October 1914, p. 8.

[19] Andrew Renshaw, *Wisden on the Great War: The Lives of Cricket's Fallen 1914-1918* (London, 2014), pp. 95-7.

[20] 'British Honour', *The Times*, 20 September 1914, p. 3.

[21] Wynn Thomas, *Nations*, p. 73; Ward, *Unionism*, pp. 78-9.   [22] 'British Honour'.

said the audience made him sick—they were far too stodgy and "comfortable"—"you had to talk your way through layers of fat".[23]

Within days of the Queen's Hall event, the Secretary of State for War, Lord Kitchener, sanctioned the formation of a Welsh Army Corps.[24] The War Office authorized the raising of Battalions in London, Liverpool, and Manchester, 'from Welshmen resident in these cities', as well as in Wales, affirming its diasporic dimension from the outset.[25] The Welsh Army Corps papers at the National Library of Wales show men from Liverpool and London requesting commissions and firms seeking business opportunities.[26] For example, throughout 1915, the Liverpool retailer, Owen Owen offered to supply Army shirts and sample kits although these overtures were largely rejected.[27] By February 1915, the Welsh Army Corps had enough men to raise the first division, which became the 38th (Welsh) Division. Once the inclusion of a London Welsh Battalion within the WAC structure was authorized, WAC badges were distributed to London Welsh recruits.[28] By early October, around 400 men had enrolled and two Battalions, the 15th and 18th, were raised.[29] In her analysis of nineteenth-century martial race ideology, Heather Streets demonstrates how imperial understandings that some 'races' were more martial than others led to the military promotion of particular masculine traits: 'inherent loyalty, honour and devotion in addition to racial hardiness'.[30] Ellis points to the popularity of notions of Welsh martiality, which by the early decades of the twentieth century largely rested 'on images accumulated during the warlike days of the distant past' when 'the Welsh and their tribal Celtic forebears were known for their ferocity, tenacity and daring in battle'.[31] When the 15th Battalion departed for training in Llandudno in December 1914, Lloyd George gave a speech at their farewell dinner in London where he lauded the hybrid unit as the embodiment of the 'martial spirit of the men of Wales'. Drawing upon the discourse of an 'imperial Welshness',[32] he also used the opportunity to emphasize Wales's historical importance within Britain: 'Let everyone say when you come back, "Gallant little Wales!" There was a notion that Wales, if Radical, was not Imperialist. Why, Wales founded the British Empire. Elizabeth Tudor was

---

[23] 21 September 1914 cited in Taylor, *Lloyd George*, p. 2. Stevenson initially refers to Lloyd George as 'C' (Chancellor) and then 'D' (David) in her diaries.
[24] 'Welsh Army Corps', *The Times*, 23 September 1914, p. 10.
[25] NLW; WAC; C8/1, Letter from Ivor Herbert to Lord Derby, 20 October 1914.
[26] NLW; WAC; A; General Correspondence, accounts and tenders for clothing and necessaries, 1914–1917.
[27] NLW; WAC; AO/14; Owen Owen Ltd, Liverpool, Jan–June 1915.
[28] NLW; WAC; C/20; 15th Battalion RWF (1st London Welsh), Letters from Rees V. Jones to Owen W. Owen, 9 October 1914, 14 October 1914.
[29] NLW; WAC; C/38; 18th (Reserve) Battalion RWF (2nd London Welsh), 1915–16.
[30] Heather Streets, *Martial Races: The Military, Race and Masculinity in British Imperial Culture, 1857–1914* (Manchester, 2004), p. 11.
[31] Ellis, 'Pacific People', p. 16. [32] Jones and Jones, 'Welsh World', p. 57.

a Welsh lady, and Wales had a separate inheritance in the empire.'[33] He also declared that he 'would not have sent his own sons into the war did he not possess the deep conviction in his soul that all he had fought for in his life was something that at last was being put to the issue of one great campaign and that Wales ought to take a leading part in it.'[34] Here, Lloyd George rhetorically equates the London Welsh battalion with 'Wales'. He also signals his commitment to the 15th by alluding to the involvement of his two sons, although both were directed into privileged staff positions.[35] By March 1915, his eldest son, Richard, was a member of Brigadier-General Owen Thomas's Welsh Army Corps staff at Llandudno and his second son, Gwilym, an aide-de-camp.[36]

In December 1915, the 15th Battalion marched to Euston Station, destined for training camps in North Wales.[37] The battalion committee members, based in London, publicly feted those who received commissions with celebratory dinners where they were presented with ceremonial swords.[38] One such recipient was Captain John Edwards, son of Rev. James Edwards; at Reggiori's Restaurant, King's Cross, his 'great talents as an actor, author and dramatist' were applauded.[39] Another was Lieutenant. V. J. Rees, the son of Mr Evan Rees, 'late of Tyddyn Mawr, Dolgelley', who was guest of honour at the Holborn Restaurant in May 1915. At this dinner, one committee member stated that they 'would not cease their labours until every available recruit in London had been secured'.[40] A second London Welsh Battalion, the 18th RWF, was sanctioned with Major Ivor Bowen appointed to its command in August 1915.[41] One of those who joined was Ludwig Lewis from Wallasey, younger brother of Saunders Lewis. Unable to gain a commission, he moved to London in January 1916 where he joined the battalion as a private. His brother commented: 'He looked, I thought, well in his uniform, but he annoyed me terribly by being ashamed of it. His only redeeming feature is that he is not ashamed of being ashamed—he is at least an honest snob.'[42] However, when the idea of a third London Welsh battalion was mooted, this illuminated some of the tensions surrounding the composition of the battalions. A correspondent to the *London Welshman and Kelt* bemoaned the fact that 'London Welsh' had 'become a very elastic term—too elastic'. He argued that the

---

[33] 'Mr Lloyd George and the London Welsh Battalion', *The Cambrian News*, 4 December 1914, p. 5.
[34] 'Mr Lloyd George'.
[35] Lloyd George initially took great measures to try to prevent his sons from serving overseas and used his influence to have both men appointed as ADCs to generals. See Ward, *Unionism*, p. 98.
[36] 'London Welsh Battalion', *Amman Valley Chronicle*, 3 December 1914, p. 6; 'Lieut. Lloyd George on Staff', *South Wales Weekly Post*, 13 March 1915, p. 8.
[37] 'London Welsh', *The Cambria Daily Leader*, 5 December 1914, p. 1.
[38] 'London', *The Cambrian News*, 21 May 1915, p. 3.
[39] 'London Welsh Officer Honoured', *The Cambrian News*, 18 December 1914, p. 3.
[40] 'London', p. 3.
[41] 'Lieutenant Colonelcy for Major Ivor Bowen', *Brecon & Radnor Express*, 5 August 1915, p. 5.
[42] *Saunders Lewis. Letters*, p. 178.

attachment of the name 'London Welsh' to the two new battalions of the RWF was a 'misnomer':

> I have seen recruits accepted with the least possible inquiry, and it would have been better to rest content with raising one battalion of 'real' London Welshmen than to have followed the course of accepting everybody and anybody who said that he was a London Welshman, or that he had London Welsh connections....
>
> It is a jesting matter for outsiders, and Llandudno Welshmen have shown strong feelings on the matter. If the third battalion is to be a real Welsh one... make it also a Welsh-speaking battalion. But we do not require another Anglo-Jewish-Welsh combination to bear the name of the London Welsh.[43]

This piece, with its repetition of the word 'real', ties into notions of authenticity, and competing understandings of who had a right to represent 'Wales' militarily. Additionally, it underlines the importance of place, implying that the London recruits were vulnerable to being rejected as 'Welsh' once training in North Wales. Mixed in with these objections was an undercurrent of anti-Jewish sentiment expressed in the final sentence. This, and the allusion to Welsh language skills, points to a narrowly exclusivist definition of Welshness. In reality, as Chris Williams notes, the 15th Battalion was a site of 'ethnic heterogeneity', contributing to a sense of 'common understanding' between both Welsh and non-Welsh soldiers within its ranks.[44] Williams notes how David Jones alludes directly to this national and racial variegation in his 1937 epic poem, *In Parenthesis,* which contrasts the 'genuine Taffies' serving in the RWF with the 'rash levied from Islington and Hackney and the... Anglo-Welsh from Queens Ferry'.[45] Furthermore, the original 1937 book wrapper underlined the deliberateness of Jones's vision, framing the text as: 'the *chanson de gestes* of the Cockney and the Welsh and the Welsh Cockney in the Great War.'[46]

One of the Londoners serving in the 15th was Lieutenant William Pugh Hinds, the only son of the Blackheath draper and MP for West Carmarthenshire, John Hinds. On 30 January 1916, the battalion's War Diary recorded Hinds, their first officer casualty, as having been 'severely wounded by a sniper in Duck's Bill'.[47] Born in 1897 and educated in Blackheath, Hinds was studying engineering at the Electrical Standardising, Testing, and Training Institution, London before he

---

[43] Cited in 'The London Welsh', *Llais Llafur*, 14 August 1915, p. 1.
[44] Chris Williams, 'Taffs in the Trenches: Welsh National Identity and Military Service, 1914–1918', in *Wales and War*, pp. 144, 157.
[45] Williams, 'Taffs', p. 144; David Jones, *In Parenthesis* (London, 1937), p. 160.
[46] Jones, *In Parenthesis* (London, 1937), Ashton Rare Books website, https://www.ashtonrarebooks.com/book/jones-david-in-parenthesis-seinnyessit-e-gledyf-ym-penn-mameu/, accessed 10 August 2023.
[47] NLW MS 10436E; The War diary, 1 December 1915–30 January 1918, of the 15th Battalion of the Royal Welsh Fusiliers, accessed via *Cymru 1914*, 23 September 2015.

enlisted in November 1914.⁴⁸ He was appointed second lieutenant in February 1915.⁴⁹ Steven John notes that it was 'possibly due to his father's political connections' that Hinds had been commissioned into the 15th in the first place.⁵⁰ John Hinds, 'of Neuadd-Deg, Carmarthen and "Bryn Teg", 30 Lee Park Blackheath' was one of the key initiators, cheerleaders, and campaigners for the 15th, displaying a vocal commitment to Welsh national ideals throughout and beyond the war.⁵¹ Born on a farm near Carmarthen, Hinds had migrated to London as a teenager and made his fortune in the drapery trade, founding the department store, Hinds & Company, in Blackheath. A one-time chair of the Welsh Liberal Foundation, he was elected as MP for West Carmarthenshire in 1910.⁵² In 1919, he presided over the formation of the London Welsh Nationalist Society whose objectives were 'to secure for Wales complete control over her own affairs'.⁵³ At the Reggiori dinner for Captain Edwards, Hinds declared that he was glad to find that 'young Welshmen' were determined to fight 'for the great cause of liberty and democracy and the principle of nationality', drawing a rhetorical veil over the Englishness of the recruits whilst also embracing a pluralistic idea of Welshness which existed beyond Wales's borders.⁵⁴ Ultimately, however, his commitment to Welsh patriotism involved a huge personal sacrifice. Under the headline, 'Welsh MP's Son', the Welsh press reported on his son William's death in France:

> He was not yet twenty years of age—a finely-built, handsome youth much liked by all the friends of the family. Brief details which have been communicated to the family show that the brave young officer was in the front trench with a bombing party of the London Welsh and that a sniper, who was at the top of a tree, shot him in the forehead.⁵⁵

Lloyd George was further drawn into the world of the 15th by the death of Hinds. During a visit to France, Lloyd George visited Hinds in an emergency field hospital and thus witnessed his protracted demise. This had such an impact on Lloyd George that when he returned to London, he confided his sense of horror to his mistress. As Stevenson records:

> I could see that the visit had told on his nerves. 'You must take my mind off it all, Pussy', were almost his first words to me. 'I feel I shall break down if I do not get right away from it all. The horror of what I have seen has burnt into my soul, and

---

⁴⁸ Edward Whitaker Moss-Blundell, ed., *The House of Commons Book of Remembrance 1914–1918* (London, 1931), p. 116.
⁴⁹ TNA; WO 339/23674; Lieutenant William Pugh Hinds.
⁵⁰ Steven John, *Carmarthen in the Great War* (Barnsley, 2014), p. 81.
⁵¹ TNA; WO 339/23674.   ⁵² 'Obituary', *Times*, 24 July 1928, p. 18.
⁵³ 'London Welsh Nationalist Society', *North Wales Chronicle*, 4 April 1919, p. 3.
⁵⁴ 'London Welsh Officer Honoured'; Scully, 'Discourses', p. 20.
⁵⁵ *South Wales Weekly Post*, 12 February 1916, p. 2.

has almost unnerved me for my work.'... The poor boy had been shot through the head, & the bullet had torn through part of his brain. He was in dreadful agony, & was paralysed all down one side. D. insisted upon fetching two more doctors to the hospital to see if they could not do anything for him, though everyone said his case was hopeless. D. later on spoke to the Commander-in-Chief, who promised that the best doctor out there should be with the boy by 5.0 yesterday afternoon. Since he has been home, D. has managed to send a brain specialist from Etaples to see him, & still hopes that it may be possible to save the boy's life. But the incident had quite unnerved him. 'I wish I had not seen him', he kept on saying to me. 'I ought not to have seen him. I feel that I cannot go on with my work, now that the grim horror of the reality has been brought home to me so terribly. I was not made to deal with things of war. I am too sensitive to pain and suffering, & this visit has almost broken me down.'[56]

John Hinds visited the Prime Minister, Asquith, at Downing Street, where Lloyd George informed him of his son's condition.[57] Stevenson's diary records the death of the officer two days later: 'Col. Lee says it is better so, for he would most probably have been an imbecile if he had lived.'[58] However, Hinds's death continued to haunt Lloyd George. When he returned to France in late 1916, he made a pilgrimage to Hinds's grave at Merville Communal Cemetery, near Bethune, subsequently receiving a note of gratitude from Hinds:

We shall never, never forget that, amongst your great work in France, that you found time to visit our dear lad's grave appeals to us more than I can express. His death took a great deal of sunshine out of our life. But such kind action as yours brings a great deal of consolation and comfort to us. We are already greatly indebted to you for all you did when he passed away and this last action places us under more obligation that we can ever hope to repay.[59]

The Welsh inscription requested on Hinds's headstone, chosen by his father, was *Yn Anghof Ni Chant Fod* (They Will Not Be Forgotten), from the poem 'Dyffryn Clwyd', so that even in death he continued to embrace his Londoner son in a Welsh martial identity.[60] Hinds was further memorialized within a London Welsh context when his father paid for a memorial at the Welsh Baptist Chapel, Castle Street for 'the young men of the congregation who gave their lives'. Lloyd George

---

[56] 1 February 1916 in Taylor, *Lloyd George*, pp. 92–3.   [57] John, *Carmarthen*, p. 82.
[58] John, *Carmarthen*, p. 94.
[59] NLW; MS 22527E; Lloyd George Correspondence 1915–45, Letter from John Hinds, 15 October 1916.
[60] Gwen Awbery, 'Longing for Peace', *Welsh Memorials to the Great War*, https://war-memorials.swan.ac.uk/?p=218, accessed 11 November 2021. For more on this phenomenon, see Chapter 6 'Mourning Dualities'.

attended its unveiling, displaying his personal closeness to this diasporic military endeavour whilst simultaneously claiming the dead as Welsh:

> It fills me with sadness; it thrills me with pride. I am proud to be a member of the church where there were fourteen of the Welshmen who laid down their lives in the Great War. They made a difference in the valuation of Welsh character, not merely now but right down through the ages.... It is to me an honour to be here today to unveil this record of these fourteen young men. Most of them I knew; I had the greatest admiration for them. I know what they gave up.[61]

Press reports note how, after delivering his address, Lloyd George 'was so overcome that he leaned against the railings of the pulpit as he wiped the tears from his face'.[62] The emergence of the 15th Battalion and its enshrouding in the language of Welsh martial identity points to a reflexive inclusion of second-generation Welsh soldiers into what Marc Scully terms a more 'pluralist' Welsh diasporic identity.[63] It also highlights the functioning of a form of militarized Welsh patriotism amongst the male diasporic elite which occasionally demanded the sacrifice of their own sons.

David Jones—'Welsh Enough'

Another of the 15th's recruits was the poet and painter David Jones. Born into the suburban milieu of Brockley in November 1895 to an English mother and Welsh father, Jones was keen to enlist in a regiment with Welsh associations. Although he lived in England for his whole life, Jones consistently asserted a strong sense of himself as Welsh, writing that, 'From about the age of six, I felt I belonged to my father's people and their land, though brought up in an entirely English atmosphere.'[64] Hooker highlights the importance of Jones's dual inheritance and of the things 'given' to Jones as a child: 'Primary among these were his mother and father, and what might be called, in a geological metaphor, the parent materials.... These included, on his father's side, the land and culture of Wales; and on his mother's... London, the Thames, ships and the sea.' He points out that Jones's dedication in his 1952 epic poem, *The Anathemata*, reads, 'To my parents and their forebears and to all the native people of the bright island of Britain.'[65] Jones

---

[61] 'A Welsh Memorial', *The Times*, 3 April 1922, p. 14; Gethin Matthews, 'What a Lloyd George Speech 100 Years Ago Today Can Tell Us', *Nation. Cymru*, 2 April 2022, https://nation.cymru/culture/what-a-lloyd-george-speech-100-years-ago-today-can-tell-us-about-welsh-attitudes-towards-the-war-to-end-all-wars/, accessed 25 May 2022.
[62] Matthews, 'What'.   [63] Scully, 'Discourses', p. 20.
[64] David Jones, *The Dying Gaul and Other Writings* (London, 1978), p. 23.
[65] Hooker, *Imagining*, pp. 112–14.

endlessly signalled his duality, which he constructed as reflecting a particular form of Britishness. Peter Lord says that, in his visual imagery and in his writing, Jones 'searched in Celtic mythology and the history of Ancient Britain for a key to his own divided identity'.[66] Jones firmly believed that, for an artist, the 'fusion' contained within the idea of being 'Anglo-Welsh' would 'necessarily show itself, however obscurely, in his works'.[67] For him, this conglomerative form of British identity was exemplified by his London Welsh battalion, as indicated in his Preface to *In Parenthesis*:

> My companions in war were mostly Londoners with an admixture of Welshmen so that the mind and folk-life of those two differing racial groups are an essential ingredient to my theme. Nothing could be more representative. These came from London. Those from Wales. Together they bore in their bodies the genuine tradition of the Island of Britain, from Bendigeid Vran to Jingle and Marie Lloyd.[68]

Jones variously spoke of himself as a 'half-Welshman', 'part-Welshmen', or a Londoner 'whose father was a Welshman'.[69] A 1949 portrait says of Jones, 'One of his earliest recollections was of his father singing a Welsh song, and he has nurtured carefully the sense, first implanted in him by his father, of belonging to the Welsh people'.[70] This patriarchal link seems particularly important to Jones and is repeated throughout his written work as a kind of incantation. In *The Dying Gaul*, Jones recalls, 'my father was a pure Welshman...he had only a rather feeble grasp of the Welsh language...but was deeply religious, and, I know, "felt" extremely "Welsh".[71] René Hague suggests that it was pressure from his Welsh father that caused the family to drop his original 'Teutonic name of Walter' in favour of David.[72] Jones often reflected on his 'Welsh tie-up'. Responding to the organizers of a retrospective exhibition of his work at the National Museum Cardiff in 1954, he wrote of his father:

> I know only that by the time I was, say, seven, that I belonged through him, to the Cymry. As to why I feel this strong attachment I do not properly speaking know. True, there was the undeniable fact that I was the son of an entirely Welsh father and an English mother of partly Italian blood. But that accident of mixed consanguinity does not, in itself, account for much.

---

[66] Peter Lord, *Imaging*, p. 386.
[67] Jones, '"Wales" Questionnaire, 1946', p. 85.   [68] Jones, *In Parenthesis*, p. x.
[69] Jones, *Dying*, pp. 32, 33, 35. In mid-life, Jones occasionally signed letters as Dai or referred to himself in letters as Dai. See Hague, *Dai Greatcoat*, pp. 99, 128.
[70] Robin Ironside, *David Jones* (London, 1949), p. 3.   [71] Jones, *Dying*, p. 31.
[72] Hague, *Dai*, p. 23.

He reiterates that his father sometimes sang 'popular Welsh songs' such as *Ar-Fyd-a-Nos, Y Deryn Pur, Dafydd y Garreg Wen*, and *Mae Hen Wlad Fy Nhadau* which 'moved me greatly' but he admits 'that alone would not account for my feeling'. Jones is also keen to point out that his father 'was not one of these Cymry Llundain' who cultivated their Welshness: 'He did not, for example, belong to some society of London Welshmen and as far as I can remember had no Welshman as a close friend.... But my father was certainly proud of his being a Welshman and knowing my feelings gave me for birthday presents such books in English about Wales as were then available e.g. O. M. Edwards, *Wales* and Rhŷs Jones, *The Welsh People* and a little later John Lloyd's great work *The History of Wales from early times to 1282*.'[73] Thomas Dilworth sees these childhood readings as indicative of Jones's 'continuing inner division between being English and identifying with the Welsh'.[74] Jones's patrilineal attachment to Wales was reinforced by his service with the RWF during the First World War.[75] When the war broke out Jones was keen to 'join a Welsh regiment of some sort'. In an undated draft letter to Hague, he wrote:

> There was being raised a unit called 'The Welsh Horse'.... I went to some place in the Inns of Court, I think, where I was taken before a perfectly round man wearing an eye-glass, and this followed:
>
> "Can you ride?"
>
> "No, sir."
>
> "Do you know anything about horses?"
>
> "Well, not really, sir."
>
> "But y'r a Welshman I take it?"
>
> "My father is a North Welshman, my mother English."
>
> "I see, that's all right, Welsh enough, and we'd like to have you, but between ourselves, if you'll take my advice, you'll enlist in some infantry mob—Welsh, by all means, but if you know nothing about horses this set-up is no place for you."[76]

In 1964, Jones found a letter dated September 1914 from Lloyd George's private secretary to his father which illuminates his father's keenness for him to undertake some form of Welsh military service:

> My father had evidently (unknown to me) written to Ll. G. personally asking him when the Government were going to make official the proposed formation

---

[73] NLW; CF1/9; David Jones Papers, Draft Letters 1929–1982; Letter to National Museum Wales, Cardiff, *c.* 1954. For more on these texts, see Wynn Thomas, *Nations*, p. 32.
[74] Dilworth, *David Jones*, p. 23.   [75] Hooker, *Imagining*, p. 39.
[76] Hague, *Dai*, pp. 26–7.

of a London Welsh battalion, as his son was anxious to enlist in such a formation and would otherwise enlist in some English regiment, which was not what he would prefer.[77]

Jones enlisted with the 15th in January 1915. Dilworth notes how the war was, for Jones, 'an immersion' in a rich mixture of Welsh and English languages and accents, in particular, 'Cockney, the vernacular of the army...became part of his own idiom, including its common obscenities—"sod", "bugger", and "fuck".'[78] When posted initially to Llandudno for regimental training, this facilitated 'an affirmation' of Jones's paternal identity.[79] During his four years of service with the RWF, Jones was wounded in the leg during the attack on Mametz Wood on the night of 11 July 1916 and later, in February 1918, left France with severe trench fever.[80] His wartime experiences eventually led to the production of *In Parenthesis* which, through its title, signified Jones's sense of dualism: an acknowledgement that he had 'written it in a kind of space between'.[81] Adrian Poole writes that *In Parenthesis* 'is given shape by the relative prominence of certain named figures...Private John Ball, and the young officer who commands his respect, Lieutenant Piers Dorian Isambard Jenkins, both Englishmen; and on the Welsh side, Lance-Corporal Aneirin Lewis, Private Watcyn and Dai Great-Coat.'[82] According to Hooker, John Ball is the character with whom Jones most closely identified:

Private John Ball is not Welsh; like Jones he is a Londoner, and his name... signifies his status as an Everyman. In this capacity, he has the longing for 'home', as a communal but also a metaphysical sense of belonging, that is especially strong among English-language Welsh poets in the twentieth century—poets who, in R. S. Thomas's terms, subsist 'in a no-man's land between two cultures', with the outsider's desire to belong.[83]

The 'emotional centre' of *In Parenthesis* 'lies in the community of the men in the trenches', from both England and Wales, which in turn invokes the shared history of an older unity, a Britain created under the Romans.[84] Hooker argues that when writing *In Parenthesis*, Jones was attempting to make sense of 'the things that constituted his sense of cultural identity. The things are, to a significant degree, Welsh,

---

[77] Hague, *Dai*, p. 195.   [78] Dilworth, *David Jones*, pp. 41–2.
[79] Dilworth, *David Jones*, p. 45.
[80] Peter Levi, 'Jones, (Walter) David Michael [*pseud*. Dai Greatcoat] (1895–1974)', *ODNB* (2009), https://doi-org.ezproxy.is.ed.ac.uk/10.1093/ref:odnb/31294. For more on the significance of Mametz Wood for the 38th (Welsh) Division see Llewelyn Wyn Griffith, *Up to Mametz* (London, 1931).
[81] Jones, *In Parenthesis: seinnyessit e gledyf ym penn mameu*, p. xv.
[82] Adrian Poole, 'David Jones', in *The Cambridge Companion to the Poetry of the First World War*, edited by Santanu Das (Cambridge, 2013), p. 149.
[83] Hooker, *Imagining*, p. 40.   [84] Hooker, *Imagining*, pp. 40–1.

the words are English. It seems reasonable to call the resulting work Anglo-Welsh.'[85] A contemporaneous review of *In Parenthesis* by the English Welsh writer Nigel Heseltine agreed, observing, 'England and Wales have very largely fused, and "In Parenthesis" is the first of a new race.' Heseltine hailed the book as 'the first truly Anglo-Welsh product'.[86]

The Welsh Guards

Another significant regiment which functioned as a site of English Welsh duality and pluralistic Britishness during the war was the Welsh Guards. Raised in February 1915 in order to complete the national complement of the Brigade of Guards identified with the countries of the United Kingdom, the Welsh Guards aimed to put Wales on an 'even standing' with the other constituent nations.[87] General Sir Francis Lloyd, the Major-General in command, insisted that, as part of the King's Guards, 'the Welsh battalion must be located in London' within the precincts of Buckingham Palace.[88] When, on St David's Day 1915, the Welsh Guards mounted guard for the first time, it was reported that its formation was a source of 'much satisfaction to the London Welsh'.[89] The regiment tended to attract, within its officer ranks, a mix of men with Welsh connections from artistic and literary worlds, as well as from the landowning and political elites. Those who served in the regiment included the artist Allan Gwynne-Jones and the architect, Bertram Clough Williams-Ellis. The latter was the son of Welsh clergyman John Clough Williams-Ellis and his wife Ellen, who was born in the rectory at Gayton, Northamptonshire, in 1883. When Williams-Ellis was four, his family moved to Glasfryn, Caernarfonshire. In his autobiography, Williams-Ellis lays a quadruple claim to Welshness, noting his Clough antecedents in Denbighshire, the Williams from Plas Brondanw, Gwynedd, Ellis forebears from Caernarfonshire and his maternal grandfather's ownership of quarries at Blaenau Ffestiniog.[90] Following education at Oundle School, Northamptonshire and Trinity College Cambridge, Williams-Ellis entered into architectural practice with chambers in Mayfair and a Victoria Embankment flat.[91] He states that he 'became more or less a Londoner' around 1905 although three years later, on his twenty-fifth birthday, he was gifted control of the Williams family property of Plas Brondanw:

---

[85] Hooker, *Imagining*, p. 6.   [86] *Wales*, 1 March 1938, p. 157.
[87] See the J. M. Staniforth cartoons: 'An Honour for Wales', *Western Mail*, 13 February 1915 and 'Making Growth', *Western Mail*, 18 February 1915' on the 'Cartooning the First World War' website, https://www.cartoonww1.org/index.htm, accessed 18 September 2022.
[88] 'Welsh Guards', *Llangollen Advertiser*, 19 February 1915, p. 4.
[89] 'The Welsh Guards', *Denbighshire Free Press*, 6 March 1915, p. 8.
[90] Williams-Ellis, *Architect Errant*, pp. 2, 18–21.
[91] Williams-Ellis, *Architect*, pp. 73, 100. It is only with the onset of the Second World War, that Williams-Ellis decides to settle permanently in Wales retaining 'a pied-à-terre in London'. See p. 157.

I have known few things in my life so intoxicatingly delightful as arriving in the star-lit dawn of a winter's morning after an all-night train journey from London and driving with my mother through the frosty air to inspect progress.[92]

On hearing of the declaration of war whilst at a weekend party in Warwickshire, Williams-Ellis headed to London to volunteer, initially serving with the Imperial Light Horse.[93] Unhappy with the ineffectiveness of his regiment, the formation of the Welsh Guards offered him a 'chance' to escape and he successfully transferred. In his memoir, Williams-Ellis places 'the glamour of joining the Brigade of Guards', over any sense of Welsh identification, as a motivating factor in his decision.[94] However, when he married Amabel Strachey in 1915 at St Martha's Church, Chilworth, Surrey it was reported in Wales under the headline 'Welsh Guards Officer', displaying an external acceptance of his Welsh martial identity.[95] At his request, his fellow officers purchased an outlook tower ruin with views of Snowdonia as a wedding present and the couple honeymooned in Wales.[96] After being sent to the front at the Hohenzollern Redoubt, Williams-Ellis recalls how he distracted himself by getting an ex-schoolmaster stretcher-bearer in his company to come round to his dug-out and 'give me lessons in Welsh with his Bible as our reading book'.[97] Gwynne-Jones, discussed in Chapter 7, also moved to the Welsh Guards due to dissatisfaction with his own regiment; in both cases it is likely that their surnames facilitated these transferrals.[98]

Saunders Lewis and the South Wales Borderers

Saunders Lewis, co-founder of Plaid Cymru and a leading figure in the world of Welsh nationalism, pointed to the importance of his military service during the First World War in his own personal and political epiphany. In a 1961 interview, he stated that he 'discovered' the novels of Maurice Barrès, *Le Culte du Moi*, whilst in the trenches which led him to a more conscious self-identification with Wales and with his own Welshness:

> From Barrès I learned that the only way to cultivate your own personality as an artist and develop your own resources, is to return to your roots, as my father had said. That you must return to your own past and take your own heritage to

---

[92] Williams-Ellis, *Architect*, pp. 88, 92, 93.   [93] Williams-Ellis, *Architect*, pp. 108–10.
[94] Williams-Ellis, *Architect*, p. 111.   [95] *Cambrian Daily Leader*, 2 August 1915, p. 5.
[96] Williams-Ellis, *Architect*, pp. 113–15.
[97] Williams-Ellis, *Architect*, p. 116. Elsewhere in his memoir, Williams-Ellis expresses unease that he can only speak English though surrounded by Welsh speakers at Brondanw, pp. 30, 114.
[98] Author interview with Emily Gwynne-Jones.

build yourself. And I think it was Barrès—after Yeats and the Irish—that turned me into a convinced Welsh Nationalist.[99]

However, Lewis's wartime letters to his future wife, Margaret Gilcriest, whom he met in Liverpool, reveal a more complex picture.[100] Lewis was born in Wallasey, Liverpool in 1893 to a Welsh Calvinistic minister and a London-born mother 'of Anglesey stock'.[101] Lewis insisted in later life: 'it was not in English England that I was born, but in a wholly Welsh and Welsh-speaking society'.[102] Lewis viewed his maternal grandfather, Rev. Owen Thomas, author of *Cofiant John Jones, Talysarn*, as a 'splendid man in many ways' and once confided to Gilcriest, 'there are many things in which I'd like to imitate him'.[103] His mother having died when he was relatively young, Lewis's family spent summer holidays in Anglesey and Welsh was spoken at home. Lewis reports that he was an object of derision at Liscard High School for Boys due to his 'lack of English'. However, Lewis also acknowledged the duality of his upbringing, drenched in English mores:

> I think I can say that all the Welsh I read when I was a schoolboy was the Bible and hymnbook and Sunday School expositions. I don't think I read much Welsh apart from that. I think that all my reading throughout my time at school was in English. Reading as everyone does at school—reading widely through the whole of English literature. And the school was a private, middle-class school, where the whole community read very extensively. And so I had the period's general knowledge of English literature.[104]

Lewis read English at Liverpool University and confirms that in this period 'my friends of my own age were English'.[105] However, during the war, Lewis indulged in an imaginative refashioning of himself as a Welsh 'peasant'. In a wartime letter, dated 12 February 1916, to Gilcriest, Lewis disavows his middle-class English background and, instead, insists on his connections to a ruralized Wales:

> My father's father was a country peasant who could neither read nor write; my mother's father before he became a preacher was a stone-mason, and all my ancestors for hundreds of years have been livers on the soil. I have never had the slightest connection with the commercial and English middle class.[106]

---

[99] Cited in Griffiths, *Saunders*, p. 4. Wounded at Cambrai, Lewis was sent to serve with British Army Intelligence in the British Embassy in Athens in 1917.
[100] Harri Pritchard-Jones, 'Lewis, (John) Saunders (1893–1985)', *ODNB* (2008), doi-org.ezproxy.is.ed.ac.uk/10.1093/ref:odnb/55454.
[101] Griffiths, *Saunders*, p. 2. [102] Cited in Griffiths, *Saunders*, p. 2.
[103] *Saunders Lewis. Letters*, p. 240. [104] Cited in Griffiths, *Saunders*, p. 2.
[105] Griffiths, *Saunders*, p. 3. [106] *Saunders Lewis. Letters*, p. 186.

Following the outbreak of the war, Lewis originally volunteered and served with the King's Liverpool Regiment. However, in May 1915 he successfully applied to join the newly formed 12th Battalion of the South Wales Borderers, stationed at Newport.[107] Williams calculates that the 12th was one of those battalions 'whose Welshness appears to have been heavily diluted': only 28 per cent of those serving were born in Wales.[108] Indeed, Lewis himself remarked that there were 'more English than Welsh officers' in the regiment.[109] As Gilcriest was Liverpool-born of Irish parentage, Lewis's wartime correspondence with her was written in English, though he sometimes signed off with Welsh endearments—'*Wyf eich anwyl, anwyl*'—and recited Welsh love verses.[110] During the war, Margaret undertook Welsh language lessons and received encouragement from Lewis, based in Chester in September 1915: 'Very soon you'll be writing to me in Cymraeg, and then we shall have for our mutual mystery those wonderful words that mean more than anything in English can ever express. Goodnight, *fy ngeneth cudd*.'[111] When on leave in London Lewis generally stayed at Hotel Gwalia, Upper Woburn Place, 'a quiet pleasant hotel, and intended especially as the name implies for Welsh folk'.[112]

When his regiment was posted to Grantham, Lincolnshire, Lewis rhapsodied about the 'typically English villages, with quaint houses and a church, a school, and a tavern' with 'sweet rustic names, Londonthorpe, Belton, Barrowby' and an air 'of repose and happy old-fashioned ease'. At the same time, he acknowledged his homesickness for his hometown of Wallasey: 'how one can hunger for the sea; feel thirsty for it'.[113] Whilst he recommends various Welsh texts to Gilcriest, including 'Prof Lloyd's two-volume history of Wales', Lewis's letters are also littered with references to Shelley, Wordsworth, and Keats.[114] On arrival in Le Havre in June 1916, Lewis self defines as English in relation to the French inhabitants: 'The people are accustomed to English soldiers, and already we have made friends with many.'[115] Once overseas he experiences the trenches as a site of 'English language, English oaths, John Bull's own ways of eating, drinking, and being generally half a gentleman by effort, and half a Bull by nature and instinct'.[116] When he is severely wounded in the legs in 1917, Lewis is 'content' to find himself transferred to Luton Hoo, 'the most luxurious hospital in England'. At the same time, Lewis expressed pleasure at encountering a Welsh nurse who 'talks Welsh to me'.[117] Indeed, his preoccupation with ideas about Welshness persists throughout his correspondence. On leave in Chester, a city close to the border with North

---

[107] *Saunders Lewis. Letters*, p. 109.
[108] Williams, 'Taffs', pp. 143–4.
[109] *Saunders Lewis. Letters*, p. 158.
[110] *Saunders Lewis. Letters*, pp. 5, 37.
[111] *Saunders Lewis. Letters*, p. 142.
[112] *Saunders Lewis. Letters*, p. 147.
[113] *Saunders Lewis. Letters*, pp. 100–1.
[114] *Saunders Lewis. Letters*, p. 203.
[115] *Saunders Lewis. Letters*, p. 208.
[116] *Saunders Lewis. Letters*, p. 211.
[117] *Saunders Lewis. Letters*, pp. 252–3.

Wales, in June 1918, Lewis muses that he likes the city 'because half the faces there are Celtic in type'.[118]

Based on the evidence of his wartime letters, of particular significance for Lewis was the move of his father from Wallasey to Swansea at the beginning of 1917. When Saunders was discharged from hospital, a few months after the death of his brother, Ludwig, he went to stay at 1 Ffynone Villas with his father, although he records: 'Everything is strange here, home is a new setting, and without my brother itself different.'[119] He reports his distaste at having to meet 'all "family", cousins, uncles, aunts, second, third, to the nth cousins' until being 'heartily sick of them'. However, Lewis is more positive about his meeting with a neighbour named Williams 'who edited the town newspaper'.[120] It seems likely from Lewis's contemporaneous letters that his father's move to Swansea and the contacts he made whilst convalescing there were relevant in consolidating his nationalist commitment to Wales. In February 1918 he wrote to Gilcriest of his ambition to 'begin for Wales what the Irish movement had done for Ireland', reporting that during his two last visits to south Wales, it had been agreed that 'a group of about six of us are going to write a book together to start things'.[121] From this point onwards, Lewis determined to write articles and reviews in Welsh and to 'speak mostly in Welsh'.[122] Significantly, he relates that his decision 'has brought my father and myself nearer together' with the former 'heartily in approval'.[123] Lewis is conscious that wartime circumstances support his new intellectual endeavour. In May 1918, his linguistic abilities in 'Welsh, French and Italian' are recognized at a War Office interview and he accepts a post in Intelligence work in Athens.[124] Once there, Lewis spends time 'translating parts of the *Iliad* into Welsh' but also acknowledges the situational nature of his activities, commenting: 'I shall go on writing Welsh as long as I have other means of getting money, but when the government's monthly charity ceases, the Lord knows whether or not Welsh will go to the wall, and I shall become an English journalist, or say, a banker, a civil servant, a tobacco company's clerk, or a strolling player!'[125] Reflecting on Lewis's post-war career as a university lecturer in Welsh at University College, Swansea, Griffiths concludes that Lewis 'adopted Wales as a man might adopt a foster-mother. He then strove mightily to shape a Wales as he visualized her, a Wales that would retrospectively justify his choice of her, and mean that his sacrifice of a career as a writer in English had not been in vain.'[126] Whilst Lewis's letters display intermittent engagement with ideas of Englishness throughout the war, ultimately he emerged from this period articulating a conscious identification with Wales,

---

[118] *Saunders Lewis. Letters*, p. 286.
[119] *Saunders Lewis. Letters*, p. 262.
[120] *Saunders Lewis. Letters*, p. 263.
[121] *Saunders Lewis. Letters*, p. 277.
[122] *Saunders Lewis. Letters*, pp. 293, 278.
[123] *Saunders Lewis. Letters*, p. 278.
[124] *Saunders Lewis. Letters*, p. 283.
[125] *Saunders Lewis. Letters*, p. 312.
[126] Griffiths, *Saunders*, p. 85.

which, in his case, led to a permanent move to Wales and a lifelong commitment to Welsh cultural and political nationalism.

'Oh, my son! my son!'—the Descended Welsh in English Regiments

Even those with a distant ancestral connection to Wales such as the poet Wilfred Owen, fighting with the 2nd Battalion Manchester Regiment, could draw martial inspiration from Wales as an imagined nation. Dominic Hibberd notes the importance of Owen's father Tom—both with his storytelling and family surname—in encouraging his children to believe themselves 'to be Welsh by distant descent'.[127] On returning to overseas service in 1918, following a period at Craiglockhart Hospital, Owen hoped to get himself attached to a Welsh regiment, partly in emulation of his literary peers, Siegfried Sassoon and Robert Graves, and partly because of 'his own Welsh blood' and vision of Wales as 'the land of soldiers as well as poets'. However, ultimately, he rejoined the 2nd Battalion.[128] When he was engaged in fierce fighting at the Hindenburg Line in October 1918—with three of his men shot in quick succession—Owen wrote: 'I had to order no one to show himself after that, but remembering my own duty, and remembering also my forefathers the agile Welshmen of the Mountains I scrambled out myself & felt an exhilaration in baffling the Machine Guns by quick bounds from cover to cover.'[129] Owen's brother Harold echoes that sense of identification in his memoir *Journey from Obscurity* by claiming to have heard 'the succouring cry from the mountains' at moments of danger.[130]

Captain Geraint Davies was an English Welsh soldier who served with the 9th Battalion Northumberland Fusiliers and died, aged twenty-two, during the Second Battle of Ypres.[131] In his memoriam card, evidence of his father's grief can be seen in the effusiveness of the tribute: 'The passionately beloved and adored elder son of Dr Morgan Davies and the late Mrs Margaret Davies, Goring Street, London, EC, who was bitterly wounded early in the morning of the 14th April, 1918, and died six hours later.'[132] The card also contains a poem by John Oxenham:

"I know! I know!...

The ceaseless ache, the emptiness, the woe,...

The pang of loss...

The strength that sinks beneath so sore a cross.

---

[127] Hibberd, *Wilfred*, p. 8.   [128] Hibberd, *Wilfred*, p. 421.   [129] Hibberd, *Wilfred*, p. 442.
[130] Cited in Hibberd, *Wilfred*, p. 8.   [131] 'Memorial Notice', *Welsh Gazette*, 29 August 1918.
[132] NLW; Clement Davies Papers (CDP); S/8/2; Memorial booklet for Capt. G. Davies.

"...Heedless and careless, still the world wags on,
And leaves me broken...Oh, my son! my son!"[133]

Scrutinizing the relationship between Morgan Davies, a prominent London Welsh doctor, and his son Geraint helps further illuminate the intricate interconnections between Wales and England during the first decades of the twentieth century. Born in London in 1854, the son of a Welsh grain merchant, Morgan Davies was brought up by his grandparents on a smallholding in Trefenter, near Aberystwyth.[134] Davies returned to London as a medical student, moved to Scotland and then qualified as a medical practitioner. According to a tribute produced by his son-in-law, Idris Griffiths, 'whilst in Scotland, he learnt to admire tremendously the Scots' strong love of country which compared so unfavourably with the extreme inferiority complex he saw in so many Welsh people...for the rest of his life he determined to create a new superiority complex amongst his own people.'[135] Griffiths claims that it was Davies's 'vision and passion for the Welsh people' that made him set up as a self-styled 'doctor for the London Welsh' with a practice in Houndsditch.[136] Davies took on 'active leadership in a London Welsh society' and wrote on themes such as religious hypocrisy for the Welsh weeklies, *Y Celt* and *Y Brython*.[137] He also presented a document to the King requesting that 'Y Ddraig Goch (the Red Dragon of Wales)' be quartered on the Royal Standard for 'recognition of Wales as an integral part of the British Isles'.[138] However, speaking in 1975, Griffiths felt it would be mistaken to claim Davies as a Welsh Nationalist, underlining his sense of dual identification:

> He was a patriot for Wales...but this does not describe his profound love for Wales and his admiration for the greatness of England. He was too big to feel the inferiority many Welsh people felt towards England....His roots were in both countries and few people outside Wales enjoyed the gifts of two cultures and two languages so fully.[139]

This rootedness in both Wales and England was shared by Davies's children Gwen, Geraint, and Gwylon, and stepdaughter Jano. His eldest son Geraint, born in 1896, attended Central Foundation Boys School in London, before moving to Cowper Street School in 1904. At the same time, strong connections with Wales

---

[133] NLW; CDP; S/8/2.
[134] Richard Phillips, ed., 'Memories of Morgan Davies, MD, FRCS (1854–1920) as Recorded by the Llate D Idris Griffiths, M.D., Ontario', *Transactions of the Honourable Society of Cymmrodorion* (1976), p. 208.
[135] Phillips, 'Memories', pp. 208–9.
[136] NLW; CDP; S/5/3, 'Memories of Morgan Davies', recorded by Dr Idris Griffiths, May 1975, p. 9.
[137] NLW; CDP; S/5/3, 'Memories', p. 2.   [138] NLW; CDP; S/5/3, 'Memories', pp. 8–9.
[139] NLW; S/5/3, 'Memories', p. 8.

were maintained; Geraint and Gwylon spent long summer vacations with their father's friend, Dr Jenkyn Lewis in Llanon, or at farms in Bryngwyn and Morfa Mawr. At the age of ten, Geraint attended Llanfair School, Bryngwyn, for a year in order to become acquainted 'with colloquial Welsh'.[140] Geraint entered Guy's Hospital as a medical student in October 1914 but enlisted a year later. He joined the Artists Rifles and after being gazetted second lieutenant with the Northumberland Fusiliers, embarked to France in October 1916.[141] Griffiths suggests that Geraint was influenced by his father, an admirer of Napoleon who 'glorified war' and believed in 'its power to bring out the strength and courage of man':

> At one time Geraint was home on leave from the fighting front and he was still suffering from trench feet [sic]. Every day home was so precious, and Gwen, who had a deep love for her brother, tried to persuade her father to write a medical certificate to prolong his leave, but this he would not do.[142]

Griffiths mentions that as a former medical student, Geraint could have accepted a discharge from the Army but 'he would not for one moment consider quitting the fight, and not one of the family tried to persuade him to do so.'[143] At the same time, his father Morgan brooded on this decision, as Griffiths recalls: 'We walked for long on this subject, and then a deep gloom fell upon him and he said, "You know Idris, I do not think I will see my son, Geraint, again."'[144] In April 1918, Geraint was fatally wounded during a counter-attack near Neuve Eglise.[145] A memorial notice records that Geraint was 'greatly endeared to his men by his interest on their behalf with local bodies and personages at Newcastle-on-Tyne (which was the home of his battalion)'.[146] Yet, in death, Davies was claimed by Wales as well as England. Under the headline 'Aberystwyth Patriot', the *Cambrian News* provided information on the death of the 'son of Dr Morgan Davies', remarking that the doctor was 'well known' in Aberystwyth.[147] Another local paper, the *Welsh Gazette,* provided an expansive obituary, attributing Geraint's health and vigour to his Welsh attachments:

> Favoured by nature from the start he grew into a tall, stalwart and exceptional handsome lad.... This gorgeous gift of perfect health in boyhood was further assured by a long summer vacation by the sea-shore given him, and his brother annually by Dr Jenkyn Lewis, Llanon.

---

[140] Phillips, 'Memories', p. 212; 'Memorial Notice'.
[141] 'Fallen Officers', *The Times*, 4 June 1918, p. 8; Alun Wyburn-Powell, *Clement Davies. Liberal Leader* (London, 2003), p. 14.
[142] NLW; S/5/3, 'Memories', pp. 19–20.   [143] NLW; S/5/3, 'Memories', p. 20.
[144] NLW; S/5/3, 'Memories', p. 19.   [145] 'Fallen Officers'.
[146] 'Memorial Notice'.   [147] *The Cambrian News*, 12 July 1918, p. 3.

The piece concluded, connecting his childhood exposure to Welsh landscapes with his martial achievements in wartime:

> The rich brooding silences of Wales withal had been pouring its lessons of wisdom and patience into this tender and pensive lad, and he found
>
> "Tongues in trees, books in running brooks
>
> Sermons in stones, and good in everything."
>
> Thus befitting him for the leadership of men in the great stresses of war.[148]

On returning to London from a German prisoner of war camp in January 1919, Griffiths was informed of Geraint's death, and, in his reminiscence, transmits the deep sense of loss felt by Morgan Davies:

> My mother told me she had never seen such human grief. To Morgan Davies it was a shattering blow and may have led on to his paralysing stroke in 1919.... When the sirens sounded and the church bells rang out to announce the signing of the Armistice ending World War I... [there was] wild rejoicing.... When my mother, whose two sons were safe, heard the news she ran joyously over to Morgan Davies to tell him. He sat, with his daughter Gwen, silent and unheeding.[149]

Morgan Davies was nursed by Gwen following a second stroke in 1919 which 'wiped out the reality of Geraint's death': 'At that time, lists of officers and men returning to England were published in the daily press. As he could no longer read he would ask one or other of us to study the list. "Don't you see the name of Captain Geraint Davies?"'[150] The nephew who was born to his sister Jano, within eight months of his death, was to die as Captain Geraint Clement Davies in the Second World War.[151]

Conclusion

By analysing the intersectionality of Welsh and English identities during the First World War, this chapter illuminates the significant expression of dual identifications functioning within mobilization and recruitment processes, and the lived experiences of military service. The war provided a moment of galvanization for diasporic Welsh patriotism in England which, in turn, encouraged some English men to volunteer to serve in Welsh-aligned regiments as 'sons of Wales'.

---

[148] 'Memorial Notice'. [149] NLW; S/5/3, 'Memories', p. 22.
[150] NLW; S/5/3, 'Memories', p. 23.
[151] See Chapter 5 'The Whole Family Turned towards Wales'.

The establishment of the 15th (1st London Welsh) Battalion RWF was a deliberate elite diasporic attempt to forge an identification with Wales via the military enlistment of the younger English generation. It also highlights the existence of a fluid and pluralistic definition of Welshness which rhetorically encompassed the second- and third-generation Welsh living in England. As well as the RWF, English soldiers of Welsh origin also sought to enlist with the Welsh Guards or other Welsh regiments. The First World War both shaped the identities of Welsh descended men in England and allowed a space for English Welsh martial masculinities to be asserted and expressed. This military and cultural elision of English Welsh identities, immortalized in the poetry of David Jones, was to re-emerge at the outbreak of the Second World War and will be discussed in the next chapter.

5
Second World War Identities

In the run-up to the Second World War, the War Office again agreed to organize territorial units which recruited specifically on the grounds of English Welsh dual identities. These formations, which comprised the 99th (London Welsh) Heavy Anti-Aircraft Regiment and the 46th (Liverpool Welsh) Royal Tank Regiment, began recruiting in 1939 from English cities with significant Welsh populations. In addition, the Welsh Guards continued to attract English men of Welsh heritage, from elite backgrounds, as commissioned officers, as did other identifiably Welsh regiments. This chapter explores the mobilization and performance of English Welsh identities during the Second World War and discusses why, at a time of global conflict, some English men opted to enlist on the basis of Welsh antecedents. Following Avtar Brah, it highlights the tensions within the lived subjectivities of some English Welsh recruits between wartime constructions of 'home' as 'a mythic place of desire' (Wales) and 'home' as the 'lived experience of a locality' and 'everyday social relations' (England).[1] Moving on to examine narratives of filiation, it also suggests that patrilineal ties often prompted romanticized constructions of Wales which compelled some men to serve on behalf of 'the Land of My Fathers'. This chapter provides a case study of Geraint and Mary Eluned Clement Davies, the English children of Liberal Welsh politician, Clement Davies, whose lives were 'turned towards Wales' and who both died whilst serving in the British Forces. Acknowledging Ellis's argument that there are competing traditions of militarism and pacifism within traditional understandings of Welsh national identity, this chapter concludes by studying the life writing of men and women living in England, with Welsh connections, who registered as conscientious objectors, reflecting upon the ways in which these individuals made use of ideas about Welshness when formulating their opposition to the war.[2]

Anthony King emphasizes how twentieth-century armies 'sought to unite their troops around common forms of social identity and civic obligation'.[3] In the late 1930s, two new English Welsh military units, based on the idea of *dual* national identifications, emerged as a result of the government's decision to double the number of Territorial Army units.[4] By 1938, the number of recruits was surging

---

[1] Brah, *Cartographies*, pp. 188–9.   [2] Ellis, 'Pacific people', p. 15.
[3] Anthony King, *The Combat Soldier: Infantry Tactics and Cohesion in the Twentieth and Twenty-First Centuries* (Oxford, 2013), p. 62.
[4] Ian R. Grimwood, *A Little Chit of a Fellow: A Biography of the Right Hon. Leslie Hore-Belisha* (Lewes, 2006), p. 112.

and the Territorial Army was shouldering 'the lion's share' of manning the nation's anti-aircraft defences.[5] This opened up a new space for the Welsh diasporic elites in London and Liverpool to attempt to (re)assert the relevance of Welshness in their localities. Indeed, Owen's notion of 'a kind of willed imagining of a Welsh identity' is relevant here.[6] It appears that the establishment of the two units was played out amid wider anxieties about the enduring visibility of the Welsh community in England; the war offered a significant opportunity for elite leaders to attempt to revitalize a sense of Welshness amongst the large and varied diaspora. At the same time, this militarized form of English Welsh duality clearly did have some resonance in mid-twentieth century England, with the units creating and performing a version of Welshness that had a wide urban appeal. King notes how, in wartime, 'the appeal to manhood was often simultaneously an appeal of nationality'. Indeed, British doctrine of the Second World War emphasized the need to develop the soldierly traits of '*patriotism*, loyalty, *pride of race* and a high sense of honour'.[7] As with the First World War, notions of Welsh military valour—promoted through the lens of diasporic patriotism—held an appeal for a significant number of English recruits with a sense of mixed heritage.

In London, a committee populated by notables such as Hon. Col. General Sir Henry Ap Rhys Pryce and the Welsh coal and press magnate Lord Kemsley[8] was set up under the chairmanship of the former Prime Minister Lloyd George to recruit and fundraise for a hybrid regiment.[9] The intention behind the 99th (London Welsh) Heavy Anti-Aircraft Battery, with its headquarters in Kensington, was that it would comprise three batteries 'to be formed from the Welsh community' residing in the capital.[10] Yet, in practice, the recruitment reach of the regiment stretched across England, suggesting that constructions of London Welshness were, by necessity, malleable and as likely to include non-Welshmen and those of Welsh heritage as those born in Wales.[11] The inaugural dinner of the regiment was held in July 1939 at the Park Lane Hotel in the presence of Lloyd George, who provided continuity between the London Welsh military formations of both world wars. His attendance enabled the Secretary of State for War, Hore-Belisha, to situate the new unit within a strongly Welsh heritage, pronouncing,

---

[5] Grimwood, *Little Chit*, p. 75.   [6] Owen, 'London', p. 123.   [7] King, *Combat*, p. 75.
[8] IWM; LBY K. 75,915; *99th London Welsh Heavy Anti-Aircraft Regiment, 1939–1945* (n.p., 1945), p. 15.
[9] Hansard, H. C., vol 391, col 2509 (5 August 1943).
[10] TNA; T 161/861, Letter from R. V. Nind Hopkins to War Office, 8 May 1939.
[11] IWM LBY K. 75,915. Johnes notes how the presence of non-Welshmen serving in Welsh regiments during the Second World War did not diminish regimental Welshness. Indeed, 'what on the surface might appear to be national symbols'—such as 'eating the leek'—'were in practice driven more by the need to create personal relationships and a common bond between diverse sets of men'. See Martin Johnes, 'Welshness, Welsh Soldiers and the Second World War', in *Fighting for Britain? Negotiating Identities in Britain During the Second World War*, edited by Wendy Ugolini and Juliette Pattinson (Oxford, 2015), p. 73. See also David French, *Military Identities. The Regimental System, the British Army, & the British People c. 1870–2000* (Oxford, 2005).

'This night will be recalled because the greatest Welshman of his age took pride of place at what might be termed your christening ceremony. By his presence alone he enshrouds you at your birth with a full panoply of tradition.'[12] The 99th batteries were initially based in Kent and Croydon with Lloyd George's son Major Gwilym Lloyd George taking command of the first battery.[13] The London Welsh Association took a proprietary interest in their affairs. In January 1940, a religious service in Welsh was conducted for the regiment in Surrey. *Y Ddolen* reported that 'the Welsh-speaking men of the Company' had complained to their padre, Rev. Brinley Jones, that 'although they are practically all "nonconformists", yet there is no Welsh Nonconformist Chaplain attached to the Battalion.'[14] A further appeal was made in April 1940 to provide entertainment for the batteries, who were confronting 'the continual monotony' of service life in the UK.[15]

The social profile of the typical recruit of the 99th is encapsulated in their in-house newsletter, *On Target*, which was produced by 303 Battery while based at Shirley Park, Croydon, and which, in its irreverent humour and lampooning style, mimics trench journals of the First World War.[16] A satirical piece titled 'The Army and the Man' alludes to the typical civilian occupations of the 99th gunners as teachers, librarians, and bank managers.[17] This mirrors Helen McCartney's depiction of pre–First World War territorial battalions as 'socially exclusive' and largely middle class in composition, drawing upon the educational and sporting milieu of public and grammar schools.[18] The newsletter also highlights the accommodation and acceptance of dual English Welsh identities with the titles of its articles interchangeably addressing both strands of identity, and the plurality of Welshness itself, in terms of language: 'Outposts of Empire: Oswestry,' 'Night Falls on Shirley,' 'Wales and War-Site,' and 'Er Cof Anwyl Am Gymry Llundain.'[19]

J. R. Davies

Originally drawn into the male world of sociability, sport, and singing offered by the local London Welsh rugby team, the bank clerk John Rhys Davies was one of those persuaded to join the 99th Territorials. Born in Wandsworth Common in July 1906 to a Post Office clerk from Ceredigion and an English mother, Davies was raised within 'a Welsh chapel background', attending 'Eisteddfods' and

---

[12] *Western Morning News*, 19 July 1939, p. 7.   [13] *Y Ddolen*, Mehefin, 1939, p. 17.
[14] *Y Ddolen*, Chwefror, 1940, p. 6.   [15] *Y Ddolen*, Ebrill, 1940, p. 4.
[16] Christopher Westhorp, Introduction to *The Wipers Times: The Famous First World War Trench Newspaper* (London, 2013), n.p.
[17] IWM; E.J.3487; *On Target* 1, no. 1, April 1940.
[18] Helen B. McCartney, *Citizen Soldiers: The Liverpool Territorials in the First World War* (Cambridge, 2005), pp. 5, 26.
[19] IWM E.J.3487; *On Target* 1, no. 1, April 1940; IWM E.J.3487; *On Target*, 1, no. 2, May 1940.

socializing within a large extended network of Welsh relations in London.[20] The Imperial War Museum holds 128 letters written by Davies while on military service overseas with the 88th Heavy Anti-Aircraft Regiment, Eighth Army, in the Middle East, North Africa, and Italy from 1941 to 1945. These letters were typed up by Davies on the occasion of the golden wedding anniversary of his parents, to whom they were originally written before being donated to the museum.[21] The manuscript is a faithful reproduction of the original letters and provides five years' worth of sustained correspondence: encapsulating what Margaretta Jolly defines as an act of 'self-preservation through perfect communication'.[22] As Davies ended the war as a lance bombardier, it also offers rare insights into the lived experience of military service from the perspective of the other ranks. Addressing letters as a historical source, Jolly underscores the importance of the relationship between the writer and recipient, observing that letters 'constructs fantasies of identity' and 'spring from and codify ideal relationships, preserving the self through appeal to the other'.[23] The focus of Davies's epistolary world was his family home, 2 Elsynge Road, London SW18, yet whilst the letters are written in English, they are littered with Welsh vocabulary, phrases, and place names. Educated at the 'semi-public' Emanuel School in Clapham from the age of eleven, Davies was a literate and well-read soldier with a self-confessed passion for 'literature' and confidence in his abilities as an epistolary communicator.[24] His letters home begin in Palestine in November 1941, when he spends a day's leave at a market in Jerusalem:

> We left the Old City by the Jaffa gate and saw something of the labyrinth of bazaars with their strange wares.... The bizarre combination of the ancient and modern shops—but what prices! They wanted 14/6 for a copy of 'How Green is my Valley.' We spent a most enjoyable evening seeing 'Gone With The Wind'.... The following morning behold me once more amidst the street scene of the old city doing a spot more mooching. I found the traditional site of Pontius Pilate's Judgment Hall, now a convent. A jovial old nun showed me round; I think I won her approval by translating a Welsh inscription for her.[25]

---

[20] IWM 26841; John Rhys Davies.
[21] IWM 13167; Private Papers of J. R. Davies, Letters to parents. Extended extracts from these letters can be found in Wendy Ugolini, '"Band of Brothers": The Mobilization of English Welsh Dual Identities in Second World War Britain', *Journal of British Studies*, 60, 4 (2021). doi.org/10.1017/jbr.2021.64.
[22] Margaretta Jolly, 'Myths of Unity: Remembering the Second World War through Letters and Their Editing', in *Arms and the Self: War, the Military, and Autobiographical Writing*, edited by Alex Vernon (Kent, 2005), p. 159.
[23] Jolly, 'Myths', p. 164.   [24] IWM 26841.   [25] IWM 13167, 10 November 1941.

Krista Cowman notes that for British soldiers serving in France during the First World War, visiting towns and cities behind the lines enabled them to make connections with urban landscapes back home.[26] At the outset of his letter, Davies remarks that Jerusalem has a 'very welcome Englishness about the landscape'. Yet within this extract there is also a double assertion of Welshness: not only is Davies clearly proud of his ability to provide a Welsh translation but he also expresses an interest in the bestselling wartime novel about South Wales, *How Green Was My Valley* (1939). His strong identification with Wales is further evidenced throughout his letters home. When he is stationed in North Africa and Italy, he always locates a local Welsh Society that provides Sunday services in Welsh.[27] In Caserta, he finds himself among a Welsh-speaking congregation and is relieved to find he has 'no great difficulty in joining in the conversation'.[28] Towards the end of the war, Davies reencounters former colleagues from the London Welsh battery at these Welsh services, demonstrating how a sense of dual identifications could be sustained even when the gunners had been transferred from their original regiment.[29]

In his letters home, Davies repeatedly expresses his nostalgia for different parts of Wales, thus expanding the notion of the imagined 'home' shared with his parental correspondents in London. In 1942, when he is based near Tobruk, he writes, 'My bivvy on a rocky crag overlooks the sea and the view from below might be reminiscent of a bit of Cardiganshire coast line'; while based in Italy from 1943 onwards, he regularly compares the surrounding landscape to Aberglaslyn in Snowdonia.[30] He always remembers to proclaim the significance of 1 March, Saint David's Day, as in a letter to his parents in 1944: 'Hope you're all wearing your leeks today or are they rationed?! We've just been listening to the midday Welsh Half Hour—a very good selection—but unfortunately they switched the current off in the middle of "O na byddai'n haf o hyd"—an outrageous bit of sabotage by our Anglo-Saxon foes.'[31] The radio is a particularly crucial medium through which Davies maintains both his sense of Welshness and a reciprocal relationship with relatives back home. The BBC ensured that more than two hours of Welsh language broadcasting on the BBC's 261-metre wavelength were transmitted, primarily for broadcasts to Europe. In early 1943, the English language production *Welsh Half Hour*, which incorporated 'regional news, commentary and a few songs', debuted on the Home Service.[32] Davies's letters regularly report on his listening habits.[33] He writes in September 1943:

---

[26] Krista Cowman, 'Touring behind the Lines: British Soldiers in French Towns and Cities during the Great War', *Urban History*, 41, 1 (2014), pp. 108, 122. doi:10.1017/S0963926813000254.
[27] IWM 13167, 30 September 1944.   [28] IWM 13167, 1 July 1945.
[29] IWM 13167, 17 April 1945.
[30] IWM 13167, 22 November 1942, 6 October 1943, 31 August 1945.
[31] IWM 13167, 1 March 1944.   [32] Hajkowski, *BBC*, pp. 182–5.
[33] IWM 13167, 18 and 23 June 1943, 11 August 1943.

'Listened with much interest to a BBC entertainment for the GIB Welsh Society. Heard some pennillion singing and some personal characteristic messages from the Rhondda and other parts of Wales. I wonder if you were listening?'[34] Here, Davies clearly positions himself as part of a transnational imagined Welsh community. There is a sense of reciprocity, a shared connection across borders, regardless of the distance between him and his family. Indeed, this vision of 'home' is crucial to him; sometimes he literally dreams of his chapel congregation back in Clapham.[35]

Johnes writes that 'it would be difficult to deny sport's place in the inventing, maintaining and projecting of the idea of a Welsh national identity within and outside Wales's blurred borders.'[36] It is notable that Davies often asserts his selfhood through an embrace of rugby as a key marker of Welshness, frequently constructing his own sense of Celtic identity in opposition to the 'Saxons': 'Yesterday morning with a boisterous wind blowing we played a great international Rugby match here—Wales V. England. We had pruned and trimmed a particular area of desert especially for this game and of course heralded it with much advance publicity and propaganda. The Saxons spilt much good red blood on the pitch but they were not quite good enough for us.'[37] On another occasion, he writes of his intention to play in an England versus Wales rugby match, noting, 'To whip our Celtic blood into the necessary fervour, we hope to preface the game with a stirring rendering of *Sospan* (Little Saucepan).'[38] At the same time, his sense of identity constantly shifts, a reflection of his own duality. When based in Italy, he both distances himself from English troops—'We tell the Anglo-Saxons here that most of the Italian language has been borrowed from the Welsh—"See Naples and Dai"'[39]—while also seamlessly representing them: 'We soon started to win legendary fame as English Milords'.[40] Furthermore, his expressions of camaraderie with Welsh servicemen are not boundless. When he encounters a Welsh driver from Aberdare whose ambition for post-war Wales is 'to patrol our frontiers when we get back...to keep those **** English tourists out,' Davies is dismissive, complaining to his parents, 'He just poured it out for half an hour.'[41]

Significantly, although Davies is keen to foreground his Welshness in terms of his social networks and preferred leisure activities, his letters underline how he is equally attuned to the nostalgic appeal of London. In March 1942, travelling on an army lorry in Cairo, he remarks on 'the exquisite music' of two former London bus conductors discussing making 'a brew'.[42] A sense of Englishness—or the classic tropes associated with wartime constructions of England—is interwoven

---

[34] IWM 13167, 20 September 1943. [35] IWM 13167, 18 March 1943, 6 December 1944.
[36] Johnes, *History*, p. 109. [37] IWM 13167, 27 December 1942.
[38] IWM 13167, 1 March 1943. [39] IWM 13167, 6 October 1943.
[40] IWM 13167, 17 May 1944. [41] IWM 13167, 14 August 1944.
[42] IWM 13167, 8 March 1942.

throughout his wartime letters.[43] In July 1942, he writes, 'it will be grand to see English flowers again after these months of sand and rock'; on another occasion, 'carpets of small bluebells, buttercups, daisies, and poppies bring vivid recollections of an English meadow'.[44] In October 1942, based near Tobruk, Davies makes specifically London references: 'Vauxhall (my pet aversion) on a damp and foggy day is a Utopia in comparison to El Adem', and he likens the movement of a tank column across the desert to the noise of 'about 10,000 Edgware to Morden underground trains'.[45] When, in January 1944, he hears a concert party rendition of 'Five Minutes in Petticoat Lane' by a Cockney comedian, he muses, 'I almost fancied I was back in Northcote Road on a Saturday night'.[46] Shifting from lowbrow to highbrow within his cultural frames of reference, Davies's correspondence includes literary references to Keats or Coleridge alongside elegiac musings about the English landscape.[47]

Thus, while Davies foregrounds allusions to Wales and Welshness in his letters and the connections he chooses to make overseas are Welsh—societies, radio programmes, rugby teams—his asserted sense of Welshness is often disrupted by his English attachments. Overall, an English sensibility is displayed alongside a deep Welsh identification within his self-narration, illuminating an almost unconscious split in his self-identity: a hybrid sense of self. Davies's letters demonstrate the equal importance of both his English and Welsh inheritances, his willingness to draw upon the tropes of English Romanticism as well as signal his Welsh attachments with his allusions to rugby, chapel, and song. This tendency supports Hickman et al.'s notion of hybridity as 'the intersection of two hegemonic domains of rootedness, nation, and authenticity' whereby, in this scenario, Wales represents Davies's 'imaginings' while England represents 'locality and citizenship'.[48] As Brah notes, the 'multi-placedness of "home" in the diasporic imaginary does not mean that diasporian subjectivity is "rootless"'; second-generation migrants often feel securely anchored and 'at home' in the place of settlement.[49] Wales is Davies's family's imagined 'home' but England is the home he writes to, where his parents and siblings live, where he and his 'Ma' were born. Essentially, England *is* home. Ironically, Davies's expressed longing or nostalgia for home, summed up by the Welsh word *hiraeth*, often takes the form of reminiscing about England within his correspondence. For Davies, his Welsh upbringing in London anchors his sense of belonging while serving overseas, underscoring the significance of English Welsh dual identifications. As a continuation of this,

---

[43] Lucy Noakes, '"Deep England": Britain, the Countryside and the English in the Second World War', in *Fighting for Britain?*, edited by Wendy Ugolini and Juliette Pattinson (Oxford, 2015), pp. 25–47.
[44] IWM 13167, 10 July 1942, 27 February 1943.
[45] IWM 13167, 24 October 1942.   [46] IWM 13167, 21 January 1944.
[47] IWM 13167, 8 August 1943, 12 September 1943, 5 December 1942.
[48] Hickman, Morgan, Walter, and Bradley Hickman, 'Limitations', p. 173.
[49] Brah, *Cartographies*, p. 194.

Davies contemporaneously positions himself as part of the British Army at war and expresses retrospective pride in being a member of the iconic Eighth Army, as evidenced by the title he gives to his unpublished manuscript, 'The Diary of a Desert Rat'.[50] Arguably, Davies's life writing demonstrates the existence of a particular strand of dual identity in wartime, which by accommodating a small number of servicemen for whom Welshness was, in Mo Moulton's phrase, a 'constitutive' part of being English, contributed to constructions of pluralistic Britishness.[51]

Shrewsbury House 'Old Boys'

The 46th Battalion (Liverpool Welsh) Royal Tank Regiment was formally constituted in April 1939 following a campaign by elite members of Welsh social networks in Liverpool, including local councillors, businessmen, and former army officers, and spearheaded by the Welsh journalist Harold Tudor, who wrote 'Cymric Causerie' columns in the *Liverpool Echo* under the pseudonym 'Talwrn'.[52] From the outset, the 'dual association' of the unit was signalled by 'its regimental crest of the Red Dragon of Wales and its brigade flash of the Liver Bird'.[53] The regiment's formation was galvanized by news of the establishment of the 99th London Welsh and also by a form of ethnic competitiveness with the Liverpool Scottish and Liverpool Irish battalions that existed in the city.[54] Streets notes how Scottish Highlanders were traditionally the 'poster boys' of the British Army, acting as 'an image of ideal masculinity and racial superiority to which all potential recruits could aspire', while the Irish were acknowledged as 'good and brave fighters'.[55] In this competitive context, the creation of the 46th can be viewed as what Katie Pickles terms the 'localized invention' of martial Welshness.[56] However, after an initial burst of enthusiasm in attestation, recruitment 'slowed down to almost a standstill', and anxieties were expressed that 'the exclusive character of the unit will have to be disturbed'.[57] This dilemma played out amid a wider anxiety that the Welsh 'community' itself barely existed. In 1943, O. E. Roberts, the

---

[50] Davies attended Eighth Army reunions every year. Personal Communication, 2012.
[51] Moulton argues that Irishness can be viewed as 'a constitutive element' of Englishness in the interwar period. Moulton, *Ireland*, p. 7.
[52] ' 'Talwrn's' Cymric Causerie', *Liverpool Echo*, 12 April 1939, p. 3.
[53] Ronald Clare, 'L'pool Welsh Disband near Corinth', *Liverpool Echo*, 22, February (1946), p. 4.
[54] 'A Cymric Causerie', *Liverpool Echo*, 22 March 1939, p. 14. See also The Tank Museum Archive (TTMA), RH87, 46 RTR 7431, *A Short History of the 46th (Liverpool Welsh) Royal Tank Regiment* (1949).
[55] Streets, *Martial*, pp. 181, 4, 169.
[56] Katie Pickles, *Female Imperialism and National Identity: Imperial Order Daughters of the Empire* (Manchester, 2002), p. 37.
[57] 'Call to Welshmen', *Liverpool Echo*, 7 June 1939; 'Welsh Tank Unit Recruiting', *Liverpool Daily Post*, 13 June 1939.

secretary of the Merseyside branch of Undeb Cymru Fydd, sent a circular to Welsh contacts in the northwest of England to ascertain the level of involvement with 'Welsh activities'; more specifically, the circular enquired whether there were 'many young Welsh people' in their locality who took 'an interest in Welsh matters'.[58] The replies from Ellesmere Port, Blackburn, and St. Helens were broadly negative. The representative from St Helens said of the second generation, 'they have tended to marry English brides and have then deserted everything Welsh.' He concluded, 'Before the boys went away they had already lost their Welsh if they had it to lose in the first place.'[59] Overall, the correspondence provides a snapshot of falling chapel attendance in England among the second and third generation, disengagement from Welsh associational culture, and a tendency for this to be attributed to intermarriage with the 'English'. Thus, although the 46th achieved full strength by the end of July 1939, there was an underlying awareness among the founders that the imagined community of Welsh people that the regiment was set up to appeal to no longer existed in any recognizable form.[60] The war provided an opportunity, to adapt Owen's phrase, to will it back into existence.[61] Fundamentally, therefore, there was a mismatch between the desires of the diasporic elite to forge a wartime vehicle of patriotic Welshness and the more prosaic realities of a long-established Welsh presence in Liverpool.

A useful way to examine this divergence is to analyse the experience of eleven troopers in the 46th who shared a pre-existent group identity as 'Old Boys' of Shrewsbury House, a youth club in the working-class Everton district, set up as part of the philanthropic public school mission movement by Shrewsbury School in 1903 (see Figure 5.1).[62] The fact that Everton was considered one of the 'three main Welsh enclaves' in Liverpool possibly explains why, in 1939, eleven of its members volunteered for the Liverpool Welsh, constituting around 20 per cent of the youth club's servicemen.[63] Since 1928, the Shrewsbury House Old Boys' Association had been run by an Old Salopian, Barr Adams. Adams was thirty-four when the war broke out, working in a directorial position at the oil refining company James Light & Son.[64] Throughout the war, Adams encouraged the 'Old Boys' who were in the forces to write to him; he then collated extracts from their letters and recirculated them as 'news sheets' to all members of the club.[65] In 1944, he gathered together the news sheets in an unpublished book, 'The Club of

---

[58] Bangor University Archive (BUA); GB 0222, BMSS OER; O. E. Roberts's Undeb Cymru Fydd Papers, Circular from O. E. Roberts, 14 April 1943.
[59] BUA; GB 0222, BMSS OER, Letter from Meurig Walters, 25 April 1943.
[60] '"Liverpool Welsh" on View', *Liverpool Daily Post*, 31 July 1939.
[61] Owen, 'London', pp. 122–3.
[62] Nigel Scotland, *Squires in the Slums: Settlements and Missions in Late Victorian Britain* (London, 2007).
[63] Jones, 'Liverpool Welsh', p. 22.
[64] Shrewsbury House Archive (SHA); BA194209SEPTb, Letter from Adams, September 1942.
[65] SHA; 'I. G. Barr Adams (O.S)'.

Figure 5.1 Members of the 46th Battalion (Liverpool Welsh) Royal Tank Regiment, Everton, Liverpool.
Reproduced with permission of Shrewsbury House Archive, Liverpool.

War' which is held in the Shrewsbury House archive. The work of Lucinda Matthews-Jones demonstrates how the existence of philanthropic organizations in poor urban areas created a space for the formation of 'cross-class friendships', which could be reinforced at a time of war.[66] In this case, the news sheets act as a conduit for the exchange of news as well as a safe forum for expressions of camaraderie and solicitude for each other. However, the correspondents, numbering around fifty servicemen in total, are also performing public roles—their awareness of a multiple audience potentially inhibits confidences, encourages jocularity, and leads to a mutual reinforcement of viewpoints.[67]

The archive also holds copies of the hundreds of letters between Barr Adams and those who were on active service covering the period 1940–46. The closeness revealed within the correspondence reflects the strength of the volunteers' emotional attachment to the club in Portland Place, also evidenced by their decision to gather there when war was declared. On the day after Germany invaded Poland in September 1939, Adams records that although their football match is cancelled, the Old Boys instinctively congregate at the club, 'talking about the

---

[66] Lucinda Matthews-Jones, '"I Still Remain One of the Old Settlement Boys": Cross-Class Friendship in the First World War Letters of Cardiff University Settlement Lads' Club', *Cultural and Social History*, 13, 2 (2016), p. 195. doi.org/10.1080/14780038.2016.1202011

[67] SHA; News Sheet 496, 1 July 1940.

uncertain future'.[68] It is at the moment of volunteering, however, when this shared group identity acquires the patina of Welshness. Their communal act of enlistment is faithfully relayed in 'The Club at War':

> Bill Foulkes was standing at the corner of Dale Street and Castle Street opposite Liverpool Town Hall. It was a brilliantly fine Monday evening towards the end of May 1939.... He was soon joined by one or two others, and they all crossed the street and walking in the direction of the Victoria Monument, turned into what had once been shop premises but was now serving as a recruiting centre for the newly 'Liverpool Welsh' Tank Regiment. After waiting about two hours among many eager volunteers those who passed their medical test and were able by some means or other to prove their Welsh origins were duly sworn in. On the question of Welsh nationality it seems that an easy view was taken. Even Jimmy Mackay who sounded like a Scotchman, looked like an Englishman, and at times behaved very like an Irishman was able to satisfy the battalion adjutant about his Welsh ancestry. For the others it was comparatively easy. And so six who had gone in as civilians, came out as troopers.[69]

It is likely that, in order to gain access to the martial masculinity of the glamorous new tank unit, these Liverpudlian volunteers were willing to draw upon a recognizable strand of Welsh identity within their local community. A newspaper article appears to allude to one of the Shrewsbury volunteers when it observes, 'Two Liverpool-Welsh-Scotsmen, insisting respectively on the "Mc" and "Mac" have been enrolled. One proudly pointed to a Welsh grandmother as his qualification for admission. The other had a Welsh mother.'[70] Within the news sheets, these volunteers are variously referred to as 'the Liverpool Welsh' 'the 46th Welsh', or 'the Taffies', and there is clear willingness among the club members to endorse the constructed Welshness of the 46th.[71] At the same time, the familial connections of the 'Old Boys' with Wales appear to have been rather distant. One of the group, Billy Reece, alludes to this with a tongue-in-cheek reference: 'They're holding a grand ball at St George's Hall on St David's Day so all we true blooded Welshmen feel that we are expected to attend'—indicating that pride in regimental traditions of symbolic Welshness possibly overlaid any sense of national identification.[72] There is also little self-reference to questions of Welsh identity in the news sheets. It is likely that the volunteers essentially used the notion of ancestral Welshness to

---

[68] SHA; Barr Adams, 'The Club at War', Chapter 2.
[69] SHA; Adams, 'Club at War', Chapter 1. Another five 'Old Boys' subsequently joined.
[70] '"Macs" Join the "Joneses"'. On the BBC People's War website, Arthur Johnstone recollects he joined the Liverpool Welsh by 'declaring a Welsh grandmother'. 'My War Years and Being a POW', Article ID A2146015, contributed 17 December 2003.
[71] SHA; News Sheet 501, 7 July 1940.
[72] SHA; News Sheet 419, 17 February 1940. See also Johnes, 'Welshness'.

further consolidate their own shared sense of fraternity, forged in the Everton youth club and summer camps in Wales. For these young working-class men, the 46th provided a site of camaraderie and togetherness, and during the war, they made use of the regimental identity to further solidify their bonds of kinship. Five of them managed to reconstitute in Egypt, Adams noting, 'The lads have stuck together marvellously so and if anything the first year of war that bound us all together more closely in many ways I think.'[73]

In terms of the interaction between English and Welsh identities, one of the most fascinating aspects of the Shrewsbury House correspondence is when they—'the Taffies'—encounter Wales. When the 46th transfers from Blundellsands on the outskirts of Liverpool to a training camp at Dinas Dinlle in Gwynedd in June 1940, a sense of dissonance appears within their correspondence.[74] One trooper writes to Adams, 'We have finally arrived and what a place!! Eight miles from the nearest town and to top it all the people here don't speak English. They just jabber away to you in Welsh. I think they must either be ignorant or they can't speak English.'[75] Another 'Old Boy', posted out in Egypt, signals back empathetically, 'Re. the opinion of [Atkinson] on Welsh people I can say the same for the wogs out here. They are too b—lazy to learn the King's English.'[76] Very similar language is deployed within the volunteers' letters to describe colonial and Italian 'others' encountered in North Africa: the 'gyppos' and the 'wogs' who are found 'jabbering' away.[77] Paul Fussell refers to the use of stereotyping by Allied troops as a mechanism through which to see themselves as 'attractive, moral and exemplary'.[78] However, while these exchanges may reflect commonplace forms of racialized military language, they also simultaneously construct the Welsh as a form of domestic 'other'.[79] Thus, while participating in the invented military tradition of the Liverpool Welsh Regiment, the troopers often, paradoxically, construct their identity in opposition to the Welsh. When Atkinson receives a posting to Criccieth, North Wales, to act as a batman to one of the officers, this soon becomes the source of dissatisfaction, as retold within 'The Club at War' in 1944, with an additional layer of anti-Welsh sentiment added by the editor:

---

[73] SHA; BA194008AUG19thBRa, Letter from Adams to Reece, 19 August 1940.
[74] For further information on the 46th, see TTMA; RH87 46 RTR; E2003.1373 *Memoir of Maj J S Routledge MC by his son Geoffrey R Routledge Lt Col (Rtd) RTR* (Taupō, 1994).
[75] SHA; News Sheet 481, 6 June 1940.
[76] SHA; News Sheet 545, 8 September 1940. As I am focusing on a negative but slender aspect of an extensive six-year correspondence for the purpose of this chapter, I have assigned pseudonyms to some of the 'Old Boys'.
[77] SHA; News Sheet 429, 4 March 1940, News Sheet 485, 10 June 1940, SHA; Adams, 'Club at War', Chapter 18. In his letters, J. R. Davies also makes reference to the Italian 'Fascist' troops as 'wogs'. See IWM 13167, 22 March 1943.
[78] Paul Fussell, *Wartime: Understanding and Behavior in the Second World War* (Oxford, 1989), p. 127.
[79] Chris Hopkins, *English Fiction in the 1930s: Language, Genre, History* (London, 2006), p. 62.

He missed his old companions and commented unfavourably on the Welsh inhabitants, the fact that no training of any sort was being done and the dullness of life at a North Welsh coast resort in winter. The only compensations appear to have been the passing attraction of the Welsh girls and by way of a link with the famous, an occasional game of billiards with Lloyd George's chauffeur—a certain Mr Dyer. He also saw the veteran statesman himself but reported that the local inhabitants held no high opinion of him judging him to be mean—a point on which the Welsh may at least claim to have gained expert knowledge through experience.[80]

These extracts suggest that the volunteers' construction of ancestral Welshness was contingent upon place and was open to challenge when they were actually based in Wales. Other elements of discord captured in the archival material hint at the complexities underlining the creation of hybrid English Welsh units. Adams mentions that while the 46th were training in Wales, 'The most local "local" had been put out of bounds following a series of disputes between the soldiers and the Welsh inhabitants. A climax was reached when the villagers declared that they would welcome the arrival of Hitler being apparently under the impression that he would liberate Wales and particularly their corner of it from the English occupation.'[81] Within the Shrewsbury House correspondence, therefore, there is a tendency to indulge in the 'othering' of Welsh civilians in ways that mirrors the crude national stereotyping of enemy troops.

The Tank Museum has collated data to show that of the 137 recorded casualties of the 46th, 31 are definitively recorded as coming from Liverpool.[82] Although the number of members with Liverpudlian associations, and certainly with Welsh heritage, substantially diminished during the war—due to the army's policy of cross-posting from 1941 onwards, and the loss of half of its tank crews at Ruweisat Ridge in July 1942—the Liverpool press continued to use the idea of militarized Welshness to frame the regiment. When covering the 46th's ceremonial dissolution in Greece in 1946, the *Echo* journalist Ronald Clare, reiterated how in 1939 'the sons of Wales in Liverpool' answered the call to form their own battalion and, with the Eighth Army at El Alamein, 'these Liverpool Welshmen fought fearlessly' and with 'native tenacity'.[83] Clare imagines the time when these men 'next meet in Liverpool, and sing, as only the Welsh can sing, "Land of My Fathers".'[84] This blurring of identity is clearly considered unproblematic: even among those who know

---

[80] SHA; Adams, 'Club at War', Chapter 43.   [81] SHA; Adams, 'Club at War', Chapter 29.
[82] TTMA, *Casualties of the 46th Royal Tank Regiment, WW2*. From the Database of The Commonwealth War Graves Commission.
[83] Clare, 'L'pool', p. 1.   [84] Clare, 'L'pool', p. 1.

this unit is no longer filled with men from Liverpool, its 'localized' Welshness still makes sense.[85]

Narratives of Filiation

Joel Morley illuminates 'the place of the Great War in the subjective worlds of Britons' at the outset of the Second World War, noting the importance of 'intergenerational transmission' between veteran fathers and their sons.[86] He highlights the tendency of First World War veterans to emphasize the 'rewarding elements of Great War service' so that the younger generation developed 'an understanding of war as a duty to accept'.[87] In Welsh diasporic families, there was an additional dynamic at play, with some Englishmen being prompted by patrilineal ties to approach their military enlistment through the lens of Welshness.[88] Born in Westminster in 1905, the author Anthony Powell liked to claim descent from Rhys ap Gruffydd (1132–97), the 'prince of South Wales'.[89] Powell followed his father into The Welch Regiment when he joined up in 1939, although he acknowledges that his father had joined this regiment 'not on account of the Powells' Welsh extraction (pretty well forgotten, and never sympathetic to my father personally)' but for financial reasons.[90] In spite of this, throughout his memoir, Powell demonstrates a strong genealogical identification with Wales, not least through their complementary regimental service. Powell recalls how he joined The Welch, when he was contacted by his wife's acquaintance at the War Office:

> "My father was a regular officer in The Welch—why not them?"
>
> "Easily get you into a funny regiment like that," said Captain Perkins. "Everyone wants to go into London units."
>
> My father would not have been pleased by Captain Perkins' estimation of The Welch Regiment (made up of the old 41st and 69th Foot), with its long roll of Battle Honours, phenomenal record for winning the Army Rugby Cup. Wellington had been an officer in the 69th, the Regiment who had served as

---

[85] Scully, 'Discourses', p. 234.
[86] Joel Morley, 'The Memory of the Great War and Morale During Britain's Phoney War', *The Historical Journal*, 63, 2 (2020), p. 440 doi: 10.1017/S0018246X19000062; Joel Morley, 'Dad "never said much" but…Young Men and Great War Veterans in Day-to-Day-Life in Interwar Britain', *Twentieth Century British History*, 29, 2 (2018), p. 199. doi.org/10.1093/tcbh/hwx063.
[87] Morley, 'Dad', p. 223.   [88] See also Chapter 8 'Affinity Welsh.'
[89] Michael Barber, *Anthony Powell. A Life* (London, 2004), p. 1.
[90] Powell, *To Keep*, pp. 11–12.

marines on Nelson's Agamemnon at St Vincent, but this was no occasion for taking offence.[91]

On discussing his enlistment with the 1/5th Battalion, The Welch, at Haverfordwest, Pembrokeshire, Powell connects himself to the locality: 'the Powell family having been associated with that neighbourhood at the end of the 18th and the beginning of the 19th centuries'.[92] Despite this ancestral link, Powell acknowledges his outsider status, remarking, 'Territorials in Wales were very much a family affair, sons following fathers.... This strongly regional background, close consanguinity, did not result in the faintest expression of coolness towards someone like myself coming in from outside.'[93] Powell later immortalized his regimental service in *Dance to the Music of Time*, in particular *The Valley of Bones* (1964). Here his protagonist, Nicholas Jenkins, also becomes a second lieutenant in a Welsh regiment and finds himself amidst 'a group of middle-class South Welsh bank officers, clerks, and miners'.[94] Nicholas Birns notes how this volume simmers 'with the intensity of firsthand experience' and suggests that Powell's regimental experience ultimately changed his writing, broadening his class perspective.[95] In *Dance*, the use of the name Jenkins was a nod to the complexion of Powell's own links with Wales, the author believing it combined 'an essential Welshness at one end of the scale, with no necessarily Welsh commitment at the other'.[96] Jenkins's opening reminiscences in *The Valley of Bones*, when he is posted to Wales, mirror Powell's own autobiographical musings about Wales:

> Although they had remained in these parts only a couple of generations, there was an aptness, something fairly inexorable, in reporting under the badges of second-lieutenant to a spot from which quite a handful of forerunners of the same blood had set out to become unnoticed officers of the Marines or the East India Company.... I was not exactly surprised to find myself committed to the same condition of service, in a sense always knowing that part of a required pattern, the fulfilment of which was in some ways a relief.[97]

Thus, like his creator, Jenkins presents his soldier-identity as one which conforms to the expectations of his Welsh heritage. However, Powell is still worried about the authenticity of his depiction; in his memoir, he acknowledges that some reviewers critiqued 'the phrasing of the Welsh-English' spoken by the fictional

---

[91] Powell, *To Keep*, p. 268. A facsimile of this conversation appears in Anthony Powell, *The Kindly Ones* (London, 1962), p. 254.
[92] Powell, *To Keep*, p. 269.   [93] Powell, *To Keep*, p. 270.
[94] Nicholas Birns, *Understanding Anthony Powell* (Columbia, 2011), p. 175. For the similarities between Powell and Jenkins, see Hilary Spurling, *Invitation to the Dance* (London, 2005), pp. 100–3.
[95] Birns, *Understanding*, pp. 170, 9.   [96] Cited in Birns, *Understanding*, p. 348.
[97] Anthony Powell, *The Valley of Bones* (London, 1964), p. 6. See Powell, *To Keep*, p. 11.

Welsh troops. In order to reassert his authority, Powell says that he consulted with the dramatist, Alun Owen—'an impeccably authentic Welshman'—who reassured him that no revision was required.[98]

Another soldier potentially motivated by strong patrilineal ties was Christopher Moelwyn Strachey Williams-Ellis, who followed his father, the architect Clough Williams-Ellis, into the Welsh Guards. After his second year, studying Moral Sciences at Kings College Cambridge, he left to enlist. Williams-Ellis was serving in Italy as a lieutenant when, on the night of March 16–17 1944, 'he was wounded and taken prisoner while leading a patrol. He must have died soon after of his wounds, for his grave was found a year later close to the place of his capture.'[99] Both father and son were born in England but the Williams-Ellis family were partly based in Wales and claimed direct descent from Owain Gwynedd. In his memoir, the senior Williams-Ellis introduces the topic of his son's death by first recalling the marriage of his daughter Charlotte at St Martin-in-the-Fields, 'an occasion that could have been gay if it had not been for the doodle bugs, V1 and V2 that threatened London and for the fact that Christopher had been posted as missing'. He continues:

> It was on the day after the wedding that I was asked to go round to the Welsh Guards Headquarters, there to be told, very gently, that he, our only son, had been killed in action before Monte Cassino. He had joined the regiment straight from his brief wartime course as an undergraduate at King's, Cambridge.... The armistice was thus a time of both pleasure and of almost unbearable pain.[100]

Williams-Ellis and his wife vowed 'to keep the wound to ourselves': the only physical memory of Christopher that remained at their Welsh residence, Plas Brondanw, was a barricaded empty bedroom.[101]

As with the First World War, another point of entry into the military for English men with a Welsh connection was the Welsh Guards. Most Guards officers at the time were recruited from the upper classes, those educated at public school, often with family connections to the regiment, and a private income to supplement their army pay. The film star, Hugh Williams, attempted to join the Welsh Guards based on his ancestry. Born in Bexhill-on-Sea in 1904 to Welsh parents, he was the grandson of Welsh Chartist lawyer Hugh Williams. Within his family, he was known as 'Tam' because when his mother, Silver, was pregnant she

---

[98] Powell, *To Keep*, p. 271.
[99] King's College Cambridge Archive (KCC); King's College Cambridge Annual Report of the Council, 26 November 1945, p. 7.
[100] Williams-Ellis, *Architect*, p. 242.
[101] Williams-Ellis, *Architect*, p. 242; Julie Brominicks, 'Snowdonian Visionary', *Countryfile Magazine*, 16 March 2018.

referred to her bump as 'Taméd' or 'Little Bit'.[102] In November 1939, Williams wrote to his partner that he 'went bang for the Welsh Guards' when asked for his regimental preference. He was unsuccessful in this endeavour, however, receiving his commission into the 8th Battalion of the Devonshire Regiment.[103] In 1941, the Regimental Lieutenant Colonel, 'Chicot' Leatham, boasted that the Welsh Guards included 'three Oxford professors, two world-famous artists, a brilliant Welsh author, a well-known film actor and a prominent racehorse trainer'. This grouping included English artists Rex Whistler and Simon Elwes, the Leicester-born grandson of the Earl of Denbigh, and the author Richard Llewellyn. Whistler, who received his commission in May 1940, went on to capture his regimental peers in a series of figurative portraits.[104] Two of these paintings portrayed Adrian Pryce-Jones, an English descendant of a Welsh commercial dynasty and fellow aesthete, who had also joined the Welsh Guards as an officer.[105] However, Whistler's wartime correspondence, held at Salisbury Museum, reveals no sense of personal affiliation with the idea of Welshness. In a letter to his friend and patron, Charles Paget, the 6th Marquess of Anglesey, Whistler admitted that he chose 'the W sort of Gs' because it was his only remaining hope of obtaining a commission.[106] The regiment also attracted descendants of the political establishment such as Intelligence Officer, Geoffrey Norris Evans ('Glob'), the English-born son of political secretary, Sir Rowland Evans, who was killed in Perugia, and the grandson of Lloyd George, Owen.[107] The latter was born in Chelmsford in 1924. He recalls his entry into the regiment in his 1999 memoir, revealing the privileged web of contacts behind his enlistment. Initially, Owen's stepfather, the barrister, David Evans, 'had a word with Sir Terence Nugent, then Brigade Major of London District', and, in 1942, Owen attended the Guards headquarters in London:

> I was duly marched into the orderly room where I faced a formidable trio in the form of the regimental lieutenant-colonel, Colonel A. M. Bankier, DSO, MC, Major the Earl of Lisburne, regimental-adjutant, and Major C. H. Dudley-Ward, assistant regimental-adjutant.... As it so happened I could claim some tenuous connection with the regiment in that my grandfather had played a significant

[102] Kate Dunn, ed., *Always & Always. The Wartime Letters of Hugh & Margaret Williams* (London, 1995), p. 1.
[103] Dunn, *Always*, pp. 13, 4.
[104] Welsh Guards Archive (WGA), Record of the Service of Rex John Whistler.
[105] 'An Officers Hut, Colchester 1940' and 'Inside the Royal Box at Sandown Park, 1940' in Jenny Spencer-Smith, *Rex Whistler's War 1939-July 1944. Artist into Tank Commander* (London, 1994), pp. 55, 60. See also Pryce-Jones, *Bonus of Laughter*, p. 69; David Pryce-Jones, *Fault Lines* (New York, 2015), p. 205.
[106] Salisbury Museum (SM), Rex Whistler Archive, Letters, n.d.
[107] For Evans, see Philip Brutton, *Ensign in Italy. A Platoon Commander's Story* (London, 1992), pp. 50, 84, 85; Queen's College Oxford, *Liber Vitae Reginensium Qui Pro Patria Mortem Obierunt 1939-1945* (Edinburgh, 1951), p. 24.

role in the raising of the Welsh Guards in February 1915....In any event, David Lloyd George's grandson was now there in the orderly room as an item of curiosity....'Bertie' Bankier was very kind and I can only recall one question, which was whether I had any private income.[108]

Lloyd George's narrative illuminates the rarefied world he entered as a member of the Welsh Guards: 'We were nearly all about the same age, public-school boys, with a preponderance of Etonians...the embryo officer had to be translated from his cocoon by a series of visits to expensive West End tailors and haberdashers.'[109] Concomitantly, Lloyd George foregrounds the regiment as a site for facilitating his Welsh identification. As part of cadet training, he was sent to Capel Curig, Snowdonia.[110] Then, whilst serving in Italy in 1944, he received letters from his father, Richard Lloyd George, musing on their shared Welsh ancestry: 'it makes you feel proud to think that you and I are descended from such a man as Owen Gwynedd [sic].' Lloyd George reflects, 'I found these philosophical disquisitions from my father strangely comforting amid the uncertainty and general discomfort that was our normal lot.'[111] Lloyd George celebrated St David's Day 1945 in Spoleto, 'in fine style, with lots of singing at our morning service and plenty to eat and drink later'. At the same time, his connection with the senior Lloyd George was ever-present: 'I remember Malcolm Richards offering up a prayer for my old grandfather at the service, which embarrassed me somewhat, though it was well meant as he was clearly in his final days.'[112] When Lloyd George died in March 1945, the Prime Minister, Churchill recalled all four of his grandsons who were on active service—Owen, David Lloyd George, and the Carey Evans brothers—to attend the funeral and act as pallbearers. Lloyd George provides a detailed account of the logistics behind his enforced pilgrimage from Italy:

> I was the farthest afield; David was firing his 5.5s across the Rhine, Robin was flying a bomber nightly from a home base, and Benjy was in the North Sea in HMS *Enterprise*. Within half an hour I was flying in a fighter from Senigallia down to Naples, where I stayed the night in Field Marshal Alexander's villa (he was away); the following morning I flew to London in a bomber....I arrived at Ty Newydd only an hour before the funeral. The little lane was up from the bridge at Llanystumdwy was already full of people....As David, Robin, Benjy and I walked beside the coffin to the graveside we were met by an amazing and very moving spectacle. There were literally thousands of men, women and children thronging the lane and on the steep hillside around the grave, with thousands more in the meadows just across the river. The singing started as the

---

[108] Lloyd George, *Tale*, p. 77.
[109] Lloyd George, *Tale*, pp. 78, 80.
[110] Lloyd George, *Tale*, p. 80.
[111] Lloyd George, *Tale*, p. 100.
[112] Lloyd George, *Tale*, p. 103.

cortege approached; many of Taid's favourite Welsh hymns—'Llef', 'Tyddyn Llwyn' (Cottage in the Spinney) and of course 'Cwm Rhondda'.... No true Welshman could have remained unmoved.[113]

The four grandsons were absorbed into this carefully choreographed funerary pageantry, to such an extent that, in the concluding sentence, Owen firmly identities as a 'true' Welshman.[114] Before returning to his regiment, Owen went to visit Clough Williams-Ellis, at Plas Brondanw: 'Clough, who had served in the Brigade in the First World War, had lost his only son Christopher, killed on Cerasola the previous February. The family had asked him to design Taid's grave and its surround at Llanystumdwy and he wanted me to see his preliminary sketches.'[115] Owen's recollection of this meeting neatly underscores the intricate thread of military connections not just between the descended Welsh but also temporally across two conflicts.

'The Whole Family Turned towards Wales'

Another example of those who performed intertwined Welsh and English identities during the Second World War is provided by Geraint and Mary Clement Davies, the children of Welsh Liberal politician, Clement Davies, who both served and died during the conflict. Analysis of the family's wartime correspondence, held at the National Library of Wales, demonstrates how their allegiances to two nations manifested and were accommodated during the course of their lifetimes. Edward Clement Davies, born in Llanfyllin in 1884, became leader of the Liberal Party at the war's close, in 1945. A successful commercial lawyer, he was elected Liberal MP for Montgomeryshire in 1929.[116] He was married to Jano Davies, who despite being raised in a London Welsh family, 'spoke Welsh fluently'.[117] In 1924, the couple purchased a large house, Plas Dyffryn, in Meifod with the intention being to spend most of the year in London, but 'for their children to spend the summer months in Wales'.[118] All four of their children were born in London, their first child David Morgan in 1914, followed by Mary Eluned in 1917, Geraint

---

[113] Lloyd George, *Tale*, pp. 104–6. Their uniformed presence at the graveside was noted. See 'Ll.G. is Buried by the Dwyfor', *Daily Mirror*, 31 March 1945, p. 5.
[114] Robin and Benjy Carey Evans were born in India and England, respectively. See Carey Evans, *Lloyd*, pp. 136, 144.
[115] Lloyd George, *Tale*, p. 110. The design was an oval enclosure of rugged masonry with the large boulder on which Lloyd George used to sit marking the grave itself. See Williams-Ellis, *Architect*, p. 147.
[116] Francis Boyd, 'Davies, Clement Edward (1884–1962)', rev. Mark Pottle, *ODNB* (2008), https://doi-org.ezproxy.is.ed.ac.uk/10.1093/ref:odnb/32736.
[117] Wyburn-Powell, *Clement Davies*, p. 10.   [118] Wyburn-Powell, *Clement*, pp. 17–18.

in 1918, and Stanley in 1920 at the family home of 11 Vicarage Gate, Kensington.[119] Alun Wyburn-Powell notes that the Clement Davies house 'rapidly became a focus for London Welsh life, attracting a circle of artists, musicians, writers and dramatists'.[120] Jano's brother, Gwylon, who had been awarded the MC 'for conspicuous gallantry and devotion to duty' in March 1918,[121] moved in with the family in London whilst he recovered from his wounds.[122] All four children attended preparatory School in Kensington.[123] David's letters home, initially from prep schools in England, then Rugby, and Trinity Hall Cambridge, consistently record his support for the Welsh national rugby team ('who is going to win at Twickenham? Gallant little Wales!') but also a sense of ease with his split existence.[124] Writing during a trip to Saint-Prix in 1933 to the physical homes themselves: 'Dear Dyffryn, Rest content. You are not forgotten. Only two days ago, I wrote to your dear friend Vicarage Gate—what is more in French—hoping that he would send the letter on to you.'[125] Though born and educated in England, however, David often self-identifies as Welsh. As a law undergraduate at Cambridge, he writes to his parents in 1934:

> My supervisor said that my partner and I represented the two types of Englishmen, the one an amateur politician and common lawyer, the other, myself, a bureaucratic expert and Roman lawyer. So I told him that I was extremely interested in politics, that Roman law gave me the pip, and that I was Welsh anyway, which ruled me out. He seemed slightly put out at the miscarriage of his diagnosis.[126]

David died suddenly in September 1939, aged twenty four, whilst working as an articled clerk.[127] His sister, Mary, also experienced a dual childhood existence before her death in 1941, a fact reflected in her mother's eulogy:

> The London of her early years meant Kensington Gardens, the Round Pond, and, of course, The Row where under the expert tuition of Miss Smith she learned to ride.... The moment term was over the whole family turned towards Wales. The children revelled in the joys of the seaside at Borth. One spring and

---

[119] NLW; Clement Davies Papers (CDP); R/1/1; David Morgan Clement Davies, birth certificate; R2/2; Mary Eluned Clement Davies, birth certificate; R/3/3; Geraint Clement Davies, birth certificate; Q1; Stanley Clement Davies, birth certificate.
[120] Wyburn-Powell, *Clement*, pp. 16–17.
[121] R. Wilfrid Callin, The Story of the 1/4th Northumberland Fusiliers during the German Offensives of March, April, May 1918 (1919); See *Cambrian News*, 28 June 1918, p. 3.
[122] Wyburn-Powell, *Clement*, p. 15.
[123] NLW; CDP; R/2/78; Transcript for Mary Clement Davies's eulogy.
[124] NLW; CDP; R/1/5, Letters from David Morgan Clement Davies 1924–36; 26 December 1932.
[125] NLW; CDP; R/1/5; 9 August 1933.   [126] NLW; R/1/5; 11 March 1934.
[127] Wyburn-Powell, *Clement*, p. 93.

summer we spent in a cottage at Dolbenmaen at the foot of Snowdon in a farm at Penrhyndeudraeth and in a little house just beneath Harlech Castle. But it was Montgomeryshire that formed the background of their childhood's experiences. Mary knew every bridle path around Meifod, was friendly with everyone and had very special privileges in her wanderings.[128]

Wartime letters reveal that Mary was attempting to learn Welsh, writing from Plas Dyffryn to her brother Geraint that 'Janet and I had our second Welsh lesson yesterday and are getting on very quickly'.[129] Mary also had a close relationship with her father, evident in their affectionate letters. When she asked for advice on applying for a passport in 1935 he responded: 'Your ordinary place of residence is 11 Vicarage Gate London W8. Your place of birth was London.... As to your distinguishing marks I think you might just put "beautiful".'[130] Her mother recalled:

> Her faith in him was absolute and she followed his public efforts with passionate interest which was to him a source of constant inspiration in his lonely efforts during 1939.... Friday was a red-letter day for the family. It was the day that brought her father down from London and the hub of things. She met him at Gobowen towards midnight and later into the small hours round a blazing hearth and laden tea-table the family foregathered to listen to one who was always brimful of news and most exciting.[131]

From the outbreak of war, Mary worked for the Women's Voluntary Service (WVS) acting as her mother's chauffeuse and secretary in Wales but the pull back to England remained significant. Mary began training as an ambulance driver in Southwark until she joined the Auxiliary Territorial Service (ATS) in August 1941, prompted by her desire to take 'a more active part in the war effort and in London'.[132] That month, Mary wrote: 'How I long to die having truly served my country. How I long to prove I am a worthy citizen.'[133]

Mary applied for a commission within three months of joining the ATS and attended a Board on 4 November 1941. However, the following night she was found dead at the foot of an electric pylon near her camp at Stoughton Barracks, Guildford.[134] *The Manchester Guardian* reported:

---

[128] NLW; CDP; R/2/78.   [129] NLW; CDP; R/2/94; 9 November 1940.
[130] NLW; CDP; R/2/174; 15 March 1935.   [131] NLW; CDP; R/2/78.
[132] NLW; CDP; R/2/72, 'Obituary', *The Express*, 15 November 1941, p. 5; NLW; R/2/78.
[133] NLW; CDP; R/2/96, Sheet of paper headed 9 August 1941.
[134] Wyburn-Powell, *Clement*, p. 123.

Miss Davies had been electrocuted. The body was found soon after blackout by an ATS officer, who saw a flash and went to investigate. Mr Clement Davies was immediately informed of the tragedy and travelled to the camp.[135]

The inquest uncovered the fact that shortly before her death, Mary had been rebuked after failing to salute an officer and went off in 'a fit of temper'; the Coroner recorded a verdict of suicide while Mary's mind was unbalanced.[136] Clement Davies disputed the verdict, the media reporting, 'The height of the anti-climbing frame was so great, combined with the happiness of his daughter in her duties, precludes in his opinion, the verdict at the inquest.'[137] However, Wyburn-Powell notes the tendency of all Clement Davies's children towards being 'very able, but highly strung'.[138] In a letter to her youngest brother Stanley, written from Guildford, Mary spoke of her dread at her forthcoming post to the Officer Cadet Training Unit and her fear of 'failure'.[139] Early on in her time at the ATS she had also confided to her mother: 'Life is sometimes most frightfully depressing.' Mary wrote that she felt forced to accept a commission, repeating a friend's opinion that 'it was my duty to accept even if I failed because of my upbringing, because I was the daughter of two parents who were most public spirited and used to taking command.'[140] Mary's funeral took place in Meifod, with a short service at Plas Dyffryn, with the coffin accompanied by a detachment of the ATS.[141]

The second-born son, Geraint, was educated at Radley College, Berkshire, before going up to read law at Trinity Hall, Cambridge in 1937. Once the war broke out, he initially joined the Royal Artillery, joining a Heavy Anti-Aircraft camp in Kent in September 1940. However, from the outset he expressed his eagerness to transfer to an infantry unit 'so that I may join the Welsh Guards' and immediately approached his superior officer with this request. In his first letter home from camp, Geraint mentioned that he had also been recommended for a commission in the RWF and signalled his own affection for Wales:

> All the men here appear to come from Wales. Their two strong points are singing and hard swearing.... We will be here for 3 weeks presumably doing parade ground drill.... I am listening to a true male voice choir typical of S. Wales, consequently my letter is very disjointed.[142]

---

[135] 'MP's Daughter Found Dead', *Manchester Guardian*, 6 November 1941, p. 5.
[136] 'ATS Girl's Death', *Manchester Guardian*, 8 November 1941, p. 8.
[137] NLW; CDP; R/2/72; 'Obituary'.   [138] Wyburn-Powell, *Clement*, p. 17.
[139] NLW; CDP; R/2/97; 12 October 1941.   [140] NLW; CDP; R/2/107, Letter to mother, n.d.
[141] NLW; CDP; R/2/72; 'Obituary'.
[142] NLW; CDP; R/3/18; Letter to Clement Davies, 17 September 1940. Stanley had also wanted to join the Welsh Guards but had been rejected on medical grounds. See Wyburn-Powell, *Clement*, p. 124.

He occasionally signs off his letters 'Cofion Geraint' and his father addresses him as 'Geraint bach'. In October 1940, Geraint was accepted as a candidate for the Welsh Guards and transferred to Sandhurst OCTU the following January. In a letter to his mother he indicates his hybrid sense of self:

> On hearing the good news I could have jumped over the moon. However, living up to the motto of the English Gentleman 'Don't be vulgar, Don't be rude', I drew myself up to my full height and breathed in God's fresh air instead...

In the same letter, he makes another linkage with Wales:

> I am writing on the floor, lying diagonally across a blanket with my feet out of the tent. To my left a fellow snoring, to my right 2 more twiddling their thumbs, and, as I suppose, cursing Hitler, Churchill, the weather and everything on earth. Our friend, 'Oye Mate!!', otherwise known as Bollard, has just come in with the news that some Welsh books and magazines are going to be provided for the Welsh boys.[143]

On hearing the news of his transfer, his father responded from London:

> Your letter to Mummy giving the good news that you had been accepted for the Welsh Guards came on Saturday morning...after reading the first few lines, [I] flew upstairs waking up Mummy from a final morning snooze with shouts of joy, in which Mummy quickly joined...the good news travelled through the family in a few seconds.[144]

However, just over two years later, Geraint was killed in an accident whilst on a training exercise on Salisbury Plain. He was returning to camp in a mortar carrier when it swerved, plunged through a barbed wire fence, and dropped five feet into a field. Geraint suffered a broken neck and was killed instantly, along with another officer. An inquest found that the accident was due to a 'broken link' in the caterpillar track of the carrier with the Coroner recording a verdict of accidental death.[145] For the second time in two years, Jano and Clement Davies received a letter from the military authorities informing them of their child's death.[146] On this occasion, Geraint's superior officer wrote, 'I cannot really express enough my distress at the accident and at losing so likeable and efficient an officer.'[147] Following Geraint's death, the family grouped together copies of letters in an

---

[143] NLW; R/3/29, Letter [n.d]. [144] NLW; CDP; R/3/31, Letter, 28 October 1940.
[145] NLW; CDP; R/3/20; 'Broken Link', *The Salisbury Times*, 12 February 1943.
[146] See also NLW; CDP; R/2/29, Letter from J. Hawke, ATS, Winchester to Jano Clement Davies, 6 November 1941.
[147] NLW; CDP; R/3/32; 5 February 1943.

envelope with a handwritten note: 'Letters of sympathy on Geraint's death from fellow officers in the Guards'.[148] Captain John Syrett, of the 1st Battalion, wrote from the Guards Club: 'To say...as one who had the privilege of serving in the same Battalion as your boy, what a very great blow his untimely death was to the Welsh Guards.'[149] Lord Delamere, another officer, recalled how when he encountered Geraint at the training ground at Esher, he had been impressed by two things: 'first, his courage both moral and physical & secondly his extreme devotion to his family'.[150] There were also civilian condolences, many acknowledging the scale of the tragedy faced in light of the consecutive child bereavements and Jano's pitiable status as a thrice-bereaved mother. Geraint's Cambridge tutor, C. W. Crawley, wrote:

> how can I say anything that is not impertinent? It seems to be more than one family should have to bear. We all admired Geraint's pluck and felt his vivid personality. I know that Stanley will be a help to you now, and he will know that he is all to you.[151]

A Welsh neighbour, Gilbert N. Phillip, commiserated with Jano, 'Your experiences of recent years resemble a Greek tragedy, as though some horrible Nemesis were pursuing you.'[152] Another Montgomeryshire neighbour firmly places Geraint in a Welsh context:

> I see before me constantly the picture of that dear boy as I saw him with you at Welshpool the other day, so handsome and attractive, so full of promise and so evidently a solace and source of pride to you and his father. Behind each young soldier in these days a grim shadow stands, but who could have imagined it would strike so swiftly in such peaceful surroundings?[153]

When Jano's half-brother, Gwylon, wrote to offer condolences, he reminisced about 'the wonderful and glorious efforts of Clem and yourself to give to your children the greatest fullness of life it was possible to give and in so doing achieved in giving them many pleasures and much happiness in their short but full lives.' In the letter, Gwylon foregrounds the memory of 'one Christmas at Vicarage Gate', their home in London:

> David was there. I arrived in the morning and found the house scintillating with decorations and lights and flowers—everything most artistically done and a

---

[148] NLW; CDP; R/3/21–6.   [149] NLW; CDP; R/3/32; 12 February 1943.
[150] NLW; CDP; R/3/32; 8 February 1943.   [151] NLW; CDP; R/3/32; 5 February 1943.
[152] NLW; CDP; R/3/32; 6 February 1943.
[153] NLW; CDP; R/3/32, Letter from Mrs Hugh Lewis, 8 February 1943.

gloriously happy dinner. The whole place was a magnificent show...It made a very deep impression on me and I will never forget it.[154]

At their parents' request, the Imperial War Graves Commission supplied temporary wooden crosses 'to mark the graves of the late Private M. E. Clement-Davies, ATS, and the late Lieutenant G. Clement-Davies, Welsh Guards' in Meifod Parish Churchyard, as shown in Figure 5.2, with the intention of arranging later for a permanent memorial.[155]

Figure 5.2 Temporary wooden crosses marking the graves of Mary and Geraint Clement Davies, Meifod Parish Churchyard.
Source: National Library of Wales; S/5/82.

---

[154] NLW; CDP; R/3/32; 18 February 1943.
[155] NLW; CDP; R/3/32, Letter from Imperial War Graves Commission, 2 June 1943.

At the funerals of all three of their children at Meifod, the Welsh hymn melody 'Crugybar' was sung in addition to English hymns, underlining the family's ties to two nations, although the choice of burial site underscored their shared emotional identification with Wales.[156] Struggling to find consolation in the face of the loss of three children in a four-year period, Clement Davies and Jano attended a sitting with the Welsh medium, Lilian Bailey in December 1944. Speaking through Bailey's Indian guide, Mary stated:

> Mummie...Mummie...Daddy...Stanley...listen to me. I didn't do this thing to you....I am with you constantly....Daddy I love you so. Don't grieve for me....I am so often with you. I tried to hold aloft the tradition of military things.

When Clement Davies asked if Mary was with her two brothers, the reply came: 'Absolutely. They put all their power at her disposal like a couple of sentinels.'[157]

Conscientious Objectors

Ellis points to the enduring sense that Welsh culture was imbued with the values of pacifism and opposition to war, suggesting that nonconformist Christianity and the advocacy of cultural and political nationalists 'have all helped to construct an image of the Welsh as a Christian people whose antipathy towards war was grounded upon religion and its own melancholy history of English conquest and domination.'[158] In the early stages of the war, members of the Welsh diasporic elite in London occasionally adhered to this pacifist interpretation of national identity. In the aftermath of the Dunkirk evacuation in May–June 1940, an opinion piece in *Y Ddolen* asserted, 'because we are imbued with the grandeur of nature, we have become passionate lovers of peace and when we awaken to the shock of war it affects us more deeply'.[159] Davies suggests that conscientious objectors (COs) in the First World War were proportionately more numerous in Wales than in the UK as a whole; of the 16, 500 registered throughout Britain at least a thousand were Welsh.[160] One of their members was George Maitland Lloyd Davies, born in Liverpool in 1880. Davies found release from what he felt to be the suffocating respectability of English Welsh suburbia in Liverpool when he moved to Wrexham, as a bank manager, in 1908. Although he initially joined the local territorial unit of the RWF, Davies resigned his commission before the First World War broke out.[161] When conscription was introduced in 1916, Davies

---

[156] NLW; CDP; S/5/16; In Memoriam card: Geraint Clement Davies.
[157] NLW; CDP; R/2/84; Notes of sitting with Mrs Lilian Bailey, 13 December 1944.
[158] Ellis, 'Pacific people', p. 15.
[159] 'Polished Armour', *Y Ddolen*, Gorffennaf 1940, p. 3.
[160] Davies, *History*, p. 515.   [161] Llywelyn, *Pilgrim*, pp. 51, 60.

objected on the grounds that all war service was 'a negation of the plain teaching of Jesus Christ'.[162] His alternative service involved working as a shepherd at Llanaelhaearn, reinforcing his perception of the Welsh countryside as an environment compatible with his belief system. His wife, Leslie Royde-Smith, herself of English Welsh parentage, wrote that 'English farmers have a very strong prejudice against conscientious objectors' whilst her husband was welcomed 'wholeheartedly' in Llŷn.[163] During the Second World War, Cragoe and Williams suggest that conscientious objection 'remained a distinctively Welsh option'.[164] Davies agrees, arguing that the refusal of more Welshmen, 'in proportional terms', than Englishmen and Scotsmen, to be conscripted, can largely be attributed 'to the strength of Christian pacifism in Wales'.[165] There was also a close identification between Welshness, conscientious objection and nationalism with political opposition to the war coming from Plaid Cymru. As Davies summarizes, its leaders believed that Wales had the right, as a small nation, to choose to be neutral. However, 'Implicit in neutrality was the denial "of the right of any other country, such as England, to force the Welsh to serve in their armed forces".' Thus the party leaders aimed 'to set "a new loyalty in place of the old loyalty to the British State"'.[166]

Beyond Wales, in England, there was also a myriad of responses, including from people of Welsh origin or those displaying an affinity with Wales. Conscientious objector, Harold Ford, was a Liverpool-born Customs & Excise officer, with a strong affective connection with Wales through his marriage to a Welsh woman. Ford's seven wartime diaries, deposited at the Imperial War Museum, delineate both his devotion to pacifism and to Wales, his adopted nation.[167] They testify to Ford's nightly attempts, in Liverpool, to teach himself Welsh, his frequent visits with his wife to her family in Wales and his thwarted attempts to gain a Customs & Excise transfer to Wales, in either Llandeilo or Newtown.[168] A diary is a more intimate form of life writing, which, Summerfield notes, can be 'a technique for managing the self' and for exploring historically 'the interaction of social and personal narratives in the creation of subjectivities'.[169] Within Ford's diaries, it is clear that Wales is a desirable imagined space, offering potential refuge from his everyday existence and dissatisfaction with his workplace. At one point he mentions listening to 'a broadcast about Wales', a rendition

---

[162] Cited in Llywelyn, *Pilgrim*, p. 90.   [163] Cited in Llywelyn, *Pilgrim*, pp. 94–5.
[164] Matthew Cragoe and Chris Williams, 'Introduction', in *Wales and War*, p. 1.
[165] Davies, *History*, p. 599.
[166] Davies, *History*, p. 598. For more on Welsh Conscientious Objection, see Denis Hayes, *Challenge of Conscience. The Story of the Conscientious Objectors of 1939–1949* (London, 1949), pp. 55–8.
[167] IWM 13417; Private papers of Harold Ford.
[168] IWM 13417; 17 October 1939, 22–23 October 1939, 3 June 1941.
[169] Summerfield, 'Subjectivity', pp. 28–9.

of *How Green Was My Valley*.[170] Eventually Ford went before a Tribunal and was directed to work on the land in Newbury but he made continued efforts to get a posting in Wales, which increasingly appealed to him as a metaphorical representation of peace.

The British Library Sound Archive holds oral history interviews with two English Welsh women who address conscientious objection in the Second World War: one undertaken with Peggy Roberts, focusing on her life in education, the other with Ifanwy Williams undertaken as part of a project on female conscientious objectors. Both women were part of large English families with Welsh fathers and, in Ifanwy's case, also a Welsh mother. As well as discussing their own attitudes towards war and peace—both said they were pacifists—the women reflected retrospectively on their Conscientious Objector (CO) brothers, who were the exception rather than the rule within their sibling group. Interviewed in 2008, retired education expert, Roberts mentioned that her eldest brother Alan became a CO during the war and linked this back to their Welsh father, a draper in Finchley: '[my father] was for peace.... I think he was more or less concerned with the underdog really. Not very competitive, certainly not aggressive; I suppose he influenced my oldest brother more than me in that [my brother] became a conscientious objector.'[171] Roberts says of her father:

> he certainly was very much identified with the country and the earth of Wales, and the traditions of Welsh individualness, in a way. Rather than to join together in any sort of gang situation. I think that's what came across really. There was this individual responsibility to belong to something that you could believe in. I think that came through the membership of the Congregational Church as well. That was very strong in Wales.[172]

Whilst her other two brothers went into the RAF and the Royal Engineers, Alan was directed into the Pioneer Corps, a fact which Roberts narrated as having negative consequences for him, whilst also linking his decision back to his sense of Welshness:

> He wanted to go out with the medical people but they put him in the Pioneer Corps and the Pioneer Corps had all the very rough roadworkers, NCOS, and they were very tough on these conscientious objectors. And he saw somebody throw themselves head forth into a barrel of water to commit suicide on one occasion. These chaps, these Pioneer Corps, were sent to Liverpool to clear up the bomb damage, particularly the drains. And he caught an infection. Then he

---

[170] IWM 13417; Diary, 11 May 1942. This identification also rested on an instability, the author Richard Llewellyn being English. See Chapter 9 'The Welsh "Pimpernel"'.
[171] BLSA; C464/68; Margaret [Peggy] Roberts.   [172] BLSA; C464/68.

was very ill with it and ended up—we got him to London and he was in the Hampstead hospital with a very severe infection.... I think that he, there were a lot of Welsh characteristics in him and he certainly knew North Wales very well.[173]

At various points in her interview, Roberts identities Welshness with a series of attributes or characteristics: peaceableness, individuality, and an affinity with Wales, providing an explanatory framework for her brother's decision. In 1998, Ifanwy Williams was interviewed in Wales where she had lived since the war, having married a Welsh Congregationalist minister. Williams had been a lifelong peace campaigner and there is a noticeable tendency to foreground her identification with Wales and ideas of peaceableness throughout the interview. Williams was born in Liverpool to Welsh parents, from Porthmadog, in 1922, the youngest of a Liberal-supporting family of nine children. Her father was an architect. Williams constructs her own journey towards pacifism as a combination of her brother's example, the influence of Aldous Huxley, and her immersion in Welsh political and religious life when she evacuated to Wales with her mother. Confronting the potential outbreak of war, she says of her family:

> There was quite a lot of talk, particularly amongst the boys. I remember—because my mother again was very anti-war—and I remember one of my brothers telling me that she'd said that if any of the boys went to the Forces, that she would either ostracise them or—she was quite strong in her words—and one of them said he was really quite afraid when war broke out. What would happen? That there would be an explosion. By this time of course, when it actually happened.... We were away in Pwllheli when war was declared. By that time, one of my brothers... he was over in France in no time. Then, my eldest sister had been in some gym class and they were suddenly converted into a unit and she became a junior commander in the ATS.[174]

Here Williams defines the military service of her siblings as being in 'defiance' of their Welsh mother's pacifism. She remarks that to conscientiously object was a 'hard' and 'difficult' decision to make at the outset of the conflict. Her brother, who did become a CO—Glyn Roberts, a London-based architect—obtained unconditional exemption and worked on ARP duties in hospitals. Williams frames Glyn's action as having the 'mettle' to go against the grain of public opinion, but she also notes that he was 'ostracised' by their brothers as a result. However, she describes Glyn as influential in her own personal development as a pacifist. She notes that, at the beginning of the war, 'knowing that I had the same

---

[173] BLSA; C464/68.   [174] BLSA; C880/21; Ifanwy Williams.

feelings', her brother recommended Aldous Huxley's pacifist tract, *Ends and Means* (1937) which she felt placed her on the 'surest foundation' regarding her beliefs. Williams would spend time living in London with 'my CO brother' from 1943 onwards: 'He had a flat just by the Marble Arch and, of course, during that period we used to go to peace meetings in Caxton Hall. I would go on Sunday night, of course, and listen to Soper. Every Sunday night.'[175] Williams pinpoints her awareness of pacifism to her schooldays when, she remembers, 'the Peace Pledge Union was active in the Welsh chapels in Liverpool. I remember seeing people I knew in Lime St, which is the centre of Liverpool, on a Saturday afternoon distributing and selling peace literature.' In addition to this, she foregrounds the importance of Wales as a *place*. At the outset of the war, Williams evacuated to Corwen, Denbighshire with her mother and felt that she 'really became a proper Welsh person there.' When she was evacuated there for a second time, she immersed herself in what she perceived as the pacifist traditions of the area:

> I went to a rural community where there was again a minister and a lecturer in WEA (Workers' Educational Association), extramural, who were practically Communist and had a great influence...in that particular area there were many pacifists and COs.... I was on a small farm looking after mother who wasn't too well and helping on the farm for this one year before going to college. People used to come there to stay and being in the middle of this community of pacifists really—and there was a great deal.[176]

As indicated above, for Williams it was her Welsh mother, rather than her father, who guided the anti-war sentiments of the family, stating that this influence 'came to me through my mother':

> My mother, definitely, would have been, at any time, anti-war. At any time. But not in a public way. That was instilled in us. So much so that the boys were never allowed to have toy guns, they were not allowed to join the Scouts, or the Guides, because it was too military. So there was that understanding although it wasn't spoken. You had the feeling.[177]

Whilst they were evacuated together in Wales, Williams remembers that her mother approved of her pacifist stance. In Williams's narrative, her wartime evacuation to Wales with her mother into a rural Welsh community is represented as symbolic of their deeper connection, allowing them to (re)connect with their shared pacific impulses. Alternately, her father, who died early in the war, 'because he was a busy man and lived in the city, he became *part of* the city in a

[175] BLSA; C880/21.   [176] BLSA; C880/21.   [177] BLSA; C880/21.

way that my mother never did.'[178] This life story interview is also significant in the way Williams discusses her decision to conscientiously object. Hazel Nicholson points out that it was harder for women to express their conscientious objection to war due to gendered assumptions around combatant roles. The government 'viewed conscientious objection as an objection to killing and direct involvement in that process, and not a wider objection to war itself.' There was also no right to conscientious objection to civilian work, which affected a far wider group of women than men.[179] In her narrative, it was symbolically important for Williams that she registered as a CO *in* Wales. Although she had returned to university studies in Liverpool in 1941, training to be a social worker:

> I went to Wrexham—by train—which would be about twenty miles from the little agricultural village that I was living in at the time, which was our home temporarily. And I did register as a CO. I remember the faces of the girls behind the counter and the real, well, cold feeling that came over. You know: How dare you? How dare you take this stand? And 'You'll be hearing from us later.' At that point, of course, I left but it was later that I heard – well I didn't hear anything— but certainly I wasn't called to any tribunal, mainly because I was doing this course in social work.[180]

Although a card-carrying member of Plaid Cymru for fifty years at the time of the interview, Williams did not align her Welsh identification to nationalism at the time of the war. Rather, she stressed that the meanings she attached to Welshness were central to her decision:

> I know that there were some COs who—some of them went to prison, of course—on nationalist grounds. That was a great part of the discussion. But at that stage, I wasn't—that wasn't part of my protest. So long as it's non-violence...things like privilege and the class struggle were part of my being Welsh and part of the things that I was.[181]

Thus, Williams's narrative ends with a clear demonstration of how closely she attaches her wartime pacifist beliefs to understandings of Welsh national characteristics.

---

[178] BLSA; C880/21.
[179] Hazel Nicholson, 'A Disputed Identity: Women Conscientious Objectors in Second World War Britain', *Twentieth Century British History*, 18, 4 (2007), p. 415. doi.org/10.1093/tcbh/hwm013.
[180] BLSA, C880/21.   [181] BLSA, C880/21.

Conclusion

The Second World War provided another opportunity for the deliberate formation of English Welsh military units, in Liverpool and London, which encouraged English men to enlist in 'hybrid' regiments that demonstrated the salience of dual English Welsh inheritances. This chapter has illuminated the existence of dual identifications among the descendants of Welsh migrants in England and, in particular, a cohort of male English volunteers for whom Wales and Welshness held some form of *meaning* at the point of their military enlistment. In a time of war, the idea of Welsh identity potentially 'trumped other factors' in determining how some English volunteers saw themselves.[182] Examining the intersectionalities between subjective wartime constructions of kin, home, and nation(s), illuminates how a sense of dual identifications could feed into recruitment patterns and potentially bolster combat motivation and morale. J. R. Davies's wartime self-construction made use of his hybridity, rooted in paternal Welshness, to signal an attachment to family and a shared imagined 'home,' while the Shrewsbury House 'Old Boys' made use of a more vestigial ancestral Welshness to consolidate kinship bonds forged in their youth club 'home'. This suggests that national identities and identifications are not just about nation(s) but are also about understandings of home, friendship groups, and kinship affiliations. Other narrators expressed a desire to follow their father's earlier military service in a Welsh regiment, paying homage to an inherited sense of Welsh affinity. These multifarious understandings of 'Welshness' could also underpin assertions of conscientious objection. The small number of conscientious objectors discussed here accessed 'ideas of the Welsh as an essentially peaceful people'.[183] These idealized constructions informed their self-representations as pacifists and of their siblings as COs. Clearly, at the outset of the Second World War, imagined Wales remained a 'powerful idea' that 'could exert a deep emotional pull' within the diaspora space of England.[184]

---

[182] Herson, *Divergent*, p. 6.   [183] Ellis, 'Pacific people', p. 32.
[184] Johnes, *Wales Since*, p. 3.

6
Mourning and Memorializing

The commanding *Recording Angel* memorial in St Stephen's Porch, Westminster Hall, shown in Figure 6.1, is dedicated to peers, MPs, officers, and their sons who lost their lives in the First World War. Inaugurated in the aftermath of the conflict, it names three English-born sons of Welsh MPs—William Glynne Charles Gladstone (1885–1915), himself an MP, William Pugh Hinds (1897–1916), and Iorwerth Glyndwr John (1894–1916).[1] This chapter explores the mourning and commemorative practices which illuminate the functioning of English Welsh dualities during and after the First World War including officially commissioned memorials, Welsh epitaphs on the tombstones of English-born soldiers, and the involvement of English sculptors and artists of Welsh origin in British memorialization activity. This chapter also analyses the multinational imagery attached to the funerals of two English Welsh soldiers from political and landed elites: the London-born Squire of Hawarden, Lt William Glynne Charles Gladstone MP, whose body was repatriated from Laventie, France and Viscount Clive of the Powis family, whose coffin was conveyed from his London home in Berkeley Square via Paddington station to Wales. Sonia Batten notes how, in the first decades of the twentieth century, the 'semi-public display' of emotion could be transmitted via 'memorials and actions' and that these forms of expression were most effectively performed by 'the upper-middle and aristocratic classes, who had the means and time of display'.[2] In the case studies examined below, we can also see how bereaved members of elite families performed expressions of English Welsh duality when mourning their war dead.

Mourning Dualities

Designed by the Australian sculptor, Sir Bertram McKennal, and unveiled in November 1922 by the Prince of Wales, the *Recording Angel* memorial in Westminster Hall demonstrates the ways in which the Houses of Parliament captured expressions of English Welsh dualities within its political iconography in the immediate aftermath of the First World War. In the centre of the memorial

---

[1] Hinds is discussed in Chapter 4 '15th Battalion (1st London Welsh)'.
[2] Sonia Batten, 'Memorial Text Narratives in Britain, *c.*1890–1930' (PhD dissertation, University of Birmingham, 2011), p. 7.

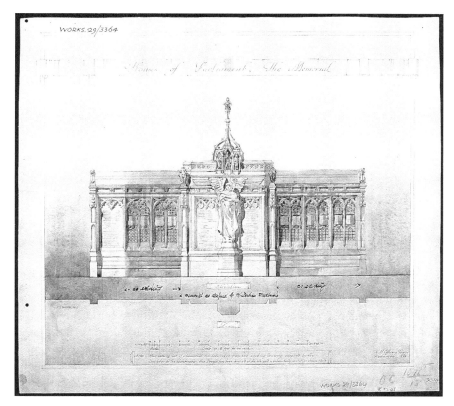

Figure 6.1 'The Recording Angel'. Houses of Parliament, The Memorial, pen, pencil and watercolour on paper by Charles Terry Pledge, c. 1921.
Source: The National Archives; WORK29/3364 (Detail).

stood a winged figure representing the Recording Angel, 'who in Abrahamic religions are said to record every person's deeds'.[3] Above the figure was a cupola in the shape of a Gothic arch surmounted by a representation of Saint George as the patron saint of England and, in the three niches below, bronze statuettes of the patron saints of Scotland, Wales, and Ireland.[4] One of the ninety-four sons recorded on the memorial was Iorwerth Glyndwr John, son of the MP for East Denbighshire, Edward Thomas (ET) John. John, a second lieutenant with the South Wales Borderers, was killed by shell from a trench mortar bomb whilst on front-line duty near Loos on 25 February 1916.[5] The *North Wales Chronicle* reported that news of his death reached his father at the Commons, where

---

[3] *Bertram McKennal's Parliamentary War Memorial* (London, 2014), p. 2.
[4] *Bertram*, p. 3. The cupola was not rebuilt after it was destroyed by a bomb in 1940.
[5] Moss-Blundell, ed., *The House of Commons Book of Remembrance 1914–1918*, p. 117.

'members on all sides expressed deep sympathy with him in his sore bereavement'.[6] The Pontypridd-born MP had been an iron ore merchant in Middlesbrough before entering parliament in 1910. He was a 'zealous advocate' of home rule for Wales[7] and repeatedly voted against the introduction of conscription via the Military Service Bill.[8] His son Iorwerth was born in Middlesbrough in 1894 and was educated at New College, Harrogate and Balliol College, Oxford, where he read jurisprudence. Employing the elite 'Lost Generation' trope of thwarted promise and also underscoring his Welsh attachments, his alma mater writes of Iorwerth's death:

> While at Oxford he showed keen interest in Welsh music and in the political and national life of Wales generally. He was Secretary and later on Treasurer of the Cambrian Society at Oxford, and was a member of the Fabian Society. Doubtless, if he had lived, he would have played a prominent part in the public life of Wales.... His Commanding Officer describes him as 'such a clever boy, always willing to do anything that was wanted'.[9]

This assertion of Welsh fidelity was reiterated in a 1931 parliamentary memorial book—which aimed to provide a 'fuller biography' of the men commemorated on the *Recording Angel* memorial—with the addendum, 'in his death Wales lost an ardent young Nationalist who, had he been spared, might have played a significant part in public life'.[10] Batten's research focuses on the personal inscriptions engraved in the cemeteries of the then Imperial War Graves Commission in the period after 1918 and 'the commemorative relationship between bodies and names' within a personal or familial setting.[11] She notes how, within prevailing wartime narratives, sacrifice was represented by the soldier himself, giving his life for an ideal such as freedom, nation or liberty, whereas 'within the bereavement narrative', it was represented by the next of kin, allowing them some agency over how the soldier was remembered.[12] At the end of the war, the Commission sent each next of kin a final verification form to provide an opportunity to choose a personal inscription for the deceased's headstone.[13] Thus, Batten argues, personal inscriptions were commonly chosen by 'the civilian bereaved' and therefore could

---

[6] *North Wales Chronicle*, 3 March 1916, p. 5.

[7] Robert Thomas Jenkins, 'John, Edward Thomas', Dictionary of Welsh Biography, http://wbo.llgc.org.uk/en/s-JOHN-THO-1857.html, accessed 2 March 2017.

[8] 'Mr E. T. John MP', *North Wales Chronicle*, 9 July 1915, p. 5; 'Mr E T John MP and Compulsion', *North Wales Chronicle*, 4 February 1916, p. 5.

[9] See Jay Winter, 'Britain's "Lost Generation" of the First World War', *Population Studies* 31, 3 (1977), pp. 449–66; *Balliol College War Memorial Book Vol 1* (Glasgow, 1924), p. 299, https://www.flickr.com/photos/balliolarchivist/albums/72157625232059789/page2, accessed 22 April 2019.

[10] Moss-Blundell, *House*, pp. vii, 117.   [11] Batten, 'Memorial', p. 19.

[12] Batten, 'Memorial', p. 183.   [13] Batten, 'Memorial', p. 67.

become 'a matter of reflected identity'.[14] We have seen in Chapter 4 how the diasporic Venmore family in Liverpool chose a Welsh epigraph on their soldier son's tombstone. The politician ET John, living at 63 Warwick Square London, chose an inscription for Iorwerth which was drenched in Welsh symbolism, using lines adapted from the bard Hedd Wyn's Welsh language poem, *Nid â'n Ango* (*[It] Will Not Be Forgotten*):

> *Un O Feibion Hoffusaf Cymru | Ei Aberth nid el heibio | a'i enw annwyl nid a'n ango* (One of Wales's favourite sons | His sacrifice will not be passed over | And his dear name will not be forgotten).[15]

The original line also appears on Hedd Wyn's memorial sculpture, which was unveiled in his birthplace, Trawsfynydd in 1923.[16] A former shepherd, born Ellis Humphrey Evans, Hedd Wyn had been killed at Pilckem Ridge in July 1917 whilst serving with the RWF. Due to the contemporaneous memorialization of his death, triggered by his posthumous award of the chair at the Birkenhead National Eisteddfod in 1917, Hedd Wyn became heavily symbolic of wartime Welsh identity and, more specifically, Welsh language identity. This poetic line was adopted in various forms: as epitaphs for individual soldiers such as Gunner Evan Evans RGA (Royal Garrison Artillery) who died on the same day as Hedd Wyn and on Welsh memorials such as Engelaim Chapel in Bangor.[17] Batten notes that the use of the Gaelic and Welsh language on headstones 'consolidated geographical links' and 'emphasised ideas of distance, absence and reunion'.[18] She points out that the next of kin, like ET John, often took the opportunity to make a political statement about the commemoration of their loved ones: 'engraved words on a common headstone ensured that they were linguistically united with members of their family, and also that family relationships could be restated and recorded.'[19] This desire to emphasize Iorwerth's Welsh affiliations extended beyond the funerary epigraph. In 1916, at the annual meeting of the Welsh Folk Song Society, it was announced that publications had been sent 'to prisoner' camps in Germany in memory of the late Lieutenant Iorwerth Glyndwr John and that there would be an annual prize, the IGJ Memorial Shield, of five guineas for the Welsh folk song competitions at the Eisteddfod.[20] At a Celtic Conference, held in Birkenhead in 1917, consisting of Gaelic, Max, Breton, and Welsh 'representatives', the trustees

---

[14] Batten, 'Memorial', pp. 121, 131.
[15] Commonwealth War Graves Commission, https://www.cwgc.org/find-records/find-war-dead/casualty-details/324993/iorwerth-glyndwr-john/, accessed 23 April 2019.
[16] IWM War Memorials Register, https://www.iwm.org.uk/memorials/item/memorial/7028, accessed 23 April 2019.
[17] IWM War Memorials Register, https://www.iwm.org.uk/memorials/item/memorial/48731, accessed 23 April 2019.
[18] Batten, 'Memorial', p. 190.   [19] Batten, 'Memorial', p. 136.
[20] 'Welsh Folk Song Society', *Carmarthen Journal,* 25 August 1916, p. 6.

of Iorwerth's estate announced an ' "In Memoriam" prize of one hundred guineas' for the best critical essay on the topic of ' "The Celtic Factor in literature at Home and Abroad" '.[21] Thus, whilst Iorwerth's English ties were recognized by his inclusion on war memorials at New College School, Harrogate and Balliol College, Oxford, there was also a series of memorial initiatives, led by his father, which deliberately emphasized the deceased's links to Wales, the Welsh language, and Celticism.

'A Veray Parfit Gentil Knyghte'

Another MP's son listed on the *Recording Angel* was William Glynne Charles Gladstone (William), also an MP in his own right. William was born at 41 Berkeley Square, London on 14 July 1885, the son of William Henry Gladstone MP and grandson of erstwhile Prime Minister, William Ewart Gladstone. He was killed in 1915 whilst serving as an officer with the RWF in France. In 1918, William's uncle, Viscount Gladstone, produced a hagiographic biography entitled *William G C Gladstone. A Memoir*, a key text through which William's short life subsequently became refracted. In preparation of the book, Gladstone contacted people to solicit their memories of William, extracted sections from letters, and sent draft copies for William's acquaintances to comment on.[22] Selling its full print run of 1500 copies, the book was extensively reviewed in the British press, with commentators repeating key quotes and regurgitating the main anecdotes about William's virtues, thus entrenching this familial representation in ink perpetually.[23] Its key function was even apparent to one contemporary reader: 'Lord Gladstone's volume is good memorial [sic] to one who deserves on personal as well as on public grounds to be thus memorialized.'[24]

As discussed in Chapter 1, Hawarden Castle in Flintshire had been an important home for the Gladstone family for many decades. When his father died prematurely, William inherited the estate, moving with his mother and sisters to the castle on the death of Gladstone in 1898; he formally became the Squire of Hawarden when he was twenty-one.[25] Cragoe underlines how a 'paternalistic ethos fostered and enforced within the aristocracy made them responsible, very specifically, for the welfare of the individuals and communities associated with

---

[21] 'Celtic Conference', *Cambrian Daily Leader*, 5 September 1917, p. 3.
[22] GG/979, Letters from members of the Gladstone family and others concerning Viscount Gladstone; William G. C. Gladstone: A Memoir (1918), Glynne-Gladstone Archive, Gladstone's Library, Hawarden, Wales, UK.
[23] GG/978, Letter from Bertram Christian to Lord Gladstone, 17 December 1918, Glynne-Gladstone Archive, Gladstone's Library.
[24] 'W. G. C. Gladstone', *The Times*, 30 May 1918, p. 9.
[25] Viscount Gladstone, *William G. C. Gladstone. A Memoir* (London, 1918), pp. 3–4, 30–1.

their land.'[26] In 1897, William's grandfather had written to him from Hawarden, spelling out his expected path in life as a Gladstone: 'It is our humble duty to apply our minds to the indications which the Providence of God may give us.... As you grow up, dearest Will, in this beautiful and attractive home which God has given you, it will devolve on you, as it belongs to all, to discharge this duty.'[27] Like his grandfather, William embodied an attachment to the four nations, with personal and political interests in England, Wales, Scotland, and Ireland. On attaining his majority, *The Northern Weekly* noted that the Gladstone family were closely connected 'with the principal Highland families' whilst via his Edinburgh-born mother, Gertrude Stuart, the 'heir of Hawarden' was 'possessed of a far-reaching Royal pedigree, Stuart, Plantagenet, and Tudor'.[28] William was educated at Eton and went to New College, Oxford; he wrote to his family from the latter in 1906, 'We are thinking of forming a Welsh Society, of which I might be either Treasurer or Secretary.'[29] He worked at the British embassy in Washington before returning home in 1911 on his appointment as Lord-Lieutenant of Flintshire.[30] That same year he was elected Liberal MP for Kilmarnock Burghs, although he sensed that the new Association of 'Young Scots' viewed him warily as 'an Englishman not understanding the Scottish viewpoint'.[31] In parliament, he focused on the Welsh Disestablishment Bill, the principle of which he 'strongly supported' whilst aiming 'to secure concessions for the Church'.[32]

On the approach to the First World War, William initially advocated a 'policy of non-intervention and peace' and at the Hawarden Flower Show, on 3 August 1914, urged Britain to remain out of the impending conflict.[33] However, he soon altered his position. Having dwelt in the opening stages of his memoir on Will's childhood sickliness,[34] his uncle frames William's decision to volunteer in the following manner:

> He wished to make personal appeals for the enlistment of young men. But how could he urge others to join the army while he, a young man not disqualified for military service, remained at home in safety? It was his duty to lead, and the best discharge of it lay in personal example. His position was Lord-Lieutenant, Member of Parliament, and Squire of Hawarden might well have suggested a

---

[26] Cragoe, *Anglican*, p. 9.
[27] GG/992, 'Letters from W. G. C. Gladstone', Letter from W. E. Gladstone, 6 June 1897, Glynne-Gladstone Archive, Gladstone's Library.
[28] GG/1902, 'Press Cuttings', *The Northern Weekly*, 19 July 1906, Glynne-Gladstone Archive, Gladstone's Library.
[29] Gladstone, *William*, p. 13.   [30] Gladstone, *William*, pp. 57, 34.
[31] Gladstone, *William*, p. 72.
[32] Gladstone, *William*, p. 74; 'Squire of Hawarden', *Flintshire Observer*, 22 April 1915, p. 3. His position was to limit disendowment to tithes, bringing him into conflict with many Welsh parliamentarians. See 'William G. C. Gladstone', *The Spectator*, 29 June 1918, p. 679.
[33] Gladstone, *William*, pp. 108, 100–1.   [34] Gladstone, *William*, p. 4.

post of comparative safety, a staff appointment, something which might be held to be quite sufficient. For there was then no talk of conscription. Moreover, his health was delicate, he possessed neither the training nor instincts of a soldier, war and fighting were repugnant to his whole moral and physical fibre. These matters had no weight with him. He was the only son of his mother, and what it meant to her he knew full well. He made up his mind in his usual quiet way.[35]

Robert Graves, a fellow RWF officer, records his belief that William was shamed into service, writing of 'Glad Eyes' in 1929:

He was in his early thirties, a grandson of old Gladstone, whom he resembled in feature, and Lord-Lieutenant of his county. While war hung in the balance he had declared himself against it, whereupon his Hawarden tenantry, much ashamed, threatened to duck him in the pond. Realizing that, once war was declared, further protest would be useless, he joined the regiment as a second lieutenant.[36]

A hint of the wider societal pressures Will faced is also present in a piece in the *Hawarden Parish Magazine* penned by the Rector, F. S. M. Bennett, in October 1914:

The Squire is with the Welsh Fusiliers at Wrexham, and the whole of Hawarden is proud to know that he is there. Some of you will have seen in last week's Punch the picture of the man who, when asked whether he didn't want to join 'Lord Kitchener's Army' and replied [sic] 'No; war's for them as likes it, which I never did.' I am sure that the Squire would say, too, that as for war 'he never did like it'; but, like or dislike, duty made its call and so he went, as all who knew him knew that he would.[37]

William had faced similar doubts over his martial credentials when he became Lord-Lieutenant of Flintshire, responsible for the Territorial Forces, with questions raised in parliament over his suitability for this position due to his lack of military experience.[38] That William potentially shared these anxieties is visible in a letter he wrote to General Sir Henry Mackinnon, Western Command, in August 1914, having made the decision to enlist: 'Heaven knows, so far from having the least inclination for military service, I dread it and dislike it intensely;

[35] Gladstone, *William*, p. 106.
[36] Robert Graves, *Goodbye To All That* (rev. edn, London, 1957), p. 65.
[37] 'The Rector's Letter', *Hawarden Parish Magazine*, October 1914, p. 1.
[38] Gladstone, *William*, pp. 34–5.

consistently with that I have no natural aptitude for it, and what is more, no training of any sort.'[39]

In spite of this brutal self-assessment, in October 1914 William received a commission as second lieutenant in the 3rd Battalion of the RWF, quartered at Wrexham.[40] A letter from his mother to his uncle Herbert acknowledges how Will's decision was made in the glare of local expectations: 'I am dreading it all very much for him, as I cannot think he is really strong enough.... People here are very appreciative, and proud of him, which is nice.'[41] William's battalion left for overseas service on 15 March 1915. After a few days in a Base Camp at Havre, William joined the front line at the Ypres Salient. In a much-cited letter, with extracts repeated in press accounts of death, at his funeral, and on his subsequent memorial, William wrote to his mother: 'I hope you have settled down now and got resigned to my departure, but really you will be wrong if you regret my going, for I am very glad and proud to have got to the Front. It is not the length of existence that counts, but what is achieved during that existence, however short.'[42] Service in the RWF also deepened William's ties with Wales. In early April, William and his mother exchanged correspondence on an orphanage at Hawarden, which was being used for RWF convalescent soldiers: 'Please let the Orphanage soldiers know that they can wander over the Park Woods and Old Castle in case they don't do it.' Here, William maintained a connection with his Welsh home through discussion of his family's patronage, on both military and domestic fronts, of RWF soldiers.[43] Following his arrival in the trenches near Laventie, on 11 April, William wrote to his mother about his first two-hour watch, still adhering to his self-image as an unsuitable warrior:

> I thoroughly enjoyed it, scrambled out over the top of the parapet to my two groups, fell prostrate over the barbed wire, was duly found by the now thoroughly awoken listening post—nearly slipped into an old deep trench full of water, and eventually got to sleep at 2.30—only to be awoken at 4 A.M. by the order to stand to, i.e. ready for an attack at dawn—everything was cold and miserable, and after such a short sleep one did not feel whether one was on one's head or feet.[44]

In this letter his mother recorded: 'This unfinished letter was his last to me. I found it in his writing pad among his things returned to me from the Front.'[45] William was shot by a sniper while standing, head exposed, behind a collapsed

---

[39] Gladstone, *William*, p. 107.   [40] Gladstone, *William*, pp. 107–8.
[41] GG 956, Letters from Gertrude to Herbert [1900–1929], 23 September 1914, Glynne-Gladstone Archive, Gladstone's Library.
[42] Gladstone, *William*, pp. 113–14.   [43] Gladstone, *William*, pp. 117–18.
[44] Gladstone, *William*, p. 121.   [45] Gladstone, *William*, p. 122.

section of parapet that he had been detailed to repair.[46] His Company Commander, Captain Blackhall, informed his family that, due to his height, he had been told to be careful, 'but Will said he could not always be crouching, his men would think he was funking'.[47] His uncle attributes William's behaviour to his strong sense of 'duty and example', yet he also produces a framing narrative which reminds the reader of the earlier accusations of failed manliness faced by William. Traces of this inference were also present in posthumous tributes. A 'soldier comrade' was cited by the Bishop of St Asaph in a 1916 memorial service, stating: 'If ever a fellow had a decent excuse not to go out he had.... He was a fine fellow. No advertisement! he just took on the often very boring job of a subaltern. No press notices; no soft jobs.'[48] At his funeral a year earlier, the Rector had noted, 'Soldiering was not congenial to him. But he threw himself into it, as he did into all else that he thought he ought to do.'[49] Whilst these tributes tangentially acknowledge William's lack of martial qualities, they also serve to underscore the nobility of his sacrifice, forged through his belief in duty. As *The Spectator* succinctly put it: 'Duty and example were always in his mind, and cost him his life.'[50]

In memorial tributes, William was commemorated in two key ways: as a Christian or saintly figure and as a four nations' representative. Will's mother gained strength from the letters of condolence she received in the aftermath of his death, writing to her brother-in-law: 'One letter I liked so much from an Oxford friend, said, what his influence had been when there, that he was the most "Christlike" man amongst them, rather an unusual adjective?'[51] This saintly imagery saturated the family's chronicle of William, with its opening statement that from the age of nine, the Bible was his 'constant companion':

> No one, not even his mother, knew what it was to him throughout his life.... All the leading passages on purity, peace, rectitude, fortitude, self-sacrifice, quietness, justice, mercy, faithfulness, personal conduct and duty to God are marked... moral truths and a never-wavering belief in God held him from the first, and guided him from day to day.[52]

These religious motifs, aligning William with Christ-like attributes, were also present in the language employed by the local rector reflecting on William's funeral:

> As on Sunday last we stood in Hawarden Church to hear the Gospel—the Gospel of the Good Shepherd—the glorious April sun came streaming through

---

[46] David Crane, *Empires of the Dead* (London, 2014), pp. 70–1.
[47] Gladstone, *William*, p. 122.   [48] *The North Wales Chronicle*, 14 April 1916, p. 5.
[49] 'The Late Lieut. Gladstone, MP', *Flintshire Observer*, 29 April 1915, p. 3.
[50] *The Spectator*, 29 June 1918, p. 679.
[51] GG/956, Letter from Gertrude to Herbert, 30 April 1915.   [52] Gladstone, *William*, pp. 5–6.

the figure of Christ in its east window, flooding with light and colour the very seat where just a month ago we saw for the last time, in his khaki tunic that became him well, him whom we knew best, not as Lieutenant Gladstone, but as the Squire.[53]

In both his death notices and the reviews of his uncle's memoir, William also emerges as the embodiment of the four nations: an Englishman with a Welsh estate representing a Scottish constituency and supporting Irish Home Rule.[54] A lot of press comments acknowledged that William was 'the best type of a serious-minded young Englishman'.[55] His Oxford tutor, Gilbert Murray, wrote, 'It does one good to think that young Englishmen like Will have existed so lately among us'[56] whilst his uncle gifted a copy of the memoir to The Central Library for Students in Tavistock Square, which aimed 'to have a set of the lives of typical young Englishmen who have lived and died for us.'[57] At the same time, the Irish nationalist press acknowledged William's 'support' for Irish Home Rule, inherited from his Prime Minister grandfather, characterizing his death as 'A Loss to Ireland'.[58] More specifically, William was viewed as 'a border hero' whose life criss-crossed the boundaries between Wales and England; the *Liverpool Post* noting, 'The border counties lost a true and devoted son in the late W. G. C. Gladstone, of Hawarden.'[59] Indeed, the duality of William's lived existence was reinforced by his mother, whose grief powered an outpouring of memorialization which crossed the borders between the two nations.

Once William had been killed, 'It was the earnest wish of his mother that the body should be brought home' and the Gladstone family used the levers of their political influence to gain access to the Prime Minister, and by permission of the King, received authority from the War Office for 'the King's Lieutenant' to be brought home. William's uncle Henry travelled to the front and, with 'every assistance from the military authorities', was able to return William's body to Hawarden nine days after his death.[60] Fabian Ware of the Red Cross, and ultimately the founder of the Imperial War Graves Commission, was unhappy that William's body had been repatriated, seeing it as an 'Old World exercise of privilege' and a form of 'social discrimination' amongst the fallen.[61] Ware wrote to a colleague on 5 May 1915:

---

[53] 'The Late Lieut.'.   [54] GG/1902, Press Cuttings.
[55] GG/1903, *Daily Telegraph*, 9 June 1918.
[56] GG/979, Letter from Gilbert Murray, 17 June 1918.
[57] GG/979, Letter from The Central Library for Students, 30 May 1918.
[58] GG/1903, *The Freeman's Journal*, 3 August 1918.
[59] GG/1903, *Liverpool Post*, 20 August 1918.   [60] Gladstone, *William*, p. 124.
[61] Crane, *Empires*, p. 72. In March 1915, General Joffre had issued a proclamation banning all exhumations on French soil. The British Expeditionary Force had also decided that the exhumation of bodies for removal to England would not be allowed in the British area. See Crane, *Empires*, pp. 68–71.

I entirely agree with your remark about Gladstone's body. Incidentally, the exhumation was carried out by British soldiers under fire. Fortunately (? or unfortunately) nobody was hit. The impression it has created among the soldiers out here is to be regretted.[62]

William's mother had achieved her aim of burying her son next to his father 'in the peaceful churchyard of Hawarden' but did not achieve equanimity, writing 'Those two Graves side by side tear one's heart out'.[63] Following the repatriation, there was an elaborate funeral procession, where William's body travelled from London to Hawarden Castle and then to his burial place at St Deiniol's Church. His Welsh regiment provided full military honours, encasing the dead Englishman in the symbolism of his Welsh obligations, both regimental and feudal. As Paul O'Leary notes, this type of large-scale public ceremonial could both reassert local hierarchy and 'set out in ritual form the ordering of status':[64]

The cortege was headed by a firing party of forty non-commissioned officers and men of the deceased officer's company of the 3rd Battalion of the Royal Welch Fusiliers stationed at Wrexham, under the command of Second-Lieutenant M'Lellan, and another contingent of sixty men from the same company under Major Macartney-Filgate.... Lining the road also were a number of wounded soldiers of the Royal Welch Fusiliers from the Orphanage, and contingents of boys and girls from the County School. There were twelve bearers, under Mr. R. S. Gardiner, the estate agent. The coffin was draped with the Union Jack, and on it rested the dead squire's hat as Lord-Lieutenant, his service sword, and a single wreath—a large and beautiful cross of white lilies from his bereaved mother.[65]

On news of William's death, the *Hawarden Parish Magazine* immediately produced a memorial supplement, and two months later, the rector produced a photographic portrait of William and a sonnet in his memory, copies of which could be 'obtained at the Post Office, 1d. each'.[66] However, the Gladstone family had more ambitious plans for William's commemoration. By February 1916, £560 had been raised by subscriptions from family, friends, and tenants and a memorial committee selected a proposal from the Chester Royal Infirmary, on the English side of the border, for a new ophthalmic theatre with wards on each side.

---

[62] Commonwealth War Graves Commission Archive (CWGCA); GRC 1; Narrative Letters and Reports, 25/2/1915–29/12/1915.
[63] GG/956, Set of notes from Gertrude which refer to the draft memoir, 'The Front', u.d; GG/868 Letters from Gertrude to Harry, 31 July 1915, Glynne-Gladstone Archive, Gladstone's Library.
[64] Paul O'Leary, *Claiming the Streets: Processions and Urban Culture in South Wales c. 1830–1880* (Cardiff, 2012), pp. 59, 73.
[65] 'The Late Lieut.'.
[66] *Hawarden Parish Magazine*, May 1915, p. 1; *Hawarden Parish Magazine*, August 1915, p. 1.

With the Gladstone family donating a lump sum towards the cost, it was agreed that 'A tablet and portrait of the squire will be placed at the entrance to the ward which will bear his name.' William's mother also financially supported the restoration of a rood screen as the main memorial for William at Hawarden Church.[67] Her brother-in-law Herbert commented, 'nothing could be more appropriate, Will's sacrifice for the nation must surely be a perennial inspiration for Hawarden.'[68] The rood, designed by Giles Gilbert Scott, the architect of Liverpool Anglican Cathedral, was dedicated by the Bishop of St Asaph on the first anniversary of William's death in April 1916.[69] It consisted of 'the figure of the crucified Saviour with the Virgin Mary His Mother on the left-hand side, and on the right-hand side the figure of St. John the Beloved.'[70] The extended inscription ended with the assertion: 'He laid down his life for his friends|Near the Laventie April 13th 1915|"He was a Veray Parfit Gentil Knyghte"|God Rest His Soule.'[71] The Rector commented:

> The line from Chaucer's Prologue, with its quaint old English spelling of 'He was a very perfect gentle knight', says in seven words just our own hearts' description of him, who, in death as in life, added worth to the name which has made our village of Hawarden famous throughout the world.[72]

The commemorative practices surrounding William, as the Squire of Hawarden, conformed to prevailing norms of 'sacrificial idealism'.[73] Stefan Goebel writes that, 'After 1914, chivalric diction translated the slaughter of the Great War into a narrative which was intelligible to Britons.'[74] Alexander Watson and Patrick Porter agree that the rhetoric of the 'ideology of sacrifice', which endured throughout the conflict, 'validated and glorified participation in mortal combat, and the act of dying in war especially was represented as nothing less than a sacred undertaking... it borrowed heavily from archetypal Christian vocabulary and ideals of sacrifice, suffering and resurrection.'[75] As with the published memoir, these memorials reflect a conscious attempt by William's family to position him within the traditional language of chivalry and sacrifice, absorbing both Christian

---

[67] *North Wales Chronicle*, 11 February 1916, p. 5.
[68] Cited in GG/956, Letter from Gertrude to Herbert, 28 September 1915.
[69] 'The Late Squire of Hawarden', *Llangollen Advertiser*, 21 April 1916, p. 4.
[70] *North Wales Chronicle*, 14 April 1916, p. 5.
[71] IWM War Memorials Archive; WM 13448 Lt W. G. C. Gladstone, http://www.iwm.org.uk/memorials/item/memorial/13448, accessed 13 May 2016.
[72] 'The Rector's Letter', *Hawarden Parish Magazine*, April 1916, p. 1.
[73] Alexander Watson and Patrick Porter, 'Bereaved and Aggrieved: Combat Motivation and the Ideology of Sacrifice in the First World War', *Historical Research*, 83, 219 (2010), p. 152. doi.org/10.1111/j.1468-2281.2008.00473.x
[74] Stefan Goebel, *The Great War and Medieval Memory. War, Remembrance and Medievalism in Britain and Germany, 1914–1940* (Cambridge, 2007), p. 202.
[75] Watson and Porter, 'Bereaved', pp. 147–8.

iconography and Chaucerian text, and in doing so, transforming him from a reluctant warrior to a revered dutiful hero.

In addition to these Welsh initiatives, there were a number of memorials for William in England, including at the Oxford Union, a memorial service in St Margaret's, Westminster and the *Recording Angel* sculpture.[76] The main English commemorative event took place at the Chester Royal Infirmary, with the new theatre and wards dedicated to William's memory. At the unveiling, Lord Bryce eulogized: 'Our best and noblest young men...had given us a proof of what our country could produce. Never had England shown herself worthier of the greatest tradition of her greatest days than she had done in these last months. An England that could do this was an England worth fighting for.'[77] The correspondence between Gladstone's mother, Gertrude and his uncles, held at Gladstone Library, shows how the former channelled her grief into a range of local commemorative projects which spanned across the border between Wales and England in both Hawarden and Chester. These aimed to 'resurrect' Gladstone in memorial form, including the installation of a religious holy rood, a hospital memorial, the circulation of a photographic portrait, and the production of a family memoir. At the same time, this almost instantaneous memorialization of Gladstone's death, whilst denoting privilege, also served to elevate and entrench the patrician expression of a bond between Wales and England.

This dynamic was also visible in the mourning practices surrounding Viscount Clive, the eldest son of the Earl and Countess of Powis, introduced in Chapter 1. Clive died on 13 October 1916 from wounds received whilst fighting with the Welsh Guards in the Battle of the Somme. On being severely wounded, he was brought back to the UK and admitted to King Edward VII Hospital.[78] However, after an operation to remove a bullet in his thigh, Clive suffered a serious haemorrhage and died. In press coverage of his death, Clive fulfils the masculine ideal of the 'young nobleman': he was 'extremely popular' with his men and a 'thorough sportsman'.[79] Press reports included first-hand testimonies from privates who served under him in the Welsh Guards, which testified to how Clive showed 'great consideration for their needs and hardships'.[80] The *Montgomeryshire County Times* records that the news of his death 'profoundly moved the town and the tenantry of the Powis Castle Estate.'[81] At the time of Clive's death, his expected inheritance was described as 'the ownership and responsibilities of about 27,000 acres with a rent roll of about £32,000 in Shropshire, and 45,000 acres with an estimated rent roll of about £40,000 in Montgomeryshire.'[82] The family also

---

[76] 'Lieut. Gladstone's Portrait', *The Times*, 18 May 1915, p. 11.
[77] 'The Toll on Youth', *The Times*, 17 April 1916, p. 4.
[78] 'Death of Viscount Clive', *Llangollen Advertiser*, 20 October 1916, p. 3.
[79] 'Death of Viscount Clive', p. 3.   [80] 'Death of Viscount Clive', p. 3.
[81] 'Death of Lord Clive', *Montgomeryshire County Times*, 14 October 1916.
[82] 'Death of Viscount Clive', p. 3.

owned a town house at 45 Berkeley Square, London, which 'had the distinction, amongst private residences', of having the name of the Earl of Powis inscribed on a brass plate on its entrance door.[83] According to a Welsh newspaper, 'It was placed there for the benefit of the family's Welsh tenants who wished to visit the earl in town but were unable to speak English.'[84]

Clive's death in England and his family's privileged status enabled the choreography of a series of elaborate funeral rituals, which again crossed the border between England and Wales. Ben Roberts notes how elite funerals often made widespread use of the urban landscape, 'touring sites associated with the life of the deceased, as a visible reminder of their community role' and, in this case, the procession involved key family sites in both London and Welshpool.[85] Clive's coffin was initially carried from the hospital chapel to a gun carriage and taken to the family home at Berkeley Square; the next day, the coffin was conveyed to Paddington station, escorted by a detachment of the Welsh Guards, before departing by train to Welshpool.[86] Poignantly, the route mirrored an earlier occasion when Clive, as a recruiter for the regiment, had accompanied a glee party of Welsh Guards from Paddington to Wales. The careful visual imagery surrounding Viscount Clive's funeral cortège, with a Union Jack-draped coffin and Welsh Guards military escort, underlines the importance of dual identifications in sustaining transnational landed influence in this period. At Welshpool, Lord Powis was the sole mourner walking behind the gun carriage as it travelled to Christ Church on the family estate, accompanied by an escort of the Welsh Guards and with estate officials in attendance.[87] Although the streets to the church were said to be 'thickly lined with sympathetic onlookers', members of the public were excluded from the churchyard. The coffin remained in the church overnight with the estate workmen acting as 'a watch guard'.[88] At the graveside, the following day, a firing party, made up of men of the King's Shropshire Light Infantry, discharged three volleys over the grave before buglers of the Welsh Guards sounded the 'Last Post'.[89] H. Avray Tipping, writing for *Country Life*, lamented how Powis Castle, 'so full of mediaeval tradition and survival, of modern taste and amenity' had become 'a home of mourning'.[90] Roberts notes the centrality of newspapers in constructing a sense of local community identity via their coverage of elite funerals such as Clive's. He points to the 'strong correlation between the local press and civic ritual of the period', noting that newspapers 'simultaneously

---

[83] Arthur Irwin Dasent, *Piccadilly in Three Centuries* (London, 1920), p. 254.
[84] 'Estate in Wales', *Cambrian Daily Leader*, 14 October 1916, p. 3.
[85] Ben Roberts, 'A Tale of Two Funerals: Civic Ritual, Public Mourning and Community Participation in Late Nineteenth-Century Middlesbrough', *Cultural and Social History*, 13, 4 (2016), p. 468. doi.org/10.1080/14780038.2016.1237448
[86] 'Death of Viscount Clive', p. 3.   [87] 'Death of Viscount Clive', p. 3.
[88] 'Death of Viscount Clive', p. 3.   [89] 'Death of Viscount Clive', p. 3.
[90] *Country Life*, 10 February 1917, p. 139.

facilitated, prompted, and encouraged public grief and connection to the deceased'.[91] The mournful and reverential tone adopted by local journalists, however, could often mask the more prosaic reasons for attendance at these extravagant public funerals:

> An elaborate funeral procession...was a form of free entertainment, irrespective of the individual emotional investment in the occasion. Ostentatious funereal decoration held considerable visual appeal. Additionally, the presence of a large number of local worthies added to the 'display' and made the funeral appear more attractive.[92]

The multinational homage visible at Clive's funeral—with wreaths from both the Welsh Guards and his former regiment, the Scots Guards—was replicated on the first anniversary of Clive's death with the erection of a memorial at his grave in Welshpool.[93] This took the form of 'a massive Celtic cross standing 8ft. 6in., in a hard red stone, with highly finished decorations'. St George and the Dragon were depicted at the top of the cross with 'the armorial bearings' of the Herberts of Powis Castle in the centre:

> The obverse side represented the crest of the Welsh Guards, surmounted by St. David, the patron saint of Wales. Lower down is a representation of the crest and motto, 'Nemo me impure lacessit' of the regiment to which the gallant young officer was first attached—the Scots Guards. On the upper half of the wheel is inscribed the legend 'Cymru am byth'. On Saturday, two beautiful laurel tributes were placed, on the grave, around one of which was entwined the colours of the Welsh Guards.[94]

The three-nation motif recurred in a stained glass window positioned on the south aisle of Christ Church, Welshpool. This depicted St George, with nimbus, holding a broken lance in his right hand and the Dragon lying at his feet and regimental cap badges of the Scots Guards and the Welsh Guards positioned next to the dedicatory inscription.[95] Whilst in the face of the high casualty rates of the First World War, elaborate funerals were increasingly on the wane, rich and powerful families such as the Powises were able to buck this trend, holding an extravagant public ritual, which served to mourn their loss, display their status, and subscribe to wider understandings of Britishness through the assertion of multinational ties.[96]

---

[91] Roberts, 'Tale', p. 471.   [92] Roberts, 'Tale', p. 469.   [93] 'Death of Viscount Clive', p. 3.
[94] *Llangollen Advertiser*, 19 October 1917, p. 4.
[95] IWM War Memorial Archives; WM 17536 Capt Viscount P. R. Clive, https://www.iwm.org.uk/memorials/item/memorial/17536.
[96] Roberts, 'Tale', p. 479; Cannadine, 'War', p. 239.

Artistic Connections

A number of English Welsh artists and sculptors became involved in post-war memorialization, including those who had been celebrated in a 1913 Cardiff exhibition dedicated to artists 'of Welsh Birth or Extraction'.[97] Frank Brangwyn became entangled in 'ill-fated' plans for a Peers War Memorial when, in 1925, he was commissioned by the 1st Earl of Iveagh to decorate the Royal Gallery of the House of Lords.[98] Brangwyn was born in Bruges in 1867, the third child of an English father and Welsh mother. His father, William Curtis Brangwin, who was born in Buckinghamshire, changed his name to Brangwyn in the early 1860s when he left to seek employment as a designer in Bruges.[99] When the family returned to London, the young Brangwyn was mentored by local artists and eventually took up mural decoration and painting.[100] During the First World War, Brangwyn produced well over 100 images on charity stamps, woodcuts, and lithographic posters, including promotion for a St David's Day fundraising event for Welsh troops at Leicester Square.[101] Due to his distinctive surname, Brangwyn was widely assumed to be Welsh, even by his closest contemporaries. His assistant, Frank Alford, was from Neath in South Wales; in a diary entry from May 1920, his wife Doris records Frank's observation about his master:

> Someone asked me the other day if Mr Brangwyn was an American and someone else questioned me as to his being of the Jewish faith. Mr Brangwyn is Welsh. His father's father was English, but his father was born and bred in Wales. His mother was a Miss Griffiths and came from Brecon. Mr Brangwyn was born in Belgium and came to Wales when quite young.[102]

This extract suggests that Brangwyn was possibly complicit in the ascription of personal Welsh identity, both to himself and to his father. As his biographer, Libby Horner, remarks, the artist revelled 'in fabrications and embellishments of the facts.... Research to date would indicate that Frank Brangwyn never set foot

---

[97] See Chapter 7 'Of Welsh Birth or Extraction'.
[98] Clare A. P. Willsdon, *Mural Painting in Britain 1840–1940. Image and Meaning* (Oxford, 2000), p. 105; Alan Powers, 'The Murals of Frank Brangwyn', in *Frank Brangwyn 1867–1956*, edited by Libby Horner and Gillian Naylor (Leeds, 2006), p. 90.
[99] Libby Horner, 'Brief Biography of Sir Frank Brangwyn RA', in *Brangwyn in His Studio. The Diary of His Assistant Frank Alford*, edited by Roger Alford and Libby Horner (Surrey, 2004), p. 123.
[100] *Frank Brangwyn Centenary* (Cardiff, 1967), Introduction.
[101] Libby Horner, *Brangwyn's War. Posters of the First World War* (Harrogate, 2014), p. 19; See National fund for the Welsh troops. Grand Matinee, St. David's day, March 1st, at the Alhambra, Leicester Square, W./designed by Frank Brangwyn; Avenue Press, Drury Lane, London, https://www.loc.gov/item/2003675356/, accessed 28 September 2022.
[102] Libby Horner, 'Brief Biography of Frank Alford FRSA', in *Brangwyn in His Studio*, p. 128; Libby Horner, 'The Diary and Letters', in *Brangwyn in His Studio*, pp. 9–10.

in Wales during his entire life.'[103] For the Peers Memorial at Westminster, Brangwyn first designed a series of compositions based on battle scenes, but Iveagh was unhappy with 'the grim realities depicted' and requested that Brangwyn start afresh on a new scheme. This series, known as 'the British Empire Panels,' colourfully illustrated different races, countries, products, flora, and fauna.[104] It was intended to evoke 'the beauty of the dominions and colonies which had fought for the British' and the 'Empire that these gallants [the sons of peers] helped to save'.[105] However, when, in 1930, five panels were placed in position at the Royal Gallery, the Royal Fine Arts Commission produced a negative report and Brangwyn's scheme was rejected.[106] Significantly, in this moment of crisis, Brangwyn turned to Wales: the panels were bought by Swansea City Council for its new Guildhall against competition from American and Commonwealth bidders.[107] Furthermore, the earlier rejected panels which illustrated war scenes, 'A Tank in Action' and 'A Heavy Gun in Action' were presented by Brangwyn to the National Museum of Wales.[108]

A contemporary of Brangwyn's, Gertrude Alice Williams, was born at 63 Shaw Street in Everton, Liverpool in 1877 to a Welsh surgeon, David Williams, and his Irish wife, Sarah.[109] Williams studied at the Liverpool School of Architecture and Applied Art before moving to Paris in 1900 on a travel scholarship from Liverpool City Council. Here, she met the Welsh artist Morris Meredith Williams, whom she married and settled with in Edinburgh, where Morris was a drawing teacher.[110] Phyllida Shaw notes how in the early years of their marriage, the couple often spent part of their long summer holiday in Pembrokeshire in Wales. Significantly, in their wartime correspondence, when they were apart, both reference St David's as a form of love language.[111] In 1915, Morris enlisted in the 17th Battalion, the Welsh Regiment.[112] Two years later, Alice was commissioned by his battalion to design a window in memory of Lt Col Wilkie for St Basil's Church in Bassaleg.[113] The window, comprising the figures of St George, St Michael, and St David, was ultimately dedicated to all the 258 men in the battalion who had died and was unveiled in February 1921. Shaw notes how, artistically, Alice's authority was enhanced via her marital link to the regiment: 'Mrs A M Williams, Edinburgh, "wife of Lieut. M Williams, an officer of the battalion"' being credited as the

[103] Horner, 'The Diary', p. 10, fn.15.   [104] Willsdon, *Mural*, p. 148.
[105] Alan Windsor, 'Brangwyn, Sir Frank William (1867–1956)', *ODNB* (2015), https://doi-org.ezproxy.is.ed.ac.uk/10.1093/ref:odnb/32046; Powers, *Murals*, p. 90.
[106] For detailed discussion of 'Brangwyn's scheme', see Parliamentary Archives, WORK 11/303, Houses of Parliament House of Lords War Memorial 1914–1918.
[107] Willsdon, *Mural*, p. 146.   [108] *Frank Brangwyn Centenary* (Cardiff, 1967), Introduction.
[109] Phyllida Shaw, *Undaunted Spirit. The Art and Craft of Gertrude Alice Meredith Williams* (London, 2018), p. 9.
[110] Phyllida Shaw, *An Artist's War. The Art and Letters of Morris & Alice Meredith Williams* (Stroud, 2017), p. 7.
[111] Shaw, *Undaunted*, pp. 41, 56.   [112] Shaw, *Artist's*, p. 7.   [113] Shaw, *Artist's*, p. 11.

designer.[114] In 1920, the architect, Sir Robert Lorimer approached Williams and they began to collaborate on major commemorative projects in Scotland, including the Paisley War Memorial and the Scottish National War Memorial (SNWM).[115] Williams worked on the bronze frieze in the shrine of the SNWM, contributing twelve separate pieces, including panels in the Women's Bay.[116] Finally, in 1925, the National Museum of Wales bought a scale bronze model of the Paisley War Memorial group, 'The Spirit of the Crusaders'.[117] Thus, during the wartime and post-war periods of creativity, Williams shifted from being a diasporic Welsh artist to demonstrating her artistic skills as a Welsh officer's wife so that, ultimately, her Welsh identity became acknowledged by the National Museum of Wales and reciprocated in their purchase of her work.[118]

Shifting Memorialization

At the end of the First World War, moves were made to commemorate the two London Welsh battalions, discussed in Chapter 4. Lloyd George agreed to become a patron of the London Welsh Regimental Association, formed in March 1919, with its headquarters at the London Welsh club.[119] A wreath was laid every year on the RWF plaque at the Gray's Inn premises and an annual service of remembrance held at Westminster Abbey. In 1939, it was considered 'impossible' to hold the latter event, although it was felt that efforts should be made to 'preserve the continuity' of a ceremony 'to which the war has added a new significance and appeal'. With the consent of the Abbey authorities, the Association instead placed a wreath on the Tomb of the Unknown Warrior on Armistice Day.[120] In Liverpool, *Y Brython,* a weekly bilingual newspaper, issued a history of the Welsh Calvinist Methodist Church, Bootle, which included photographs of the twenty-six members of the congregation who lost their lives in the First World War.[121] On the grounds of the church, a stone obelisk war memorial listing their names was also inaugurated and two names were later added in commemoration of the Second World War dead under the inscription *Yr Ail Ryfel Byd* (the Second

---

[114] Shaw, *Undaunted*, p. 59.   [115] Shaw, *Undaunted*, pp. 79, 84.
[116] Shaw, *Undaunted*, pp. 5, 107.
[117] Shaw, *Undaunted*, p. 5. Also 'Mrs Meredith Williams', *The Times*, 7 March 1934, p. 16.
[118] The father and son duo of James Havard Thomas and George Havard Thomas were other artists of 'Welsh extraction' who ventured into both English and Welsh memorialization work. George produced memorials in Lancashire and completed his father's work on the Mountain Ash War Memorial unveiled in 1922. See Gill Abousnnouga and David Machin, *The Language of War Monuments* (London, 2013), p. 152.
[119] 'London Welsh Battalion', *Carmarthen Journal*, 7 November 1919, p. 7.
[120] *Y Ddolen*, Rhagfyr, 1939, pp. 6–7.
[121] Hugh Evans, *Camau'r Cysegr sef Hanes Eglwys y Methodistiaid Calfinaidd Stanley Road Bootle* (Liverpool, 1926).

Figure 6.2 Park Road Welsh Congregational Chapel font with names of chapel members killed during the Second World War.
Source: National Museums Liverpool; MOL.2011.37.1.

World War).[122] Similarly, a memorial plaque was commissioned at the Grove Street Welsh Congregational Chapel for seven members killed in the First World War with the subsequent addition of a separate plaque commemorating two members who died in the Second World War.[123] For the latter conflict, as shown in Figure 6.2, there was also a simple memorial font created at the Park Road Welsh Congregational Chapel in memory of Dennis Roberts and Owen Leonard Woodward.[124]

This subdued memorialization—where names were often added to existing memorial spaces—mirrored wider societal trends in terms of remembering the dead of the Second World War.[125] It also perhaps encapsulates a lessening of the need amongst well-established diasporic families to commemorate their loss in a specifically Welsh space, with the Second World War acting as a watershed moment. By the end of the conflict, the devastation wrecked on cities such as Liverpool and London by aerial bombardment, including on Welsh chapels, and wartime evacuation, had encouraged the return or retirement to Wales of many

---

[122] IWM, War Memorials Register, https://www.iwm.org.uk/memorials/item/memorial/2433, accessed 30 September 2022.
[123] National Museums Liverpool (NML); Museum of Liverpool; Accession No. MOL.2011.37.3, Plaque for chapel members of Grove Street Welsh Congregational church who died in World War Two.
[124] NML; Museum of Liverpool; Accession No. MOL.2011.37.1, Park Road Welsh Congregational Chapel font with names of chapel members killed during Second World War.
[125] Nick Hewitt, 'A Sceptical Generation? War Memorials and the Collective Memory of the Second World War in Britain, 1945–2000', in *The Postwar Challenge 1945–1958*, edited by Dominik Geppert, p. 88.

prominent members of the community elite, further fragmenting associational life.

Conclusion

The inauguration of the *Recording Angel* memorial in the Palace of Westminster provides a useful vehicle through which to examine the commemorative performance of English Welsh dual identities in the aftermath of the war and the fluidity of identity formation back and forward across the borders of the two nations. In his study of the material culture within the Houses of Parliament between 1834 and 1928, James Ford suggests that, at times, Welsh national identities could 'combine or collide with Englishness to form an overriding Britishness.'[126] The *Recording Angel* memorial, and its companion remembrance volume acknowledged the existence of English Welsh dualities within Westminster memorialization, which, in turn, shored up a sense of shared Britishness. In a similar way, the cross-border symbolism of the mourning processes surrounding the privileged war dead articulated a more patrician expression of the bonds between Wales and England, often within an extended three- or four-nation identity. The inclusion of artists of Welsh origin, such as Brangwyn and Williams, in commemorative endeavours which crossed the borders between Wales and England further deepened these interconnections. In gravestone epitaphs, some English-born soldiers were posthumously positioned within a Welsh linguistic community which signalled the importance of their families' Welsh diasporic, and Welsh language, identity above their day-to-day existence lived out in England. However, there was a noticeable decline in post-war memorialization which differentiated the English Welsh war dead between the two conflicts, indicating the subtle erosion of English Welsh duality as a meaningful assertion of identity by the end of the Second World War.

---

[126] Ford, 'Art of Union', p. 14.

PART THREE
CREATING AND FAKING

7
Imagining Wales from England

In *Imaging the Nation*, addressing Welsh art since the sixteenth century, Peter Lord refers to the phenomenon of diasporic artists in England being 'accorded the status of Welsh' by their contemporaries on the basis of their family origins.[1] This chapter addresses the artistic and literary works, and drama initiatives, which emerged from, and reflected, the functioning of English Welsh dualities in the first half of the twentieth century. It explores the influence of Welsh painter, Augustus John, addressing the network of English Welsh artists who congregated around John in London around the time of the First World War, as well as assessing his children's relationship with their Welsh heritage. It also investigates how some English writers living within diasporic communities, in the borderlands with Wales, or with homes in Wales, creatively made use of imagined interconnections, providing a case study of the author Richard Hughes. Finally, this chapter explores attempts by the arts patron Lord Howard de Walden, 'an Englishman turned Welshman' to establish a national drama movement in Wales.[2] Overall, this chapter seeks to establish the meaning and wider appeal of Welshness amongst English creatives with a Welsh connection, raising questions of authenticity, acceptance, and belonging.

'Of Welsh Birth or Extraction'

By the time of the First World War, there was certainly a willingness on the part of the Welsh cultural establishment to promote a fluid conception of Welshness which accommodated English painters and sculptors of Welsh heritage as representatives of Wales. From December 1913 to February 1914, the National Museum of Wales hosted an 'Exhibition of Works by Certain Modern Artists of Welsh Birth or Extraction' who had 'influenced and enriched modern British art by bringing into it new ideas and fresh methods.'[3] The exhibition, at Cardiff City

---

[1] Peter Lord, *Imaging the Nation* (Cardiff, 2000), p. 337.
[2] T. Seymour, *My Grandfather, A Modern Medievalist* (Swindon, 2012).
[3] Mapping Sculpture website, https://sculpture.gla.ac.uk/mapping/public/view/reference.php?id=msib1_1203340874&search=Works%20by%20Certain%20Modern%20Artists%20of%20Welsh%20Birth, accessed 23 March 2015.

Hall, Cathays Park, displayed around 100 works of art by the 'most reputed of modern Welsh artists' including almost twenty works of sculpture. English Welsh patron Howard de Walden gifted £100 towards the expenses of the exhibition.[4] A *Welsh Outlook* reviewer viewed the exhibition as 'a striking vindication of the assertion that Wales is in no way deficient in those creative forces which find most beautiful and vital expression on canvas and in stone.'[5] Yet, the Museum's decision to actively include those of Welsh descent was recognition of both the need for a broad conception of Welshness when celebrating national artistic heritage and a tendency for Wales to position itself in terms of its 'contributionism' to the wider British imperial project.[6] Indeed, Lord notes how, on the cusp of the First World War, the Welsh establishment 'sought to locate itself in a symbiotic, rather than a combative, relationship with the English'.[7] Artists admitted 'on the strength of their Welsh forbears' included G. F. Watts, Arthur Hughes, and Sir Edward Burne-Jones.[8] Mark Evans points out that the 'incoherence' of the list of participants 'emphasises the exhibition's lack of any guiding principle other than that of including artists who were (or were fancied to be) Welsh'.[9] English sculptor James Havard Thomas acted as the project consultant for the production of ten marble sculptures to fill the Pantheon of National Heroes in Cardiff City Hall, inaugurated in 1916.[10] Lord points out that 'all the main strands of early twentieth-century national sentiment' were expressed in the Pantheon: the early church (Saint David), nonconformity (William Williams, Pantycelyn), poetry (Dafydd ap Gwilym), and both Anglophile British political sentiment (Sir Thomas Picton) and the independent Welsh tradition (Owain Glyndwr) yet the statues were 'carved mostly by younger English sculptors of conservative inclinations'.[11] This willingness to use English creatives when constructing Welsh national iconography is supported by Ford's study on decorative art of the Palace of Westminster, which points out that, in 1897, the St David mosaic commissioned to represent Wales was created by English painter Edward Poynter with 'no Welsh involvement'.[12] It also hints at the multiplicity of artistic interrelationships which crossed back and forward across the border between the two nations in the opening decades of the twentieth century.

---

[4] Mark L. Evans, *Portraits by Augustus John: Family, Friends and the Famous* (Cardiff, 1988), p. 9.
[5] 'Art and National Life', *Welsh Outlook*, 1, 1 (1914), p. 25.
[6] Peter Lord, 'Homogeneity or Individuation? A Long View of the Critical Paradox of Contemporary Art in a Stateless Nation', in *Globalization and Contemporary Art*, edited by Jonathan Harris (Chichester, 2011), p. 59.
[7] Lord, 'Homogeneity', p. 59. [8] Evans, *Portraits*, p. 9. [9] Evans, *Portraits*, p. 9.
[10] Lord, *Imaging*, p. 337. [11] Lord, *Imaging*, pp. 337–8.
[12] Ford, 'Art of Union', pp. 221–2.

Augustus John and His Circle

The work of the Welsh artist Augustus John was shown at the 1913 Exhibition.[13] John was born in Tenby in 1878 to a Welsh father and an English mother, spending his early years in Haverfordwest.[14] After studying at the Slade he married an English woman, Ida Nettleship, and moved to Liverpool where he found a temporary position at the School of Art.[15] John purportedly liked the city because it was 'full of Germans, Jews, Welsh and Irish and Dutch'.[16] Here he made contact with the university librarian, John Sampson, who produced *The Dialect of the Gypsies of Wales*. When John's first son, David, was born in Liverpool in 1902, he struggled to name him: according to Michael Holroyd, 'he would fix upon his son a good Welsh name—Llewelyn or maybe Owen or even Evan.... But which? Perhaps, since the child would after all be only one-quarter Welsh this too was wrong.'[17] Ida died in 1907 after giving birth to their fifth son Henry who joined David, Caspar, Robin, and Edwin.[18] John subsequently had four children with Londoner Dorelia McNeill: Pyramus, Romilly, Poppet, and Vivien. According to Caspar John, in the years following their mother's death, the eldest five siblings 'journeyed constantly between London and Paris' and spent time in Norfolk and North Wales.[19] With their Nettleship family at Wigmore Street, they were taken on 'the ritual round' of middle-class activities: trips to the park, zoo, Madame Tussaud's, and the pantomime.[20] With John, they would spend time at his cottage Nant Ddu, situated in a valley near Bala Lake: 'It was surrounded by stacks of peat which David and Caspar used to rob for the fire. A local train ran through the valley, and the boys used sometimes to be taken to the stop called Cwm Prysor, about a mile away, and introduced to Mrs Evans, the station-mistress.'[21] This sense of duality also took sartorial form: at prep school in Dorset the John siblings were known for their 'long hair and strange clothing' but on holidays with their Nettleship grandmother in Mevagissey, Barmouth and Harlech, 'A barber would be summoned and outfits of orthodox school clothing bought.'[22] As his English Welsh children grew older, John 'began to see them as the very subject-matter of his work'.[23] As well as individual portraits, he captured his offspring in *Lyric Fantasy c.* 1913–14, a mural commissioned by a private dealer Hugh Lane, to decorate the hallway of his Cheyne Walk residence in Chelsea (see Figure 7.1). John used his family and friends as models, including his late wife Ida, positioned on the right. In correspondence with the Tate, Caspar confirmed that the male figures consisted of Pyramus drumming on the left with Caspar, Romilly, and

---

[13] Lord, *Imaging*, p. 370.
[14] Michael Holroyd, *Augustus John. A Biography* (London, 1987), pp. 13–16.
[15] Holroyd, *Augustus*, p. 142.   [16] Holroyd, *Augustus*, p. 143.
[17] Holroyd, *Augustus*, pp. 160–1.   [18] Rebecca John, *Caspar John* (London, 1987), p. 20.
[19] John, *Caspar*, p. 21.   [20] John, *Caspar*, p. 28.   [21] John, *Caspar*, p. 32.
[22] John, *Caspar*, pp. 35–6.   [23] Holroyd, *Augustus*, p. 308.

Figure 7.1 Augustus John, 'Lyric Fantasy', c. 1913–14.
Reproduced with permission of Tate Images and the Estate of Augustus John.

Edwin on the right. John's daughter, Poppet, was held in the arms of the unknown central figure. The landscape is thought to be Alderney Manor-inspired, John and his family having moved there in 1911, 'although the mountains in the background suggest Wales'.[24]

Beyond painting, however, John had a tense relationship with his children, and, in particular, 'found it hard to bear the physical presence of his maturing sons'. Holroyd notes how, 'overawed by his great presence', his sons 'fell, one by one, into privacy and other lines of self-preservation'.[25] David, occasionally known as 'Dafydd', was an oboist and then a postman, Edwin a professional boxer and landscape painter.[26] Caspar, born in London in 1903, was the most successful in breaking loose from life in their father's shadow, ultimately becoming a naval captain.[27] He wrote in an unfinished autobiography, 'I was saddled with the name Caspar, awkward enough on its own without the addition of the surname John, a combination which harried me for life'.[28] His daughter Rebecca John comments that Augustus's hostility to his son's proposed naval career 'in no way soured Caspar's interest in his father's work as a portrait painter', the former writing to his maternal grandmother in 1916: '"I hear Daddy's picture of Lloyd George is done".'[29] Another son, Romilly, born in 1906, remembers visits to Tenby staying

---

[24] Tate, 'Augustus John OM, Lyric Fantasy', Catalogue Entry, http://www.tate.org.uk/art/artworks/john-lyric-fantasy-t01540, accessed 18 March 2016.
[25] Holroyd, *Augustus*, p. 498.
[26] Holroyd, *Augustus*, p. 663; 'Edwin John, Painter, Is a Fighter as Well', *Deseret News*, 12 Dec 1931, IV, https://news.google.com/newspapers?nid=336&dat=19311212&id=y7JOAAAAIBAJ&sjid=_bUDAAAAIBAJ&pg=4060,4195491&hl=en.
[27] Holroyd, *Augustus*, pp. 497, 665.   [28] Cited in John, *Caspar*, p. 17.
[29] John, *Caspar*, p. 39.

with his Welsh grandfather who indulged in 'the same impenetrable silences' as his father:

> it is true that he provided us with black stockings for Sunday wear, but the meals were curiously similar to some of those at Alderney, not a word being spoken from start to finish. However, he was not able to inspire much awe in the minds of the third generation, though he may well have been an object of terror to his own children.[30]

In a 1975 postscript to his 1932 memoir, *The Seventh Child*, Romilly emphasizes a sense of distance from his own father, which is reflected in an expressed ambivalence about Wales. He describes his father as tyrannical, melancholic, and uncommunicative and recalls that as a child he could pass his father on King's Road, London, 'without ever receiving a flicker of recognition'.[31] When remembering Wales, both as a child and adult, it is a place of incessant rain and dreariness.[32] When in the early 1920s Romilly hiked through North Wales, en route to stay with the poet Roy Campbell near Pwllheli, he was discomfited when encountering local inhabitants. At one railway station:

> The porters gathered round, and I was subjected to a friendly but interminable cross-examination. Either the Welsh are the most inquisitive of races or the unaffected openness of their character gives their curiosity unusual play. I was relieved when at last the train drew in which was to bring me to the end of my journey.[33]

At his final destination, Romilly is further disorientated: 'Its environs, moreover, did not seem to correspond at all to Roy's description of the country round him, where half the people knew no English.'[34] When the friends move to another cottage, 'an ancient man called on us and began pouring out a flood of eloquence, unfortunately in the Welsh tongue. After some lively pantomime we made out that he was the former tenant of the cottage.'[35] Thus, in his life writing, Romilly tends to indulge in a dismissive 'othering' of the Welsh people he encounters. When he completed his 1932 memoir, Romilly submitted the typescript to his father: 'He dismissed the entire thing with the single word "Rotten". On my pressing him for some constructive criticism, he was able to point out that I had misspelt—and who would not?—the name of a Welsh mountain.'[36] Here we see a

---

[30] Romilly John, *The Seventh Child. A Retrospect* (London, 1975), p. 184.
[31] John, *Seventh* (1975), pp. 179–80.
[32] Romilly John, *The Seventh Child. A Retrospect* (London, 1932), pp. 78, 209.
[33] John, *Seventh* (1932), p. 209.   [34] John, *Seventh* (1932), p. 209.
[35] John, *Seventh* (1932), p. 213.   [36] John, *Seventh* (1975), p. 181.

tension between father and son, reflected in a tussle of authenticity over their respective knowledge of Wales. Whilst Romilly employed the usual lyrical motifs about Wales found within the narratives of the descended Welsh—mountains, holidays, farms, relatives—he did so in a more negative tone, possibly in an attempt to reflect his emotional distance from his father.

In London, John's circle included his English Welsh muse, 'Birdie', aka Gwendolyn Rosamund Schwabe, née Jones. Born in London in 1889, Birdie was the youngest child of the financially independent Herbert Jones and his wife Elizabeth. She was gifted the nickname 'Birdie' by John because of her habit of 'perching on the lockers' at the Slade School of Art; her appearance was also much commented upon by her peers.[37] Her neighbour, Charles Tennyson, wrote that 'with her sleek black head, clear, ivory skin and long limbed angular grace' Birdie resembled 'some exquisite ibis or crane picking a delicate way through the mysterious reed-beds of the Oxus; and what zest for life she had...flashing through wild studio parties.'[38] In 1923, a fellow Slade student, Camilla Doyle, published a poetic tribute 'To Birdie (GS)' which rhapsodizes: 'No peacock ever danced and preened|His beauty more audaciously...In curving blackbird-coloured hair|Her brow stands white.'[39] In 1915, Birdie was painted at John's Chelsea studio 'where he insisted on her posing with her lips slightly apart and wearing a narrow red hat-band around her neck, both against her wishes.' Originally known as *Birdie: The Black Hat*, this was one of the three 'Birdie' portraits John produced.[40] After Birdie's 1913 marriage to artist Randolph Schwabe, they lived at 43A Cheyne Walk, 'a large rather dilapidated house...next to Terrey's greengrocers'. Fellow artist Allan Gwynne-Jones lived above their flat. Gill Clarke notes how, the Schwabes introduced Gwynne-Jones to 'their wide circle of artist friends, including Augustus John, James Dickson Innes, and Albert Rutherston whose parties they frequented in Fitzroy Street', thus expanding the pool of English Welsh artistic interconnections.[41] Gwynne-Jones's daughter, Emily, relates how Birdie 'dressed in a way that all the Johns did, wore wonderful reds and yellows and berets.'[42] When the Schwabes' child, Alice, born in 1914, was a baby, she would be taken to parties at the Johns and be put down on a bed.[43] In addition, Alice's school fees at Bedales were paid by her godfather, Gwynne-Jones, who shared Birdie's English Welsh heritage.[44]

---

[37] David Fraser Jenkins and Chris Stephens, eds, *Gwen John and Augustus John* (London, 2004), p. 186.
[38] Charles Tennyson, *Stars and Markets* (London, 1957), pp. 196–7.
[39] Camilla Doyle, *Poems* (Oxford, 1923), pp. 40–1.
[40] Jenkins and Stephens, *Gwen John*, p. 186.
[41] Gill Clarke, *Randolph Schwabe* (Bristol, 2012), pp. 32–3.
[42] Author interview with Emily Gwynne-Jones.
[43] Gill Clarke, *The Diaries of Randolph Schwabe. British Art 1930–48* (Bristol, 2016), p. 200.
[44] Clarke, *Diaries*, p. 552.

Gwynne-Jones was born in Richmond in 1892 to solicitor, Llewellyn Gwynne Jones, of Welsh parentage, and his Irish wife Evelyn Clara. Ancestrally, his father's family had links to John Jones Maesygarnedd, one of the regicides of King Charles I.[45] Educated at Bedales School, Gwynne-Jones was articled with solicitor and MP, W. Joynson-Hicks, and had just started as an art student at the Slade when he volunteered to serve in the First World War. Keen to get 'to the Front as soon as possible',[46] Gwynne-Jones initially served with the Public Schools Battalion, then the East Surrey Regiment, and the 1st Cheshire Regiment. As a second lieutenant, he was awarded the DSO for 'conspicuous gallantry in action' in October 1916, before transferring to the Welsh Guards in January 1917.[47] Based on his wartime letters, his daughter believes that this transfer was largely due to his dissatisfaction with the Cheshires, but the Welsh Guards also became important to him.[48] Significantly, in Randolph Schwabe's interwar diaries, the author often frames Gwynne-Jones via his military association with the Welsh Guards. In 1930, Schwabe recounts an incident whereby Gwynne-Jones paints his model, 'Rogers the Guardsman', without rest until the latter 'went green with faintness'. Schwabe surmises that the artist played on 'Rogers's respect for him as an ex-Guards officer'.[49] In 1933, Schwabe recounts an anecdote about when Gwynne-Jones was in the Welsh Guards, and 'with the help of two Welsh ex-poachers in his regiment', secured hens to feed the Scots Guards.[50] David Brown notes that while in the army, Gwynne-Jones occasionally found time to draw and paint a few watercolours; he also 'decorated a few small objects, candlesticks, boxes and a mirror for "Birdie" Schwabe, whom he admired greatly'.[51] These included a box from 1917 with 'Here lies a most beautiful lady' inscribed on the inside lid in gold on a deep pink background.[52] In 1914, Gwynne-Jones painted 'Andantino-Schumann Opus 22' which depicted two identical female figures in a style reminiscent of Augustus John's pictures. According to Brown, the facial features of both the figures 'are those of "Birdie" Schwabe' with the *Andantino* movement being 'intensely romantic in feeling'.[53] Following demobilization, Gwynne-Jones pursued his artistic career; in a landmark 1919 exhibition at the Twenty-One Gallery of articles of everyday use designed by artists, Birdie contributed two illuminated manuscripts with Gwynne-Jones who provided the lettering for her miniatures.[54] After the war Gwynne-Jones concentrated his artistic focus on English scenery often staying with his mother near Petersfield,

---

[45] A. H. Dodd, ed., *A History of Wrexham* (Wrexham, 1957), pp. 48–9, 58–9.
[46] TNA; WO 339/46416; 2nd Lieutenant Allan Gwynne-Jones; Letter from W. Joynson-Hicks to War Office, 10 November 1915.
[47] *London Gazette,* 29,793, 20 October 1916; TNA; WO 339/46416.
[48] Author interview. In one letter, he wrote 'I can't tell you how fed up I am at leaving my platoon after what we have done together'.
[49] Clarke, *Diaries*, pp. 23–4.   [50] Clarke, *Diaries*, p. 140.
[51] David Brown, *Allan Gwynne-Jones* (Cardiff, 1982), p. 13.   [52] Brown, *Allan*, p. 68.
[53] Brown, *Allan*, p. 21.   [54] Clarke, *Randolph*, p. 49.

Hampshire, and making a number of etchings of Froxfield subjects; his first work purchased in 1924 by a public gallery was *Spring Evening: Froxfield*.[55] As his post-war career developed, Gwynne-Jones became lauded for the 'poetic sensibility' of his English landscapes.[56]

At the same time, Gwynne-Jones's association with the Welsh painters, John and Innes—who painted together in North Wales and southern France[57]—was also important. Emily Gwynne-Jones recalls that her father 'looked up to' John; their socializing together meant that John's children in their Romany style of dress also informed Gwynne-Jones's 'aesthetic' in that period.[58] He was also affected by John's enthusiasm for French painting and 'his admiration of things being painted... *alla prima*'. Similarly, the paintings of Innes 'had an incredible influence' on Gwynne-Jones's early work. Here, it could be argued that Gwynne-Jones's relationship with Wales was forged as much through his awareness of the work of contemporary Welsh artists with whom he socialized in London as his own ancestral links.[59]

Later Exhibitions

In 1935, there was another attempt to showcase the work of Welsh artists: a travelling Contemporary Welsh Art Exhibition, led by Cedric Morris and supported by 'several affluent patricians' including the architect, Clough Williams-Ellis and author Richard Hughes. However, Lord suggests that this endeavour was limited by its 'reversion to the definition of a Welsh artist as a person whose ancestry was Welsh'. This resulted in the inclusion of Wyndham Lewis and Allan Gwynne Jones 'who had no practical connection with Wales'. Indeed, Lord notes the refusal of Welsh artist Timothy Evans to participate because he believed 'it is not for some half-English snobs like Clough Williams-Ellis and his cronies to control and chatter about art in Wales'.[60] The use of the term 'half-English' is interesting here, not just because it dismisses Clough's diasporic claim to Welshness—both his parents were Welsh—but because it possibly reflects the perception of Williams-Ellis as someone who spent half his time in Wales and half in England. It illustrates how easily a sense of acceptance, even for establishment figures, could be flipped on its head and the person relegated to the boundaries of Welsh belongingness.

David Jones was included in the 1935 exhibition; by this time, writes Lord, 'his mediations on the matter of Wales as part of the idea of Britain were beginning to

---

[55] Brown, *Allan*, pp. 22, 10.
[56] Humphrey Brooke, 'Introduction', *Allan Gwynne-Jones. An Exhibition to Mark His 80th Birthday* (London, 1972), p. 6.
[57] Holroyd, *Augustus*, p. 450.   [58] Author interview.
[59] Author interview.   [60] Cited in Lord, *Imaging*, p. 380.

secure for him a place in the intellectual life of the nation.'[61] Jones's most direct painterly association with Wales stems from the period he spent with Eric Gill and his circle based at the former monastery at Capel-y-ffin in the Vale of Ewyas. Between 1924 and 1927, Jones spent much of his time 'painting and engraving at Capel and on Caldy, an island off the south coast of Pembrokeshire'.[62] According to Ariane Bankes, it was while at Capel-y-ffin that Jones's 'powerful feelings for the landscape around him coalesced into paintings of real beauty and distinction'. For him, Wales was both the 'home of his forefathers' and '"a land of enchantment"'.[63] In this period, Jones produced works such as *Ponies on a Welsh Hillslope* (1926), *Y Twmpa, Nant Honddu* (1926), *Capel-y-ffin* (1926–7), and *Sandy Cove, Caldy* (1927).[64] However, his close friend René Hague writes that whilst Jones was widely read in Welsh history and myth, he had 'no more than a sentimental love' for Wales with 'little or no knowledge' of modern Wales.[65] Indeed, Hague alludes to the disconnect between Jones's mythic vision of Wales and the reality of living there. He points out that when in Capel, Jones had no contact with the inhabitants of the valley who were 'very Welsh in their intonation and very different in their ways'. He suggests that Jones hardly spoke with them and 'found them strange and frightening'.[66] Hague points out that Jones was seldom in the country, except at the 'almost completely anglicized' Caldey Island and Capel-y-ffin, and 'could never have lived there'.[67] It is worth noting that Jones mainly accessed Wales through sharing Gill's habitat, rather than as a result of his own agency. When Gill left Capel-y-ffin, Jones did too, moving on to paint a series of seascapes from his parent's newly acquisitioned bungalow near Brighton.[68] As discussed in Chapter 2, Jones's English suburban output was equally important in reflecting his own sense of selfhood; however, the perception of Jones as a Welsh artist has endured. In 1954, a touring exhibition of Jones's work was organized by the Welsh Committee of the Arts Council of Great Britain, in consultation with the artist, and shown at Aberystwyth, Cardiff, Swansea, Edinburgh, and London.[69] There was another major exhibition on Jones from 1972–73 jointly organized by the National Museum of Wales and Welsh Arts Council Exhibition.[70] In the latter decades of the twentieth century, there were also national Welsh exhibitions dedicated to Allan Gwynne-Jones and Ivor Roberts-Jones, both English artists of Welsh ancestry. Although Gwynne-Jones's output was heavily focused on English landscapes, his 'protégé', the Welsh artist Kyffin Williams, unproblematically included him in a list of Welsh painters in a 1991 speech:

[61] Lord, *Imaging*, p. 384.
[62] Paul Hills, 'Engraver of Signs', in Bankes and Hills, *Art of David Jones*, pp. 30–2.
[63] Ariane Bankes, 'Tutelar of Place', in Bankes and Hills, *Art*, p. 47.
[64] Bankes and Hills, *Art*, pp. 38, 46, 52.   [65] Hague, *Dai*, pp. 23–4.
[66] Hague, *Dai*, p. 33.   [67] Hague, *Dai*, p. 24.
[68] Paul Hills, 'Watercolour Vision', in Bankes and Hills, *Art*, p. 91.
[69] 'Current and Forthcoming Exhibitions', *The Burlington Magazine*, 115, 838 (1973), p. 55.
[70] 'Current', p. 55.

there is no room in the whole of Wales devoted solely to the best of Welsh art. I believe it is important that there should be one in order to show to the world and to our own land that we have produced many distinguished artists. I envisage a gallery showing...the paintings of Augustus John and his sister Gwen, David Jones and many other like Ceri Richards and Allan Gwynne-Jones.[71]

In an exhibition at Agnew's in 1972, the catalogue records that Allan Gwynne-Jones was 'of Welsh, Cornish, Irish and English ancestry',[72] but ten years later, on the occasion of a Welsh retrospective for Gwynne-Jones, his Welshness was foregrounded. Indeed, the National Museum of Wales, the Welsh Arts Council, and the Royal National Eisteddfod of Wales celebrate their 'combined tribute' to the ninety-year-old artist which aims to showcase 'the work of one of the Principality's finest artists'.[73] A similar trend can be seen with Ivor Roberts-Jones who was born in 1913 in the English market town of Oswestry, close to the Welsh border, to a Welsh solicitor father and an English mother. Educated at Oswestry Grammar School and Worksop College, Roberts-Jones went up to Goldsmiths College, London, to study painting aged eighteen.[74] In 1940 he moved to 31 St James's Gardens, London which was to be his home until the mid-1960s.[75] At the outbreak of the Second World War, Roberts-Jones volunteered to serve in the Royal Artillery and, in 1940, was posted to Northern Ireland, as a lieutenant in the 83rd Field Regiment, Royal Artillery, as part of the 53rd (Welsh) Division.[76] He saw active service in north-eastern India and Burma, fighting at Arakan.[77] Jonathan Black notes that the destruction of Roberts-Jones's pre-war sculpture due to a direct hit on his Chelsea studio meant that the war 'created a tabula rasa for him'.[78] Although in 1946 he obtained a teaching post at Goldsmiths which secured his base in England, in the post-war era Roberts-Jones gained a significant amount of artistic and commercial support from the Welsh arts establishment which possibly accentuated his own identification with Wales. In the 1960s, the National Museum of Wales paid to have his large sculpture *Mrs Griffiths* cast in bronze for its sculpture collection and also purchased his head of the Welsh painter Kyffin Williams.[79] In 1978, the Welsh Arts Council held a retrospective exhibition for Roberts-Jones at the Oriel Gallery, Cardiff and subsequently commissioned a monumental sculpture to stand outside Harlech Castle, Gwynedd.[80] Inspired by a story from the 'tale of Branwen' in the Mabinogion, Roberts-Jones devised a 'horse and rider' depicting Bendigeidfran's return to Wales with the dead body of

---

[71] Author interview; 'Cyflwyno Medal', *Transactions of the Honourable Society of Cymmrodorion* (1991), p. 37.
[72] Brooke, 'Introduction', p. 5.   [73] Douglas A. Bassett, 'Foreword', in Brown, *Allan*, p. 7.
[74] Jonathan Black, 'Ivor Roberts-Jones', in *Abstraction and Reality. The Sculpture of Ivor Roberts-Jones*, edited by Jonathan Black and Sara Ayres (London, 2013), p. 13.
[75] Black, 'Ivor', p. 16.   [76] Black, 'Ivor', pp. 16–17.   [77] Black, 'Ivor', pp. 17–19.
[78] Black, 'Ivor', p. 20.   [79] Black, 'Ivor', pp. 26, 28.   [80] Black, 'Ivor', p. 30.

his nephew Gwern, to which he gave the alternate titles, *The Two Kings/Janus Rider*.[81] Black points to the 'inherent duality' in the work's message.[82] Roberts-Jones wrote that working on the project, even though it faced criticism from the Welsh Language Society due to the sculpture's location 'outside an "English" castle', left him feeling 'a closer affinity to Wales'.[83] The Welsh Arts Council press release about the artwork described him as 'Wales's most distinguished and best-known living sculptor', confirming his external acceptance as a Welsh artist.[84] The extent to which Robert-Jones gained such a central position in the Welsh art world is testimony to both Roberts-Jones's liminality and the willingness of influential Welsh friends—including the artist Kyffin Williams and Labour MP Cledwyn Hughes—to treat him as a Welsh artist.[85] Williams once said of Roberts-Jones that their 'Welshness' was a shared bond, although his tribute serves to emphasize the vulnerabilities contained within this perceived identity:

> Ivor was small and bird-like, in fact a typical Welshman to look at. However, he did not sound Welsh, if anything he had an Oxford accent. Ivor always had an odd relationship with Wales. He couldn't keep away from the place, yet, he didn't like it.... Like so many Welsh, spontaneity was his thing: the lightning sketch of an animal, the brilliant characterisation of a sitter, achieved in one sitting.[86]

English Welsh Literary Spaces

The backdrop to English Welsh cultural production in the first half of the twentieth century was the longstanding debate over who could speak creatively on behalf of Wales and in what language; even Welsh-born writers who wrote in English could come under critical scrutiny. 'Anglo-Welsh' was a term used to describe the English language writers of Wales who began to publish their work in the 1930s.[87] In his 1968 text, *The Dragon Has Two Tongues*, Glyn Jones defined Anglo-Welsh writers of the twentieth century as 'Welshmen [sic] who write in English about Wales'; most commonly, individuals who were cultural products of the South Wales coalfield.[88] In this analysis, Jones 'cheerfully' rejects what he termed 'writers of remote Welsh ancestry', lumping together the rather eclectic group of 'Wilfred Owen, Charles Morgan, Anthony Powell, Wyndham Lewis and

---

[81] Black, 'Ivor', p. 33, Jonathan Black, 'Catalogue Raisonné', in Black and Ayres, *Abstraction*, p. 262.
[82] Jonathan Black, 'The Last Icon-Maker', in Black and Ayres, *Abstraction*, p. 126.
[83] Black, 'Last', p. 127; Black, 'Catalogue', p. 264.   [84] Black, 'Catalogue', p. 262.
[85] Black, 'Ivor', p. 33.   [86] Cited in Black, 'Ivor', p. 28.
[87] Jeremy Hooker, *Imagining*, p. 6.
[88] Glyn Jones, *The Dragon Has Two Tongues* (London, 1968), p. 39; Gwyn Jones, 'Anglo-Welsh Literature, 1934-46', *Transactions of the Hon. Society of Cymmrodorion* (1987), pp. 177–92.

the Powys brothers'.[89] However, Hooker points out that whilst 'the ability of the English language to mediate Welshness' has always been contested, 'the positive interaction of English and Welsh elements' in Anglo-Welsh writing should not be overlooked.[90] Following Hooker, this section focuses on 'the sense of imaginative possibility that different writers find in the "border" or "frontier" situation between their Welsh and English inheritances'.[91] It will briefly address the careers of authors John Owen, Charles Morgan, and the 'borderlands' novelist Margiad Evans before providing a case study of dramatist Richard Hughes who determinedly self-fashioned as Welsh from his teenage years onwards.

At the beginning of the Second World War, Ernest Rhys, editor of the Everyman's Library series, published his autobiography, *Wales England Wed*, which alluded to his mix of cultural identity. Rhys was born in Islington in 1859 to a Welsh father and an English mother, a fact which he alludes to in the opening lines of his poem, 'Wales England wed, so I was bred|'twas merry London gave me breath.' The stated intention of his autobiography was to pay tribute to 'my own people, Welsh and English'.[92] Throughout the text, he underscores the 'two very different strains' which were woven into the texture of his character and which led to a strong sense of himself as 'a dual personality'.[93] When he mentions his adult friendship with the Irish poet, W. B. Yeats, he ruminates again on his hybrid self: 'I was complicated in ways he was not. A Londoner born, as well as a Welshman in exile, I suffered from the mixed sympathies that are bound to affect a man of mixed race.'[94] Another writer who encapsulated this sense of two worlds was the novelist Frank Elias, known by his Welsh pen name as John Owen. During the Second World War, Owen, the descendant of a Welsh-building dynasty in Liverpool, produced novels such as *The Beauty of the Ships* (1940) and *Blitz Hero* (1942), which uniquely reflected the responses of the Welsh diaspora to the exigencies of war. Owen was born in Liverpool in 1878; his builder father, William Owen Elias, also born in Liverpool, was heavily involved with Welsh affairs.[95] A series of streets in Walton are named so that the consecutive initials spell out the names of Owen's grandfather and father, Owen and William, in a unique form of 'street memorial'.[96] In the 1930s, Owen was praised as a novelist of 'books with a local setting' who documented 'the familiar suburbs, restaurants, cafes, clubs' of Liverpool.[97] He drew on his own apprenticeship experience as the basis of his first novel, *The Cotton Broker* (1921), and it was noted how

---

[89] Jones, *Dragon*, p. 41. Interestingly, Jones includes Richard Llewellyn in his list of Anglo-Welsh writers.
[90] Hooker, *Imagining*, pp. 7, 13.   [91] Hooker, *Imagining*, p. 2.
[92] Ernest Rhys, *Wales England Wed* (London, 1940), p. 270.
[93] Rhys, *Wales*, pp. 3, 18.   [94] Rhys, *Wales*, p. 104.
[95] J. R. Jones, *The Welsh Builder on Merseyside: Annals and Lives* (Liverpool, 1946), p. 33.
[96] Jones, *Welsh Builder*, p. 31.
[97] Jones, *Welsh Builder*, p. 34; John Brophy, 'Writers of Merseyside. John Owen', *The Liverpolitan*, December 1932, p. 16.

throughout Owen's work, 'his material is drawn from his own experience and observation'.[98] Owen's fictional setting of Weftport—which features in his wartime novels—was clearly inspired by his home city of Liverpool: 'The Welsh population of Weftport comprises a tenth of the whole. A great part of the town was built by men who came from Carnarvonshire and Anglesey and Denbigh…. Has not Weftport been dubbed the capital of Wales?'[99] *The Beauty of the Ships* follows the life of shipping company owner, Gwyn Ravelston Jones, 'born in the great maritime city of Weftport' in 1905.[100] Throughout the novel Jones is positioned within a Welsh diasporic context. He inherits the company from John Ravelston Hughes, 'the natural gentleman that Welsh peasant stock so easily produces' who had 'put several young Welshmen into good places in Weftport because he'd known their fathers in Anglesey'.[101] In contrast, Jones's father, Ethelred, is depicted as profligate in his habits, with a family who could 'fill two pews' in the local chapel.[102] He tells the local Welsh minister, 'Well, Mr Williams Ellis, I have, I dare say, nine children or thereabouts. I have buried one or two—in Anfield mostly. Yes, though one was buried in Anglesey.'[103] Jones himself is described as a dark, medium 'Celt' with 'clear eyes inclined to show excitement'.[104] In the novel, he joins the Peace Pledge Union and develops 'strongly pacifist views', a trait for which he is apparently punished by drowning on a ship due to sabotage by an espionage ring.[105] There is evidence that Owen's work found a readership amongst the Liverpool Welsh: in 1940, Selwyn Lloyd's mother wrote, 'I have just read Frank Elias's new book "The Beauty of the Ships", not so sad as his usual one it is rather drawn out.'[106] Owen's next novel, *Blitz Hero*, also addressed the experiences of the 'Weftport Welsh', focusing on their evacuation to Llanfair-on-Sea during the Blitz.[107] The main character is Morrow Charlton-Davies, a timber merchant with a Welsh father and an English mother. After encouraging his Welsh wife, Ruby, to evacuate to their rented home at 'Meganwy' near Conwy Valley, Charlton-Davies becomes an ARP warden and spends most of the novel wrestling with notions of personal courage (or the lack thereof).[108] His wife observes his overexcitement following air raids and mediates, 'unlike an Englishman's, a Welsh-man's egotism is oftener naïve than vulgar, and resembles a child's more often than a self-seeking adult's, so she rejoiced that his derivation was from his Welsh rather than his English side.'[109] This sentence encapsulates the many subtle ways in which ideas of duality, diaspora and hybridity were threaded through Owen's wartime books.

[98] Brophy, 'Writers', pp. 16–17.
[99] John Owen, *The Beauty of Ships. A Story of the Present War* (London, 1940), p. 40.
[100] Owen, *Beauty*, p. 9.   [101] Owen, *Beauty*, pp. 10, 12.   [102] Owen, *Beauty*, p. 29.
[103] Owen, *Beauty*, p. 13.   [104] Owen, *Beauty*, p. 44.
[105] Owen, *Beauty*, p. 115. 'Stories of Ships and Seafarers', *The Scotsman*, 16 May 1940, p. 7.
[106] SELO 1/63, Letters to Selwyn Lloyd from his mother, Mar–Dec 1940; Letter, May 1940.
[107] John Owen, *Blitz Hero* (London, 1942), p. 30.
[108] Owen, *Blitz*, pp. 59–62.   [109] Owen, *Blitz*, p. 77.

Border Identities

Keith Robbins notes that border counties in nineteenth-century Britain, 'straddling the boundaries between England and Wales...frequently had more in common with each other that they had with their respective national hinterlands.'[110] In her 1933 travelogue, *Pilgrim from Paddington*, English Welsh writer Naomi Royde-Smith adopts an expansive view of this perspective, writing, 'Wales, so far as the northbound traveller is concerned, begins at Shrewsbury, at which point the Welsh language is heard, spoken freely, in trains. Should you wish to stay at The Raven, or to visit a young relative at school on the heights above the Severn, you will hear as much Welsh as English in the streets of the town, but you will not need to speak it yourself...Wales also begins at Chester, an unquestionably English city.'[111] M. Wynn Thomas depicts the borderlands surrounding the Wales–England border as 'regions of cultural exchange, limbo-lands, areas of negotiation' which 'generate distinctive forms of consciousness'. He cites Herefordshire's Margiad Evans, Abergavenney's Raymond Williams, and Nigel Heseltine of Powys as notable examples of 'border-country' writers.[112] Evans is one of the most celebrated of these border writers.

Evans was born Peggy Whistler in Uxbridge, Middlesex, in 1909 to English parents, insurance clerk Godfrey Whistler and Katherine Wood.[113] Aged eleven, Evans stayed for a year with her Aunt who had a farm at Benhall near Ross-on-Wye, a market town in Herefordshire, near the border with Wales. Ceridwen Lloyd-Morgan believes that this year 'later came to represent for Peggy a golden age, a lost world of innocent, irresponsible childhood' and provided 'a store of vivid impressions and memories which were to inform her writing throughout her life.'[114] Evans's family then moved to Bridstow, just west of Ross, where she was educated locally.[115] As Evans emerged onto the literary stage, she adopted a Welsh pen name, using the surname of her paternal grandmother, Ann Evans who was 'believed to be of Welsh extraction' and the Caernarfonshire equivalent of Peggy/Margaret for her first name.[116] As Barbara Prys-Williams notes, Evans's elected identity indicates a 'degree of attachment to a specifically Welsh persona.'[117] In 1930, Evans boarded at a farm, Coch-y-bûg, in Pontllyfni, Gwynedd, where she worked on the manuscript of her first novel and imbibed local culture.[118] Her

---

[110] Robbins, *Nineteenth-Century*, p. 11.   [111] Royde-Smith, *Pilgrim from Paddington*, p. 179.
[112] M. Wynn Thomas '"A Grand Harlequinade": The Border Writing of Nigel Heseltine', in *Welsh Writing in English. A Yearbook of Critical Essay*, 11 (2006–7), p. 51.
[113] Ceridwen Lloyd-Morgan, *Margiad Evans* (Bridgend, 1998), p. 7.
[114] Lloyd-Morgan, *Margiad*, p. 9.   [115] Lloyd-Morgan, *Margiad*, p. 10.
[116] Lloyd-Morgan, *Margiad*, pp. 7, 21.
[117] Barbara W. Prys-Williams, 'Variations in the Nature of the Perceived Self in Some Twentieth Century Welsh Autobiographical Writing in English' (PhD dissertation, Swansea University, 2002), p. 44.
[118] Lloyd-Morgan, *Margiad*, p. 21.

subsequent book, *Country Dance*, published in 1932, explores the themes of border identities, dualities, and national identifications. It tells the story of Ann Goodman, a woman of 'mixed blood', born on the English side of the border between Herefordshire and Monmouthshire, to an English father and a Welsh mother.[119] Ann frequently crosses the border between her English birthplace and her cousin's farm in Wales, where she works. Ann is also caught between two male suitors, one English, one Welsh, the marriage plot being used 'as a metaphor for the "union" of two nations'.[120] In a number of set pieces, Evans highlights the fluidity of identity construction in the borderlands. At a country dance, Ann resists Evan ap Evans's overtures in the Welsh language insisting, 'I am English' but he counters, 'Half. No, not that even, for you have lived in the mountains'. Through the voice of one of her main characters, Evans thus suggests that Welshness can be accessed in multiple ways.[121] The narrative moves 'between Wales and England, two contrasting languages, Welsh and English, church and chapel, father's people and mother's people', purposefully illuminating the 'ease' of crossing amongst the populations on both sides of the Welsh/English border.[122] Evans's following three novels, *The Wooden Doctor* (1933), *Turf or Stone* (1934), and *Creed* (1936) were all set in Ross and the surrounding district and drew on her own life experiences.[123] Lloyd-Morgan emphasizes the continual inspiration Evans found at 'the Border, with its strange mixture of Welsh and English people and place-names'.[124] Fundamentally, Evans was drawn to the notion of the border 'as a place where she could explore her duality'.[125]

Evans often communicated a clear attachment to Wales. Prys-Williams reports that Evans's personal journal records 'the intense lifting of the heart she regularly experienced on catching sight of the Welsh mountains spread out against the sky, often from the Hereford road as she returns home after an absence'. Indeed, during Evans's year at Benhall, 'the mountains of Wales became imprinted on her consciousness as part of the landscape of security and joy'.[126] At the same time, Clare Morgan notes how, in Evans's poetry, the borderland which 'abuts the ancient Celtic heritage' is something that she 'views longingly' but at a distance.[127]

---

[119] Evans, *Country*, p. 3.
[120] Diana Wallace, '"Two Nations at War Within it": Marriage as Metaphor in Margiad Evans's *Country Dance* (1932)', in *Rediscovering Margiad Evans. Marginality, Gender and Illness*, edited by Kirsti Bohata and Katie Gramich (Cardiff, 2013), p. 24.
[121] Evans, *Country*, p. 20.
[122] Lloyd-Morgan, *Margiad*, pp. 25–6; Lucy Thomas, '"Born to a Million Dismemberments": Female Hybridity in the Border Writing of Margiad Evans, Hilda Vaughan and Mary Webb', in *Rediscovering*, p. 50.
[123] Ceridwen Lloyd-Morgan, 'Williams, Peggy Eileen [*pseud*. Margiad Evans] (1909–1958)', *ODNB* (2010), https://doi-org.ezproxy.is.ed.ac.uk/10.1093/ref:odnb/96737.
[124] Lloyd-Morgan, *Margiad*, p. 32.   [125] Wallace, '"Two Nations"', p. 33.
[126] Prys-Williams, 'Variations', p. 45.
[127] Clare Morgan, 'Exile and the Kingdom: Margiad Evans and the Mythic Landscape of Wales', in *Welsh Writing in English. A Yearbook of Critical Essays*, Vol 6, edited by Tony Brown (Cardiff, 2000), p. 90.

For example, in her poem, 'To the Mountains', Evans writes of 'Mountains, before whose form and cast|Of exquisite severity, all nearness blurs|To insignificance unnoticed.'[128] It is significant that Evans includes 'scraps of traditional Welsh verses and songs' and common Welsh phrases in her 1932 novel. Lloyd-Morgan notes that Evans sent these extracts to a Welsh professor, Ifor Williams, for checking before submitting her manuscript.[129] Thus, at the same time as she is positioning herself as an educator of 'an implied English reader about the history and language of this "other" country',[130] Evans felt insecure in terms of her authoritativeness on Welsh matters. Like others who followed, such as Richard Llewellyn and Anthony Powell, Evans felt the need to have her work checked by Welsh acquaintances for authenticity. Essentially, although she was 'glad of my drop of Welsh blood', Evans saw herself as a border writer, observing daily life mainly from the English perspective.[131] In a letter to the Welsh scholar Gwyn Jones, in 1946, she wrote:

> I'm *not* Welsh. I never posed as Welsh and it rather annoys me when R[obert] H[erring] advertises me among the Welsh short stories because *I am the border*—a very different thing. The English side of the border too...people who judge my 'characters' as Welsh can't understand much, with the exception of *Country Dance* of course. Most of them are stolid English, flavoured with Celtic ancestry and named from a very far past.[132]

Morgan firmly places Evans within the English Neo-Romantic movement of the 1930–50 period, arguing that Evans's themes of 'childhood, vision, man-and-nature' are shared with contemporaneous English artists such as John Piper, John Craxton, and W. A. Poucher who also visited and drew inspiration from Wales.[133] Indeed, during the Second World War, they set out to map 'an "other" Britain', drawing on ideas of ' "Celtic" supremacy' and the desirability of Wales.[134] In works such as *Country Dance*, Morgan argues, Evans shows a similar desire, as an outsider, 'to appropriate the rural, and particularly the Celtic, past in terms of the anxieties of the present'.[135] For Evans, Wales represents cultural rootedness and belonging: she is 'forever attempting to...appropriate an "otherness" whose liminal condition at once mirrors her own but speaks of that very indigenous quality to which the desire to belong inevitably refers.'[136] It is interesting to note that Evans encouraged her sister Nancy to adopt the name Sian Evans and become a writer, reflecting her desire to reinvent her family 'as a Welsh equivalent of the

---

[128] Margiad Evans, *Poems From Obscurity* (London, 1947), p. 40.
[129] Lloyd-Morgan, *Margiad*, p. 23.   [130] Wallace, ' "Two Nations" ', p. 29.
[131] Cited in Lloyd-Morgan, *Margiad*, p. 32.
[132] Cited in Lloyd-Morgan, 'Archivist's Tale', p. 14.   [133] Morgan, 'Exile', pp. 90–6.
[134] Morgan, 'Exile', pp. 91, 92, 117.   [135] Morgan, 'Exile', pp. 98, 113.
[136] Morgan, 'Exile', p. 113.

Brontes'.[137] Prys-Williams also suggests that Evans's creative attempt to align with Welshness possibly 'came from an area of vulnerability', pointing out that her father's alcoholism 'totally overshadowed her young life'.[138] Ultimately, Evans's vision of Wales was always refracted through an English lens.

Other prominent authors of the interwar period accessed Welshness in a myriad of imaginative ways. Charles Morgan, author of the acclaimed 1929 novel, *Portrait in a Mirror*, was born in Bromley in 1894 of English and Welsh heritage. Morgan had perhaps a more oblique relationship with his sense of Welshness than the writers discussed above. His English-born father had married his mother in Australia, both of Morgan's grandfathers having emigrated there from Pembrokeshire.[139] A 1933 profile, however, noted that Morgan was 'proud to boast Welsh blood on both sides'.[140] This duality is reflected in his 1958 *Times* obituary which commemorated Morgan as an 'English novelist',[141] whilst in his lifetime, the Welsh journalist Glyn Roberts described him as 'young and Welsh'.[142] In a 1967 biography, Welsh author Eiluned Lewis notes that, as Morgan's upbringing was English, he referred to himself as '"a Celt trained down"'.[143] However, throughout the text, Lewis makes repeated references to Morgan's connection with Wales; she argues that because Welsh people tend to be 'rooted in their own land', this meant that, all his life, Morgan 'knew the handicap of rootlessness'. He believed that his father's death in 1941 had cut him off from both his childhood and his 'origins'.[144] Marriage had, however, offered a way for Morgan to reconnect with his roots. Serving as a naval officer during the First World War, Morgan subsequently met his wife, the Welsh novelist Hilda Vaughan in 1922. Adding fresh sediment to Morgan's seam of Welshness, Lewis notes that Vaughan was 'the daughter of Hugh Vaughan Vaughan of Builth, Breconshire, of Welsh blood sprung from the borders of Brecon and Radnor' and was possibly descended from Henry Vaughan, the seventeenth century 'Silurist'.[145] Whilst many of Morgan's letters, covering the period 1915–58, contain explanations of English national characteristics, from his own vantage point as an English writer, Morgan still couldn't resist the appeal of Welshness.[146] In a 1936 lecture to Sorbonne students, he pronounced '*J'ai du sang celte moi-même* (I have Celtic blood myself)'[147] and in a review of a book on his wife's putative ancestor, Henry Vaughan, he asserted, 'though Welsh by blood, I am English by upbringing.... But I know that Vaughan's

---

[137] Prys-Williams, 'Variations', pp. 47–8. [138] Prys-Williams, 'Variations', p. 48.
[139] Eiluned Lewis, ed., *Selected Letters of Charles Morgan* (London, 1967), pp. 2–3.
[140] Glyn Roberts, 'Charles Morgan. Novelist and Critic', 14.11.33, http://cynonculture.co.uk/wordpress/london-welsh/charles-morgan-1894-1958/, accessed 30 March 2022.
[141] 'Mr Charles Morgan', *The Times*, 7 February 1958, p. 11. [142] Roberts, *I Take*, p. 146.
[143] Lewis, *Selected*, p. 1. [144] Lewis, *Selected*, p. 3. [145] Lewis, *Selected*, p. 17.
[146] Lewis, *Selected*, pp. 137, 179, 180. A set of wartime essays by Morgan also contains many ruminations on 'we English'. See Charles Morgan, *Reflections in a Mirror* (London, 1944).
[147] Charles Morgan, 'Creative Imagination', in *The Queen's Book of the Red Cross* (London, 1939), p. 33.

conception of the whole universe being indissolubly interconnected and of the perpetual "commerce" between earth and heaven is familiar to the Welsh mind.'[148] However, as Mary Auronwy James acknowledges, Morgan's 'closest connections with Wales came through his wife'.[149] Writing in 1933, Glyn Roberts points out that Morgan 'has never lived in Wales, and has not as much first-hand knowledge of it as he would like. He gets a great deal of second-hand knowledge of it, however, from his wife, Hilda Vaughan, herself a writer of power and distinction.'[150] For Morgan, an English novelist living in London, marriage to Vaughan added a patina of credibility to his own occasional assertions of a specifically Welsh sensibility.

Richard Hughes

The English-born writer Richard Hughes, best known for his bestselling first novel, *A High Wind in Jamaica* (1929), wrote about Wales consistently throughout his lifetime and was feted as a 'modern Welsh author' by his contemporaries.[151] From an early age, Hughes demonstrated a willed desire to be Welsh which he managed to enact in his own lifetime; when he published a personal anthology in 1931 at the height of his fame, the back piece referred to 'the powerful and disturbing pen of this young Welshman'.[152] In reality, Hughes was born in 'a substantial family house' in Caterham on 19 April 1900 into 'middle-class Edwardian prosperity'; his civil servant father, Arthur Hughes, worked in the Public Record Office.[153] Like other case studies examined in this book, Hughes always felt himself to be an 'outsider' in his childhood environment and turned to Wales for solace.[154] In a 1931 memoir, Hughes states that, after his first visit to Barmouth, North Wales in 1911, 'I determined then and there to live in Wales as soon as I was able'.[155] Whilst studying at Charterhouse, Hughes befriended Charles Graves, younger brother of Robert Graves. In November 1918, Graves invited Hughes to the family's holiday home, Erinfa in Harlech, to which a delighted Hughes replied:

---

[148] Lewis, *Selected*, p. 30.
[149] M. A. James, Morgan, Charles Langbridge, *Dictionary of Welsh Biography* (2001), https://biography.wales/article/s2-MORG-LAN-1894, accessed 30 March 2022.
[150] Glyn Roberts, 'Charles Morgan. Novelist and Critic', 14 November 1933, http://cynonculture.co.uk/wordpress/london-welsh/charles-morgan-1894–1958/, accessed 30 March 2022.
[151] Richard Poole, *Fiction as Truth. Selected Literary Writings by Richard Hughes* (Bridgend, 1983), p. 10; 'Bibliographies of Modern Welsh Authors. No. 3 Richard (Arthur Warren) Hughes', *Wales*, no. 4, March 1938, p. 156.
[152] Richard Hughes, *An Omnibus* (New York, 1931).
[153] Richard Perceval Graves, *Richard Hughes* (London, 1994), p. 2.
[154] Graves, *Richard*, p. 12.
[155] Richard Hughes, 'Autobiographical Introduction', in *Hughes. Omnibus*, p. xvii; Graves, *Richard*, p. 12.

'This damned flat country is stifling me. Oh to be back among the hills!'[156] The latter's recollection, in 1951, of how he connected Hughes both with his family at Erinfa and the wider Harlech landscape hints at a slight bemusement at the extent to which Hughes went on to transform himself into 'being' a Welshman:

> Years previously Hughes had told me of his earnest desire to go to Wales, instead of spending his holidays with his widowed mother at Caterham. Mother invited him at my suggestion and he revelled in the Harlech atmosphere, recreating in his mind the Welsh ancestry which his name suggested and which his request to be called Diccon, instead of Dick or Richard, accentuated.... Later on, he was to write *A High Wind in Jamaica* and, after marriage, to grow a beard and buy himself an old Welsh castle.[157]

In 1919, after his first term at Oxford, Hughes spent most of the Easter vacation in Harlech, including time with Robert Graves and his wife Nancy Nicholson at the latter's holiday home, Llys Bach.[158] Charles records how Hughes was 'a tremendous fan of Robert's works and of Robert himself' and began spending as much time as possible in Robert's company; the younger man admired the poet as both 'an exemplar of the "modern" literary life' and 'of what he believed to be his own ancestral past'.[159] At this time, Charles's sister Rosaleen also gave Hughes 'elementary' Welsh lessons.[160] Inspired by the Graves family, Hughes decided to sublet Ysgol Fach, a tiny cottage in the Maes-y-neuadd grounds.[161] In Hughes's recollection:

> This little stone Cromwellian hovel had only one room; there were large holes in the slate roof; and a spring, rising under the fireplace, ran across the stone floor and out of the front door; but I mended the roof and drained the spring, and decorated the house and furnished it at the total cost of the four pounds I then had in the Savings Bank. There I firmly established myself, alone. I taught myself to cook, and refused ever again to regard as my home the house in England where I had been brought up.[162]

Hughes links finding this space to the beginning of his creative productivity.[163] He also refers to his ancestral connection and the insignificance of his family's 'little absence of three hundred years' from Wales, writing:

---

[156] Graves, *Richard*, pp. 29–30.
[157] Charles Graves, *The Bad Old Days* (London, 1951), pp. 39–40.
[158] For more on Robert Graves, see Chapter 8 'Affinity Welsh'.
[159] Graves, *Bad,* p. 40; Graves, *Richard*, pp. 34–6.   [160] Graves, *Richard*, p. 35.
[161] Stephens, 'Hughes'.   [162] Hughes, 'Autobiographical', p. xvii.
[163] Hughes, 'Autobiographical', p. xviii.

It is almost impossible to describe the hold which this cottage, and this whole Welsh countryside...immediately established over me. It was not only the beauty of the mountains and the sea and my little ancient shell of stone and blackened oak, or the friendship of Robert Graves (who had been brought up in the neighbourhood) and his family.... The feeling I had that I was in the right place—in other words, that I was at home—was so strong that it was almost magical.[164]

The Graves family remained important in soldering his link to Wales; on New Year's Day, 1923, Hughes called on the father, Alfred Perceval Graves, who had produced pageants at Harlech Castle, to discuss his life plans.[165] Another pivotal contact for Hughes, and part of the same English Welsh social network, was Clough Williams-Ellis. When Hughes was looking for a new home he met Williams-Ellis's wife, Amabel, on a train from London to Penryndeudraeth. The couple suggested he live at Garreg Fawr, a deserted cottage within a few minutes' walk of their home, Plas Brondanw.[166] From here, with playwright A. O. Roberts, Hughes formed the Portmadoc Players in 1924 with the intention of selecting the best Welsh dramatic talent from a network of district companies across Wales.[167] Significantly, even at this point of immersion in Welsh cultural life, Hughes sensed his own lack of legitimacy. He resigned from his share in the management of the company after it performed at the Lyric Theatre, Hammersmith, commenting: 'I did not feel it was fitting...that a mongrel such as myself should remain at their head. It was a post which only a pure Welshman ought to fill.'[168]

Hughes's prolific dramatic output, however, confidently straddled both the Welsh and English worlds he inhabited. His first play, *The Sisters' Tragedy*, opened at the Little Theatre, London in May 1922 and was critically acclaimed.[169] The main characters were characterized by Hughes as being 'bitten with the prevalent Welsh piety of the neighbourhood'.[170] His 1926 short story, 'The Stranger', was set in the village of Cylfant and employed the characters 'Mrs Grocery-Jones', 'Mrs Boot-Jones', and Mr Williams the rector.[171] Another short story from the same era, 'Poor Man's Inn', was set in Clun Forest on the Welsh borderlands.[172] A story about a simpleton, eponymously titled 'Llwyd', informed the reader that

---

[164] Hughes, 'Autobiographical', pp. xvii–xviii.
[165] Graves, *Richard*, pp. 94–5.   [166] Graves, *Richard*, pp. 68–70.
[167] Richard Hughes, 'The Theatre in Wales', *Manchester Guardian*, 18 January 1933, p. 9. Hughes conceded that 'the idea did not spread to other districts as we had hoped it would'.
[168] Richard Hughes, 'The Relation of Nationalism to Literature', *Transactions of the Hon Society of Cymmrodorion* (1930–31), pp. 123–4.
[169] Stephens, 'Hughes'.   [170] Richard Hughes, *The Sisters' Tragedy* in *Hughes. Omnibus*, p. 61.
[171] Richard Hughes, 'The Stranger', in *A Moment in Time*, edited by Richard Hughes (London, 1926), pp. 57–70.
[172] Richard Hughes, 'Poor Man's Inn', in *Moment*, edited by Hughes, pp. 85–103.

'Llwyd was born in Cwm-y-Moch, in a small grey house with thick walls.'[173] However, other stories published in 1926, 'Leaves' and 'Martha' were both set in London.[174] In Hughes's 1924 play, *The Man Born to be Hanged,* one of the characters is Davey, a twenty-year-old youth who 'talks in a nondescript accent half Welsh, half Manchester', explicitly acknowledging the existence of dual identity.[175] In 1924 Hughes scripted 'Danger', the first play to be broadcast by radio, an experimental piece 'for effect by sound only'.[176] The characters, Jack, Mary, and Mr Bax, are all 'English visitors' trapped in a Welsh coal mine and fearing that they are about to die. Also audible are 'Voices: A party of Welsh miners who say a few words and are heard singing off'.[177] In one scene where Mary asks if there has been an accident the older Mr Bax (who dies at the end) responds:

> Goodness knows! I'd expect anything of a country like Wales! They've got a climate like the Flood and a language like the Tower of Babel, and then they go and lure us into the bowels of the earth and turn the lights off! Wretched, incompetent—their houses are full of cockroaches—Ugh![178]

When the voices off are heard 'singing: "Ae hyd y Nos"' the following exchange occurs:

BAX. Gad! those chaps have courage.
JACK. You're finding some good in the Welsh, then, after all?[179]

In Hughes's work, we can sense a determination to transmit the importance of Wales and the Welsh people to English audiences. In these writings, Hughes often positions himself as an expert on Welsh traditions and language. For example, in his short story, 'Cornelius Katie', he writes: 'There are fewer gypsies, probably, in North Wales than in any other part of Great Britain, for two reasons: it is a hard, poor country... there are not many rich spots.'[180] And: 'They called her Gwennol, which in Welsh means a swallow.'[181] As a dialogist, he also included short phrases or words in Welsh to underline his insider knowledge: ' "Diawl, you'll be waking dad!" '[182] In a fascinating expression of this, his 1924 play, *A Comedy of Good and Evil,* first performed at the Royal Court Theatre, London, contains detailed 'instructions' on pronunciation to the actors:

---

[173] 'Llwyd', in *Hughes. Omnibus,* p. 329.
[174] Richard Hughes, 'Leaves', in *Moment,* edited by Hughes, pp. 160–4; Richard Hughes, 'Martha', in *Moment,* edited by Hughes, pp. 165–92.
[175] Richard Hughes, *The Sisters' Tragedy. And Three Other Plays* (London, 1924), p. 33.
[176] 'Danger', in *Hughes. Omnibus,* p. 205.   [177] 'Danger', p. 206.   [178] 'Danger', p. 209.
[179] 'Danger', p. 212.   [180] 'Cornelius Katie', in *Hughes. Omnibus,* p. 197.
[181] 'Cornelius Katie', p. 200.   [182] 'Cornelius Katie', p. 199.

The accent is that of the South Snowdon district. The dialect is not intended for a translation of Welsh idiom, but for the English spoken, when occasion demands, by Welsh-speaking country people.[183]

In the published script, Hughes provides phonetic pronunciations and translations at the foot of the page:

MINNIE. *Duw anwyl, what's that? Pwy sydd 'na? Oooo! Tyd yma, the poor darling!
*Pronunciation: Dew anwyl (Good gracious!) Poo-y-sithna? (Who is there?) Tid Uma (Come here).[184]

Charles Graves notes that in the play, Hughes 'introduced all kinds of local Harlech characters like Evan Flat Fish, Mrs "Face" Jones, Mr Humphrey "Station."'[185] Hughes's detailed descriptions of his characters do, however, stray into national stereotyping, employing tropes of the Welsh as 'dirty', and fixating on Welsh idioms. The character Owain Flatfish is disreputable and 'incredibly dirty'. The Rev. John Williams is described as having a Welsh accent which 'is very noticeable, but attractive' and continues, 'On no account must the audience be allowed to laugh at him.' A blue-eyed, golden-haired character called Gladys has an 'unimpeachable' English accent whilst Timothy Ysgairnolwen, 'a young Saxonate' has a noticeable accent 'especially when excited'.[186] Of this rather tortuous performance of knowledge, Hughes's daughter Penelope, born in London in 1934, surmises:

Sometimes I felt that Diccon was a snob. When my parents took me to see a revival of his three-act play *A Comedy of Good and Evil*, at the Arts Theatre, a play set in a Welsh rectory kitchen, I had the uneasy feeling that stage-Welshmen such as Owain Flatfish could never appear on any stage in Wales itself, they were too artificial.[187]

Alyce Von Rothkirch notes that Welsh audience members were 'disappointed' when they saw the play as it was 'symbolic rather than realistic'. She cites the *Western Mail*'s observation, 'if the Welsh national theatre movement is to succeed, there must be something more essentially Welsh, both in the players and in the play.'[188] The Welsh dramatist, J. O. Francis, pinpointed Hughes's lack of authority in his review, writing that '"Mr Hughes would do well to...acquire a

---

[183] 'A Comedy of Good and Evil', in *Hughes. Omnibus*, p. 337.
[184] 'A Comedy of Good and Evil', p. 354.   [185] Graves, *Bad*, p. 40.
[186] 'A Comedy of Good and Evil', pp. 338–9.
[187] Penelope Hughes, *Richard Hughes. Author, Father* (Gloucester, 1984), pp. 111–12.
[188] Alyce Von Rothkirch, *J. O. Francis, Realist Drama and Ethics* (Cardiff, 2014), p. 87.

minimum of Welsh speech without which he will not make the race yield up the heart of its mystery".[189] In the face of this backlash, Hughes blamed the English cast, stating, 'Few actors could be found who had any knowledge of the Welsh accent.... As a result, a play which I feel sure would have appeared simple enough and clear enough if it had been performed by Welshmen for Welshmen, seemed wild and incomprehensible when performed by Englishmen for Englishmen.'[190] This critical response to the play goes to the heart of Hughes's own identity crisis. Hughes was clearly sensitive to accusations of inauthenticity and aware of his own lack of legitimacy. In an address to the Cymmrodorion Section of the National Eisteddfod at Bangor in 1931, he said of *A Comedy of Good and Evil*: 'although what little reputation I have as a Welsh dramatist is almost entirely founded upon that play, it has never, since I wrote it, received a single performance within the borders of Wales.'[191] In his speech on the relationship between 'the Welsh writer of today and his sense of nationality', Hughes opened with the question: 'Am I, for humble instance, a Welsh writer myself?'[192] He reflected:

> When I first came to live in Wales towards the close of my school-days, living in a little one-roomed cottage at Talsarnau, I came there as a stranger. For though I am Welsh by blood, and Welsh by sympathy, and Welsh now by domicile, I am not Welsh by birth or education: and it is therefore only with the greatest diffidence... that I can pretend to being a Welsh author at all.[193]

At the close of his speech Hughes adopts an almost abject position, concluding: 'I offer you an apology: that I, who have no claim to call myself a scholar, and so poor a claim even to call myself a Welshman, should have had the temerity to occupy the time of so learned a Welsh Society.'[194] This speech highlights the situational nature of Hughes's claim to 'being' Welsh—with this speech laced with words which suggest his own sense of artifice. In a 1933 profile by Glyn Roberts, Hughes was assumed to be Welsh even when identified as living in London. Roberts refers to a 'Welshman with an equally high reputation among the discriminating is Richard Hughes, the tall, bearded man with the dreamer's face and the adventurer's physique. He has an immense telescope in his London house, with which he gazes at the stars and generally amuses himself.'[195] Thus, even though Hughes was publicly endorsed as Welsh by journalists, he could still feel discomfited when confronted with Welsh audiences. This ties in with the social awkwardness of the English Welsh poets Edward Thomas and David Jones, when they also encountered 'real' Welsh people in Wales.

---

[189] Cited in Von Rothkirch, *J. O. Francis*, p. 8.   [190] Hughes, 'Relation', p. 125.
[191] Hughes, 'Relation', p. 126.   [192] Hughes, 'Relation', p. 107.
[193] Hughes, 'Relation', p. 120.   [194] Hughes, 'Relation', pp. 127–8.
[195] Roberts, *I Take*, pp. 227–8.

In 1934, following the advice of Williams-Ellis, Hughes took out a long-term lease on a house attached to Laugharne Castle in Carmarthenshire and moved there with his wife Frances.[196] All of his children were born in London, although his daughter Penelope remarks that, as siblings, they were 'very conscious' of their Welshness.[197] However, by the late 1940s, Penelope was beginning to question her own sense of identity. She recalls how when 'Granny Hughes' died in London:

> Her ashes were brought back to be buried in North Wales. There was a Memorial Service with prayers read beside the grave in the rain. The whole scene seemed unreal to me, or rather, hyper-real, with the intensity of a dream. Angrily I realised that I was not actually Welsh, and neither was my grandmother, for all her long love-affair with Wales.[198]

From 1940 to 1945, Hughes served as a civilian in the Admiralty, living in Bath and Chelsea, but after the war, he moved to Môr Edrin, Talsarnau. He died thirty years later and was buried in the nearby churchyard.[199] In a critical reflection on her father's own place within Wales, Penelope acknowledges that although her father cared deeply about the landscape of Wales, 'he couldn't get accepted as a Welshman'. She concludes:

> Diccon was uneasy with other Welsh, and hid behind his personality as a 'Man of Letters.' I realised that from his marriage onwards he had always lived on the fringe of Wales. For Laugharne was an odd exotic place...almost a separate Principality.... Mor Edrin was in some ways an outpost of 'Clough country' and that wasn't Wales either.[200]

Dramatic Endeavours

At the 1902 National Eisteddfod, Lloyd George had encouraged the development of a national Welsh drama movement. The key figure who responded to this call in the following decades was landowner, writer, and arts benefactor Lord Howard de Walden, alongside a few influential figures such as Owen Rhoscomyl, D. T. Davies, and J. Eddie Parry.[201] Described by his grandson as 'an Englishman turned Welshman', Thomas Evelyn Ellis Scott succeeded to his title in 1899 at the age of nineteen.[202] According to his granddaughter, de Walden 'made up for an

---

[196] Graves, *Richard*, p. 226. [197] Hughes, *Richard*, p. 107.
[198] Hughes, *Richard*, p. 109. [199] Stephens, 'Hughes'.
[200] Hughes, *Richard*, p. 112. [201] Von Rothkirch, *J. O. Francis*, p. 46.
[202] Seymour, *My Grandfather*; Margherita Lady Howard de Walden, *Pages From My Life* (London, 1965), p. 41, fn.1.

unglamorous appearance by living like a Renaissance prince'.[203] He became a generous benefactor and patron of the arts in Wales, supporting pageants, Eisteddfodau, and ultimately supporting the founding of the Welsh National Theatre. His son records how, in 1911, de Walden became 'infatuated' with Chirk Castle, 'a fourteenth-century fortress in the Marches, the borderlands that divide England from Wales'.[204] As a wealthy landowner, fascinated in heraldry, he made 'a snap decision' and took out a twenty-year lease.[205] In her 1965 memoir, de Walden's wife, Margherita, plugs into an elite English attraction to the notion of a Welsh historical pedigree, establishing a linear link for her husband:

> Castell y Waun (Chirk) which Tommy made his home at the time of our marriage was built by Edward I on the site of an old fortress called Castell Crogan.... Roger Mortimer built Chirk Castle as we know it... and more or less completed it in 1310... [his grandson] sold the place to Richard Fitzalan, Earl of Arundel, and after three generations it passed to Thomas Mowbray, Duke of Norfolk. So Tommy felt pleased that his own ancestors had owned and lived at Chirk in his so dearly loved fourteenth century.[206]

Margherita pinpoints their extended residence at Chirk as a time when de Walden 'first learnt the language and then did a great deal for the music and theatre in Wales'.[207] She also paints a clear picture of her husband's esoteric absorption into his Welsh surroundings and his desire for genealogical authenticity:

> His after-dinner conversations were on history mostly, or horses or armour or ancestors.... His stories of the early Welsh or talks about the Greeks or mythologies were most enjoyable but at times he would get stuck on the breeding of his race horses or on his own ancestry. Then one just did not listen for it could be tedious.... Kicking the logs until the sparks turned to flames, Tommy might begin to wander about among his Welsh Ellis forebears. He believed they came from near Wrexham.[208]

When the First World War broke out in 1914, de Walden left with his regiment, the 2nd County of London Yeomanry Westminster Dragoons, for Egypt, was involved in the Gallipoli campaign of 1915, and, in November 1916, became Second-in-Command of the 9th Battalion of the RWF in France. His wife recalls that de Walden was 'very happy' with his leadership position in the RWF: 'He

---

[203] Miranda Seymour, *In My Father's House* (London, 2008), p. 110.
[204] Lord Howard de Walden, *Earls Have Peacocks. The Memoirs of Lord Howard de Walden* (London, 1992), p. 31; Seymour, *In My*, p. 110.
[205] de Walden, *Pages*, pp. 89–90.   [206] de Walden, *Pages*, p. 101.
[207] de Walden, *Pages*, p. 102.   [208] de Walden, *Pages*, pp. 98–9.

liked being with a Welsh Regiment and was able to practice Welsh. He asked for books and band music, for his little Welsh dictionary and for a photograph of the children.'[209] In a nod to his antiquarian obsessions, de Walden equipped his regiment with Welsh medieval 'machette' swords from his own collection: 'The very same shape as had been in use in the Battle of Crecy by the Welsh.'[210] However, de Walden returned from the war a changed man, writing in 1921 that he was a man 'living out a life that he finds infinitely wearisome'.[211] In the interwar era he became increasingly absorbed in Welsh folklore and pageantry. Before the war, de Walden had started sponsoring a £100 prize for the best play in English or Welsh, which dealt with 'Welsh life'.[212] In 1915, when The London Welsh Musical and Dramatic Union was formed, the Chair, W. A. Bayley, noted 'the effort which Lord Howard de Walden had made to stimulate interest in the Drama among Welsh people' and suggested that he be made president of the society on his return from 'doing his duty for his country'.[213] In the post-war era, de Walden developed a 'Touring Welsh National Repertory Theatre', offering prizes for 'the best plays both in Welsh and in English by Welshmen'.[214] In addition, in 1920, de Walden organized a historical pageant at Harlech Castle where his wife dressed as Queen Margaret of Anjou, he as the Earl of Plymouth, and their twins as their pages.[215] Alfred Graves recalls producing this event in collaboration with Ernest Rhys: the pageant was 'handsomely supported' by the de Waldens, 'who took part in it and helped with dresses and armour, even bringing their own falcons for a medieval scene'.[216]

In reflecting upon her husband's support for the arts in Wales, Lady de Walden exudes an air of *noblesse oblige*, often adopting a patronizing tone and constructing the Welsh people as grateful recipients of their largesse. For example:

> When the miners were out of work in that dreadful black despairing time Tommy subsidised the whole of Beecham's orchestra and sent them touring round the distressed areas of South Wales. Those people had never heard an orchestra, and they absolutely loved it.[217]

Similarly, when Margerhita gave an amateur performance at the Queens Hall, London in 1923, she included 'Dafydd y garreg wen' which 'gave great pleasure to the Welsh who were listening in on their radios'.[218]

In 1933, de Walden joined forces with Richard Hughes in setting up a 'new venture', the Welsh National Theatre. This would consist of a body of professional actors, acting as 'a window through which Wales can look on the rest of

---

[209] de Walden, *Pages*, pp. 138, 144.　[210] de Walden, *Pages*, pp. 113–14.
[211] de Walden, *Earls*, p. 36.　[212] Von Rothkirch, *J. O. Francis*, p. 30.
[213] 'Welsh Dramatic Art', *Llangollen Advertiser*, 12 March 1915, p. 6.
[214] De Walden, *Pages*, p. 149.　[215] De Walden, *Pages*, p. 152.
[216] Graves, *To Return*, p. 339.　[217] De Walden, *Pages*, p. 151.
[218] De Walden, *Pages*, pp. 72–3.

civilization and the rest of the world can look on Wales'. When Hughes made a public call for donations, he said of de Walden: 'it is hardly fair that he should be expected to be the sole milch-cow for all Welsh theatrical endeavour.'[219] De Walden became chair of the organizing committee and committee meetings were held at his Belgrave Square address.[220] Alyce von Rothkirch points out that as Welsh dramatists were mostly amateurs, they found that they could not compete with non-Welsh professional playwrights; by 1936, de Walden sensed that the movement had stalled.[221] However, he remained involved with the Welsh National Theatre at Plas Newydd, Llangollen in the run-up to the Second World War. According to his son, de Walden's life during the Second World War was 'sad and lonely' confined to involvement with the local Home Guard.[222] Once his tenancy at Chirk expired, he moved to Ayrshire and died in London shortly afterwards.[223] This brought to an end one Englishman's determination to project a certain version of Welshness from his rented castle in Chirk. Ultimately, despite his best endeavours, de Walden only 'inhabited' this Welsh space for a time-limited period.

Conclusion

By illuminating the ability of those with dual identifications to imaginatively travel backwards and forwards across the borders between Wales and England, this chapter demonstrates how English writers, painters, and dramatists with a sense of personal commitment to Wales, often found themselves at the heart of cultural representations of Welshness in the first half of the twentieth century. Formal renditions and representations of Welsh national identity, which accommodated English artists 'of Welsh extraction', also underscore the multiplicity of constructions of Welshness—the different 'nations of Wales'—functioning in the late nineteenth and early twentieth centuries.[224] This chapter highlights a willingness on the part of Welsh cultural institutions to embrace English Welsh artists which persisted throughout the twentieth century; what Lord terms 'the ambiguities of allegiance embedded in Welsh consciousness'.[225] There was also a level of reciprocity where the Welsh artist Augustus John, based in England, inspired clusters of English Welsh mixing both within his own family and the wider artistic circle which he dominated. From the English side of the border, authors variously chose to use their diasporic, ancestral, or borderland links with Wales in either their writing or the construction of their authorial identities. Some, like Hughes and the architect Williams-Ellis, transplanted themselves partially to Wales yet still remained vulnerable to discourses of inauthenticity.

---

[219] Hughes, 'Theatre', p. 9.   [220] Graves, *Richard*, pp. 221–2, 230.
[221] Von Rothkirch, *J. O. Francis*, p. 54.   [222] de Walden, *Earls*, p. 43.
[223] Seymour, *In My*, p. 137.   [224] See Wynn Thomas, *Nations*, p. 36.
[225] Lord, *Imaging*, p. 354.

8
Constructing Wales as a Site of Solace

In Christmas 1939, the BBC Home Service broadcast 'They, Too, Loved Wales', a programme which highlighted 'how certain great English writers of the early nineteenth century discovered the beauty of Wales and revealed it in their work'.[1] The chosen topic reflects what Lord refers to as the 'fashion for Welsh landscape which resulted in setting mountain scenery at the centre of English ideas about Wales'.[2] Morgan notes how English poets, Coleridge and Wordsworth, went on walking tours of North Wales at the time of the Napoleonic Wars and were part of a wider travel writing movement which informed a 'narrative of Wales as an English construct'.[3] George Henry Borrow was one of the most noted Victorian 'observers' of Wales, producing *Wild Wales: The People, Language and Scenery* (1862). Jodie Matthews points out that Borrow 'distinctively constructs an exotic, authentic, noble and eccentric Welshness to match his own self-image'.[4] In the text, Borrow takes pride in his ability to speak Welsh, 'a manifestation of his desire to be *of* a people'.[5] Yet whilst the text is littered with 'the possibilities for an identity shaped by affiliation', the Welsh people he encounters are largely constructed as 'a British other'.[6] This dynamic was replicated by English Neo-Romantics of the 1940s, whose involvement in initiatives such as the wartime 'Recording Britain' project across England and Wales mapped out competing representations of Britishness and tended to interpret Wales as an exotic Celtic 'other'.[7]

This chapter addresses the experiences of those whose sense of affiliation with Wales meant that they indulged in some form of othering of the Welsh nation, whilst also constructing it as a site of solace. Within twentieth-century lifewriting, Wales often appears as a site of refuge, healing, or personal rejuvenation both for members of the Welsh diaspora and for those who displayed an 'affinity' for Wales. Selwyn Lloyd's housemaster at Fettes said of Lloyd George, 'He goes to Wales to recoup from his dissipations, as King Edward used to go to Carlsbad [sic]'.[8] For the poet, Edward Thomas, Wales became a place to which he withdrew in times of crisis whilst for the former MP, Eliot Crawshay-Williams, Wales was

---
[1] 'Genome', BBC Home Service, 14 December 1939.   [2] Lord, *Imaging*, pp. 10–11.
[3] Morgan 'Exile', p. 117, fn. 20, p. 116, fn. 13.
[4] Jodie Matthews, 'Borrowing Welshness: Wild Wales, Affiliation and Identity', *North American Journal of Welsh Studies*, 6, 1 (2011), p. 55.
[5] Matthews, 'Borrowing', p. 56.   [6] Matthews, 'Borrowing', pp. 54, 61.
[7] Morgan, 'Exile', pp. 89–96.
[8] SELO 1/14, Letters to Lloyd from his housemaster at Fettes, K. P. Wilson, 1922–23; Letter, September 1922.

somewhere to disappear in the summer months.[9] This chapter also addresses the emotional investment in Wales as a site of healing by English artists and servicemen. It discusses the Royal Welch Fusiliers poet, Robert Graves, who dreamed of living, with his friend Siegfried Sassoon, in a cottage in Harlech after the First World War, viewing this as a restorative site where they could recover from their combat experiences. It also examines the experiences of Royal Engineer, Alex Cordell, whose military convalescence in Harlech during the Second World War served to reignite an authorial connection with his ancestral homeland, informing his postwar literary output which focused on Welsh history. For these case studies, Wales is constructed as a place where mental and physical wounds can be healed. The final focus of this chapter is on the 'affinity' Welsh: English cultural figures with no ancestral connection with Wales but who expressed a strong affinity with the nation, such as the artist John Petts and Robert Graves. In particular, it looks at how Graves's identification with Wales, forged in childhood, was reinforced by his First World War experiences. It then addresses the potential implications of this affinity Welshness for the war service of his eldest son David. The traumatic loss of David, whom Graves had encouraged to serve with the Royal Welch Fusiliers (RWF), and who died in Myanmar in 1943, will also be discussed in relation to the wartime production of *The White Goddess,* published in 1948, which Graves defined as a 'Welsh' concept.

Refuge and Recuperation

David Peters Corbett, Ysanne Holt, and Fiona Russell note the links between constructions of national identity and native traditions, writing how concepts of nationality 'are made to signify place and time, implying a consensus about qualities, a series of intangible attitudes and formal traits, which have been variously interpreted as embodying national and racial attributes.'[10] In the case of English observers of Wales, the idea of 'deep Wales' was often attached to the pastoral vision of a mountainous landscape. In her 1933 travelogue, Naomi Royde-Smith wrote: 'Five minutes out of Shrewsbury, but on the left-hand side of the carriage now, the mountains of Wales showed like flat indigo silhouettes cut out of paper against the western sky.'[11] She also noted that, 'North Wales has been painted so often and by so many English landscape painters, especially by David Cox and the water-colourists, that the fleeting views of its more famous mountains as they melt into one another past the carriage windows suggest that Welsh Nature has

---

[9] Bodleian Library; MS. Eng. c6365, p. 39.
[10] David Peters Corbett, Ysanne Holt, and Fiona Russell, 'Introduction', in *The Geographies of Englishness. Landscape and the National Past 1880–1940*, edited by David Peters Corbett, Ysanne Holt, and Fiona Russell (London, 2002), pp. ix–x.
[11] Royde-Smith, *Pilgrim*, p. 193.

imitated British Art.'[12] In June 1918, the recuperating South Wales Borderers veteran Saunders Lewis was in England waiting for a posting with the British Legation in Athens. Applying for a weekend pass, he travelled on an early morning train from Chester to Bangor, walked to Anglesey and had tea at the Menai Bridge. A letter to Margaret Gilcriest captures his sense of rejuvenation:

> The sea, the Straits, the woods, the mountains, they are all about me, the hedgerows, the wayside flowers, the grass—and oh! the children talk Welsh at play and old men and women everywhere pass the time of day in the old way; and I kissed the earth, the grass, the flowers for my happiness... somehow, queerly, this land kindles me, excites me, its touch is like a sweetheart's, it thrills the heart, and I cannot help it awhile if all the troubles of the war pass from me, and all the havoc of my self; and in that spirit I stopped some kiddies who were playing in English and swore terribly at them till they promised me never again to play except in Welsh.[13]

On his return, Lewis reflected further on how his trip confirmed his rejection of English mores, embodied in his British officer's uniform, and his sense of 'belonging' to Wales:

> I may go again next weekend, and if so, I'll go to Caernarfon this time to be right close by the hills. The trouble is my uniform. The Welsh folk hate the dress and feel shy of officers even when they speak Welsh. It's strange how a conquered people are timid of the very show of caste. But I console myself that had I not taken a commission I should not have even this little freedom. You see, I don't belong to a people swanky by nature, like the English. I had to cultivate it carefully. You may congratulate me on my success.[14]

In December 1918, whilst posted in Athens, Lewis writes of the urge to visit the Conwy Valley and 'have two months quiet to put myself right'. However, he also acknowledges: 'But coming home to England will for me be essentially coming to my family and coming to you. They are what the years have left me.'[15] So, whilst Wales was somewhere that Lewis needed to recharge his sense of self, at this point, England could still function as 'home'.

In his 1913 semi-autobiographical novel, *The Happy-Go-Lucky Morgans*, Thomas characterizes the daughter of the Morgan household in London, Jessie, as subdued because 'She went back to Wales too seldom'.[16] Daniel Huws notes that for Thomas himself, Wales became a 'place of renewal' and notes how 'at several

---

[12] Royde-Smith, *Pilgrim*, pp. 242–3.   [13] *Saunders Lewis. Letters*, p. 288.
[14] *Saunders Lewis. Letters*, p. 289.   [15] *Saunders Lewis. Letters*, p. 318.
[16] Thomas, *Happy*, p. 25.

times of crisis it was to Wales that he withdrew'.[17] When Thomas was suffering from depression in late 1911, he moved to Laugharne as 'a suitable location for his recuperation', confident that 'a visit to Wales would "soon put me right"'.[18] Also sent to recuperate in Wales was the protagonist of Naomi Royde-Smith's 1930 novel, *The Island. A Love Story*, which depicts an unequal love affair between two women. Jill Benton notes how Royde-Smith 'mined issues earned through her lived experiences, transforming them into imagined situations and characters'.[19] In this case, Royde-Smith divided 'aspects of her poetic sensibilities into two women characters' mirroring her own sense of dualities.[20] In the novel, Myfanwy Hughes, 'a pale, sickly creature', is sent from living with her Welsh milliner aunt in Liverpool to recuperate on her Welsh aunt's farm, Porth Gwyn in Tonfanau.[21] Being raised in 'a small suburban street' and struggling to recover from scarlet fever, Myfanwy is sent to Wales for the restorative 'sea air'.[22]

In the aftermath of his divorce case and abrupt return from military service overseas, Eliot Crawshay-Williams wrote repeatedly to his mother, based at the family home in Bridgend, about his need to spend time in Wales. In 1918, he wrote from London: 'I think you are lucky to be quiet down in Wales. When the war is over I shall hope to get a little rest with you down there.'[23] Four years later, he stated, 'It has been rather trying in London lately, and I shall be glad to get into the country' and in 1923, 'I hope soon you will let me come down to Wales.... I could get away if you will have me.'[24] For Crawshay-Williams, in this period, Wales often acted as a temporary hideaway. At the time of the Second World War, the family of Selwyn Lloyd, whether singly or together, often travelled to Wales to take a break, especially during the Blitz period. Lloyd's sister Dorice wrote to him from Criccieth in 1940, 'This is about the most peaceful spot you could imagine. Just as it is when there is no war. No protected windows or guns and the few soldiers and sailors we see are from camps round about.'[25] The following year, his sister Rachel wrote from the Wynnstay Hotel, Machynlleth:

> Daddy and I came here last Monday after the fourth night of Blitz...Saturday was the most awful night, the drone of enemy planes never ceased, it sounded as if thousands were coming over....I'm afraid I didn't feel a bit like coming and leaving Mummy & Nurse to cope with the Blitz, but when I suggested to Daddy

---

[17] Daniel Huws, 'Edward Thomas's Private Writing', *Times Literary Supplement*, 4642, 20 March 1992, p. 13.
[18] Cuthbertson, *Edward Thomas*, p. 330; Thomas, *Edward Thomas*, p. 180.
[19] Benton, *Avenging*, p. 120.   [20] Benton, *Avenging*, p. 117.
[21] Naomi Royde-Smith, *The Island. A Love Story* (London, 1930), pp. 81, 84.
[22] Royde-Smith, *Island*, pp. 92, 85–6.
[23] NLW; D3/1, Crawshay-Williams Correspondence, Letter, 8 June 1918.
[24] NLW; D3/2, Crawshay-Williams Correspondence, Letter, 23 November 1922; Letter, 3 April 1923.
[25] SELO 1/66, Letters from Dorice to Lloyd, March–November 1940; Letter, 18 August 1940.

that he went to Machy by train, he said, "It's not much fun going away by yourself" so I realised he wouldn't go if I didn't go with him. We tried to get in at Oswestry but it was full so we came here.... It is certainly very peaceful...Daddy and I went by bus to Aberystwyth yesterday and came back by train. The country looks awfully pretty.[26]

The Broken Soldier

The novelist Alexander Cordell rose to fame in the late 1950s due to the popularity of his novel set in Wales, *Rape of the Fair Country,* the first in a trilogy. Having served with the Royal Engineers before and during the Second World War, Cordell carried himself with the demeanour of a typical British officer, with his 'ex-Army binoculars' and 'clipped military moustache'.[27] When he moved to Abergavenny in 1959, Cordell even named his home 'Ubique' after the Royal Engineers' motto.[28] However, he also alluded to the dual allegiances which informed his sense of Britishness, describing himself 'as an Englishman deeply in love with both England and Wales' who had 'adopted' Wales as a country.[29] Cordell was born George Alexander Graber in Ceylon in September 1914. His father, Frank Graber, a Regimental Sergeant-Major with the Royal Engineers, had a German father and a Welsh mother. When Cordell moved to Belfast as a child, his Welsh grandmother lived with the family; he later wrote that she 'came from the wild places of the Rhondda Valley'.[30] However, after a short time in London, the family emigrated to China in 1925, leaving his grandmother behind. Cordell remembers their final farewell: 'She came to me and with her face next to my ear whispered, "Goodbye, my precious. May the baby Jesus bring you back to me", and then something in Welsh I did not understand.'[31] Following his return to England, Cordell joined the Royal Engineers in 1932. He was posted to Shrewsbury, close to the Welsh border, and when he transferred into a civil service post, he visited Wales for the first time. His biographers suggest that, based in Shrewsbury, 'with the looming nearness of the hills, Alexander became more conscious of the Welsh blood in his veins.'[32] However, when he returned to the Royal Engineers in 1939 and fought in France as part of the British Expeditionary Force, his thoughts of Wales were spasmodic.[33] Having analysed his wartime diaries, his biographers suggest that he was more likely to note St George's Day within its

---

[26] SELO 1/70, Letters from family to Lloyd, January–June 1941; Letter, 9 May 1941.
[27] Mike Buckingham and Richard Frame, *Alexander Cordell* (Cardiff, 1999), p. 1.
[28] Buckingham and Frame, *Alexander*, p. 65.
[29] 'The Englishman in Wales', *London Welshman,* September 1961, p. 2.
[30] Buckingham and Frame, *Alexander*, pp. 2–3, 15.
[31] Cited in Buckingham and Frame, *Alexander*, p. 15.
[32] Buckingham and Frame, *Alexander*, pp. 22–3.
[33] Buckingham and Frame, *Alexander*, p. 51.

pages than St David's Day and to think of himself as British. On 7 May 1940, when involved in the BEF retreat to the French coast, he observed the fleeing French refugees and soldiers, and wrote, 'Thank God for being British!'[34] Things began to change for Cordell when he was severely injured during the evacuation at Boulogne and moved to a hospital at St David's Hotel, Harlech, in order to convalesce. Cordell's wartime recuperation here was crucial in his personal and literary development, allowing him to reconnect with his patrilineal Welshness. As Mike Buckingham and Richard Frame write, 'in this quiet corner of Wales long walks, sea air and the time to think and plan all played a part in healing both physically and mentally. Alexander always said that China had shaped his social conscience but it was Wales that offered him something gently lyrical.'[35] Whilst convalescing, Cordell read Robert Graves's *Goodbye to All That* and began to seriously consider writing as a career. His biographers suggest that his quest to become a commissioned officer was also tied into this literary ambition and point to his awareness that Wilfred Owen had been born at Oswestry and had studied at Shrewsbury Technical College before going into the Army.[36] Thus, at Harlech, Cordell had a moment of awakening which appeared to fuse his Welsh sense of self with his literary and military selves. In the immediate aftermath of the war, Cordell returned to Shrewsbury leading a dual life as a quantity surveyor and a short story writer. However, following a move to Llanellen in 1950, he started to write seriously publishing the first of his Welsh historical trilogy, *Rape of the Fair Country*, in 1959.[37] These books offered 'a romantic but essentially accurate picture of life in early industrial Wales, in the iron districts of Monmouthshire'.[38] From thence forward, Cordell's commercial success relied heavily on demonstrating his passion for 'Wales and its past' although his attempts to replicate Welsh cadences of speech created some unease.[39] Buckingham and Frame astutely note that, 'From reading Alexander Cordell's books it is easy to imagine that he had always been saturated in the stories and life of Wales. In fact it impinged upon his consciousness very slowly.' They point out that although Cordell felt genuine affection for his Welsh grandmother 'much of the influence he would ascribe to her was with the benefit of hindsight'.[40] At the same time, Phil Carradice acknowledges that 'many people living outside Wales formed their initial opinions of the country—and possibly still do—from reading the historical novels of Alexander Cordell.'[41] Cordell's extended period of convalescence in Harlech clearly triggered

---

[34] Buckingham and Frame, *Alexander*, p. 32.
[35] Buckingham and Frame, *Alexander*, p. 38.
[36] Buckingham and Frame, *Alexander*, p. 36.
[37] Buckingham and Frame, *Alexander*, pp. 48, 51.
[38] Phil Carradice, 'Alexander Cordell—A View of Wales', 1 February 2013, BBC Wales, http://www.bbc.co.uk/blogs/wales/entries/9a3fbffe-f8d0-32a4-a9d2-6495cefbd95b, accessed 23 November 2015.
[39] John Harris, 'Popular Images', in *Welsh Writing in English*, edited by M. Wynn Thomas (Cardiff, 2003), pp. 218, 220; Buckingham and Frame, *Alexander*, p. 54.
[40] Buckingham and Frame, *Alexander*, p. 51.
[41] Carradice, 'Alexander'.

an affinity with Wales through his patrilineal line which was to blossom fully when he moved to Wales. Cordell's biographers mention the hostility he faced throughout his life due to his 'Germanic-sounding' surname, Graber, and posit this as a reason why he altered his surname to Cordell when he became a published author in 1957.[42] This sense of outsider or 'enemy' status could also provide a reason for his desire to find escapism in Wales and the idea of Wales. Ultimately, the commercial success he achieved with his historical novels compounded Cordell's connections with the Welsh nation which were, originally, rather 'slight'.[43]

Affinity Welsh

In his study of 'Affinity Scots', focusing on north-western Europeans who celebrate and re-enact Scottishness in kilts at Highland Games competitions, David Hesse points to the importance of the Scottish 'dreamscape'—'a well-established romantic fantasy of Scottish history' which broadly appeals to people with no Scottish roots.[44] There were also English cultural figures who had 'no proven roots' but cared greatly, for whom 'dreams' of Wales were important and who could be termed 'Affinity Welsh'.[45] This group includes the artist and conscientious objector, John Petts. Born in London in 1914, Petts defined himself in later life as 'a naturalised Welshman' pointing to his love of Wales, his relationship with Welsh painter Brenda Chamberlain, and their decision to remove themselves from London to a remote part of Wales before the Second World War.[46] In a recorded interview with the Imperial War Museum about his life, Petts provides repeated contrasts between his birthplace, 'the Big Smoke' and Wales, a place full of 'magic and promise'.[47] Petts grew up 'in a typical suburban street without any magic at all in North London: 22 Danvers Road', where 'the mystery of God's creation' had been forgotten. Petts was born with an acute curvature of his spine and was wheeled about in a spinal carriage, surrounded, he recalls, by male relatives 'half destroyed' by the First World War. Due to his disability, he had to lie on his back for hours:

---

[42] Buckingham and Frame, *Alexander*, pp. 17, 58.
[43] Buckingham and Frame, *Alexander*, p. 60.
[44] David Hesse, 'Home is where the Heart is: Affinity Scots in the Scottish Diaspora', in *Global Migrations. The Scottish Diaspora Since 1600*, edited by Angela McCarthy and John M. MacKenzie (Edinburgh, 2016), p. 228.
[45] David Hesse, *Warrior Dreams. Playing Scotsmen in Mainland Europe* (Manchester, 2014), p. 13; Hesse, 'Home', p. 232.
[46] IWM 9732; Sound Archive; John Ronald Petts, interviewed by Lyn E. Smith, 2 March 1987.
[47] IWM 9732.

> I knew every crack on the bedroom ceiling, in the plaster. Fine, fine cracks. Because that was the profile of a mountain that I would climb. I would climb up a precipice and rest panting on a shelf but then tackle the next pitch—as I learnt later myself when I became a climber myself later of rocks in North Wales...lying on my bed I used to draw mountains, so to speak, along these cracks, and then climb them.[48]

Petts came to equate his ability to overcome his disability with the sensation of scaling mountains. From early childhood he imagined mountainous landscapes as a form of challenge and a place of potential healing, thus heightening the likelihood of his subsequent rapport with Wales. In the mid-1930s, Petts studied at the Royal Academy Schools in London where he fell in love with Chamberlain. He recalls her 'wearing a white smock like an angel rolling down in the darkness with a beautiful smile on her face' and says that he would 'ask her about the mountains'. Chamberlain was 'one of about half a dozen students from Wales and Ireland who brought to my ignorant London mind an awareness of different cultures, different attitudes, different accents from not very far away', including Alfred Janes, Mervyn Levy, and their friend Dylan Thomas:

> This talk of Wales and, of course, Brenda's particular enthusiasm led me to follow my gaze, which had always been to the West.... From London, I always used to look West. There was in my mind the phrase, 'Go West, young man'![49]

Meeting Chamberlain provided the catalyst for Petts's long-held desire to move to Wales:

> I reacted against city life more and more. I wanted to live the simple dream of growing one's own food in a cottage up in the hills...[Chamberlain] used to talk like mad about the beauties of Snowdonia so in the holidays, I would travel to Snowdonia and she would take me round the hills of Snowdonia that she knew very well and subsequently we married and bought our little freehold: a pair of ruined cottages and half an acre of land for the magnificent sum of £16 in 1936/7.[50]

Sickened by the artificiality of the art world, Petts says, 'I came to Wales—I turned my back on London.' The desire to move to Wales was further compounded by his pacifist beliefs and identification as a conscientious objector.[51]

The poet John Betjeman is famed for his elegiac tributes to a lost English world and in particular, his lifelong love of Cornwall. Yet Philip Payton points out that,

---

[48] IWM 9732.   [49] IWM 9732.   [50] IWM 9732.   [51] IWM 9732.

'beneath Betjeman's enthusiasm for his "own" North Cornwall...was a deeper search for personal identity'. Indeed, for Betjeman, there were instabilities surrounding his own heritage and 'English credentials' as his ancestors, the Betjemanns, were of Dutch or German origin.[52] During the anti-German hostility of the First World War, his mother altered their surname to one 'n', but Betjeman 'remained convinced that at root he was an outsider in England'.[53] As such, he sought an alternative identity which was founded in both a rejection of urban industrial society and an identification with 'Celtic Christianity'. This meant he was attracted not only to Cornwall but also to the idea of Wales.[54] A relative had informed Betjeman that his great-great-grandfather, William Merrick, was born in a mansion at Bodorgan, Anglesey into a family 'descended from Cadafel, lord of Cedewain in Powys'.[55] As Payton writes, 'For Betjeman, if he was not really English, then here at least was a genuine Welshness, an authentic Celticity that would allow him to claim common kinship with Wales and the wider Celtic world.'[56] This sense of attachment was reinforced by Betjeman's reading of *The Secret Glory* (1922) by the Welsh author Arthur Machen, whilst a schoolboy at Marlborough.[57] The main character, coincidentally named Ambrose Meyrick, 'found salvation—and martyrdom—through his embrace of Celtic Christianity and pursuit of the Holy Grail...in deepest Wales.'[58] A. N. Wilson notes that lines from Machen, such as 'I saw golden Myfanwy, as she bathed in the brook Tarógi' are echoed in Betjeman's extravagant poems about his English Welsh friend, Myfanwy Piper née Evans, 'Myfanwy' ('Golden the lights on the locks of Myfanwy') and 'Myfanwy at Oxford' ('Gold Myfanwy, kisses and art') which appeared in his 1940 collection, *Old Lights for New Chancels*.[59] Wilson notes how in the latter poem, 'the willowy figure of Myfanwy Evans blends in the incense-choked shrines of St Paul's and St Barnabas's with the Celtic Myfanwy of Arthur Machen's *The Secret Glory*.'[60] In a further signalling of his Welsh knowledge, Betjeman includes a Welsh version of his poem, 'In Westminster Abbey', in the anthology, thanking '"Gwylim" for his Welsh translation'.[61] Whilst an undergraduate at Oxford, Betjeman had insisted on learning medieval Welsh. Although this has been viewed by observers as being deliberately perverse—his college 'had been put to all the trouble and expense of importing a don from Aberystwyth twice a week'—Payton suggests that Betjeman was, in fact, being sincere in 'expressing his sense of ancient kinship' and affinity with Wales.[62]

---

[52] Payton, *John*, pp. xvii–xviii.
[53] Bevis Hillier, *Young Betjeman* (London, 1989), p. 3; Payton, *John*, p. 15.
[54] Payton, *John*, pp. xviii–xix.   [55] Hillier, *Young*, pp. 5, 411, fn. 23.
[56] Payton, *John*, p. 16.   [57] Hillier, *Young*, p. 122.   [58] Payton, *John*, p. 97.
[59] A. N. Wilson, *Betjeman* (London, 2007), pp. 42–3, 321; Betjeman, *Old Lights*, pp. 48, 49.
[60] Wilson, *Betjeman*, p. 125.   [61] Betjeman, *Old Lights*, pp. 58–60, xix.
[62] Hillier, *Young*, p. 192; Payton, *John*, p. 92.

The poet and author Robert Graves is culturally the most significant example of someone who demonstrates a strong 'affinity' towards Wales. Graves was born in Wimbledon in 1895 to an Irish father and a mother of German parentage, and defined himself as being 'partly of Scottish blood' with 'no Welsh or English in me'.[63] However, having spent a significant amount of his childhood in Wales, Graves also liked to say that he was 'Welsh by adoption'.[64] Graves's sister Rosaleen recalls how they grew up with a Welsh under nurse at their Wimbledon home and were brought up with music, singing folksongs in Welsh, as well as French, German, Italian, and Scots.[65] This was largely due to their Irish father, poet and folklorist, Alfred Graves, who had expertise in Celticism and pan-Celtic studies. As part of this, he collected and translated Welsh folk songs into English, published in the volumes *Welsh Poetry Old and New* and *Ceiriog Hughes's Poems*.[66] In a 1917 review of his *Celtic Psaltery*, the *Cambria Daily Leader* referred to Alfred Graves as 'an old and ever-faithful friend of Wales'.[67] Graves was keen to underline his early imbibing of Welsh scholarship, stating in a letter to the Welsh poet Lynette Roberts:

> I was the first Englishman, so far as I know, to write a Welsh *englyn* according to the fixed ninety-odd rules. I did this when I was thirteen and the result is in my father's not very profound book *Welsh Poetry Old and New*.[68]

Of particular significance to Graves was the establishment of a family base in Harlech, where Graves's parents set up a second home, Erinfa, in 1897. Rosaleen recalls how they would visit Harlech each spring and summer:

> Our Welsh house, planned by Mother, looked right across an enormous plain to the Snowdon mountains on the right. In the foreground was the sea where we gathered shells, learnt to swim and played games in the sand-hills. To the left was Harlech Castle where we climbed and played.[69]

In *Goodbye To All That*, Graves states, 'Having no Welsh blood in us, we felt little temptation to learn Welsh, still less to pretend ourselves Welsh...but above Harlech I found a personal peace independent of history or geography.'[70] He goes on to say, 'The first poem I wrote as myself concerned those hills' and rhapsodizes about:

---

[63] Robert Graves, *But It Still Goes On. An Accumulation* (London, 1930), p. 27.
[64] Miranda Seymour, *Robert Graves. Life on the Edge* (London, 1995), p. 5.
[65] Rosaleen Cooper with Ann Palmer, *Games From an Edwardian Childhood* (Newton Abbot, 1982), p. 11.
[66] Graves, *To Return*, pp. 267–8, 284.
[67] 'Welsh Singers', *Cambria Daily Leader*, 29 November 1917, p. 3.
[68] 1 September 1943. Cited in O'Prey, *In Broken*, p. 317.   [69] Cooper, *Games*, p. 12.
[70] Robert Graves, *Goodbye to All That* (rev. edn, London, 1957), p. 30.

the blueberries on the hills near Maes-y-garnedd; or the cranberries at Gwlawllyn; or bits of Roman hypocaust tiling (with the potter's thumb-marks still on them) in the ruined Roman villas by Castell Tomen-y-mur; or globe flowers on the banks of the upper Artro; or a sight of the wild goats which lived behind Rhinog Fawr, the biggest of the hills in the next range; or raspberries from the thickets near Cwmbychan Lake.[71]

Graves's identification with Wales was reinforced via his regimental connection with the RWF, with whom he served from 1914 to 1919. When the First World War broke out in August 1914, Graves volunteered almost immediately, taking advantage of a contact at the local golf club in Harlech to get a commission in the RWF (he concedes in his 1930 book, *But it Still Goes On* that his presence in the regiment was 'accidental').[72] Graves was initially posted to oversee an internee camp in Lancaster where he commanded a detachment of fifty Special Reservists, 'a rough lot of Welshmen from the border counties'.[73] He went overseas in 1915 and was severely wounded at the Somme in 1916; it was mistakenly reported that he had 'Died of Wounds' in *The Times* on 4 August.[74] As a result of his wartime service, Graves developed a deep—and abiding—attachment to the regiment and its *esprit de corps*. In *Goodbye To All That*, he shows pride in the RWF's regimental tradition—their twenty-nine battle-honours—and their link, signalled through the spelling of 'Welch' with a 'c', to 'the archaic North Wales of Henry Tudor and Owen Glendower'.[75] In February 1916 he wrote to Eddie Marsh:

> I have to live up to my part here as I have learned to worship my Regiment: in sheer self-defence I had to find something to idealise in the Service and the amazing sequence of R W Fus. suicides in defence of their 'never-lost-a-trench' boast is really quite irresistible.[76]

Graves acknowledged that, 'in peacetime, the regular battalions of the regiment, though officered mainly by Anglo-Welshmen of county families, did not contain more than about one Welsh-speaking Welshman in fifty. Most recruits came from Birmingham.'[77] However, there were increasing numbers of Welsh recruits during the course of the war, and for Graves, the regiment provided a site of emotional identification, crystallizing his attachment to Wales. In his 1930 *Memoirs of an Infantry Officer*, Sassoon paints a vivid picture of Graves at this time, referring to him as 'David Cromlech'. Jean Moorcroft Wilson observes that this pseudonym not only emphasizes Graves's Welsh connections but also contains a pun around

---

[71] *Goodbye*, pp. 29–30. [72] Graves, *Goodbye*, p. 61; Graves, *But It Still*, p. 27.
[73] Graves, *Goodbye*, p. 63. [74] 'Roll of Honour', *The Times*, 4 August 1916, p. 5.
[75] Graves, *Goodbye*, pp. 72, 75. [76] O'Prey, *In Broken*, p. 39.
[77] Graves, *Goodbye*, p. 70.

'Cromlech' being the Welsh word for a megalithic grave.[78] It also suggests that Graves's affinity with Wales was visible to his contemporaries. Indeed, in his wartime correspondence he often testifies to this attachment, writing to Sassoon in May 1916 of 'the Welsh, whom I love'.[79] This affection was reciprocated. In its review of Graves's poetry volume, *Fairies and Fusiliers* (1917), *Welsh Outlook* comments, 'That the author has lived in and loved Wales is shown in the "Letter to SS from Mametz Wood", and although he does not speak Welsh one feels that Wales can claim credit for at least one part of the book.'[80]

Another dimension of Graves's affinity with Wales was his consistent wartime construction of Wales as a restorative site of refuge from conflict and a place of solace. Miranda Seymour believes that during their military service together in the RWF, Graves and Sassoon were akin to 'two poets planning a farming future', with the unchanged landscape of Wales coming to 'symbolise a lost idyll in wartime'.[81] Mary Ann Constantine believes that it is impossible to overstate the importance of Harlech to Graves's 'poetic development and emotional survival'; for Graves, it was not 'so much a place as a state of mind'.[82] In a letter to Sassoon in August 1916, whilst recuperating in a London hospital, he wrote, 'I'm as right as rain and hope before many days to be up in glorious Merioneth again basking in the sun and storing up a large mass of solar energy'.[83] Earlier that year, he had purchased a small cottage from his mother on the Erinfa estate, which, he recalled, 'was done in defiance of the war: something to look forward to when the guns stopped'.[84] This act had been pre-imagined in his poem, 'Over the Brazier', composed in 1915, and reflecting on the life he would lead after the war: 'I'd thought: "A cottage in the hills, North Wales ... I'd live there peacefully and dream and write."'[85] Graves employs the notion of this sun-imbued white Welsh cottage as a form of commune with Sassoon, using the idea of Wales as a way of establishing or forging a new site of intimacy. In a 1916 letter to Sassoon from Erinfa, he writes, 'Merioneth now is nothing but bright sun and misty mountains and hazy seas and sloe blossoms and wild cherry and grey rocks and young green grass. I am writing in my small, white-walled cottage of which I must have told you.'[86] Furthermore, the poem, 'Familiar Letter to Siegfried Sassoon', written in 1916, includes the section: 'Well, when it's over, first we'll meet | At Gweithdy Bach, my

---

[78] Jean Moorcroft Wilson, *Siegfried Sassoon: The Journey from the Trenches* (New York, 2003), p. 241.
[79] O'Prey, *In Broken*, p. 48.
[80] H. Ll J, '"Fairies and Fusiliers" by Robert Graves (Capt., R.W.F)', *Welsh Outlook*, 5, 3 (March 1918), p. 103.
[81] Seymour, *In My*, p. 115.
[82] Mary-Ann Constantine, 'Rocky Acres: Robert Graves, Harlech and the Great War', *Planet. The Welsh Internationalist*, 215 (2014), pp. 58, 64.
[83] Cited in O'Prey, *In Broken*, p. 57.   [84] Graves, *Goodbye*, p. 178.
[85] *Over the Brazier* (1915), in *Robert Graves. Collected Poems, Volume 1*, edited by Beryl Graves and Dunstan Ward (Manchester, 1995), p. 21.
[86] O'Prey, *In Broken*, p. 45.

country seat.' Graves identifies Gweithdy Bach as the place where they will 'dress our wounds and...store up solar energy'.[87] Here, Graves poetically reproduces sentiments already expressed in letters to Sassoon and they represent recurring themes which can be seen in other poems from this period such as *The Cottage* and *Rocky Acres*.[88] For Graves, during the First World War, Wales provided a 'dreamscape', a simplified landscape of wild berries, mountains, and sunshine.[89] In this wartime poetry, Graves echoes the earlier travel writers such as Borrow, displaying a literary pull towards Wales but also producing an outsider's observations and romanticized version of Wales.

Graves and Sassoon did spend some time together convalescing in Harlech when both were on sick leave in September 1916.[90] In an intriguing way, Graves' poetic longing, as well as its realization, anticipates the work of the Welsh writer, Hilda Vaughan, who in two post–First World War novels, *The Soldier & the Gentlewoman* (1932) and *Pardon and Peace* (1945), focuses on English ex-servicemen seeking psychic recovery in Wales.[91] In particular, Vaughan uses the symbol of the broken English soldier citizen to embody the tensions between the two nations in the post-war landscape. The earlier novel focuses on the story of the English veteran, Captain Dick Einon-Thomas, of Welsh paternity, who on his return from war service learns that he has inherited Plâs Einon, a country estate in Carmarthenshire. In the novel, Wales is initially configured as 'home', a site of security and refuge:

> When he was alone, he drew a long breath. The air was newly washed by rain. It held the saltness of the sea, and the sweetness of rising sap. The pungency of wet leaf mould and of moss was in it, rank woodland scents, stealing up from the dingle below and blending with the tonic breeze that swept the hilltops. Cool, he thought, clean, restful, safe! He shut his eyes and smiled. *Safe*, he repeated to himself, and then—*home*.[92]

As Lucy Thomas writes, for Einon-Thomas, 'the Welsh landscape represents the safety he has longed for during the terrifying years of battle'.[93] It also promises restoration of peaceability, promising succour to his embattled self:

> To Dick, whose weak blue eyes had not long ago been blinking at the arid glare of Mesopotamia, the colours of this landscape—the rich brown of peat bogs, the bronze of last year's bracken, the mauve cloud shadows and pale cobalt of ocean

---

[87] Graves and Ward, *Robert Graves. Collected Poems, Vol. 1*, pp. 44–5.
[88] See Robert Graves, *Fairies and Fusiliers* (London, 1917).   [89] Hesse, 'Home', p. 228.
[90] Seymour, *Robert*, p. 54.
[91] See Lucy Thomas, 'Introduction', in *The Soldier and the Gentlewoman*, edited by Hilda Vaughan (Dinas Powys, 2014), p. 7.
[92] Vaughan, *Soldier*, p. 29.   [93] Thomas, 'Introduction', p. 6.

and sky, the gay sprouting green of the foreground—were magically soft.... Never had he seen any land so wet and soft and harmless.[94]

This pastoral Welsh vision is contrasted with Einon-Thomas's previous English suburban existence of 'neat fields, crossed by footpaths, where, before the war, he had taken girls to picnic on fine Sundays'; he is presented as a 'common little suburban with a pale moustache' who has been 'bred on pavements'.[95] The novel ultimately recounts Einon-Thomas's inability to settle in his new home and marriage due to his Englishness and sense of alienation living amongst 'a lot of jabbering foreigners'.[96] Similarly, in Vaughan's 1945 novel *Pardon and Peace*, another First World War veteran, English soldier, Mark Osbourne, purposefully sets out to revisit an 'unchanged' Welsh village, Bryn-Tawel, in order 'to be made whole again':

> The village lay hidden in its orchards, four miles up from the valley's mouth. It scarcely suggested the work of man, for the abiding rains and the mists which rose from the stream or curled down from the mountains caused lichens, grey and yellow to mottle the slate of roofs and to fur the branches of fruit trees. The apples and damsons were green now, but later, Mark promised himself, he would hear them fall with a plop on to the unpaved street.[97]

Graves and his first wife Nancy Nicholson spent their honeymoon in Wales and, in 1918, lived at Bryn-y-Pin, a farmhouse near Kinmel Park camp where Graves was stationed. In his memoir, Graves even frames his recollection of the 1918 Armistice through a Welsh lens: 'The news sent me out walking alone along the dyke above the marshes of Rhuddlan (an ancient battle-field, the Flodden of Wales) cursing and sobbing and thinking of the dead.'[98] After demobilization, Graves wrote that he intended to 'retreat to my lovely Wales and grow cabbages'.[99] In the immediate post-war period, Graves was selected as a visible representative of Welsh veterans in Harlech enabling him to further forge a relationship between himself, the RWF, and Welsh wartime experience:

> The Harlech villagers treated me with the greatest respect. At the Peace Day celebrations in the castle, I was asked, *as the senior Man of Harlech who had served overseas*, to make a speech about the glorious dead. I spoke in commendation of the Welshman as a fighting man and earned loud cheers [my italics].[100]

---

[94] Vaughan, *Soldier*, p. 24.
[95] Vaughan, *Soldier*, pp. 25, 51, 61.
[96] Vaughan, *Soldier*, p. 60.
[97] Hilda Vaughan, *Pardon and Peace* (London, 1945), pp. 2–4.
[98] Graves, *Goodbye*, p. 246.
[99] Cited in O'Prey, *In Broken*, p. 104.
[100] Graves, *Goodbye*, pp. 253–4.

This bond with his Welsh regiment continued for the rest of Graves's life, exemplified through the correspondence he received from RWF veterans and his attendance at regimental dinners.[101] He dedicated *Fairies and Fusiliers* to the RWF and referred to the regiment as 'the only organisation of any sort (school, college, society etc.) that I am childishly proud of having belonged to myself'.[102] At the outbreak of the Second World War, Graves reimmersed himself in this regimental identity, having embarked on the production of the Sergeant Lamb novels about an eighteenth-century RWF soldier fighting in the War of Independence. The first book, *Sergeant Lamb of the Ninth* (1940), was followed in 1941 by *Proceed, Sergeant Lamb* where the Preface underlines Graves's emotional commitment to the regiment:

> The chief link that I have with Lamb is that I had the honour of serving, like him, in the Royal Welch Fusiliers during a long and bloody war; and found their character as a regiment, and their St David's Day customs, happily unaltered since his day.[103]

This residual Welsh regimental loyalty had implications for Graves's eldest son, David Graves, shown in Figure 8.1, at the onset of the Second World War. By this time, Graves had returned to England, settling in Galmpton, Devonshire, with his partner Beryl Hodge and his second family of small children. Graves was desperately keen for David to join the RWF; in January 1940, he wrote to his son, who was studying at Jesus College Cambridge:

> I got in touch with my old battalion commander "Scatter-cash" Ford alias Major General J R Minshull-Ford CB, DSO, MC now the Colonel of the Regiment as a whole. He told me his son is now in the Regiment and I replied that I had a son who thought of applying for a Commission in it when he finished with Cambridge in June.
>
> Hence enclosed; please return.
>
> It would <u>greatly please me</u> if you did go into the Regiment, because it is and always was a corps d'elite and thus has always had the pick of the market in recruits and officers. As I think I told you, one feels much <u>safer</u> in a really good regiment, does not have to worry about being let down by one's men or brother-officers. <u>Please let me know as soon as possible about this.</u>

---

[101] Robert Graves Collection (RGC) St John's College, Oxford; Robert Graves Collection (RGC); GB 473; RG/K/WW1 Correspondence from former comrades; RG/H/SH Speech Given at the Savoy Hotel.
[102] Cited in Richard Perceval Graves, *Robert Graves and The White Goddess 1940–1985* (London, 1998), p. 68.
[103] Robert Graves, *Proceed, Sergeant Lamb* (London, 1941), p. vii.

CONSTRUCTING WALES AS A SITE OF SOLACE 237

Figure 8.1 Portrait of David Graves taken during his service with the Royal Welch Fusiliers.
Reproduced with permission of William Graves and The Robert Graves Copyright Trust.

Graves enclosed an application form for a commission, ending his letter with the remark 'make friends with the Brass Hat Hammer of Privilege!'[104] Graves was clearly willing to make use of his RWF network of contacts and patronage to get David a commission. He circumvented normal channels by going directly to Minshull-Ford, the Colonel-in-Chief of the regiment, who then 'applied for David join the RWF and, presumably, had him posted to the 1st (and best) battalion.'[105]

Graves's desire for his son David to join 'the Regiment' sits within a wider military pattern of filial enlistment whereby the English-born sons of men with Welsh connections felt compelled to join Welsh regiments during the Second World War. As discussed in Chapter 5, it was quite common for sons confronting the outbreak of the war to want to follow in their father's regimental footsteps. Graves

---

[104] Robert Graves Collection (RGC) St John's College; Box 5 Group 31; Letters to David Graves; Letter January 22 1940. Original punctuation shown.
[105] RGC; Box 5 Group 30; Letters to Nancy Nicholson; Letter from Graves, 4 April 1943.

showed clear pride at the intergenerational regimental link he shared with his son, writing in early 1943, 'David by the way is in my old battalion (& Lamb's) under orders for the East.'[106] To wartime correspondents, he referred possessively to 'My David' and gave them updates on his son's regimental career.[107] Reciting news of David's training course at the Woolacombe Bay School—including an '11 mile run, 75 mile march, swimming a reservoir in full equipment, scaling 100 foot precipice'—Graves predicted, 'He will be a very good soldier.' Taking pride in their shared martial experience, he wrote, 'David and I had a talk about the functions of the RSM and CSM and decided that the former's task was to shoot inefficient CO's [sic] and the latter to shoot inefficient Coy Commands.'[108]

However, when David, as a lieutenant with the 1st RWF (2nd Div.), died in combat at Arakan on 18 March 1943, it triggered a desperate response in Graves. In April 1943, Graves notified the Liddell Hart family that he had received 'news that David was "missing since March 19th in the Indian Theatre of Operations," and then came the second blow of his being "missing believed killed March 18th". I imagine it was the Mayu River show.... Of course it isn't final yet, but it seems pretty hopeless.' Graves remarked on the fact that David's sister, Jenny, had 'strained her heart with the suppressed shock' and was hospitalized.[109] On the news that David was 'missing, believed killed', Graves wrote to his former wife, and David's mother, Nancy, 'This is not final, of course, but the margin of hope shrinks.' However, he also mentioned that he had received a communication from General Scaife, of the RWF, which allowed him to cling to the hope that David had survived:

The only gleam is that in action where there has been a forced retirement soldiers are always liable to report officers killed if they are wounded and incapacitated, and very often report fictitious last messages. It is something to do with the group psychology of defeat. And if the officer is popular it is a sort of excuse for not having gone back to fetch him to safety.[110]

As Corinna Peniston-Bird notes, in times of bereavement, fathers often function as 'activists seeking answers'.[111] On 2 June 1943, the *Daily Worker* reported that David 'the 22-year-old son of Mr Robert Graves, the author, is missing, believed

---

[106] King's College London (KCL): Liddell Hart Centre for Military Archives, LIDDELL HART 1/327/201, Letter from Graves to Barry Sullivan, 2 January 1943.
[107] See LIDDELL HART 1/327/58, Letter from Graves to Liddell Hart, 13 December 1941.
[108] KCL: Liddell Hart Centre for Military Archives, LIDDELL HART 1/327/67, Letter from Graves to Liddell Hart, 9 April 1942.
[109] KCL: Liddell Hart Centre for Military Archives, LIDDELL HART 1/327/200, Letter from Graves to Kathleen Liddell Hart, 19 April 1943.
[110] RGC, Box 5 Group 30; Letters to Nancy Nicholson; Letter from Graves, 14 April 1943.
[111] Corinna Peniston-Bird, 'The Grieving Male in Memorialization: Monuments of Discretion', *War & Culture Studies*, 8, 1 (2015), p. 42. doi.org/10.1179/1752628014Y.0000000017.

killed on the Arakan front'.[112] Writing to his friend, military theorist, Captain Basil Liddell Hart, Graves enclosed the press cutting and wrote, 'there still seems a faint hope, as the batt. got chucked out almost at once by infiltration and "believed killed" is a commonplace on such occasions.'[113] Liddell Hart immediately responded that the report offered 'a distinct ray of hope—as well as a fine tribute. For if one man goes forward alone in this way, it is a common assumption among those who are behind that he has been killed, when he may just as well have been wounded and taken prisoner. That happened so often in the last war.'[114] It is likely that Graves was keen for a distinguished expert such as Liddell Hart to endorse his view on the possibility of David surviving the offensive attack, with the latter becoming complicit in raising Graves's hopes. Graves also pursued his elite network of Royal Welch contacts in an attempt to find out information about his son, including Minshull-Ford and Brigadier A. D. Buchanan-Smith at the War Office.[115] Graves received a communication from David's ex-colonel, Hopkins, that he thought David was 'definitely killed', but Grave remained resistant to the news, commenting that Hopkins 'had not been in command of the regiment at the time'.[116] In September 1945, Field Marshall General (Sir) Archibald Wavell, who had been Commander-in-Chief of British troops in India, responded to an approach from Graves with the sobering words: 'I should like to wish you good news of your son but I am afraid that...the hopes of his being alive are very slender.'[117] In a letter to his son Sam the next month, Graves mentions that the evidence about David's death had been 'carefully sifted at Wavell's personal orders'.[118] It is worth noting that the memory of his own mistakenly reported death in the Great War appears to have hindered Graves's capacity to accept David's death. In the same letter, he wrote, 'personally I have now given up hope; with a mental reservation that my own "death" seemed final enough and that one never knows.'[119]

Around this time, Graves focused on producing an imaginative melding of his own and his son's military service with the RWF. In his Lamb novels, the first edition of *Proceed, Sergeant Lamb*, published in 1941, referred solely to Graves's service in the RWF. Yet, in the second edition, published in 1946, Graves

---

[112] 'Japs Attack in Burma', *Daily Worker*, 2 June 1943, p. 4.
[113] KCL: Liddell Hart Centre for Military Archives, LIDDELL HART 1/327/102, Letter from Graves to Liddell Hart, 18 June 1943.
[114] KCL: Liddell Hart Centre for Military Archives, LIDDELL HART 1/327/103, Letter from Liddell Hart to Graves, 22 June 1943.
[115] See RGC; RG/J/SmithA, Letter 15 December 44; Box 5 Group 30 Letters to Nancy Nicholson; Letter from Graves, 4 April 1943.
[116] KCL: Liddell Hart Centre for Military Archives, LIDDELL HART 1/327/105, Letter from Graves to Liddell Hart, 21 July 1943.
[117] University at Buffalo; Martin Seymour-Smith Collection MS-S 211-001; Letter from Field Marshal Archibald Wavell to Robert Graves, 7 September 1945.
[118] RGC; Box 5 Group 29; Letters to Sam Graves; Letter from Graves, 31 October 1945.
[119] RGC; Box 5 Group 29; Letter, 31 October 1945.

retrospectively added a mention of David's service to the original foreword: 'My eldest son is now an officer of the same regiment, in a new war.'[120] And then, in the 1946 Note to the Second Edition, Graves adds:

> My son, whom I mentioned in the above foreword, Lieutenant David Graves, was killed with the 1st battalion of the Royal Welch Fusiliers on March 20th 1943, at Donbaik in Burmah [sic] while making a single-handed assault with grenades on the third of three Japanese strong points, having destroyed the garrisons of the other two.[121]

Here, we can see Graves's determination to signal the cyclical relationship between himself, the regiment, and David. By retrospectively inserting the new text, he underlines David's own commitment to the regiment, and through fatherly loss, his own. Similarly, his biography in a 1945 *Lilliput* article about the origin of 'Thomas Atkins', is framed in the following manner:

> Robert Graves, poet and novelist. Is the author of *Sergeant Lamb of the Ninth* and *Proceed, Sergeant Lamb*, the latter containing an account of the Royal Welch Fusiliers' part in the campaign of 1779–81.... He was himself a captain in the Royal Welch Fusiliers (1914–19) and was officially reported 'Died of Wounds' at the Somme in July 1916. His eldest son, Lieut. David Graves, of the 1st Royal Welch Fusiliers, is still 'missing, believed killed' since March 20, 1942 [sic]. After capturing two Japanese strong-points at Donbaik, Burma, the second single-handed, he fell in an assault on a third.[122]

A similar eulogizing reference to David appears in the epilogue to the 1957 revised edition of *Goodbye to All That*.[123] Thus, there appears to be a continual requirement from Graves for his readers to bear witness to David's sacrifice for the regiment. It was also clearly important to Graves that David had an honourable death. The *Daily Worker* reported that David was 'known to be shot after taking a Japanese strongpoint single-handed, armed only with grenades'.[124] To his sister-in-law Evelyn Neep, Graves wrote, 'David was recommended for a DSO for his single-handed attack and capture of a Jap strong-point, but won't get it because a) he's believed killed b) the whole battle ended in a retreat.'[125] To Liddell Hart, he comments in a postscript, 'David's Colonel writes that the "finest thing he had ever seen in his life" was David's coolness as he returned to advanced Batt HQ to

---

[120] Robert Graves, *Proceed, Sergeant Lamb* (2nd edn, London, 1946), p. vii.
[121] Graves, *Proceed, Sergeant Lamb*, p. ix.
[122] 'The Search for Thomas Atkin', *Lilliput*, 16, 2 (1945), p. 168.   [123] Graves, *Goodbye*, p. 304.
[124] 'Japs Attack'.
[125] RGC, Box 8 Group 42; Letter from Graves to Evelyn Neep, 18 July 1943.

collect an armful of bombs for a renewed attack on the Jap strong point, after his sergeant & Bren gunner had been knocked out and he was left alone—"it was as though he was on an assault course".[126] When Graves's friends, Molly and Brian Bliss, meet a gardener in Brecon in 1946 who had served with David and reported his view that 'he was a Hercules; he went in with a grenade in either hand', Graves craved further information.[127] Indeed, all his correspondence is filled with an incessant search for knowledge about his son's service and death.

Around this time, the idea of sacrifice became increasingly foregrounded in Graves's literary outputs. In a letter to Liddell Hart in May 1944, he deliberated on the religious context of different European faiths, referring to 'a deeply rooted religious habit of sacrificing one's eldest son'. He concluded, '"So and so worshipped the Old Gods and was punished by the New Gods by being tricked into killing his son & marrying his daughter, after which he killed himself in a fit of remorse".'[128] Seymour suggests that here, indirectly, Graves was acknowledging responsibility for the fact that he had encouraged his son to go to war and agitated for him to join his regiment. She writes that David's death 'acted as a catalyst for [Graves's] backward leap, into a world where the death of a heroic young man could be seen as a poetic sacrifice'.[129] Fran Brearton agrees that when Graves produced a book on poetic mythology, *The White Goddess*, in the latter half of the war, the 'cycles of male sacrifice' at the heart of the text—'of the sacred king "crucified to the lopped oak", or of the child burned to death as the king's "annual surrogate" map onto the story of Graves's own mistakenly reported death and metaphorical rebirth in World War I, and of his eldest son's death (with the same regiment, the Royal Welch Fusiliers) in World War II.'[130] As well as alluding to tropes of sacrifice within *The White Goddess*, Graves also draws upon that strand of Welsh culture which Tony Conran defines as *traddodiad* (tradition), the ancient culture of Wales, rooted in a devotion to history and myth, finding its main expression in texts such as the *Mabinogion*.[131] In a 1970 interview, Graves stated: 'The actual bones of my poetry are different from the spirit behind them; and that started strangely in the Second World War when I was reading the Mabinogion.' He went on: 'From that started this whole White Goddess concept, which is really a Welsh one.'[132] Whilst producing the book, Graves relied on a familial store of

---

[126] KCL: Liddell Hart Centre for Military Archives, LIDDELL HART 1/327/107, Letter from Graves to Liddell Hart, 18 August 1943.
[127] RGC; GB 473; RG/J/BlissB; Letters from Brian Bliss, 22 July 1946, 13 August 1946.
[128] KCL: Liddell Hart Centre for Military Archives, LIDDELL HART 1/327/126, Letter from Graves to Liddell Hart, 1 May 1944.
[129] Seymour, *Robert*, p. 305.
[130] Fran Brearton, 'Robert Graves and The White Goddess', *Proceedings of the British Academy*, 131 (2005), pp. 273, 283–4.
[131] Tony Conran, *Frontiers in Anglo-Welsh Poetry* (Cardiff, 1997), p. 72.
[132] 'Where the crakeberries grow—Robert Graves gives an account of himself to Leslie Norris'. *The Listener*, 28 May 1970, vol. 83, issue 2148, p. 716.

knowledge, mentioning to Karl Gay in November 1945 that on a recent trip to Wales, he had 'found a set of learned book on the subject of Taliesin and the bards generally in my father's library'.[133] He also had a detailed correspondence with his half-brother Philip during the war about competing interpretations of iconic Welsh texts such as the *Mabinogion* and *Taliesin*. Philip, who wrote a book on Welsh language, warned that misspelling or mixing up Welsh names would make Graves look 'a proper laughing stock'.[134]

As a form of memorial to his son, Graves determined to publish one of David's surviving poems, entitled 'In Conclusion':

> It will be small loss, never to return.
> The summer-house will be cobwebbed,
> The plaster flaked;
> The nets over the unpruned fruit-bushes
> Holed and torn.
> [...]
> The engine in the boiler-house will have ceased its beating;
> The known voices will no longer be heard about the house,
> There will be weeds and crumbling and desolation only.
> We should be sorry we returned.[135]

Sam Graves identified the inspiration for this poem as novelist Richard Hughes's Welsh residence, writing to his father that the poem 'is next to my heart, being about Laugharne Castle (Diccon's place) apparently his favourite place as well as mine'.[136] In the poem, David makes an imaginative connection with Wales as some form of 'home', colluding in his father's affinity Welshness. Indeed, in a further illustration of this, whilst on service with the RWF overseas in 1943, David also composed an 'Ode on the difficulties of celebrating St David's Day in a foreign clime in a proper and fitting manner' which was reproduced in the regimental newsletter.[137] In a final act of reclamation of David's narrative, Graves wrote a short story, 'Kill them! Kill Them!', published in 1956, based on events which Graves insists 'really happened'.[138] In this tale, Graves firmly positions David in a wartime Welsh context. He describes a post-war car trip with his daughter Jenny, close to the Welsh borders, beginning:

---

[133] O'Prey, *In Broken*, pp. 332–3.
[134] RGC; GB 473; RG/J/GravesPhilip; Letter from Philip Perceval Graves, 9 May 1944.
[135] *Cambridge Review*, 25 May 1946. Reproduced with the permission of The Robert Graves Copyright Trust.
[136] RGC; GB 473; RG/J/GravesSam; Letter, 4 April 1946.
[137] *Informer*, Vol II No C 8, Aug 1943. Cited in Graves, *Robert Graves and The White Goddess*, p. 65.
[138] Robert Graves, *Catacrok! Mostly Stories, Mostly Funny* (London, 1956), p. 8.

Wales reminded us both of David, who had done his battle training in this region…

Green Welsh hills and wild-eyed Welsh sheep and the syllable *Llan* appearing on every second fingerpost. Hereabouts David had commanded his platoon in aggressive tactical schemes; perhaps had sten-gunned the imaginary garrison of that farmhouse at the top of the slope.[139]

Graves recollects how as a child in Oxford, David had once seen 'a great pack of black-coated, dog-collared parsons' swarming across the street and had shouted out: '"Kill them! Kill them!"'[140] When they stop for tea in Wales they are suddenly confronted by a group of 'black-coated, dog-collared clergymen' each holding seed cake, which David hated. The story concludes: 'I had a vision of a serious apple-cheeked little boy, sitting between Jenny and me and shaking his fist in a fury…. "Kill them, kill them!" I shouted involuntarily.'[141] It is worth noting that the motif 'Kill Them! Kill Them!', is reminiscent of the chant of: 'Kill! kill! kill!' by the dancers of the sacrificial fires around the Naked King in *The White Goddess*.[142] This autobiographical tale also allows Graves to reconnect himself, David, and Wales in an act of commemoration. Finally, David's death was recorded with the Commonwealth War Graves Commission in the following style: 'Son of Capt. Robert Graves, formerly of The Royal Welch Fusiliers, of Deya, Majorca, Spain. M.A. (Cantab.); Jesus College.'[143] Within this memorial inscription, Graves and his son are enclasped within their shared regimental identity: Graves is not only a bereaved father but, as a 'fellow soldier' has privileged status within 'the hierarchy of mourners'.[144] As we have seen with the persistent literary references to David's death, and the focus on his heroism, this dedication reinforces Graves's allegiance to the regiment to which he has now sacrificed his son. It also suggests that David's paternal connection with the regiment confers additional layers of meaning on his life, and death.

'I have never really got over David's death', Graves admitted to a correspondent in 1961.[145] In the 1970s, he received a letter from a former RWF soldier which mentions David's death in Myanmar and asks, 'Was it his choice to go to the 2/3rd Sir?'[146] This innocent question pierced to the core of Graves's sense of loss. In order to find meaning in David's death, Graves continued to place his son posthumously within a wider communion with their shared Welsh regimental identity.

---

[139] Graves, *Catacrok!*, pp. 148–50. [140] Graves, *Catacrok!*, p. 149.
[141] Graves, *Catacrok!*, p. 150. [142] See Brearton, 'Robert', p. 298.
[143] 'Lieut. John David Nicholson Graves', https://www.cwgc.org/find-records/find-war-dead/casualty-details/2510140/john-david-nicholson-graves/, accessed 8 June 2023.
[144] Peniston-Bird, 'Grieving Male', p. 45.
[145] Beryl Graves and Dunstan Ward, *Robert Graves. Collected Poems, Volume 3* (Manchester, 1999), p. 557.
[146] RGC; GB 473; RG/K/WW1, Letter from Charles E. Griffiths, 14 February 1977.

In 1974, he attended a regimental dinner in London: 'a splendid occasion with a speech in honour of David—and of me—which moved me very much'.[147] Indeed, this affinity with Wales, and in particular, with the RWF, afforded Graves some personal solace in his later years. At his own memorial service in London in 1985, the Last Post was played by a bugler of the RWF; it was reported that his loyalty to the Royal Welch had 'never wavered'.[148]

Conclusion

When going through the process of gender transition in the 1970s, English Welsh travel writer Jan Morris spent time at Llanystumdwy where their house lay 'blessed I thought like a healer's presence with a cure for my sickness'.[149] Morris was carrying on a tradition which has been made apparent during the course of this chapter: English people who, via vestigial ancestral connections or a sense of affinity, identified and experienced Wales as a site of refuge, healing, and personal renewal. The conscientious objector John Petts felt a sense of recognition amongst the Welsh mountains, whilst John Betjeman used the idea of Wales to mitigate his outsider status. For Graves and Cordell, who served as soldiers in the First and Second World Wars, respectively, the Welsh nation promised a chance to recuperate and recover, the Welsh countryside acting as an inspirational 'dreamscape'. It is clear that for many creative English figures, including those with the most tenuous of Welsh connections, Wales functioned as an appealing mirage in which they could invest their fantasies of belonging. In many ways, the construction of Wales as an entrancing mountainous landscape within life writing narratives mirrored the travel writing movement of the early nineteenth century, where English observers constructed Wales as a culturally distinct 'other', offering a tantalizing promise of an alternative form of existence.

[147] Cited in Seymour, *Robert*, p. 457.
[148] D. M. Thomas, 'Good Riddance to All That', *New York Times*, 5 November 1995, https://www.nytimes.com/books/99/09/19/specials/seymour-graves.html, accessed 20 November 2015.
[149] Morris, *Conundrum*, p. 114.

9
Welshness as Masquerade

Richard Llewellyn achieved worldwide fame in 1939 with his novel, *How Green Was My Valley* (*HGWMV*), a story of the South Wales coalfield. The book was an instant bestseller, both in Britain and America, and in 1941, it was made into an Academy award-winning film, linking Llewellyn indelibly in the public mind with a particular vision of Wales and Welshness. Yet, after his death in 1983, it emerged that Llewellyn was not born in Pembrokeshire, as he had claimed, but rather in London to Welsh parents, a revelation which attracted accusations of fakery.[1] This chapter addresses the notion of masquerade, or the use of Welshness to mask Englishness, addressing both Llewellyn's life story and other examples of elective Welshness: the soldier-writer, Owen Rhoscomyl, the novelist Naomi Gwladys Royde-Smith, and William Emrys Williams, director of the Army Bureau of Current Affairs (ABCA), who, at various life moments, masked their English roots, by implying that they were born in Wales. Efrat Tseëlon points out that whilst the use of a mask has come 'to connote disingenuity, artifice and pretence', it is perhaps more accurate to see it as providing 'partial covering' amongst those with dual identifications.[2] Christie Davies agrees that those who opt to wear 'masks' are often attempting 'to resolve an uncertain identity'.[3] Therefore, rather than dismissing these cultural figures as frauds or imposters, this chapter explores the intersections between their assertions of Welsh identity and understandings of the authentic self. Following Alexis T. Franzese, authenticity is defined here as 'an individual's subjective sense that their behaviour, appearance, self, reflects their sense of core being' which, in turn, is composed of their values, identities, and self-meanings.[4] Whilst authenticity is part of the 'process of becoming' it is also 'socially constructed, evaluative, and mutable'.[5] Rebecca J. Erickson writes that since all personal identities develop through 'an actor's reflective observations of self-in-interaction with others', they will be 'closely related to the content

---

[1] 'How Phoney Was My Valley', *The Observer*, 5 December 1999.
[2] Efrat Tseëlon, 'Introduction', in *Masquerade and Identities. Essays on Gender, Sexuality and Marginality*, edited by Efrat Tseëlon (London, 2001), pp. 1–10.
[3] Christie Davies, 'Stigma, Uncertain Identity and Skill in Disguise', *Masquerade*, p. 38.
[4] Alexis T. Franzese, 'Authenticity: Perspectives and Experiences', in *Authenticity in Culture, Self, and Society*, edited by Phillip Vannini and J. Patrick Williams (London, 2009), p. 87.
[5] Phillip Vannini and J. Patrick Williams, 'Authenticity in Culture, Self, and Society', *Authenticity*, p. 3.

of social identities imputed by these others'.[6] At the same time, she points to the fundamentally 'self-referential' nature of authenticity and the importance of the 'meanings' attached to particular identities within constructions of self.[7] In particular, this chapter underlines the importance of these English individuals' close diasporic links with Wales. Ellis highlights how, in the late nineteenth and early twentieth centuries, 'the construction of Welsh identity was not confined to those within the geographic boundaries of Wales, but was in many senses a global project concurrently undertaken across Britain, the colonies and the world beyond.'[8] In the first half of the twentieth century, those discussed in this chapter were often at the forefront of global diasporic projections of ideas of Wales and Welshness.

The Precursor: Owen Rhoscomyl

Ellis's case study of author Owen Rhoscomyl discusses an Englishman who pre-dates Llewellyn in his self-crafting of a 'public image as an imperial Welshman par excellence'.[9] Born Robert Scowfield Mills in Southport in 1863, the son of a Rochdale mason, Rhoscomyl forged an identity 'as a popular Welsh author, patriot and hero' and was responsible for promoting the investiture of the Prince of Wales in 1911 as 'a public celebration of Welsh nationhood'.[10] For Rhoscomyl, raised in the town of Droylsden, Englishness became 'negatively associated in his mind with the difficulties of his youth, the squalor of industrial Manchester and the straitjacket of working-class life' and represented 'the drab, harsh and oppressive background from which he wanted to escape'.[11] Significantly, Rhoscomyl was largely raised by his maternal Welsh grandmother, heightening his emotional connection with Wales.[12] She told 'romantic tales of her childhood home (in Tremeirchion) and the martial and patriotic virtues of Welsh warriors like Arthur, Llewellyn and Owain Glyndŵr.' Thus, suggests Ellis, 'In her telling Wales was a land of romance and heroes whose ancient glories were superimposed on those of their own family and ancestry.'[13] Wynn Thomas notes that, as a cultural influencer, Rhoscomyl consciously renounced the '"feminised" representation of the "Celtic" character...made popular in the cartoon figure of Dame Wales' and, instead, 'set out to advertise Welsh "manliness".'[14] Under the alias Arthur Owen Vaughan, he served in irregular units in the South African war; on his return to Wales, Rhoscomyl began to 'develop basic abilities in the Welsh language and

---

[6] Rebecca J. Erickson, 'The Importance of Authenticity for Self and Society', *Symbolic Interaction*, 18, 2 (1995), p. 126. doi.org/10.1525/si.1995.18.2.121.
[7] Erickson, 'Importance', p. 134.
[8] John S. Ellis, 'Making Owen Rhoscomyl (1863–1919): Biography, Welsh Identity and the British World', *Welsh History Review*, 26, 3 (2013), p. 485.
[9] Ellis, 'Making', p. 485.   [10] Ellis, 'Making', p. 489.   [11] Ellis, 'Making', pp. 493–4.
[12] Ellis, 'Making', p. 485.   [13] Ellis, 'Making', pp. 494–5.
[14] Wynn Thomas, *Nations*, p. 20.

ornamented his speech with Welsh expressions and exclamations'.[15] In 1905, Vaughan published *Flame-bearers of Welsh History*, 'a romantic narrative written in English'. He was then invited to script the 1909 National Pageant of Wales in Cardiff, and moved to Dinas Powys.[16] By the time of the 1911 census, Rhoscomyl claimed Llandudno as his birthplace and said he spoke both English and Welsh.[17] With the outbreak of the First World War, when there were discussions within the Welsh Army Corps of the need for 'some well-known capable writer on Welsh affairs' to be permanently attached to the 38th Welsh Division in France, Rhoscomyl was mooted for the role. However, as the requirements were for someone who was bilingual, he was rejected on the grounds of 'his lack of knowledge of Welsh'.[18] Following his death in October 1919, Rhoscomyl was buried in Rhyl with full military honours.[19] However, whilst Rhoscomyl increasingly adhered to a Welsh identity through the course of his life, Ellis points out that in letters written from America, he also spoke of 'his homesickness for England'.[20] This lingering duality was also visible in his self-construction as a 'Britisher' in one of his autobiographical short stories.[21]

Ambiguous Heritage

Naomi Gwladys Royde-Smith, introduced in Chapter 3, was a high-profile literary journalist, of Rhoscomyl's generation, who also weaved an inaccurate story about being born in Wales. Royde-Smith was born in Halifax in 1875 to a Welsh mother, Anne Williams, and an English father, Michael Holroyd Smith. In an unpublished memoir, she acknowledges multiple identifications within her family, writing that 'French, Irish, Welsh and Yorkshire blood runs in our beings'.[22] Royde-Smith expresses pride in her father's involvement with the Yorkshire firm of Frederick Smith & Co, which 'made the copper wire for the first Atlantic cable'.[23] She also establishes her specifically Welsh credentials via her mother, 'the only daughter of the Reverend Ebenezer Williams... a great-nephew of William Williams of Pant-y-celyn, the great Welsh poet who wrote the hymn "Guide me, O thou great Jehovah".'[24] However, biographer Jill Benton notes how, in public, Royde-Smith went further, claiming Wales, rather than England, as her birthplace:

> In published biographical blurbs, including decades of entries in *Who's Who*, she claimed she was born in Llan*wrst*, a no-place, her fabrication making clever use

---

[15] Ellis, 'Making', pp. 487–8, 493.   [16] Ellis, 'Making', p. 488.   [17] Ellis, 'Making', p. 493.
[18] NLW; WAC; AD/46, Letters from Owen Owen to William Davies J. P., 22 February 1916; 7 April 1916.
[19] Ellis, 'Making', p. 509.   [20] Ellis, 'Making', p. 492.   [21] Ellis, 'Making', p. 492.
[22] VATPA, 'Nine Lives', p. i.   [23] VATPA, 'Nine Lives', p. i.   [24] VATPA, 'Nine Lives', p. i.

of a Welsh orthographic boggle, for the word is similar to Llan*rwst* [my emphases], a real place where her parents did finally reside as elders retiring to the countryside to live in Maenan Hall in the late 1920s.[25]

Similar to Ellis's analysis of Rhoscomyl's motivations, Benton believes that Royde-Smith claimed a Welsh birthplace in order to 'slough aside industrial bourgeois entanglements while romanticising her image as a girl from the West Country, an area eulogized by poets'.[26] However, Royde-Smith's attachment to Wales was clearly visible throughout her memoir, albeit rather whimsical in tone. She often frames Wales as a site of fantasy, mentioning that she once saw 'a fairy's house' near a wooden post whilst on a visit to her grandmother in Wales.[27] Within her family, Royde-Smith was known by her second name 'Gwladys' until the age of twenty.[28] Throughout her life, she continued to holiday in Wales, including visits to her parents at Maenan in the Conwy Valley where they had retired. Royde-Smith writes of 'the years when I took my summer holidays alone, wandering among the mountains of Merioneth'.[29] In her 1933 travelogue, *Pilgrim from Paddington*, she admits her tenuous linguistic connection to Welsh Wales: 'I know no Welsh beyond the words for the simpler forms of food and the times of day, learnt years ago when I needed them in order that life might be sustained on long days tramping the mountains, where, at such farms as were passed, no English was spoken. The equivalent for "the minister," "grandfather," "darling," "uncle," "little," "cheerful," and "graveyard" were also familiar to my ear.'[30] In her 1930 novel, *The Island*, the dedication is to her sister Leslie, who married English Welsh pacifist George Maitland Ll. Davies: 'To Leslie, In Towyn', deliberately situating a close family member within a Welsh context, and reinforcing her own position as a Welsh 'insider'.[31] Royde-Smith often used Wales as a topic for her work, including novels and travelogues. In *Pilgrim from Paddington*, Royde-Smith narrates a series of rail journeys across England and Wales and occasionally flashes her superior knowledge of the latter. A typical example is the retelling of a conversation with a porter on Manorbier Station who advises that the local castle is nearby: 'Knowing what Welsh miles are and what Welsh rain can be, I decided to go to Pembroke.'[32] Overall, Royde-Smith's insistent references to Wales in her writing reflect a desire to validate her own sense of dual affinities.

William Emrys Williams, who was the director of ABCA during the Second World War and 'one of the most powerful cultural mandarins in the country',

[25] Benton, *Avenging*, p. 5.   [26] Benton, *Avenging*, p. 5.
[27] VATPA, 'Nine Lives', pp. 11–12.   [28] Benton, *Avenging*, p. 28.
[29] Benton, *Avenging*, pp. 157, 203, 208; VATPA, 'Nine Lives', p. 86.
[30] Royde-Smith, *Pilgrim*, p. 216.   [31] Royde-Smith, *The Island* (London, 1930).
[32] Royde-Smith, *Pilgrim*, p. 93.

shares this sense of ambiguity within his self-presentation.[33] Williams rose to prominence through his work in adult education and the arts as well as his role as editor-in-chief at Penguin Books from 1936 onwards. When Malcolm Ballin emphasizes how 'notions of Welshness reverberated in the epi-centre of British cultural life in the middle of the twentieth century', he places Williams at the heart of this phenomenon.[34] Williams was born in Hulme, Manchester, in 1896 to Welsh parents who became part of 'the expatriate Welsh community gathered together around the Booth Street Congregational Chapel'.[35] However, Williams's biographer, Sander Meredeen, admits that when attempting to write about his subject's early life, he was 'confronted with a brutal conflict of "facts"'.[36] In his 1977 *Times* obituary, Williams was said to have been 'born at Capel Issac, a village in Carmarthen'.[37] Similarly, his widow's private memoir asserts that Williams was born 'in a small farm in Morfa Bychan, a neighbouring village to Criccieth, the village where Lloyd George was born'.[38] Ballin notes how this latter account both preserves Williams's 'rural Welsh authenticity' and adds 'an intriguing geographical connection with an even more famous Welshman'.[39] As noted in Chapter 1, declaring proximity to Lloyd George was often a useful shorthand to confirm Welshness amongst diasporic *aficionados* of Wales in England. Ballin suggests that the main problem with these 'factual discrepancies' is linked to the fact that 'so much of Williams's proclaimed persona seems to have stemmed from the notion of being born as "Welsh of the Welsh"'.[40] As with those mentioned in previous chapters, Williams's personal contradictions were 'bound up to some extent with the perception of Williams as an outsider, "on the edge" perhaps, someone not always wholly comfortable in the centres of metropolitan power.'[41] For figures like Williams, this sense of liminality could provide fruitful terrain 'for elaborating strategies of selfhood' and perhaps clinging to a form of authentic identity, in his case, Welshness.[42]

Meredeen ultimately concludes that Williams was a Welshman 'despite his English birth'. He points out that Williams was educated for a period in his father's hometown, Morfa Bychan, until the age of eight, when his parents returned to Manchester.[43] At high school in Manchester, Williams wrote essays about 'wild Wales'—aping Borrow's book title—which reflected his abiding 'emotional

---

[33] Robert Hewison, *Culture and Consensus. England, Art and Politics since 1940* (London, 1995), pp. 80–1.
[34] Ballin, 'Welshness', pp. 81–2.
[35] Sander Meredeen, *The Man Who Made Penguins: The Life of Sir William Emrys Williams* (London, 2008), pp. 10, 18, 23.
[36] Meredeen, *Man*, p. 10.   [37] *The Times*, 1 April 1977, p. 16.   [38] Meredeen, *Man*, p. 10.
[39] Ballin, 'Welshness', p. 87.
[40] Ballin, 'Welshness', p. 87. This is how he was introduced by Professor Gwyn Jones when he received an Honorary Degree at the University of Wales in 1963.
[41] Ballin, 'Welshness', p. 86.   [42] Ballin, 'Welshness', p. 86.
[43] Meredeen, *Man*, pp. 11, 17.

attachment' to Welsh cultural heritage.[44] As Meredeen notes, these school essays, which he signed 'Emrys', provide an insight into how Welsh lore and legend 'fed his youthful imagination' and helped form his own self-image and identification with Wales.[45] As a young adult, Williams was befriended by Dr Thomas Jones, 'arguably the most influential Welshman of his generation', who acted as his mentor. Jones was behind his first significant appointment, in 1934, as Secretary of the British Institute of Adult Education, and when he became Director of ABCA in 1941.[46] Johnes notes that, during the Second World War, heightened contact between England and Wales 'promoted a sense of Welshness as well as Britishness'.[47] Whilst firmly based in England, Williams continued 'to champion Welsh themes and cultural figures' in his lifetime although he acknowledged to Jones in a 1940 letter that he was a Welshman primarily through 'blood and association'.[48] Williams was so successful in his desire 'to emphasise his links with Wales' that his contemporaries came to treat his Welshness 'as a factor in the way they constructed his identity'.[49] For example, Williams's colleague at Penguin, J. E. Morpurgo, recalled:

> William Emrys Williams was a Welshman to every letter of his unmistakeably Welsh name; even if he did come from Manchester. The rich rhythms of his Welsh voice, cunningly modulated by a controlled stammer, freed him from the suspicion of patronizing the audience that hung over so many of the Oxonian and metropolitan popular educators of that era.[50]

The Welsh 'Pimpernel'

Another leading cultural figure who was perceived as 'Welsh' by his contemporaries was author Richard Llewellyn. His 1939 novel, *How Green Was My Valley* (*HGWMV*), the story of a Welsh mining community seen through the eyes of a child, Huw Morgan, was, in Dai Smith's view, 'the most popular novel ever written by a Welshman about Wales'.[51] It fixed Llewellyn's status as a Welsh writer in permanent aspic. When the news emerged that Llewellyn was not born in Wales as he had stated throughout his lifetime but rather as Richard Vivian Herbert Lloyd in Willesden in 1906, it is significant that much of the negativity attached to

---

[44] Meredeen, *Man*, p. 12. [45] Meredeen, *Man*, pp. 24–5.
[46] Meredeen, *Man*, pp. 12, 55–6, 129; Hewison, *Culture*, p. 41. [47] Johnes, *Wales Since*, p. 29.
[48] Meredeen, *Man*, p. 12. [49] Ballin, 'Welshness', p. 81.
[50] J. E. Morpurgo, *Allen Lane. King Penguin* (London, 1979), p. 120.
[51] David Smith, 'Myth and Meaning in the Literature of the South Wales Coalfield – the 1930s', *The Anglo-Welsh Review*, 25, 56 (1976), p. 28.

this revelation arose from contested notions of authenticity.[52] Analysing Llewellyn's complex negotiation of selfhood during the Second World War allows us to examine the historical tensions between Welshness 'as the preserve of the nation-state'—what Marc Scully terms a largely 'territorialised assumption' of identity—and Welshness as 'a pluralist, diasporic identity'.[53] Charles Burdett, Loredana Polezzi, and Barbara Spadaro point out that narratives of a nation can be produced outwith a country's own boundaries, including from members of diasporic communities. Following their argument, these narratives can often be endorsed by international organizations or the state, thus creating multiple representations of what it means to be 'Welsh', inside or outside of Wales's border.[54]

From the moment of his literary success, Llewellyn allowed himself to be perceived as Welsh, weaving a story about his cultural hinterland that essentially asserted that he was born in Pembrokeshire and that his paternal grandfather was a superintendent at the Britannic Colliery in Gilfach Goch, rather than as an ironworks foreman in Middlesbrough.[55] According to Meic Stephens, Llewellyn 'laid down these false trails all through his life'.[56] Any biographical profile, such as that by Mick Felton, tends to reproduce the same mythic elements:

> Richard Llewellyn was born…in the cathedral village of St. David's, Pembrokeshire, on approximately 10 December 1906. His birth was not registered because his anglophobic maternal grandfather considered birth registration to be an English practice.… Until the age of six, when his family moved to London, Llewellyn spoke only Welsh.[57]

Commentators such as Sam Adams are puzzled by Llewellyn's lifetime reluctance 'to disclose the circumstances of his upbringing'.[58] However, there is a strong case, put forward by John Harris, that the text of *HGWMV* was itself an expression of Llewellyn's struggle to construct a composed identity: to deal with 'his own inner conflicts regarding Wales', his warring 'two worlds'.[59]

Llewellyn was born in Willesden to Welsh parents: restaurant manager, William Llewellyn Lloyd and his wife Sarah Ann and was the product of a lower

---

[52] Sam Adams, 'Letter from Wales', *PN Review*, 35, 6 (2009), p. 7; Aidan Byrne, '"The Male Shoutings of Men": Masculinity and Fascist Epistemology in How Green Was My Valley', *International Journal of Welsh Writing in English* (2013), p. 169.
[53] Scully, 'Discourses', pp. 17, 20.
[54] Burdett, Polezzi, and Spadaro, 'Introduction: Transcultural Italies', p. 1.
[55] Email communication from David Asprey, 9 September 2014. Llewellyn's paternal grandfather, Joseph Lloyd, raised a family in Middlesbrough, including Llewellyn's father, and died there in 1892.
[56] NLW; 'Richard Llewellyn' [video recording]/CambrensisBBCWales, BBC1, 15 December 1999.
[57] Mick Felton, 'Richard Llewellyn', in *Dictionary of Literary Biography, Vol. 15. British Novelists 1930-1959, Part 1*, edited by Bernard Oldsey (Detroit, 1983), p. 324. The 1911 Wales census records Llewellyn as an 'English' speaker.
[58] Adams, 'Letter', p. 9.   [59] Harris, '"Hallelujah"', p. 45.

Figure 9.1 Childhood portrait of Richard Llewellyn, on the left of the picture, with his siblings Gladys, Lorna, and Trevor, London.
Reproduced with permission of David Asprey.

middle-class English suburban childhood (see Figure 9.1).[60] By the time he was a teenager, the Lloyd family were living at 21 Hewitt Avenue, Wood Green; his father William was working as a catering manager with the Slough Trading Company.[61] William organized the catering at the 1924–5 British Empire Exhibition at Wembley and eventually became manager of the Rose and Crown in Watford.[62] Richard's three siblings, Trevor Llewellyn, Gladys Ethelwyn, and

---

[60] Harry Ransom Center, The University of Texas at Austin (HRC), Richard Llewellyn Papers 1939–1952, Birth certificate.
[61] FindMyPast 1921 census, accessed 23 April 2022.
[62] Email communication from David Asprey, 25 August 2014.

Lorna, were also born in part of a significant Welsh diaspora in London. After leaving school, Richard worked as a catering apprentice at his father's employers, the Slough Trading Company.[63] He joined the British Army in 1924, serving for six years, largely in India and Hong Kong.[64] Returning to London, he worked as a reporter for *Cinema Express* and then as a scriptwriter for Fox-British studios producing quota quickies.[65] In 1937, Llewellyn experienced his first taste of critical success when he wrote a play, *Poison Pen*, which transferred to the West End the following year. From this point onwards, Llewellyn appears to have publicly asserted a Welsh identity which was widely accepted. In 1938, he was introduced by the *Daily Mail* as 'a young Welsh author'.[66] That same year, another newspaper profile characterized him as:

> a grandson, on his father's side, of the late Mr and Mrs Joseph Lloyd, of Gilfach Goch, and on the other, of Mr and Mrs Richard Thomas, of Old Belle Vue House, St David's. Much of his time has been spent at Aberdare and at St David's. He speaks Welsh, and his new novel of industrial Wales, 'How Green Was My Valley' is awaited with interest.[67]

Within months of this press item, the publication of this novel was to sweep Llewellyn to a new level of international celebrity and fame, one in which he was firmly anointed as a 'Welsh' author.

The process by which Llewellyn produced *HGWMV* is significant in illuminating his determined self-identification as Welsh, which could also be framed as a search for authenticity. Llewellyn first contacted the publisher Michael Joseph in 1936 via an intermediary, the society photographer, Howard Coster, who tipped off Joseph about 'a novel with a Welsh setting'.[68] There appears to have been a general assumption amongst his English contemporaries that Llewellyn was Welsh; his assertion of Welshness was either taken at face value or widely indulged.[69] His publisher Robert Lusty recollects Llewellyn as 'an irresistibly charming Welshman' who, after receiving a contract and an immediate payment of 150 pounds, 'disappeared into the depths of the Wales from which he had come'.[70] Llewellyn stated later in life, 'I found I didn't know enough about my country or its people' and, adhering to contemporary 'territorial understandings'

---

[63] FindMyPast 1921 census, accessed 23 April 2022. [64] Felton, 'Richard', pp. 324–5.
[65] James Mason, *Before I Forget* (London, 1981), p. 100.
[66] Harold Conway, 'Much Tested Play', *Daily Mail*, 5 April 1938, p. 6.
[67] NLW; GB 0210 DRDIES; 1/108 1936, D. R. Davies Collection of Drama Scrap Books, Richard Llewellyn, 'New Llewellyn Play', 18 July 1938.
[68] Robert Lusty, *Bound to be Read* (London, 1975), pp. 83–4.
[69] In their wartime correspondence, Bertram Rota occasionally addresses Llewellyn as 'Dafydd'. See NLW; MS 21752E Richard Llewellyn Agency Papers 1937–1948; Bodley House Literary Agency, Draft letter, December 1943.
[70] Robert Lusty, 'Writers Remembered: Richard Llewellyn', *The Author* (1991), pp. 20–1.

of Welshness, clearly felt the need to situate himself in Wales in order to secure both personal, and literary, authenticity.[71] In the late 1930s, he travelled repeatedly to Wales before settling in Llangollen. The Welsh actor Meredith Edwards testifies to his presence at Plas Newydd in 1938 as part of the venture by arts patron Howard de Walden to form a Welsh National Theatre.[72] Harris suggests that Plas Newydd acted as 'an important cultural contact' for Llewellyn, providing a meeting point with the Welsh scholar T. Gwynn Jones and Saunders Lewis, both members of the National Theatre Council.[73] Edwards recalls how Llewellyn was holding auditions on de Walden's behalf whilst writing his novel:

> He came to one of our sessions one day and asked me what my name was. My first name was Gwilym and that was the name I used then.... 'Right,' he said, 'that will be the name of the father in my novel.'[74]

In 1938, Llewellyn also pursued the Welsh dramatist and broadcaster Jack Jones, a 'self-educated working-class writer of high talent'.[75] Significantly, Jones laces his recollection of their meeting with an implicit hint at Llewellyn's inauthenticity alongside an assertion of his own territorial and generational authority:

> He told me he was writing a book, a novel about mining life, so he wanted to have a talk with me. He stayed to lunch and we talked and after lunch I went down to Cardiff on the bus with him. *Cymru am byth*, which means Wales for ever, he cried as he left me. He did not know much about the life and work of the mining community of South Wales, but he was very much in sympathy with them and had made up his mind to try and do them justice in the novel he was writing. Good luck to you, son, was what I said.[76]

Llewellyn did have an ancestral connection to Gilfach Goch which was less immediate than the one he claimed: his father's maternal grandfather, David Thomas Jones, was a cashier at one of the collieries in the 1880s.[77] Thus, Llewellyn undertook fieldwork in the South Wales coalfield in order to learn more about his 'home' of origin. Adams insists that Llewellyn primarily found out about the area of Gilfach Goch through a local miner, Joseph Griffiths, who had worked underground for over fifty years.[78] In a 1999 BBC Wales documentary, Joseph's grandson, Teifion Griffiths, produced his father's diary which confirmed that Llewellyn visited the family on 21 November 1938. Griffiths said of his grandfather:

---

[71] *Western Mail*, 12 August 1968; Scully, 'Discourses', p. 109.
[72] von Rothkirch, *J. O. Francis*, p. 85.   [73] Harris, '"Hallelujah"', p. 44.
[74] *Western Mail*, 4 January 1989.   [75] Jones, *Dragon*, p. 58.   [76] Jones, *Me*, p. 62.
[77] Email communication from David Asprey, 5 September 2014.   [78] Adams, 'Letter', p. 7.

He walked Llewellyn around Gilfach up and down the valley, pointing out various things, telling him where the first pit had started and so on.... The feeling in my family is that Llewellyn actually gained quite a lot of information from my grandfather.[79]

More significant, however, is that Llewellyn initially made the Gilfach Goch contact via the Welsh Department of Foyles bookshop on Charing Cross Road, London, which was managed by Joseph's son, Will Griffiths.[80] This bookshop, described by the poet Keidrych Rhys as a 'London-Welsh cultural centre', was a significant meeting place for the diasporic exiled Welsh in London.[81] It regularly hosted 'All-Welsh Luncheons' and produced its own publications under the imprint 'Gwasg Foyle.'[82] During the war, Llewellyn's friend, the bookseller Bertram Rota, reminded him of 'the old days of the Welsh Circle at Foyle's' signifying Llewellyn's participation in this diasporic cultural grouping.[83] There is also evidence that Will Griffiths himself had a closer editorial role in Llewellyn's novel than has previously been acknowledged. A letter written by Llewellyn in July 1939 shows that the author sent Griffiths the draft manuscript of *HGWMV*, requesting, 'Please read it and correct where you find it wrong, and I shall be in your debt. But quickly, Willie, for it is near to publication.'[84] Llewellyn also contacted T. Gwynn Jones at this time, inviting 'any criticism you may have to offer in the matter of proper names', particularly the correct rendition of Welsh spellings.[85] This demonstrates both the importance of London Welsh diasporic networks in Llewellyn's evolution as a writer as well as his painstaking attempts to achieve authenticity through his dependency on Welsh contacts. Adams notes how, in the finished product, Llewellyn's dialogue 'imitates Welsh idiom and word order'.[86] Even more significantly, the book 'is predicated on the notion that the characters are speaking in Welsh and that what is on the page is an English translation',[87] thus indicating an insider's knowledge. The inclusion of a 'Guide to the Pronunciation of Welsh Names' at the close of the book is also significant, with Llewellyn consciously positioning himself as an expert interlocutor between Wales and England.

---

[79] NLW; 'Richard Llewellyn' [video recording].
[80] Adams, 'Letter', p. 9.
[81] Keidrych Rhys, 'Editorial', *Wales*, 4, 6 (1945), p. 7.
[82] Jones, *Me*, p. 108; Adams, 'Letter', p. 9.
[83] NLW; MS 21752E; Draft letter from Bertram Rota, 19 January 1944.
[84] Invaluable Online Auction Catalogue (2013). 'Lot 216: Collection of literary ephemera, formed by Mr William Griffiths', Letter from Llewellyn to Griffiths, 19 July 1939, http://www.invaluable.com/auction-lot/collection-of-literary-ephemera,-formed-by-mr-wil-216-c-07ebe01fb3, accessed 23 September 2015.
[85] NLW; G3691; Papers of Thomas Gwynn Jones, Letter from Richard Llewellyn, n.d.
[86] Adams, 'Letter', p. 8.
[87] Derrick Price, 'How Green Was My Valley: A Romance of Wales', in *The Progress of Romance. The Politics of Popular Fiction*, edited by Jean Radford (London, 1986), p. 85.

How Green Was My Valley

Set during the late nineteenth century in a South Wales mining village, *How Green Was My Valley* is concerned with the story of the Morgan family narrated through the memories of the youngest child, Huw. As well as promoting a powerful vision of family, the novel addresses 'manual colliery work, English ownership of the coal mines, strikes, lockouts, industrialization, emigration, hostility toward the Welsh language, and the political and social power of Nonconformist religion.'[88] Glyn Jones defines the interwar 'Anglo-Welsh' novel as having emerged from the South Wales coalfield, 'an industrial area which knew widespread, perhaps unparalleled, unemployment, and during a period of violent unrest and bitter suffering'. He identifies Richard Llewellyn as one of its key practitioners alongside Jack Jones, Rhys Davies, Gwyn Jones, and Lewis Jones.[89] More recently, Daniel G. Williams notes how Welsh writings of the 1930s 'document and occasionally celebrate the emergence of a new, cosmopolitan, urban Wales, while also conveying some unease about what the *Welsh Review* described in 1939 as "the coming of a mongrel race".' In this context, Llewellyn's *HGWMV* offers 'a simplified, bestselling, treatment of a theme that reappears in the period's novels, and reverberates beyond the fiction into other discourses relating to 1930s Wales.'[90] At the same time, Chris Hopkins notes how, in this period, 'Wales became a subject for writing and viewing *from England* in a way which it had never been before.' The reasons for this, he suggests, lay not in a particular recognition of Wales as a nation in its own right but rather, an association of Wales with 'a particular political response' and a 'literary aesthetic'.[91] Dai Smith identifies how the trend for government-commissioned industrial and sociological surveys investigating the 'plummeting decline' of the South Wales coalfield in the 1930s was matched by literary endeavors to 'enlighten' sympathetic readers.[92] In this period, some London publishers actively sought to publish work by writers about working-class subjects, particularly in 'Distressed Areas' such as South Wales, to such an extent that Wales came to 'represent a kind of domestic otherness'.[93] Llewellyn clearly benefited from these trends; indeed, Felton detects one major source of contemporary criticism for his novel being the sense that it was 'profiting from the Welsh vogue in England'.[94]

HGWMV was published a month after the outbreak of the Second World War on 2 October 1939, becoming an instant bestseller. Making an unprecedented investment in a first-time novelist, Michael Joseph set a run of 25, 000.[95] In the UK, it sold a thousand copies a week over the next two years and 60,000 in 1942 after the release of the film; this success was duplicated in America and with

---

[88] Felton, 'Richard', p. 325.
[89] Jones, *Dragon*, p. 56.
[90] Williams, *Black*, p. 197.
[91] Hopkins, *English*, p. 61.
[92] Smith, 'Myth', p. 550.
[93] Hopkins, *English*, pp. 61–2.
[94] Felton, 'Richard', p. 325.
[95] Lusty, *Bound*, p. 96.

colonial sales.[96] Hajkowski argues that the enduring cultural image of the Welsh mining village carried special significance during the war with coal being vital to the war effort and the dangers faced by miners symbolizing the wider dangers faced by the British people. Most importantly, 'the values of the miners and the mining villages interlocked effectively with the ideals of a nation fighting a total war for its survival: community, camaraderie, resilience, and cheerfulness in the face of great tribulation.'[97] Overall, the book was well-received, receiving effusive reviews. *The New York Times* viewed it as 'The most magnificent novel ever produced about Wales', whilst the editor of *The Bookseller* proclaimed, 'Llewellyn has done for Wales what Synge did for Ireland.'[98] The poet David Jones reviewed the novel for the *TLS* in October 1939 under the title 'Light from Wales', enthusing about 'the breath of Welsh incantation in Mr Llewellyn's flow of language' whilst Edwin Muir praised Llewellyn's skill in 'writing English as a Welshman'.[99] Some, however, sensed falsity. From Wales, in particular, there were accusations that the novel was a 'misrepresentation of Welsh life' and a typical product of those who 'wrote about Wales for a market'.[100] For Keidrych Rhys, the editor of the arts journal *Wales*, which promoted Welsh writing in English, 'Llewellyn was another "merchant-hack", trimming his material for London publishers.' Glyn Jones's verdict in 1942 was that it was 'a fake, but a charming fake', believing that the novel 'ignored the grimness of the Valleys'.[101] Overall, Harris surmises, the leading figures within Welsh writing in English were irritated by 'Llewellyn's presumption of speaking for Wales' conjoined with a sense of unease at his 'professional Welshman' persona.[102] To adopt Scully's argument, this suggests that Llewellyn's personal construction of Welsh identity was not 'felt' as authentic within wider collective understandings of Welshness.[103] Ironically, the book, which sold well in both Wales and England, was successful because it was experienced as emotionally authentic by its readership even though it was often framed as inauthentic by contemporary Welsh reviewers.[104]

A key point of dissonance within Welsh contemporary observations of Llewellyn appears to have been the way in which he ostentatiously embraced his commercial success. This perhaps sat uneasily after years of economic depression

---

[96] John Harris, 'Not Only a Place in Wales', *Planet: The Welsh Internationalist*, 73 (1989), p. 11.
[97] Hajkowski, *BBC*, p. 187. These ideas were reinforced by the 1941 film which Richards describes as a 'potent mixture of myth, romance, idyll, dream, memory, melody and emotion' Jeffrey Richards, *Films and British National Identity. From Dickens to Dad's Army* (Manchester, 1997), p. 220.
[98] *Daily Express*, 13 March 1940; Harris, 'Not', p. 12.
[99] Cited in Thomas Dilworth, 'From the Archive', *The New Welsh Review*, 75, 1 (2007), p. 43; Edwin Muir, 'New Novels', *Listener*, 12 October 1939, 561, p. 734.
[100] NLW; GB 0210 DRDIES; 1/108 1936, 'How Green Are Welsh Authors?', 8 August 1944.
[101] Harris, ' "Hallelujah" ', p. 56.
[102] Harris, 'Not', p. 15; Huw Osborne, *Rhys Davies* (Cardiff, 2009), p. 36.
[103] Scully, 'Discourses', p. 9.
[104] John Harris, 'Popular Images', pp. 203–21; Byrne, ' "Male" ', p. 169. See NLW; Richard Llewellyn papers; Correspondence 1970–1983, 5/1–137.

which had seen the decimation of coalfield communities, particularly in South Wales, and when Welsh visibility in interwar London was often embodied by hunger marchers calling attention to their plight.[105] Meredith Edwards recalls how Llewellyn's ownership of dozens of suits and shoes at Plas Newydd was 'very impressive to a Welsh boy with one suit and one pair of shoes'.[106] Lusty also recalls how Llewellyn 'moved into a lavish Mayfair flat which he crammed with pictures and many treasures', including forty-eight toothbrushes in the bathroom.[107] For Rota, it was 'an enchanting haven' full of 'good and elegant things'.[108] Yet, this extravagance also worked to set Llewellyn apart from Welsh writers such as Jack Jones whose play *Land of My Fathers*—which highlighted the plight of 'idle and good men rotting for want of something to do'—was performed in London in 1938.[109] In his memoir, Jones describes being buttonholed by Llewellyn in a Strand restaurant, and being smothered by the latter's excessive display of hospitality. Jones's narrative subtly constructs Llewellyn as misguidedly attempting to assert authority over a more legitimate representative of Wales:

> As I entered the room where Richard Llewelyn [sic], looking ever so vivid and vital, was entertaining the producer and cast, he greeted me with '*Cymru am byth*', Wales for ever, and escorted me to the place of honour which he said was reserved for me. I thought him most kind though a little too attentive and solicitous. Three of the young men of the cast had already noted and resented this and had gone to sit apart at a small table, and when I went across to them one of them said: It's no before you ask, Jack. We're on our own and we're paying for our own. No ill-feeling, said the other. It's just that our host is a shade too flamboyant for us chaps. The third said something rather offensive and I went back to where our host was doing all in his power to honour and entertain the people up from Wales.[110]

Implicit here is the suggestion that Llewellyn does not fully comprehend the current plight of the people of Wales; he is constructed oppositionally to the people 'up' from Wales. Later on in Jones's memoir, his perplexing wartime discovery of Llewellyn serving as 'Capt Richard Lloyd of the Welsh Guards' in Fano, Italy, again hints that Llewellyn is not what he appears to be.[111]

Significantly, whilst English contemporaries of Llewellyn also picked up on dandified elements of Llewellyn's appearance, they still firmly construct him as a 'Celt', often employing stereotypical motifs of Welshness. Theatre producer Basil Dean, who employed Llewellyn as his 'right-hand man' at Entertainments

---

[105] John Stevenson, *British Society 1914–45* (London, 1990), pp. 114–15.
[106] *Western Mail*, 4 January 1989. [107] Lusty, 'Writers', p. 21.
[108] NLW; MS 21752E; Draft letter from Bertram Rota, 4 November 1943.
[109] Jones, *Me*, p. 19. [110] Jones, *Me*, p. 68. [111] Jones, *Me*, p. 393.

National Service Association (ENSA) from October 1939, described his 'quick intelligence and Celtic gift of fantasy where the facts of a situation required embellishment'.[112] At the Ministry of Economic Warfare, where Llewellyn was seconded between 1941 and 42, the author Peter Quennell encountered him as 'a small neat dark Celt, now wearing the elegant uniform of a captain in the Welsh Guards' and looking 'enviably smart and rich'.[113] In these accounts Llewellyn often appears as a liminal figure, positioned on the boundaries of belonging. The ENSA employee Stephen Williams recalls the presence of Llewellyn at a meeting in 1940 between ENSA grandees and senior BBC staff, including the producer, Greatorex Newman.[114] On this occasion, Llewellyn arrived in attire consisting of 'a startling shade of green, with shirt and collar of paler hue, suede shoes and a violet tie'.[115] Williams recalls the arrival of his 'flamboyant' colleague:

> It really was something quite extraordinary. So much so that Rex Newman turned round to us in a quiet voice and said, 'He's just written that book *How Green Was My Valley*, hasn't he? Well, how green was *his* valley, to let him go out like that?'[116]

The ENSA founder, Basil Dean, also present, relates Newman's comment as follows: 'he leaned across the table to me and whispered, "How keen was my valet!"'[117] Using a slightly different iteration of Newman's pun, Dean's account underlines the same point: that Llewellyn was perceived as an outsider. Arguably, Llewellyn was still struggling to find a place where he fully 'belonged' despite the fact that his asserted claim to Welshness had been culturally endorsed. It is worth noting that, in this period, Llewellyn also ventured into representations of contemporary England. Before the war, Llewellyn was drafting a new play about Italian 'gangster-life' in Soho which he intended to call either 'Murder in Soho' or 'Lid Off London'.[118] Llewellyn's second novel, *None But the Lonely Heart* (1943), which he worked on whilst serving in the Welsh Guards, also focused on the theme of metropolitan criminality, charting the life of delinquent Ernie Mott. This was an aspect of English society which Llewellyn said he had witnessed in the 1930s, as an observer in juvenile courts.[119] However, Llewellyn's decision to write 'in Cockney English—written to be read aloud'[120] was again critiqued on the grounds of perceived inauthenticity. Peter Quennell was unimpressed by the

---

[112] Richard Fawkes, *Fighting for a Laugh. Entertaining the British and American Armed Forces 1939–1946* (London, 1978), p. 187; Basil Dean, *The Theatre at War* (London, 1956), p. 98.
[113] Peter Quennell, *The Wanton Chase* (New York, 1980), p. 28.
[114] IWM 8741; Sound Archive; Stephen Williams interviewed by Lyn E. Smith, 10 December 1984.
[115] Dean, *Theatre*, p. 99.   [116] IWM 8741.   [117] Dean, *Theatre*, p. 99.
[118] *Daily Mail*, 26 October 1938, p. 21; John Rylands Special Collections (JRSC); Basil Dean Archive 1/1/1509; Letter from Llewellyn, 7 July 1939.
[119] *Western Mail*, 12 August 1968, p. 6.   [120] *Western Mail*, 12 August 1968, p. 6.

'rambling cockney jargon' and whilst collating the reviews for Llewellyn, Rota noted their generic complaint 'that this is not the real East End and the real cockney'.[121] Whilst Llewellyn subsequently rejected the novel as 'unfinished', his experimentation with Welsh and English idioms in both wartime novels suggests someone who was attempting to shift between two potential identities but remained an outsider in both.[122] Indeed, Quennell's review of *None But the Lonely Heart* perceived the 'Welshman' Llewellyn as 'approaching his subject from the point of view of the romantic outsider'.[123]

The success of *HGWMV*, however, conferred immediate legitimacy upon Llewellyn in the sense that it positioned him as an authority on all matters Welsh. Throughout the war, he was in demand from a range of cultural agencies, including the BBC, who were keen for him to promote ideas of Britishness, making use of his 'Welsh' profile to plug into wider narratives of national togetherness to global audiences. As the war progressed, significant attempts were made by key institutions to refine conceptions of Britishness whilst working to recognize 'the diversity of the British Isles'.[124] Jeffrey Richards has shown how British wartime cinema was 'careful to characterize its forces units as embracing all regions, countries and classes of the United Kingdom', with films such as *Millions Like Us* (1943), *The Way Ahead* (1944), and *The Captive Heart* (1946) including Welsh and Scottish characters alongside English ones.[125] Similarly, in the documentary films *Scotland Speaks* (1941), *Ulster* (1941), and *Wales—Green Mountain, Black Mountain* (1942), Stuart Allan notes how the producers used this space to confidently narrate a sense of cultural distinctiveness within the framework of British unity.[126] For Hajkowski, the BBC was 'the most important arena, in which regional cultures interacted with and interrogated a normative English culture, buttressing the hybrid "dual identities" of contemporary Britain'.[127] Throughout the conflict, the BBC maintained its production of 'regionally flavoured' programmes thus emphasizing national unity whilst recognizing 'the national diversity of Britain'.[128] Hajkowski points out that special programmes were dedicated to all of Britain's patron saints, Welsh region prepared talks in Welsh and the series *In Britain Now*, which included contributions from Scotland, Wales, Northern Ireland, and the English regions, 'admirably represented the multinational character of Britain'.[129]

What is clear from archival research is that Llewellyn responded somewhat ambivalently to the demands placed upon him in this wartime role as an

---

[121] *Daily Mail*, 9 October 1943, p. 2; NLW; MS 21752E; Letter from Bertram Rota, 1 March 1945.
[122] *Western Mail*, 12 August 1968, p. 6.　　[123] *Daily Mail*, 9 October 1943, p. 2.
[124] Hajkowski, *BBC*, p. 8.　　[125] Richards, *Films*, p. 109.
[126] Stuart Allan, '"Some Idea of Our Country": Scotland, Wales and Northern Ireland in Early Wartime Documentary Film', in *Fighting for Britain?*
[127] Hajkowski, *BBC*, p. 2.　　[128] Hajkowski, *BBC*, p. 121.　　[129] Hajkowski, *BBC*, p. 122.

authority on Wales. Hajkowski notes that once BBC Wales became fully integrated into the BBC's unified Home Service in September 1939, Welsh broadcasters focused on their nation's contribution to the war effort and 'produced programs that connected the Welsh experience, or Welshness, to larger propaganda themes'.[130] In autumn 1940, a flurry of internal memos circulated within the BBC attempting to locate Llewellyn as a potential 'speaker.' When BBC Overseas in London assumed that 'Welsh Region' would know his whereabouts, the latter responded, 'as far as we know Mr Llewellyn is still working for ENSA at Drury Lane' confirming his address as the St Regis Hotel, London.[131] In early 1941, Nan Davies, of the Features and Drama Section in Wales, attempted to contact Llewellyn asking him to participate in the programme, 'Welsh Chords', one of a series of monthly broadcasts to the Empire with 'a Welsh bias'.[132] When Llewellyn proved hard to track down, Davies contacted the BBC in London stating:

> I have been trying to get hold of Mr Richard Llewellyn's address but he appears to be rather an elusive gentleman. I noticed an article by him in a recent issue of 'London Calling' so it occurred to me that you might have his address in your files. If so, I should be very grateful if you could let me have it as soon as possible.[133]

The reply came the following day, revealing that Llewellyn's 'real name is Lloyd' and providing a Welsh Guards contact address, an allusion to his military enlistment.[134] Davies made contact with Llewellyn via his regiment and tried to encourage his participation by stating that his speech would appear alongside 'Welsh News-Letter' (Gossips from Wales) by A. G. Prys Jones and 'The Welsh corner of the British empire' by a French commentator. The broadcast would also include a Welsh folk song performed by a group of evacuated London schoolchildren. Davies resorted to enclosing a telegram form with 1/- in stamps to encourage a reply.[135] In a subsequent communication, Davies elaborates on the intention behind the programme:

(a) To let Welshmen abroad have some news of what is happening in 'yr hen wlad'.

---

[130] Hajkowski, *BBC*, pp. 182, 186.
[131] BBC Written Archives Centre (WAC), WA8/370/1; Llewellyn Richard, Internal Circulating Memos, 26 August–2 September 1940.
[132] WAC; WA8/370/1; RP/9/ND, 24 January 1941.
[133] WAC; WA8/370/1; RP/9/ND, Internal Memo—Wales, 3 February 1941.
[134] WAC; WA8/370/1; RP/9/ND, Internal Memo to Nan Davies, 4 February 1941.
[135] WAC; WA8/370/1; RP/9/ND, 7 February 1941.

(b) To show listeners in the Empire generally how a small nation living in close proximity to England is able to preserve its own way of life and foster its native language and culture.

Specifically, the programme makers wanted Llewellyn to aim for a 'lighter and more chatty' talk that 'throws light on the Welsh temperament, or a description of some old Welsh character that may have impressed you at some time'.[136] Llewellyn eventually did respond and recorded a four and a half minute talk in London entitled 'A Welsh Cameo' but his evasiveness hints at his metaphorical and literal distance from Welsh cultural life at this time. However, Llewellyn continued to be pursued by cultural agencies that identified him as a leading representative of the Welsh nation. In October 1941, the publishers William Collins contacted Llewellyn to see if he would contribute a volume to the series *Britain in Pictures* on the subject of Wales and provide 'some description of the character of the country and its people', concluding, 'the Committee and the Publishers are most anxious that the volume on Wales should be as good as possible and feel that no author could write this book so well as yourself'.[137] Llewellyn turned this opportunity down. This suggests that Llewellyn was uneasily aware that he could never fully match the expectations of others in terms of his own constructed Welsh identity. It also suggests that he lacked faith in the authority of his diasporic claim to Welshness: that acknowledgement of his English birthplace and upbringing would somehow dilute the sincerity of his personal commitment to Wales. Increasingly, with his phenomenal literary success, Llewellyn became publicly confined within a Welsh identity which overlaid his diasporic roots. In response, he appears to have behaved during the war as a 'Welsh Pimpernel': sought here and there to present a vision of Wales but often proving elusive.

The Welsh Guards

One way in which Llewellyn attempted to resolve these contradictions was to join the Welsh Guards. In June 1940, Llewellyn wrote to his former ENSA boss, Basil Dean, from Portmeirion, 'The news is wretched, yet I am confident that we are not in a losing patch. Dunkirk was an Act of God. There will be more.'[138] As a former guardsman in the British Army, Llewellyn was able to volunteer from the Officers Emergency Reserve and was commissioned in September 1940, at the rather advanced age of thirty-four. Importantly, the uniform of the Welsh Guards

---

[136] WAC; WA8/370/1; RP/9/ND, 10 February 1941.
[137] NLW; MS 21752E; Letter from Sheila D. Shannon, 21 October 1941.
[138] JRSC; Basil Dean Archive; 1/1/1512, 6 June 1940.

enabled him to readily access a recognizably Welsh martial identity.[139] When he was commissioned, Llewellyn recorded his birthplace as St David's on his army forms and recorded his own nationality as 'Welsh' alongside that of his parents. On this documentation, he also inserted 'Dafydd' and 'Llewellyn' into his name to become Richard Dafydd Vivian Llewellyn Lloyd.[140] Although he was living at Claridge's Hotel, Llewellyn borrowed the address of his family's temporary residence in Merionethshire, North Wales, where he had arranged for them to be evacuated in September 1940: 'Cynlas' near Bala, itself highly symbolic as the birthplace of influential Welsh Liberal politician, and founder of Cymru Fydd, T. E. Ellis.[141] Furthermore, a journalist's report of a private film viewing of *HGWMV* shows how Llewellyn's military persona, in this newly patriotic context, served to consolidate his Welshness:

> Richard Llewellyn, now a lieutenant in the Welsh Guards and wearing the uniform, sat with me through the film which he, too, was seeing for the first time....Mr Llewellyn's Welsh associations are with St David's, where he was born, and Gilfach Goch, where his family lived for many years.[142]

As Lieutenant Lloyd, Llewellyn served in the UK for two years until overseas service in North Africa and Italy from 1943 onwards.[143] A young subaltern who served alongside Llewellyn, Philip Brutton, wrote of their time stationed in Lake Trasimeno living in the property of the Marchesa Bourbon del Monte Ranieri di Sorbello but, interestingly, constructs Llewellyn as sitting outside of conventional norms:

> The Marchesa, like most Italian women, is rather beautiful but also very selective...one of our officers [Richard Llewellyn Lloyd—Richard Llewellyn who wrote *How Green Was My Valley*] remarked that the house was under military control and that she must consider herself very lucky not to have had it demolished like most others. Later Richard Lloyd had the Marchesa's cook put in prison in Passignano for a month. The circumstances were as suspicious as Richard Lloyd was capricious. He was in the charge of the mess. He also supplied the cook with Army rations. She taught him kitchen Italian wherever was most comfortable. They fell out. She called him names. He called in the police. The 'evidence' was there. The house, as he had inelegantly expressed it, was under military occupation. The cook returned to the Marchesa who has never forgotten the talented but complexed little man.[144]

---

[139] Welsh Guards Archive (WGA); Papers of Captain Richard Lloyd.
[140] WGA; Papers of Captain Richard Lloyd.   [141] *Evening Express*, 5 April 1899.
[142] NLW; GB 0210 DRDIES; 1/108 1936, 'The Author Pleased', [27] April 1941.
[143] WGA; Papers of Captain Richard Lloyd.   [144] Brutton, *Ensign*, p. 88.

Here, the implication is that Llewellyn's display of poor manners towards the Marchesa was linked to his failure to adhere to the correct 'form' of a Guards officer; a factor underlined by his liaison with the Italian cook. With his lower-middle-class suburban upbringing, it appears that Llewellyn struggled to fit in with the other, often privately educated, upper-class Welsh Guards officers. Interestingly, an *Observer* profile from 1975 picks up on this distance between Llewellyn and his fellow officers, stating that following the publication of *HGWMV*, Llewellyn was 'accused in the officers' mess of being a "bloody Red"' due to the fact that many of his fellow officers were 'the sons of coal barons'.[145] Ultimately, these articulated class frictions suggest that, for Llewellyn, the wartime identity of the Welsh Guardsman also proved, at times, to be ill-fitting.

Llewellyn's particular form of shape shifting, reflected in his adoption and shedding of different forenames and surnames, was not accidental but, arguably, a reflection of his own conflicted sense of duality. Although Llewellyn dedicated *HGWMV* 'To my father and the land of my fathers', he also associated his Welsh-born father William Lloyd primarily with Englishness. In 1968, he reminisced about being raised within a dual and competing heritage:

> With my grandfather during school holidays we were all Cambrians. We fought again with Caradoc and Llewelyn, recited the poetry, sang the songs. At home, with my father, we charged at Waterloo and stormed the Great Redan. We were English of the English.[146]

Here, Llewellyn acknowledges his English heritage but does not categorically state that he grew up in England. It could reasonably be argued that, in his public pronouncements, Llewellyn was engaged upon the act of masquerade, electing to emphasize his Welsh identity and mask his English upbringing. However, in terms of Llewellyn's personal identity construction, it is also crucial to acknowledge the significance of his diasporic links with Wales. By 1931, there were over 50,000 Welsh-born men and women living in the city, contributing to a diasporic presence which had comfortably reached its third generation of settlement.[147] As discussed in earlier chapters, the concept of diaspora 'opens up new cultural spaces beyond the boundaries of homeland', enabling an emphasis on identity as historically constructed rather than fixed.[148] Merfyn Jones points out that for the descendants of Welsh immigrants growing up in English cities in the early twentieth century, being Welsh 'offered few problems' compared to the settler generation: 'with the English language, but without their Welsh accents, they only

---

[145] Road, 'How green', p. 37. Road observes that Llewellyn is, rather, 'a true-blue right-wing Welshman'.
[146] *Western Mail*, 12 August 1968, p. 6.   [147] Jones, 'Flow – and Ebb', p. 128.
[148] Kenny, *Diaspora*, p. 12.

needed to choose'.[149] For Llewellyn, his Welsh parentage and heritage clearly mattered. He spent childhood holidays in Wales, particularly with his maternal grandparents in St David's.[150] In a 1992 TV documentary, his sister Lorna Llewellyn Lloyd was filmed in St David's where she recalled:

> This was the Wales he knew. This is why he was able to reproduce, years later, the language because St David's was the centre point of his life at that time and he absorbed it all because of the large family, you see? My mother had many sisters as well as this one brother and they all spoke Welsh. Nobody spoke English. You wouldn't dare. So, this was the part of the world that inspired him.[151]

Both of Llewellyn's parents were born in Wales, although his father was raised in Middlesbrough from a young age. Llewellyn is also recorded in the 1911 census as staying with his paternal aunt, Kate Poulsen, at 18 Windsor Esplanade, Cardiff, a place his cousin recalls as a popular holiday destination amongst the younger generation of the extended Lloyd family.[152] Writing in 1968, Llewellyn linked the genesis of his first novel to his father:

> It was in 1927 that I got the idea of writing about an ordinary Cambrian—not a Lloyd George—of modest birth, little more than the 3Rs, and finding out what he might have done with his life at about the time my father was born.[153]

Llewellyn also pointed to the influence of his Welsh mother, whose relatively early death in 1928 is of potential significance in nurturing his identification with Wales. In a private letter to his cousin, David Asprey, in 1975 Llewellyn mentions 'my beautiful Mama'.[154] He also reminisced in his *Western Mail* column, 'A man thinking back across his life can be gentle with himself in boyhood. Because of his Mama. The most important influence in any man's life.'[155] Whilst not reflecting Llewellyn's own lived experience, Osmond acknowledges that the emotional power of *HGWMV* is rooted in the iteration of 'Huw's love for his "Mam"'.[156] Another matrilineal factor which bolstered Llewellyn's attachment to Wales was his relationship with his grandmother Elizabeth Thomas who lived in St David's until her death in 1915. In wartime correspondence with an American girlfriend,

---

[149] Jones, 'Liverpool Welsh', p. 29.
[150] St David's as a historical site of Welsh 'Anglicanism' could also be significant here. See Davies, *History*, p. 229.
[151] NLW; 'How Green Was My Valley', BBC2 Wales, Agenda Production for BBC Wales, dir. John Osmond, 30 April 1992.
[152] David Asprey, '"Number Eighteen". A Fond Memory of Childhood' (2013), unpublished memoir (private hands).
[153] *Western Mail*, 12 August 1968, p. 6.
[154] David Asprey, 'Fact or Fiction', unpublished notes (private hands).
[155] *Western Mail*, 17 June 1968, p. 4.   [156] *Western Mail*, 29 April 1992.

Sarah R. Steinman, whom he met whilst serving in Italy, Llewellyn reminisced about 'My Grannie' who used to spend time in bed 'in red flannel with a fichu of beerstains & biled ham'. During his 1942 affair with the double agent Mathilde Carré, the latter confided to her MI5 minder that there were 'only two women' in Llewellyn's life, 'one his grandmother and the other she'.[157]

In addition, wartime correspondence between Llewellyn and his father, held at the Harry Ransom Center, University of Texas at Austin, testifies to a closeness between the author and his father as well as illuminating a wider familial connection with Wales. Whilst evacuated in Bala, Llewellyn's father, William Lloyd wrote a series of letters to his son, 'Darling Vivian.' Although he was raised in Middlesbrough, it is interesting to note how in their correspondence William signals his own sense of Welshness and connection to the Welsh landscape. Writing from his rented farmhouse, he muses:

> The wild life and open spaces might sound good in books but in reality it does not appeal to me on the side of a mountain with wind, rain and the water rushing down from the hills or I ought to say mountains, yet, there is something in my old blood when I realise it is Wales.

Lloyd also expresses pride in his English granddaughters who are attending a local school: 'I am pleased to let you know that Ann & Sally speak & sing Welsh, it is the funniest thing to hear them and it is not parrotwise, it's real'.[158] The letters also provide an insight into how the success of *HGWMV* propels the author's family into a closer identification with Wales. For example, Llewellyn's father became involved in dealings with the producers of the film version of *HGWMV*, including the arrangements for Welsh auditions for cast members. In November 1940, he writes to Llewellyn:

> I enclose a letter from Mr Baker of the 20th Century Fox for your perusal.... I feel sure he will like my reply in which I conveyed to him the extraordinary interest the North Walians are taking and looking forward to the film. My taking the two boys and the schoolmaster to Cardiff created quite a sensation and it is in all the North Wales papers (in Welsh).[159]

Llewellyn's literary reputation is certainly a key factor in explaining his foregrounding of his Welsh sense of self, suggesting a complex reciprocity with the overwhelming popular success of *HGWMV*. There is evidence that, during the

---

[157] NLW; MS 23710D; Richard Llewellyn letters 1944–1945, Letter No. 9, January 1945; TNA; KV2/928; Mathilde Lucie Carré, Memo by S. Barton, 17 May 1942. Both these files provide fascinating insights into Llewellyn's wartime relationships with women.

[158] HRC; Letter from William Lloyd, 4 December 1940.

[159] HRC; Letter from William Lloyd, 20 November 1940.

war, he purchased a cottage in Wales as a 'mountain retreat'.[160] Llewellyn also collected antiquarian items relating to Wales, Rota reassuring him whilst he was on military service: 'We snap up odd trifles like old Welsh maps from time to time, to show you when you return.'[161] Thus, through a network of familial ties, beginning in childhood and reinforced during the war, it is clear that being Welsh held *meaning* for Llewellyn.

Papers held at the BBC Written Archives provide further evidence of Llewellyn's distinctive brand of 'self-fashioning' as well as the often precarious nature of his wartime performance of Welsh identity.[162] As discussed above, the promotion of images of Wales and Welshness was central to the BBC's imperial and global projection of the British nation. The BBC Overseas Service was particularly interested in Llewellyn's appeal to US audiences and was keen for him to broadcast to North America where his novel had been 'well received'.[163] In a letter, Llewellyn's father describes one such broadcast as 'the feature of the evening at gatherings in many places in America of Welsh speaking people'.[164] In January 1941, Llewellyn provided four talks for the BBC's Overseas North American Transmission under the series title *Democracy Marches*. He also provided an earlier talk in December 1940 entitled 'Britain Speaks.' In this script, the key theme is the composure of women in the face of war. It focuses primarily on London and suggests an intimate, insider knowledge of the capital city.[165] Overall, Llewellyn ruminates on the British character at war plugging into the popular discourse of British fearlessness and stoicism simultaneously being promoted by US commentators Ed Murrow and Quentin Reynolds, the former an acquaintance of Llewellyn's.[166] In a talk transmitted on 18 January 1941, Llewellyn waxes lyrical about St David's, his supposed birthplace in Wales, and artfully manages to convey the impression that this is where he was raised and, indeed, still lives. Lynn Abrams notes how narrative self-fashioning is 'a project which requires much sifting and selection, omission as well as inclusion' in order to achieve a coherent or composed self.[167] Llewellyn's talk begins with a recollection of the city of St Davids and his maternal grandmother, 'a Welsh woman whose eyes, as I remember them, held the grey brave fire of one who has experienced all that can decently happen to any good

---

[160] NLW; MS 21752E; Draft letter from Bertram Rota, 4 November 1943.
[161] NLW; MS 21752E; Letter from Bertram Rota, 6 March 1944.
[162] Matt Houlbrook, '"A Pin to See the Peepshow": Culture, Fiction and Selfhood in Edith Thompson's Letters, 1921–1922', *Past & Present*, 207, 1 (2010), pp. 215–49. doi.org/10.1093/pastj/gtp049.
[163] WAC; WA8/370/1; Internal Memo—Welsh Region, 30 August 1940.
[164] HRC; Letter from William Lloyd, 20 November 1940.
[165] WAC; Talks Llewellyn, Richard, 'Britain Speaks', B/C 21/22.12.40.
[166] Ed Murrow, *This is London* (New York, 1989), p. 176.
[167] Lynn Abrams, 'Liberating the Female Self: Epiphanies, Conflict and Coherence in the Life Stories of Post-war British Women', *Social History*, 39, 1 (2014), p. 19. doi.org/10.1080/03071022.2013.872904.

woman in a space of sixty years.'[168] In his script, Llewellyn notes how she lived in a house 'overlooking a chapel, whose front is my earliest memory'—stating 'where every Sunday we went, all of us'—and then elaborates on his 'childhood' memories:

> Then came the Great War, which I remember very well, for I was then a very small boy. In that day my grandmother was alive. I remember her, in grey silk, among the sweet-peas in her garden.[169]

With clever verbal dexterity, Llewellyn presents his childhood self within a Welsh context whilst the monologue also makes sense if viewed from the perspective of an English schoolboy on his holidays. In a closing statement, Llewellyn signals his own historic rootedness and connection to the area:

> Up on a shoulder of the valley that overlooks the Cathedral you will find two headstones: one in the memory of Richard Darrog Thomas, and the other to Elizabeth Walters Thomas. They rest in the soil that bore them, tranquil in the knowledge that their sons and grandsons will comport themselves no less faithfully than they and their fathers.[170]

At the same time, Llewellyn places himself firmly within present-day Wales:

> In this war I have found no difference among the people. If you walk down the valley road, you will still hear, from up on the right hand side, the voices of the children reciting their twice times table. You will still see a small boy chasing geese out of the clover and down to the pond at the fork of the road, as I once did. And you will still see the choirboys, in their mortarboards, with the tassels shadowing their faces, with their clean white collars, their short jackets and long trousers, with jewels flashing in their boots, running in the sunshine of a Sunday morning down to the Cathedral vestry.[171]

He ends the talk triumphantly, with a proprietorial assertion of Welshness:

> If Mr Hitler prosecutes his threat of invasion, he may be quite certain that he shall have his fill of it; for if it is merely a question of invasion, the people of my country have served their time to it, and we still can say, in our own language, 'Cymru am byth'.[172]

---

[168] WAC; Talks Llewellyn, Richard, 'Democracy Marches' script, B/C 18/19.1.41, p. 1.
[169] WAC; Llewellyn, 'Democracy Marches', B/C 18/19.1.41, pp. 1, 4.
[170] WAC; Llewellyn, 'Democracy Marches', B/C 18/19.1.41, pp. 5–6.
[171] WAC; Llewellyn, 'Democracy Marches', B/C 18/19.1.41, p. 5.
[172] WAC; Llewellyn, 'Democracy Marches', B/C 18/19.1.41, p. 6.

Essentially, however, Llewellyn's experience of Wales was largely gained during childhood holidays and visits, as was the case with many second-generation Welsh children growing up in English towns and cities.

Finally, it could also be significant for Llewellyn's self-fashioning as Welsh that by the end of the war he had lost most of the immediate members of his family. His father died at Westminster Hospital in 1942. Two years later, in June 1944, his stepmother, Marion Lloyd, his sister, Gladys Moore-Wood, and his two nieces, Sarah and Ann Toogood, were killed during a V-1 bombing raid whilst residing at his flat at 36 Buckingham Gate, London.[173] The *Evening Telegraph* reports that Moore-Wood, an ENSA welfare officer, and her brother were 'devoted friends', citing a colleague: '"Richard now an army captain in Italy will be heartbroken when he hears of her death".'[174] In September 1944, Rota wrote to Llewellyn to offer his 'profound sympathy' on the news of 'the tragedy about which I can hardly bear to write'. He continues, 'We knew your nieces a little, having met them in the Royal Academy and taken them to tea. The younger girl and I hit it off at once.... In the case of such insensate murder there is nothing remotely adequate one can say, but it breeds a cold fury in the heart which, multiplied a million-fold against us, will, please God, wipe such evil off the earth for ever more.'[175] In May 1945, Llewellyn wrote to Sarah Steinman, from Italy, that he had received a letter from his surviving sister, Lorna, 'She's much better, and from the tone of her letter, appears to be taking more interest in life; and that's a little satisfaction, anyway.'[176] These multiple family deaths potentially allowed the fictions of Llewellyn's life to take flight, affording a further moment of reinvention. For example, Felton notes how Llewellyn's date of birth—subsequently the source of debate—was recorded 'in the traditional Welsh fashion', in the family Bible, which was destroyed by the 1944 bombing.[177] To paraphrase Jonathan Black, the destruction of the war possibly 'created a tabula rasa' for Llewellyn from which to further consolidate his Welsh persona.[178] In the press report of his sister Gladys's death—which describes her as his 'most valued critic'—she is transformed into the Welsh reiteration, 'Gwladys'.[179] Furthermore, his sister Lorna Toogood, whose children were killed in the bombing raid, changes her surname to Llewellyn Lloyd

---

[173] When Llewellyn appeared on BBC *Woman's Hour* in April 1974, it triggered correspondence from people who had known his immediate family in London, one former associate writing: 'I shall never forget...the shock I experienced when Mrs Lloyd, Gladys and the children were killed.' See NLW; Richard Llewellyn papers; Correspondence 1970–1983, 5/31, Letter from Miss Taylor, 12 April 1974. Llewellyn also dedicated his 1966 novel, *Down Where the Moon is Small*, 'To the memory of my sister Gwladys, Commandant, Royal Red Cross, and her nieces, Ann and Sally, and Marie, nicest of women, killed in the bombing of London, June 1944, ever, with love, Richard.'
[174] 'Author Loses Sister-Critic', *Evening Telegraph*, 27 June 1944, p. 5.
[175] NLW; MS 21752E; Letter from Bertram Rota, 8 September 1944.
[176] NLW; MS 23710D; Letter to Sarah R. Steinman, 6 May 1945.
[177] Felton, 'Richard', p. 324.   [178] Black, 'Ivor', p. 20.   [179] 'Author Loses'.

following her 1946 divorce.[180] Thus, it can be seen how the slipstream of Llewellyn's success pulled his immediate family into a heightened identification with Welshness, even posthumously.

Conclusion

According to Ellis, Rhoscomyl 'found that identity was incredibly fluid within the British world' and that 'he could fashion his identity and sense of self with relative ease'.[181] Rhoscomyl 'consciously sought to raise the international image of the Welsh through his fiction, integrating the Welsh identity into the imperial narrative and introducing it to the English speaking world not merely as a matter of local interest but as a global concern and commodity.'[182] At the same time, 'the British world provided a liberating element of choice and allowed for multiple and evolving identities.'[183] A generation later, Richard Llewellyn negotiated similar dynamics. At the outset of his writing career, in the late 1930s, Llewellyn demonstrated an apparent keenness to align himself with the Welsh aspect of his identity and to mask his Englishness. It is likely that in his determination to succeed as a 'Welsh author', Llewellyn felt unable to counter prevailing fixed and 'essentialist discourses' of national identity as dependent on birthplace.[184] Rather than assert his own hybridized identity, Llewellyn felt the need to deny his diasporic roots in order to situate himself within 'collective' constructions of authentic Welshness.[185] With the publication of *HGWMV*, Llewellyn appears to have set out with a dual objective: to pay homage to Wales, 'the land of my fathers', and to assert his own claim to Welshness. Ian Bell suggests that, motivated by his status as an 'outsider', Llewellyn constructed his identity as Welsh in order 'to gain a kind of authenticity'.[186] The largely positive reception of *HGWMV* provided Llewellyn with validation of his imagining of Wales. Through his literary success and interaction with cultural agencies, he was increasingly positioned as a representative of Welshness in wartime society. Yet in the afterglow of his success, he remained in a liminal position, viewed as both authentically and 'inauthentically' Welsh.[187] With his dandified appearance, commercial success, and ostentatious behaviour, Llewellyn arguably failed to correspond to 'socially shared constructions' of what an authentic Welsh identity constituted.[188] His reluctance to engage with Welsh cultural agencies also suggests an uneasy self-awareness that his own

---

[180] *The London Gazette*, 16 July 1946, 3693.   [181] Ellis, 'Making', p. 491.
[182] Ellis, 'Making', p. 503.   [183] Ellis, 'Making', p. 510.   [184] Scully, 'Discourses', p. 12.
[185] Scully, 'Discourses', p. 19.
[186] NLW; 'Richard Llewellyn' [video recording]/CambrensisBBCWales; See also Scully, 'Discourses', p. 103.
[187] Scully, 'Discourses', pp. 105, 316.   [188] Scully, 'Discourses', p. 10.

personal construction of Welshness was open to contestation.[189] Yet, Llewellyn's assertion of Welsh identity is ultimately an example of what Scully terms 'authenticity through diasporic claim.'[190] Llewellyn accessed and performed an imagined Welshness through his diasporic Welsh contacts in London, cultural networks in Wales, and sojourns in Wales, as well as memories of his childhood visits and familial links to Wales which continued into the Second World War. The war afforded another opportunity for Llewellyn to attain Welsh legitimacy through military service in the Welsh Guards. In his wartime broadcasts to Welsh diasporic and imperial audiences, Llewellyn's construction of Welshness also held a clear transnational appeal. Moreover, *HGWMV* was accepted for many decades as a 'Welsh' novel because it was felt to be 'authentic' by its readership. The complexities which lay behind Llewellyn's wartime construction as a leading representative of Wales point to the multilayered and fluid nature of British identity formation during the Second World War and offer a particular vantage point from which to scrutinize notions of English Welsh duality, emerging from the Welsh diasporic population in England, as an important underpinning of pluralistic Britishness in wartime.

[189] Scully, 'Discourses', p. 105.   [190] Scully, 'Discourses', p. 12.

Conclusion

Writing in 1933, the journalist Glyn Roberts observed, 'It is good fun being Welsh (outside Wales).... I never know when I shall see a Welsh inscription in a London churchyard, or a Welshman's statue in a London street. It happens surprisingly often.'[1] This book has aimed to recapture both these material fragments which hint at the once-thriving historical Welsh presence in England and to recover the narrative traces of what has become a largely forgotten sense of dual identity amongst the descended Welsh. It has retrieved these shards of subjective lived experience through the analysis of personal letters, diaries, and unpublished memoirs as well as more tangential pieces of evidence transmitted intergenerationally: the image of a dead child in a gold locket, inherited family portraits, or a signature in a hotel register. Cumulatively, it demonstrates how, in the first half of the twentieth century, Wales and Welshness held meaning for hundreds of English men and women, their lived subjectivities reflecting the coexistence of an imagined 'home' of origin (Wales) and their 'home' of birthplace and residence (England). Above all, it demonstrates that, in this period, understandings of what it meant to be British were manifold and multistranded.

By foregrounding ideas of 'nation, migration and mobility' and focusing on the political, social, cultural, and military interconnectedness of the descended Welsh in early twentieth-century England, this book illuminates the 'dynamic and plural nature' of Welsh identities and cultures, outside the boundaries of Wales.[2] Following Moulton, it acknowledges the ways in which Wales influenced and informed the vibrancy of modern English society, as well as the existence of 'very human connections' between the two nations.[3] Furthermore, the 'mixing' between Welsh and English identities, which emerged from the Welsh diasporic presence in twentieth-century England, highlights the multistranded nature of English national identity construction and 'adds a certain slipperiness to the idea of Englishness'.[4] Smith notes how the Victorian migration of Edward Thomas's father to London, creating a family of six sons affluent enough to hire a succession of Welsh servants, was just one version of 'a whole history of transplantings which give lie to the myth of England as one people living perpetually in the same place'.[5]

---

[1] Roberts, *I Take*, p. 270. [2] Burdett, Polezzi, and Spadaro, 'Introduction', p. 4. [3] Moulton, *Ireland*, pp. 4, 47. [4] Smith, *Edward*, p. 12. [5] Smith, *Edward*, p. 14.

In the context of the multiplicity of cultural interconnections between England and Wales in the first half of the twentieth century, therefore, 'different "structures of feeling"' underpinned the construction of personal identities amongst English-born people of Welsh origin.[6] In *The Dying Gaul*, Brockley-born David Jones writes that, 'from the age of about seven, I myself, for reasons that I suppose only psychologists could fathom, "felt" Welsh.'[7] Anthony Powell, with a more vestigial genealogical claim, was still keen to attach himself to Wales. Despite 'the quintessentially English character of his writing' and the fact that he was born and raised in England, Powell 'thought of himself as Welsh' and had *Cwm Rhondda* played at his memorial service.[8] Meanings of Welshness could be 'deeply personal and idiosyncratic'[9]: they could symbolize love of a remembered parent or grandparent, nostalgia for a time of family togetherness, a personal sense of exoticism, or even, simply, an appreciation of a mountainous landscape. Hooker believes that some early twentieth-century English-born writers found in Wales 'a numinous aura…that they did not find in England'.[10] Furthermore, as this book indicates, the idea of Wales and Welshness could offer a form of escapism from an unhappy or disordered childhood, an opportunity to downplay wartime enemy status or a site to locate a sense of personal authenticity. For the descended Welsh in England, Wales was somewhere to visit but also an imagined space. This grouping consisted of a broad and richly variegated grouping representing elite Anglo Welsh identities as well as working-class citizens, Welsh and anglophone speakers, the outwardly nonconformist, and the irreligious. The vast majority of case studies examined in this book were not heavily embedded in Welsh diasporic associational life in England and few could speak Welsh beyond self-taught phrases or remembered fragments. For some, the Welsh aspect of their personal identity mattered more than for others.

For those living in early to mid-twentieth century England, a sense of Welsh identification could translate into renting property in Wales in order to spend time there whilst for those in less privileged positions, it was likely to endure as an imagined association, possibly bolstered by short family trips or holidays. Constructions of selfhood which foregrounded a sense of Welshness could also prove unstable, especially when individuals spent time in Wales. There was often a disassembling amongst the English Welsh on encountering the 'real' Welsh: for example, Edward Thomas's awkward encounter with the dairymaid in Dryslwyn and David Jones's reported social shyness whilst based in Capel-y-ffin. Gunner J. R. Davies, discussed in Chapter 5, was self-aware enough to

---

[6] Ballin, 'Welshness', p. 102. This alludes to Raymond Williams's famous cultural hypothesis which defines a 'structure of feeling' as 'meanings and values as they are actively lived and felt'. Raymond Williams, *Marxism and Literature* (Oxford, 1977), p. 132.
[7] Jones, *Dying*, p. 31.   [8] Barber, *Anthony Powell*, p. ix; Birns, *Understanding*, p. 192.
[9] Moulton, *Ireland*, p. 7.   [10] Hooker, *Imagining*, pp. 197–8.

differentiate himself from Welshmen when he recorded in a wartime letter from the North African desert: 'Calling at the Naafi on the way to a hot shower I heard someone whistling "Sospan"; it was the assistant, a true Celt hailing from Bangor (I got an extra packet of fags on the strength of it!).'[11] For the descended Welsh in England, ideas of authenticity, often located in understandings of their own Welshness, remained ever open to challenge and contestation. As Barbara Prys-Williams observes, amongst English people, a love of Wales could often 'stem from an imaginative affinity and a romantic attachment to the idea of the country rather than from any extensive experience of its reality'.[12] As the life writing analysed within this book has demonstrated, this could be the case amongst both the descended Welsh and those with looser or even more fragile connections who nevertheless felt a strong sense of 'affinity' with Wales and a desire to align themselves with the characteristics of an imagined Welsh landscape.

Chapter 1 illuminated the intricate English Welsh social, cultural, aristocratic, and military networks operating in England in the first half of twentieth century—with the talismanic and dominant political figure of Lloyd George initially positioned at the fulcrum of these reciprocal 'chains of connection'.[13] One case study who epitomizes the functioning of these social networks is the Northamptonshire-born architect, Clough Williams-Ellis, who first appeared, within this book, as the solicitous neighbour of Robert Graves and Richard Hughes in Gwynedd, then as the memorialist for Lloyd George at Llanystumdwy, and finally as the grieving father of a dead Welsh Guards veteran in London.[14] Although at the culturally elite end of the social spectrum, Williams-Ellis embodies the intertwined relationships between English people of Welsh heritage stretching over the first five decades of the twentieth century. Whilst in the political sphere the presence of Lloyd George framed the aspirations of subsequent generations of English Welsh politicians, transnational landed elites with estates in both Wales and England also provided the wellspring for a cohort of privileged English men who often displayed their sense of dual identifications by volunteering for Welsh regiments in the First World War. However, these cross-border connections and associations were also played out in a multiplicity of ways across the social classes, including within England's suburbs and streets of terraced housing.

Chapter 2 highlights how, in many of the life writing sources analysed within this book, there were suggestions of liminality: second-generation Welsh men and women in England could grow up experiencing an 'outsider' status, reflected in their culturally distinctive narratives of childhood. For the descendants of

[11] IWM 13167, Letter 25 May 1943.
[12] Barbara Prys-Williams, 'Writing it Out: Margiad Evans (1909–1958)', in *Twentieth-Century Autobiography. Writing Wales in English*, edited by Barbara Prys-Williams (Cardiff, 2004), p. 34.
[13] Scott, *Social Network*, p. 14.
[14] Jan Morris also encountered Williams-Ellis in later life, seeing him as 'a man who had known suffering in his time'. See Morris, *Conundrum*, p. 115.

Welsh migrants raised in England, 'contrary ethnic positionings are often simultaneously maintained and claimed', an expression of what Brah terms 'contingent positionality'.[15] Furthermore, as Burdett, Polezzi, and Spadaro emphasize, the 'inherent transculturality' of national cultures suggests that dual identities could emerge from the transcultural spaces created by Welsh migration into England.[16] For English Welsh authors such as Edward Thomas, David Jones, Norman Lewis, and John Osborne, growing up in English suburbia, their sense of 'belongingness' was not just confined to the local but also served to remodel 'national collective imaginaries'.[17] It would, therefore, be helpful to view these case studies as transcultural subjects. Indeed, their upbringing in the English suburbs—'Welshburbia'—and sense of a mixed dual heritage, often inspired their artistic creativity. Chapter 3 analysed the life writing of those with Welsh origins born and raised in England, touching upon the importance of naming, material culture, language, and kinship in facilitating a sense of duality or dual identification with both Wales and England. These personal narratives both revealed how the second-generation Welsh could, at times, experience a sense of alienation or 'difference' in England but also attach importance to their connection with Wales maintained, to varying degrees, through family rituals, holidays, honeymoons, and short visits. All these domestic moments of engagement, the intimate pulsations of lived experience, underpinned the existence of an almost subterranean connectivity between Wales and England. Fundamentally, this chapter underscored how the existence of powerful family and cultural ties operating across the border ensured the close relationship between the two nations, which did not just simply exist as a political and economic entity in the period from 1914 to 1945.

Chapters 4 and 5 underlined how a sense of dual identifications was made particularly visible during the two world wars through military recruitment and mobilization practices. For a cohort of male English volunteers, Wales and Welshness held some form of *meaning* at the point of their military enlistment in both conflicts. In the First World War, politicized displays of Welsh patriotism in the metropolis, primarily through the raising of the 15th (1st London Welsh) Battalion, were implicated in the military voluntarism of a select category of English soldiers. The Second World War again illuminated 'a range of identifications' across Englishness and Welshness among the descended Welsh in England and provided the opportunity for the expression of dual identifications through military service.[18] In wartime, Britishness functioned in a 'conglomerative' way, gathering together distinct national identities and accommodating subcultures

---

[15] Murray, 'A Diasporic Vernacular?', p. 76; Brah, *Cartographies*, p. 148.
[16] Burdett, Polezzi, and Spadaro, 'Introduction', p. 3.
[17] Keshav Nath, 'Transcultural Literature, Nationalism and its Adequacy in World Literatures: Pedagogical Requirements', *postScriptum: An Interdisciplinary Journal of Literary Studies* (2019), pp. 2, 3.
[18] Walter, 'English/Irish Hybridity', p. 20.

such as English Welsh duality.[19] The 99th (London Welsh) Heavy Anti-Aircraft regiment and the 46th (Liverpool Welsh) Royal Tank Regiment provided useful vehicles for English men to access martial masculinity by claiming identification with Wales, but the evidence suggests that they also valued their wider participation in the British war effort, particularly those who served in the iconic Eighth Army. In this sense, it is possible that, for soldiers of dual heritage, military service within localized hybrid units shaped, and contributed to, their overarching sense of pluralistic Britishness. At the same time, during both conflicts, multiple understandings of 'Welshness' could also underpin assertions of conscientious objection whereby English individuals deployed ideas of an inherently Welsh pacifism when articulating their objection to military service. As Chapter 6 demonstrated, the involvement of English Welsh artists and sculptors in post-war memorialization, often undertaken within a three-nation framework, and the signalling of English Welsh experience within commemorative iconography, reinforced the intersectionality of dual identities and constructions of Britishness, especially in the aftermath of the First World War. Intentional commemorative expressions of English Welsh duality were less visible following the Second World War. By the end of this conflict, the aerial bombardment of sites of Welsh settlement in English cities had prompted the return or retirement to Wales of many members of the community elites, further diminishing those long-established networks instrumental in deliberate acts of diasporic memorialization.[20]

Chapter 7 highlighted the extent to which English cultural figures with Welsh connections, variously defined, operated at the centre of artistic, literary, and dramatic representations of Wales and Welshness, beginning with the National Museum of Wales's 'Exhibition of Works by Certain Modern Artists of Welsh Birth or Extraction' in 1913. Indeed, the accommodation of English artists within representations of the Welsh nation persists into the present day. In a 1998 review of Welsh poetry, Patrick Crotty observed 'the habit of claiming poets for Wales on the basis of parentage and emotional affiliation'.[21] A current National Museum Wales website reproduces a portrait of the explorer Teddy Evans—'Admiral Sir Edward Evans'—of the Antarctic. The website mentions that Evans was one of a series of twenty portraits of 'eminent Welshmen and women' commissioned by the museum in 1937, undertaken by the artist Sydney Morse-Brown. However, it also acknowledges that Evans's 'Welsh roots are obscure'.[22] Other online selected representatives of Wales include English Welsh case studies featured in this book such as Clough Williams-Ellis, Richard Hughes, and Charles Morgan. A recent

[19] Hickman, Morgan, Walter, and Bradley, 'Limitations', p. 178.
[20] Jones, *Welsh Builder*, Foreword.
[21] Patrick Crotty, 'Nothing Fancy', *Times Literary Supplement*, 20 February 1998, 4949, p. 11.
[22] 'A Portrait of Teddy Evans of the Antarctic', National Museum Wales, https://museum.wales/articles/1062/A-portrait-of-Teddy-Evans-of-the-Antarctic-Evans-of-the-Broke-1880-1957/, accessed 30 September 2014.

filmic portrayal of the English Welsh politician Eliot Crawshay-Williams, born in London in 1879, presented him as a Welsh language speaker even though, by his own admission, he 'never learnt Welsh'.[23] The accommodation of English-born artists within institutional representations of the Welsh nation was most recently demonstrated by the high-profile positioning of David Jones and Edward Thomas during First World War centenary commemorations. In 2016, the Welsh National Opera in Cardiff hosted a world premiere of an opera adapted from Jones's *In Parenthesis* by Iain Bell.[24] The following year, both the National Library of Wales and the University of Cardiff held exhibitions on Thomas: *Fallen Poets: Edward Thomas & Hedd Wyn* and *Edward Thomas 100*, respectively. As a result of this institutional keenness to claim artistic figures of dual heritage as 'Welsh', there is a risk of losing sight of their Englishness. Similarly, on the centenary of Ivor Roberts-Jones's birth, in 2013, National Museum Cardiff held the exhibition, *The Double Edge: The Portrait Sculpture of Ivor Roberts-Jones,* as part of their 'Welsh Artists in Focus' series, reaffirming his acceptance as a Welsh artist.[25] Webb notes that Edward Thomas is often adjudged by commentators to be a 'Welshman' because 'he regarded himself as Welsh' and the same can be said for many of the second- and third-generation Welsh case studies discussed in this book.[26] But an analysis of original English Welsh life writing sources also indicates that, for English-born men and women, self-identification as 'Welsh' was dependent on context, audience, and reception, which can shift and evolve through time.[27] Some case studies who were claimed, and even lauded, as 'Welsh' in their lifetimes, such as the middlebrow writer, Richard Llewellyn, are now largely neglected within Welsh academic discourse, whilst literary authors such as Margiad Evans, born in Uxbridge to English parents, are increasingly embraced.

Chapter 8 recovered the experiences of English people who identified and experienced Wales as a site of refuge, healing, and solace. This included those with no familial connection with Wales who nevertheless expressed a strong affinity with the nation, and for whom fantasies of Wales were important. Creative English figures such as Robert Graves and John Petts became emotionally invested in the perceived 'romanticism' of Wales, with its beautiful mountainous landscapes, in close proximity to England, offering both a sense of comfort and escape. These narrations of Wales suggest a selective appreciation of the contemporaneous Welsh landscape which tended to prioritize rural nostalgia over

---

[23] *Morfydd*, dir. Andy Newbery, S4C broadcast, 6 December 2018; Eliot Crawshay-Williams, 'The Tragedy of Morfydd', *Ddwias* (Mar 1959), pp. 17–18.
[24] Wise Music Classical website, 'In Parenthesis', 8 April 2016, https://www.wisemusicclassical.com/news/3463/In-Parenthesis--World-premiere-of-new-opera-by-Iain-Bell/, accessed 2 November 2022.
[25] Polly March, '20th century leading Welsh figures in National Museum Cardiff exhibition', BBC Wales, http://www.bbc.co.uk/blogs/wales/entries/de738c97-5031-3797-9150-463a26ae9814, accessed 3 November 2015.
[26] Webb, *Edward*, p. 55. [27] See McCrone et al., 'Who Are We?', p. 651.

industrialized realities. Chapter 9 contained an exploration of the desire amongst English-born individuals, such as the writer Richard Llewellyn, to 'masquerade' as Welsh in order to gain a cultural foothold and a sense of personal authenticity. It also highlighted how constructions of Welshness by these high-profile figures could often hold a wider transnational appeal. These case studies served to underline the historical tensions between understandings of Welshness as a 'territorialised assumption of identity' and as a pluralist diasporic identity upon which claims of authenticity and belonging could be made.[28] Ultimately, those studied in this book cover a diverse range of allegiances, stretching from those who could be described as English-born with strong Welsh identifiers to those who were simply English-born with an affinity with Wales, with a whole mass of English-born individuals with a sense of dual identifications in between. In conclusion, this book underscores the importance of dual identifications *across and within* the borders of England and Wales in advancing our historical understanding of British society and complicates the notion of fixed singular national identities within the constituent countries of the United Kingdom. In particular, it has recaptured the experiences of artists, writers, soldiers, politicians, and ordinary men and women in the two world wars, foregrounding the multiple ways in which English Welsh dual identifications were mobilized, and subsequently memorialized, in England during both conflicts. By examining the cultural interaction between English and Welsh identities, this book hopes to deepen historical understanding of how dual identities within the constituent countries of a multinational British state informed—and potentially supported—the functioning of a pluralistic Britishness in wartime. As well as stimulating future interest in the historical construction of English personal, cultural, and national identities in Wales, I am hopeful that this book will encourage explorations of the significant cross-border movements of peoples between England and Scotland/Northern Ireland, and between Wales and Scotland/Northern Ireland, and the implications for the diasporic construction of other forms of 'dual identities' within the United Kingdom, and their mobilization in wartime.

Finally, whilst the available archival sources have tilted this book towards a representation of the elite, literate, and literary interconnections between Wales and England, there have been spaces where I have also been able to recover the perspectives of working and lower middle-class English people of Welsh origin. This is something I was keen to do to reflect the lived experience of my English Welsh grandfather, John Herbertson, who grew up in a terraced house in Liverpool during and following the First World War with his Welsh mother and English father, Welsh grandparents, and Welsh aunts living in nearby streets. He took the time to share his memories with me when I was a teenager in the 1980s,

[28] Scully, 'Discourses', pp. 17, 20.

driving me to his childhood haunts and illuminating a lost world of Welsh families, chapels, and burial sites within the city. His determined expression of English Welsh dual identifications, which would otherwise have remained out of sight, formed the inspiration for this research. So I will end this book thinking of the young Liverpudlian boy, leaning up against the local bakery wall in Kirkdale for warmth, but connected in multifarious ways, both near and far, to an imagined Wales.

Bibliography

Key Primary Sources

Author Interviews
  School of Scottish Studies Archive; SA2013.019; Enid Martin-Jones, 11 April 2013.
  Emily Gwynne-Jones, 2 August 2016.

British Library Sound Archive
  C467/36; Patrick Gwynne interviewed by Neil Bingham, Architects' Lives, 12 October 1997.
  C466/25; Myfanwy Piper, interviewed by Margaret Garlake, Artists' Lives, 21 November 1994.
  C464/68; Margaret [Peggy] Roberts, interviewed by Mary Stewart, 17 October 2008.
  C464/37; David Traherne Thomas interviewed by Linda Sandino, 14 February 2003.
  C880/21; Ifanwy Williams interviewed by Rena Feld, Women Conscientious Objectors, 19 May 1998.

Imperial War Museum
  13,167; Private Papers of J R Davies.
  13,417; Private papers of Harold Ford.
  E.J.3487; *On Target* (1940).

Imperial War Museum Sound Archive
  26841; John Rhys 'Jack' Davies, interviewed by Peter M Hart, March 2003.
  9732; John Ronald Petts, interviewed by Lyn E Smith, 2 March 1987.
  8741; Stephen Williams interviewed by Lyn E Smith, 10 December 1984.

BBC Written Archives Centre
  WA8/370/1; Llewellyn Richard.
  Llewellyn, Richard; Talks Llewellyn, Richard.

Liverpool Record Office
  Liverpolitan February 1935–July 1936.
  West Lancs Territorial Association Cuttings.

London Welsh Centre
  London Welsh Yearbooks.
  Y Ddinas.
  Y Ddolen.
  Young Wales Association material.

National Archives
  WO 339/23674; Lieutenant William Pugh Hinds. The Royal Welsh Fusiliers.
  WO 339/43155; 2/Lieutenant Iorwerth Glyndwr John. The South Wales Borderers.
  WO 339/8852; Captain Pyers George Joseph Mostyn. The Royal Welsh Fusiliers.

National Library of Wales
    GB 0210 CLEIES Clement Davies (Liberal MP) Papers.
    GB 0210 DJONES David Jones (Artist and Writer) Papers.
    GB 0210 ELICRAAMS Eliot Crawshay-Williams Papers.
    GB 0210 RICLYN Richard Llewellyn Papers.
    GB 0210 WELARMRPS Welsh Army Corps Records.
    MS 21752E Richard Llewellyn Agency Papers.
    MS 23710D Richard Llewellyn Letters.

Parliamentary Archives
    Lloyd George Papers
    Houses of Parliament; House of Lords War Memorial 1914–1918.

The Tank Museum Archive
    RH87, 46 RTR 7431:
    A Short History of the 46th (Liverpool Welsh) Royal Tank Regiment (1949).
    E2003.1373 *Memoir of Maj J. S. Routledge MC by his son Geoffrey R. Routledge* (1994).
    Casualties of the 46th Royal Tank Regiment, WW2.
    The Tank. Journal of the Royal Tank Regiment.

Welsh Guards Archive
    Papers of Captain Richard Lloyd.
    Record of the Services of Rex John Whistler.

Private Papers
    Bangor University Archive; O. E. Roberts's Undeb Cymru Fydd Papers.
    Bodleian Library, Oxford; Papers of Lady Greenwood.
    British Library Manuscripts; Dilys Powell Papers.
    Cardiff University Special Collections and Archives; Papers of Edward Thomas (1878–1917).
    Churchill Archives Centre, Cambridge; Papers of Selwyn Lloyd.
    Gladstone's Library, Hawarden; Glynne-Gladstone Archive.
    Harry Ransom Center, The University of Texas at Austin; Richard Llewellyn Papers.
    John Rylands Special Collections; Basil Dean Archive.
    King's College London; Liddell Hart Centre for Military Archives, LIDDELL HART 1/327.
    St John's College, Oxford; Robert Graves Collection.
    Shrewsbury House Archive, Liverpool.
    University at Buffalo; Martin Seymour-Smith Collection.
    V & A Theatre and Performance Archives; Ernest Milton Collection.

Published Life Writing

Barber, D. H., *The House on the Green* (London, 1960).
Casson, John, *Lewis & Sybil. A Memoir* (London, 1972).
Crawshay-Williams, Eliot, *Simple Story. An Accidental Autobiography* (London, 1935).
de Walden, Margherita Lady Howard, *Pages From My Life* (London, 1965).
Gladstone, Viscount, *William G C Gladstone. A Memoir* (London, 1918).
Graves, Robert, *Goodbye To All That* (rev. edn, London, 1957).

Hague, René, ed., *Dai Greatcoat. A Self-portrait of David Jones in his Letters* (London, 1980).
Richard Hughes. *An Omnibus* (New York, 1931).
John, Rebecca, *Caspar John* (London, 1987).
John, Romilly, *The Seventh Child: A Retrospect* (London, 1932).
Jones, Diana Wynne, *Reflections on the Magic of Writing* (Oxford, 2012).
Jones, David, *The Dying Gaul and Other Writings* (London, 1978).
Jones, Mervyn, *Chances. An Autobiography* (London, 1987).
Lewis, Eiluned, ed., *Selected Letters of Charles Morgan* (London, 1967).
Lewis, Norman, *Jackdaw Cake* (London, 1987).
Lloyd George, Owen, *A Tale of Two Grandfathers* (London, 1999).
Morgan, Gwenda, *The Diary of a Land Girl* (Risbury, 2002).
Morris, Jan, *Conundrum* (2nd edn, London, 2002).
Osborne, John, *Looking Back. Never Explain, Never Apologise* (London, 2004).
Picton-Turbervill, Edith, *Life is Good. An Autobiography* (London, 1939).
Powell, Anthony, *To Keep the Ball Rolling* (London, 1983).
Rhys, Ernest, *Wales England Wed* (London, 1940).
Saunders Jones, Mair, Thomas, Ned, and Pritchard Jones, Harri, eds, *Saunders Lewis. Letters to Margaret Gilcriest* (Cardiff, 1993).
Thomas, Edward, *The Happy-Go-Lucky Morgans* (London, 1913).
Thomas, Edward, *The Childhood of Edward Thomas. A Fragment of Autobiography with a Preface by Julian Thomas* (London, 1938).
Thomas, Helen with Myfanwy Thomas, *Under Storm's Wing* (London, 1988).
Williams-Ellis, Clough, *Architect errant* (Gwynedd, 1991).

Key texts

Ballin, Malcolm, 'The Welshness of William Emrys Williams: Strands from a Biography', in Katie Gramich, ed., *Almanac: Yearbook of Welsh Writing in English,* 13 (Cardigan, 2009), 81–108.
Bankes, Ariane, and Hills, Paul, *The Art of David Jones. Vision and Memory* (Farnham, 2015).
Batten, Sonia, 'Memorial Text Narratives in Britain, *c.* 1890–1930', PhD dissertation, University of Birmingham, 2011.
Bechhofer, Frank, McCrone, David, Kiely, Richard, and Stewart, Robert, 'Constructing national identity: arts and landed elites in Scotland', *Sociology,* 33, 3 (1999), 515–34.
Black, Jonathan, and Ayres, Sara, *Abstraction and Reality. The Sculpture of Ivor Roberts-Jones* (London, 2013).
Bohata, Kirsti, and Gramich, Katie, eds, *Rediscovering Margiad Evans. Marginality, Gender and Illness* (Cardiff, 2013).
Brah, Avtar, *Cartographies of Diaspora. Contesting Identities* (London, 1996).
Buckingham, Mike, and Frame, Richard, *Alexander Cordell* (Cardiff, 1999).
Burdett, Charles, Polezzi, Loredana, and Spadaro, Barbara, eds, *Transcultural Italies. Memory, Mobility and Translation* (Liverpool, 2020).
Cannadine, David, *The Decline and Fall of the British Aristocracy* (New Haven & London, 1990).
Cragoe, Matthew, and Williams, Chris, eds, *Wales and War. Society, Politics and Religion in the Nineteenth and Twentieth Centuries* (Cardiff, 2007).
Cuthbertson Guy, *Edward Thomas. Prose Writings. A Selected Edition. Volume 1 Autobiographies* (Oxford, 2011).

Davies, John, *A History of Wales* (London, 1993).
Davies, J. Glyn, *Nationalism as a Social Phenomenon* (Liverpool, 1965).
Ellis, John S, 'Making Owen Rhoscomyl (1863–1919): Biography, Welsh Identity and the British World', *Welsh History Review*, 26, 3 (2013), 482–511.
Erickson, Rebecca J, 'The Importance of Authenticity for Self and Society', *Symbolic Interaction*, 18, 2 (1995), 121–44.
Ford, James, 'The Art of Union and Disunion in the Houses of Parliament 1834–1928', PhD dissertation, University of Nottingham, 2016.
Giles, Judy, and Middleton, Tim, *Writing Englishness: An Introductory Sourcebook* (London, 1995).
Hajkowski, Thomas, *The BBC and National Identity in Britain, 1922–53* (Manchester, 2010).
Hapgood, Lynne, *Margins of Desire. The Suburbs in Fiction and Culture 1880–1925* (Manchester, 2009).
Harris, John, '"A Hallelujah of a Book": *How Green Was My Valley* as Bestseller', in Tony Brown, ed., *Welsh Writing in English. A Yearbook of Critical Essays*, 3 (Cardiff, 1997), 42–62.
Herson, John, *Divergent paths: Family histories of Irish emigrants in Britain 1820–1920* (Manchester, 2015).
Hickman, Mary J, Morgan, Sarah, Walter, Bronwen, and Bradley, Joseph, 'The Limitations of Whiteness and the Boundaries of Englishness', *Ethnicities*, 5, 2 (2005), 160–82.
Hooker, Jeremy, *Imagining Wales. A view of modern Welsh writing in English* (Cardiff, 2001).
Hopkins, Chris, *English Fiction in the 1930s: Language, Genre, History* (London, 2006).
Johnes, Martin, *Wales Since 1939* (Manchester, 2012).
Johnes, Martin, *Wales: England's Colony?* (Cardigan, 2019).
Jones, Aled, and Jones, Bill, 'The Welsh World and the British Empire, c. 1851–1939: An Exploration', *Journal of Imperial & Commonwealth History*, 31, 2 (2003), 57–81.
Jones, Emrys, ed., *The Welsh in London 1500–2000* (Cardiff, 2001).
Jones, Merfyn, 'Welsh Immigrants in the Cities of North West England. 1890–1930: Some Oral Testimony', *Oral History*, 9, 2 (1981), 33–41.
Jones, R. Merfyn, 'The Liverpool Welsh', in R. Merfyn Jones and D. Ben Rees, eds., *Liverpool Welsh & Their Religion* (Liverpool, 1984), 20–43.
Kumar, Krishan, *The Making of English National Identity* (Cambridge, 2006).
Longley, Edna, *Edward Thomas. The Annotated Collected Poems* (Tarset, 2008).
Lord, Peter, *Imaging the Nation* (Cardiff, 2000).
McCrone, David, Stewart, Robert, Kiely, Richard, and Bechhofer, Frank, 'Who Are We? Problematising National Identity', *Sociological Review*, 46, 4 (1998), 629–52.
Moulton, Mo, *Ireland and the Irish in Interwar England* (Cambridge, 2014).
Owen, Tomos, 'The London Kelt 1895–1914: Performing Welshness, Imagining Wales', in Katie Gramich, ed., *Almanac: Yearbook of Welsh Writing in English*, 13 (Cardigan, 2009), 109–25.
Payton, Philip, *John Betjeman and Cornwall. "The Celebrated Cornish Nationalist"* (Exeter, 2010).
Prys-Williams, Barbara W., 'Variations in the nature of the perceived self in some twentieth century Welsh autobiographical writing in English', PhD dissertation, Swansea University, 2002.
Readman, Paul, Radding, Cynthia, and Bryant, Chad, eds, *Borderlands in World History, 1700–1914* (Basingstoke, 2014).
Robbins, Keith, *Nineteenth-Century Britain. England, Scotland, and Wales. The Making of a Nation* (Oxford, 1989).
Scully, Marc, 'Discourses of Authenticity and National Identity among the Irish Diaspora in England', PhD dissertation, The Open University, 2010.

Shaw, Phyllida, *Undaunted Spirit. The Art and Craft of Gertrude Alice Meredith Williams* (London, 2018).
Teng, Emma Jinhua, *Eurasian. Mixed Identities in the United States, China, and Hong Kong, 1842–1943* (Berkeley, 2013).
Thomas, M Wynn, *The Nations of Wales 1890–1914* (Cardiff, 2016).
Travers, Daniel, and Ward, Paul, 'Narrating Britain's War: A "Four Nations and More" Approach to the People's War', in Manuel Braganca and Peter Tame, eds., *The Long Aftermath. Cultural Legacies of Europe at War 1936–2016* (Oxford, 2016), 77–95.
Ugolini, Wendy, and Pattinson, Juliette, eds, *Fighting for Britain? Negotiating Identities in Britain During the Second World War* (Oxford, 2015).
Walter, Bronwen, 'English/Irish Hybridity: Second-generation Diasporic Identities', *International Journal of Diversity in Organisations*, 5, 7 (2005/6), 17–24.
Walter, Bronwen, Morgan, Sarah, Hickman, Mary J., and Bradley, Joseph M., 'Family Stories, Public Silence: Irish Identity Construction Amongst the Second-generation Irish in England', *Scottish Geographical Journal*, 118, 3 (2002), 201–17.
Ward, Paul, *Unionism in the United Kingdom, 1918–1974* (Basingstoke, 2005).
Williams, Chris, 'Problematizing Wales: An Exploration in Historiography and Postcoloniality', in Jane Aaron and Chris Williams, eds., *Postcolonial Wales* (Cardiff, 2005), 3–22.

Index

For the benefit of digital users, indexed terms that span two pages (e.g., 52–53) may, on occasion, appear on only one of those pages.

2nd Battalion Manchester Regiment 117–18, 135
5th Battalion RWF 118–19
9th Battalion Northumberland Fusiliers 117–18, 135–7
12th Battalion South Wales Borderers 133
15th (1st London Welsh), RWF 9, 36–7, 117–30, 138–9, 275–6
17th Battalion, the Welsh Regiment 188–9
18th (2nd London Welsh), RWF 121–2
38th Welsh Division 121–2, 247
46th (Liverpool Welsh) RTR 9, 25, 140, 147–53, 275–6
53rd (Welsh) Division 204–5
99th (London Welsh) HAA 9, 140–2, 147, 275–6

Aaron, Jane 7, 98–9
Aberaeron 19–20
Aberdare 90, 145, 253
Abrams, Lynn 267–8
Acts of Union 4–5
Adams, Barr 148–52
Adams, Sam 251, 254–5
'adoption' of Wales 226–8, 231 *see also* affinity Welsh
affiliations with Wales 222–44
affinity Welsh 21, 29, 166–7, 171, 222–3, 228–44, 273–4
Alford, Frank 187
Ammanford 74, 78–9
ancestral Welshness 20, 118, 135, 150–4, 171, 213–14, 221, 244
anti-Welsh prejudice 84–9, 113–14, 151–2
Ap Rhys Pryce, Henry 141–2
aristocracy 49–58, 176–7, 184–6, 218–19
art exhibitions 195–8, 202–5, 276–7
associational culture 15, 66, 148, 191, 273
authenticity 93, 123, 195, 199–200, 209–10, 217, 219, 221, 245–6, 250–5, 270–1, 273–4, 277–8
Auxiliary Territorial Service (ATS) 160–1, 164, 168

Baden-Powell, Olave 55
Baden-Powell, Robert 53–5

Bailey, Lilian 165
Bala 197, 262–3, 266
Balham, London 67–8, 71–2, 78–9, 95
Ballin, Malcolm 18–20, 248–9
Bankes, Ariane 69, 202–3
Barmouth 105, 197–8, 212–13
battalions
  2nd Battalion Manchester Regiment 117–18, 135
  5th Battalion RWF 118–19
  9th Battalion Northumberland Fusiliers 117–18
  12th Battalion South Wales Borderers 133
  15th (1st London Welsh), RWF 9, 36–7, 117–30, 138–9, 275–6
  17th Battalion, the Welsh Regiment 188–9
  18th (2nd London Welsh), RWF 121–2
Batten, Sonia 172, 174–6
Battle of Crecy 120, 219–20
Battle of the Somme 55, 117, 184–5, 232
BBC 8, 144–5, 222, 258–62, 267–9
Beddoe, Deirdre 93
Belchem, John 12–13
Bell, Iain 276–7
Bell, Rachel 60–1
Benbough-Jackson, Mike 11, 62
Benton, Jill 224–5, 247–8
Betjeman, John 21–2, 229–30, 244
Bhabha, Homi K. 15–16
biographical turn 23
Birkenhead 90, 106, 111–12, 175–6
Birns, Nicholas 154
Black, Jonathan 204–5, 269–70
Blue Books *see* 'Treason of the Blue Books' (1847)
borders
  border counties 181, 208, 232
  border crossings 14, 26, 49–57, 103–7, 114, 181, 274, 277–8
  border identities 208–12
  borderlands 3, 15–16
Borrow, George Henry 74, 222, 233–4
Bournemouth 19, 67, 92, 95–7, 102, 113

Bowen, Ivor 122–3
Brah, Avtar 2, 15–16, 22–3, 140, 146, 274–5
Brangwyn, Frank 187–8, 191
Brearton, Fran 241–2
Brecon & Radnor Express 55–6
Bridgend 39–43, 108, 225
British Empire 4–9, 121–2, 187–8, 261
British identity, and war 7–9
Brockley, London 15, 69, 126
Bron y Garth 106–7
Brutton, Philip 263
Bryant, Chad 15–16
Brynawelon 43–4, 46
Buckingham, Mike 226–8
Burdett, Charles 26–7, 68–9, 250–1, 274–5
burial practices 103, 165, 182
Burne-Jones, Edward 195–6
Butler, Marilyn 111–12

Caerleon upon Usk 74
Caernarfon 35, 224
Caldey Island 202–3
Cambria Daily Leader 55–7, 231
Cambrian News 137
Cannadine, David 49–50, 52, 98–9
Capel-y-ffin 202–3, 273–4
caricatures of Welsh people 87–9
Carmarthen 103–4, 123–4
Carradice, Phil 226–8
Casson, John 106–7
Casson, Lewis 106–7
Casson, Randal 106
Celtic mythology 126–7
Celtic 'other,' 19–20, 222
cemeteries 98–9, 101–2, 174
censuses
 1911 12–13, 246–7, 265
 1921 89
Chamberlain, Brenda 228–9
chapels
 in diaspora 12–13
 falling attendance 147–8
 Liverpool 23, 64–5, 168–9, 189–90
 Lloyd George family 36–7
 London 63–5
 nonconformist 12–13, 63–5
 war memorials 189–90
chaplains 141–2
Chester 133–4, 184, 208
Chester Royal Infirmary 182–4
childhood narratives 84–92, 267–9
Chirk Castle 218–21
Clare, Ronald 152–3

class 3, 25, 67–8, 148–51, 106, 246, 256, 264, 273, 278–9 *see also* middle class experience; upper class experience; working class experience
Clement Davies, David 158–9
Clement Davies, Edward 111, 140, 158–9, 161
Clement Davies, Geraint 140, 158–9, 161–5
Clement Davies, Jano 136, 138, 158–9, 162–3, 165
Clement Davies, Mary Eluned 140, 158–61, 164–5
Clement Davies, Stanley 158–9, 161, 163–5
Clive, Percy Robert Herbert (Viscount Clive) 52–3, 172, 184–6
coal 5, 48, 254, 256–8
Colley, Linda 2
Colls, Robert 22–3
Commonwealth War Graves Commission 243
Conran, Tony 241–2
conscientious objectors 23–5, 28, 59, 140, 165–71, 228–9, 244, 275–6
Constantine, Mary Ann 233–4
Cordell, Alex 29, 222–3, 226–8, 244
cosmopolitanism 10, 60–1, 256
Coster, Howard 253–4
countryside 103–11, 165–6, 199 *see also* rural landscapes; mountains
Cowman, Krista 144
Cragoe, Matthew 5, 33–4, 49–50, 165–6, 176–7
Crawshay-Williams, Eliot 37–43, 56–7, 107–11, 222–3, 225, 276–7
Crawshay-Williams, Gillian *see* Greenwood, Jill
Crawshay-Williams, Olwen 39–40, 108
Criccieth 35, 37–9, 43–6, 105–6, 151, 225
croquet 67–8, 108
Crosland, T. W. H. 87–8
cultural capital 16–17
cultural memory approach 24–5
Curtis, Thomas Figgis 36–7
Cuthbertson, Guy 37–9, 70–2
Cymru Fydd 33–4, 262–3

Daily Worker 238–41
dairy trade 12–13, 111–12
Das, Santanu 2–3, 23
David, Anna 86
Davies, Christie 245–6
Davies, Elizabeth 35
Davies, George Maitland Lloyd 59, 63–4, 165–6, 248
Davies, Geraint 117–18, 135–7, 140
Davies, Gwen 136–8
Davies, Hazel 75
Davies, Idris 33
Davies, J. Glyn 60–2, 89
Davies, John 7–10, 12–13, 103, 111–12, 165–6
Davies, J. R. 19–20, 23, 97, 142–7, 171, 273–4

Davies, Morgan 117–18, 135–6, 138
Davies, Nan 260–1
Dean, Basil 258–60, 262–3
death as theme in writings 98–102
'deep Wales,' 223–4
de la Mare, Walter 70–1
Denbigh 46–7
Depression period 10, 48, 257–8
de Walden, Howard 195–6, 218–20, 253–4
de Walden, Margherita 219–21
diaspora *see also* Liverpool; London
    gendered diasporic initiatives in First World War 36–7
    identity formation 84–5
    isolation 96–7
    literature about 205–6
    Lloyd George as talisman 7–9, 37–9, 57–8
    returning to Wales to be buried 103
    Welsh diasporic space in England 10–14
    Welsh language 89–91
difference, sense of 86 *see also* second-generation identities
Dilworth, Thomas 37–9, 128–9
Dinas Dinlle 151
disestablishment 33–4, 49–50
Doan, Laura 48–9
Douglas-Pennant, Violet 48–9
drama 195, 214–21
drapery business 12–13, 64, 123–4, 186
dual identification
    15th (1st London Welsh), RWF 118–26
    Alex Cordell 226–8
    BBC 260
    both/and identities 2, 9
    definition of 84–5
    and dual language 6
    Edward Thomas 70–8
    English Welsh duality 15–16
    English Welsh subculture 9
    inherent transculturality 274–5
    lack of research on 2, 9
    second-generation identities 14–17
    soldier poets 56–7
    women 47–9
Duffy, Michael 87–8
Dunn, J. C. 119

Easthope, Hazel 14
education 61–2, 87–8
Edwards, John 122
Edwards, Meredith 253–4, 257–8
Edwards, O. M. 74–5, 128
Eisteddfodau
    Aberystwyth National 37–9

aristocracy 49–50
art exhibitions 204–5
    Birkenhead National 175–6
    Eliot Crawshay-Williams 45
    Ernest Thomas 79
    Gladstone at 34–5
    IGJ Memorial Shield 175–6
    J. R. Davies 142–3
    Lloyd George at 37–9
    London 53
    national drama movement 218–19
    Richard Hughes 216–17
elective Welshness 22, 245
Elias, Frank *see* Owen, John
Elias, William Owen 205–6
elites 49–57, 209–10, 274 *see also* aristocracy
Ellis, John S. 2–3, 23, 140, 165–6, 246–7, 270–1
Ellis, Steffan 56–7
Ellis, Thomas E. 33–4, 263
Elwes, Simon 155–6
Enfield, London 80–1
England, mythology of 22–3
England-Wales historical relationship 4–7
English language
    literary spaces 205–6
    Liverpool Welsh 90
    London Welsh 90
    middle-class suburbia 64
Englishness *see also* dual identification
    Edward Thomas 70–1, 76
    J. R. Davies 145–7
    porosity 22–3
    sense of English superiority 87–8
    and the suburb 60–1
    Welshness in contrast to 7–9, 272
English Review 76
English Welsh life writing 80–2
epigraphs 117, 174–5
evacuation 111–13, 168–70, 190–1, 207, 262–3
Evans, Caradoc 13–14, 64, 103
Evans, D. H. 12–13, 35
Evans, Ellis Humphrey *See* Hedd Wyn
Evans, Geoffrey Norris 155–6
Evans, Julian 81
Evans, Margiad 15–16, 87–8, 205–6, 208–11, 276–7
Evans, Mark 195–6
Evans, Myfanwy *see* Piper, Myfanwy
Evans, Neil 14
Evans, Olwen Carey (nee Lloyd George) 36–7, 43, 100–1
Evans, Thomas Carey 36–7, 157
Evans, Timothy 202
Evans, Trevor 111

Everton, Liverpool 60–1, 188–9
Ewenny Priory Estate 47
extended family 97, 103–4, 274–5 *see also* grandparents

Farjeon, Eleanor 76
fathers, Welsh 92–8, 153, 266
Felton, Mick 250–1, 256, 269–70
Ffrangcon-Davies, Gwen 19–20
filiation, narratives of 153–8
Finchley, London 67
Firbanks, Ronald 56–7
First World War 117–39, 275–6
　centenary celebrations 276–7
　conscientious objectors 165–6
　David Lloyd George 35, 37–9
　Edward Thomas 59, 76–8
　Evan Morgan 56–7
　gendered diasporic initiatives 36–7
　Howard de Walden 219–20
　identity formation 7–9
　memorials 172–91
　Owen Rhoscomyl 246–7
　Philipps family 55–6
　Robert Graves 232, 235–6
　soldier poets 56–7
　Viscount Clive 52–3, 172, 184–6
　William Glynne Charles Gladstone 172, 176–84
fluid conceptions of Welshness 28–9, 138–9, 191, 195–6, 270–1
folklore 70–1, 219–20
Ford, Harold 166–7
Ford, James 57–8, 191, 195–6
Foyles bookshop 255
Foyles Welsh Luncheon 48
Frame, Richard 226–8
Francis, J. O. 216–17
Franzese, Alexis T. 245–6
Fulham, London 81–2, 93
funerals 53, 78–80, 103, 157–8, 165, 172, 179–80, 182, 185–6, 218
'funk holes' 113
Fussell, Paul 151

Gaffney, Angela 7–9, 42
Garner, Steve 10
gendering dualities 47–9
Gilbert, David 60–1
Gilcriest, Margaret 86, 132–4, 223–4
Giles, Judy 7–9, 22–3, 77–8
Gilfach Goch 254–5
Gill, Eric 202–3
Gilleman, Luc 93
Gladstone, Gertrude 176–7, 179–84

Gladstone, Henry Neville 45, 181
Gladstone, Herbert John (Viscount) 176–81, 183
Gladstone, Maud 45
Gladstone, William Ewart 34–5, 62–3, 176, 181
Gladstone, William Glynne Charles 172, 176–84
Gladstone family 45
Glamorgan Gazette 42–3
Glyndŵr, Owain 5–6, 47, 195–6, 232, 246–7
Glyn-Jones, Hildreth 90
Goodbye To All That (Graves, 1929) 119, 227, 231–2, 240
Gothic literature 98–9
Gramich, Katie 1–2
grandparents
　Alex Cordell 226–8
　Augustus John 198–9
　Diana Wynne Jones 112–13
　Dilys Powell 95
　Edward Thomas 95–6, 104
　importance of Welsh family 84–98, 273
　Jill Greenwood 108–10
　John Herbertson 23, 94–5
　John Osborne 81–2, 95–6
　Myfanwy Piper 105
　Myfanwy Thomas 67–8, 78–9
　Naomi Royde-Smith 104, 248
　Owen Rhoscomyl 246–7
　Richard Llewellyn 254, 265–6, 268
Graves, Alfred 37–9, 214, 219–20, 231
Graves, Charles 212–13, 216
Graves, David 222–3, 236–44
Graves, Jenny 238, 242–3
Graves, Philip 241–2
Graves, Richard Perceval 100
Graves, Robert 21, 37–9, 51, 118–19, 135, 178, 213–14, 222–3, 226–8, 231–44, 277–8
Graves, Rosaleen 213, 231
Graves, Sam 239, 242
Greenwood, Jill 84, 97–8, 107–11
Greenwood, Tony 110
Griffiths, Bruce 134–5
Griffiths, Idris 136–8
Griffiths, Joseph 254
Griffiths, Teifion 254
Griffiths, Will 255
Grove St Welsh Congregational Chapel 189–90
Gunn, Simon 60–1
Gweithdy Bach 233–4
Gwili (preacher-bard) 74–5
Gwynedd, Owain 21, 155, 157
Gwynfryn School 74, 78–9
Gwynne, Patrick 19–20, 97–8
Gwynne-Jones, Allan 19–20, 130, 200–5
Gwynne-Jones, Emily 200, 202
Gwynn Jones, T. 253–5

Hague, René 69, 127, 202–3
Hajkowski, Thomas 256–7, 260–1
Halfway House, The (film, 1944) 6–7
Hapgood, Lynne 59, 71–2
Happy-Go-Lucky Morgans, The (Thomas, 1913) 26–7, 71–3, 224–5
Harlech 197, 204–5, 213, 216, 219–20, 222–3, 226–8, 231–6
Harmsworth, Cecil 48–9
Harris, John 64, 251, 256–7
Hawarden estate 34–5, 45, 176–83
Hawarden Parish Magazine 178, 182–3
headstone inscriptions 117, 125–6, 175–6, 243
healing, Wales as site of 222–3, 277–8
Hedd Wyn 174–6, 277
Heilpern, John 93
Herbertson, John 9, 23, 90, 94–5, 97–8, 103–4, 278–9
Herson, John 16–17, 84–5
Heseltine, Nigel 15–16, 129–30, 208
Hesse, David 228
Hibberd, Dominic 88–9, 135
Hickman, Mary J. 15–16, 146–7
Hinds, John 117–18, 123–5
Hinds, William Pugh 117–18, 123–6, 172
hiraeth 17–18, 26, 57, 73, 146–7
holidays in Wales 43, 46–7, 74, 78, 84, 92, 94–5, 104–8, 131–2, 136–7, 158–9, 197–8, 200, 248, 264–5, 269, 273–4
Holroyd, Michael 197–9
Home Rule 33–4, 62–3, 77–8
Honourable Society of Cymmrodorion 12–13
Hooker, Jeremy 20, 74, 126–7, 129–30, 205–6, 273
Hopkins, Chris 256
Hore-Belisha, Leslie 141–2
Horner, Libby 187–8
How Green Was My Valley (Llewellyn, 1939) 144, 166–7, 245–6, 250–1, 253–4, 256–64, 266, 270–1
Hughes, Arthur 195–6
Hughes, Cledwyn 204–5
Hughes, Penelope 216, 218
Hughes, Richard 20, 91–2, 99–100, 111–12, 195, 202, 205–6, 212–18, 220–1, 242, 276–7
Hughes, Robert Elistan Glodrydd 91–2
Huws, Daniel 224–5
Huxley, Aldous 168–9
hybridity *see also* dual identification
    Ernest Rhys 205–6
    J. R. Davies 146–7
    Liverpool Welsh regiment 152
    and mobility 14
    second-generation identities 14–17
hyphenated identities 15–16

identity construction 3–4, 7–9, 12–13, 84–5
'imagined communities,' 12–13
imagined nation, Wales as 135, 144–5, 147–8, 195–221, 273
imperialism 4–5, 22, 65–6
Imperial War Graves Commission 164, 174–5, 181
    See Commonwealth War Graves Commission
Imperial War Museum 24–5, 142–3, 166–7, 228–9 *see also* Commonwealth War Graves Commission
'imperial Welshness,' 121–2
Innes, James Dickson 200, 202
In Parenthesis (Jones, 1937) 38, 117–18, 123, 127, 129–30, 276–7
Irish Home Rule 34–5, 181
Islington, London 60–1
isolation 96–7

Jefferies, Richard 75
Jenkins, Elis 75
Jenkins, John *see* Gwili (preacher-bard)
John, Angela V. 26, 47
John, Augustus 195, 197–202, 221
John, Caspar 197–9
John, David 197–9
John, Edward T. 118–19, 172–6
John, Edwin 197–9
John, Iorwerth Glyndwr 118–19, 172–6
John, Rebecca 197–9
John, Romilly 105–6, 197–200
Johnes, Martin 4–9, 12–13, 111–12, 145, 250
Jolly, Margaretta 142–3
Jones, Aled 4–5
Jones, Bill 4–5
Jones, Diana Wynne 111–13
Jones, David 15–18, 21, 37–9, 59, 68–9, 117–18, 123, 126–30, 202–3, 217, 256–7, 273–7
Jones, Emrys 11, 103
Jones, Ernest 92–3
Jones, Glyn 205–6, 256–7
Jones, Gwyn 209–10
Jones, Gwynfor 4–5
Jones, Jack 48, 254, 257–8
Jones, J Graham 39–40
Jones, Mervyn 84–5, 92, 100–1
Jones, Peter 12–13
Jones, Rhŷs 128
Jones, R. Merfyn 11, 13–14, 16–17, 61–4, 264–5
Jones, Thomas 249–50

Kemsley, Lord 141–2
Kenny, Kevin 2–3
King, Anthony 140–1
Kirkdale, Liverpool 23, 90, 279

292   INDEX

Kuchta, Todd 68–9
Kumar, Krishan 4–5, 7–9, 22–3, 49–50

"Land of My Fathers," 21, 140, 152–3, 264, 270
Larkin, Philip 76
Laugharne Castle 218, 224–5, 242
Leatham, 'Chicot,' 155–6
letters, as sources 25, 143
Lewis, Eiluned 211–12
Lewis, Ludwig 122–3, 134–5
Lewis, Norman 19–20, 59, 67–8, 80–2, 91, 101–4, 274–5
Lewis, Saunders 18–19, 59, 67–8, 86, 117–18, 122–3, 131–5, 223–4, 253–4
Liddell Hart, Basil 238–42
liminality 60, 83, 104, 205, 248–9, 258–9, 274–5
literary spaces, English Welsh 205–7
Liverpolitan 61
Liverpool
   area of Wales migrants came from 11
   Augustus John 197–8
   building industry 12–13
   cosmopolitanism 10
   evacuation 111–12
   Gertrude Alice Williams 188–9
   Irish population 10, 62–3
   John Herbertson 9, 23, 90, 94–5, 97–8, 103–4, 278–9
   John Owen 205–6
   Liverpool Welsh and Welsh identity 13–14
   middle-class suburbia 59, 63–4, 67, 165–6
   proximity to North Wales 97–8
   research into Welsh diaspora 11
   social mobility of Welsh diaspora 61–2
   'street memorial,' 205–6
   war memorials 189–90
   Welsh Army Corps (WAC) 121–2
Liverpool Echo 61, 147–8, 152–3
Liverpool Welsh National Society 11
Llandudno 105–6, 121–2, 129
Llangollen Advertiser 52–3
Llewellyn, Richard 19–20, 22, 29, 91, 94–5, 155–6, 209–10, 245–6, 250–71, 276–8
Lloyd, Dorice 97–8, 105–6, 225
Lloyd, Jack 43–5
Lloyd, Lorna Llewellyn 251–3, 264–5, 269–70
Lloyd, Rachel 225
Lloyd, Richard *see* Llewellyn, Richard
Lloyd, Selwyn 18–19, 39–40, 43–7, 88–9, 105–6, 205–6, 222–3, 225
Lloyd, William Llewellyn 251–3, 264, 266, 269–70
Lloyd George, David 18–19, 33–50, 57–8, 70–1, 87–8, 117–22, 124–6, 141–2, 157–8, 189–90, 222–3, 248–9, 274

Lloyd George, Gwilym 6, 36–7, 43–4, 121–2, 141–2
Lloyd George, Mair Eluned 36, 100–1
Lloyd George, Margaret 36–7, 46
Lloyd George, Megan 36–9, 43–6
Lloyd George, Olwen *see* Evans, Olwen Carey
Lloyd George, Owen 90, 155–8
Lloyd George, Richard 35–7, 121–2, 157
Lloyd-Morgan, Ceridwen 208–9
Llywelyn, Jen 63–4
London
   15th (1st London Welsh), RWF 9, 36–7, 117–30, 153, 275–6
   area of Wales migrants came from 11
   chapels 64–5
   cosmopolitanism 10, 60–1
   diaspora 62, 64–5
   evacuation 111–12
   Lloyd George family 35–7
   performative Welshness 13–14
   Richard Llewellyn 251–3
   suburbia 60–1
   trades of Welsh immigrants 12–13
   Welsh language 89
London Welsh Association 35–7, 113, 142
London Welsh Battalion Committee 119–23
London Welsh Centre 65–6
London Welshman and Kelt 13–14, 122–3
London Welsh Nationalist Society 123–4
London Welsh Regimental Association 189–90
Longley, Edna 68–9, 77
Lord, Peter 126–7, 195, 202
Lorimer, Robert 188–9
Lusty, Robert 253–4, 257–8

Mabinogion 70–1, 74, 91–2, 204–5, 241–2
Machen Arthur 229–30
MacRaild, Donald M. 4–5, 11–13
Manchester 11, 18, 35, 121, 246–9
marginality 73, 81
martial race ideology 121–2
Martin-Jones, Enid 90, 97–8, 104
masking 245–71
material culture 97–8, 272
Matthews, Jodie 222
Matthews-Jones, Lucinda 148–9
McCartney, Helen 142
McCrone, David 84–5
McKennal, Bertram 172–4
McNeill, Dorelia 105–6, 197–8
Meifod 111–12, 158–61, 164
memorials 125–6, 158, 164, 172–91, 273, 275–6
memories of the dead 98–102
'Men of Harlech,' 105, 120–1

Meredeen, Sander 248–50
middle class experience 3, 26, 43, 59–64, 119, 132, 142, 197
Middlesbrough 11, 118–19, 173–4, 265–6
Middleton, Tim 7–9, 22–3, 77–8
migration
 and diaspora 2–3 *see also* diaspora
 second-generation identities 14–17
 Second World War 113
mixed marriages 84–5, 147–8
Montgomeryshire County Times 184–5
Moore-Wood, Gladys 252, 269–70
Morfa Bychan 248–9
Morgan, Charles 205–6, 211–12, 276–7
Morgan, Clare 209–11
Morgan, Evan 56–7
Morgan, Gwenda 1, 102
Morgan, Owen 102
Morgan, Prys 12–13, 87–8
Morley, Joel 153
Morris, Jan 84–5, 244
Morse-Brown, Sydney 276–7
Morton, H. V. 22–3, 87–8
Mostyn, Lord 11
Mostyn, Pyers George Joseph 50–2, 118
Mostyn, Pyers (Sir) 51
Mostyn family 45–6, 50–1
mothers, Welsh 92–5, 169, 265–6
Moulton, Mo 22–3, 66, 146–7, 272
mountains 93, 105–6, 135, 199–200, 209–10, 222–4, 229, 231–4, 248, 266, 273, 277–8
mourning 172–91
MPs
 David Lloyd George 35, 57–8
 Edith Picton-Turbervill 48–9
 Edward Clement Davies 4–5, 158–9
 Edward T. John 118–19, 172–6
 Eliot Crawshay-Williams 39–40
 interests of Wales 33–4
 John Hinds 123–4
 Selwyn Lloyd 43
 memorials to sons of 172–4
 William Glynne Charles Gladstone 176–7
Muir, Edwin 256–7
Murray, Tony 24

naming practices 84–5, 91–2, 197–8
narrating the self 23–5
Nash, Margaret 76
Nash, Paul 76
Nath, Keshav 96
National Library of Wales 5, 121–2, 158–9, 276–7
National Museum of Wales 5, 127, 188–9, 195–6, 202–5, 276–7

National Pageants 53–5, 219–20, 246–7
Neo-Romanticism 210–11, 222
Nettleship, Ida 197–8
Newlyn, Lucy 73, 75
Newman, Greatorex 258–9
Newport 56–7, 81–2, 93, 133
Newtown 106, 166–7
Nicholson, Hazel 169–70
Nicholson, Nancy 213, 235, 238
Nid â'n Ango 174–5
nonconformist chapels 12–13, 63–5
North Wales Chronicle 172–4
nostalgia 96, 133–4, 144–7, 273

obituaries 36–7, 55–6, 111–12, 117–18, 137, 248–9
Offa's Dyke 14, 86–7
O'Leary, Paul 7–9, 182
On Target 142
Osborne, John 59, 81–2, 93, 95–6, 100–2, 274–5
Oswestry 88–9, 204–5, 226–8
'otherness'
 Diana Wynne Jones 112
 Edward Thomas 75
 John family 199–200
 Lloyd George family 36–7
 Margiad Evans 210–11
 Richard Llewellyn 256
 romance of 17–18
outsider status 19–21, 80–2, 86, 97, 154, 210, 212–13, 229–30, 244, 248–9, 259–60, 274–5
Owen, Alun 154–5
Owen, Harold 88–9, 135
Owen, John 19–20, 97–8, 101, 205–6
Owen, M. M. 88–9
Owen, Morfydd Llwyn 39–40
Owen, Tomos 13–14, 33, 140–1
Owen, Wilfred 37–9, 88–9, 117–18, 135, 205–6, 226–8
Owen, Owen W. 117
Owen Owen 37–9, 121–2
Oxford 10–11, 75

pacifism 140, 165–9, 229, 275–6
Pantheon of National Heroes 195–6
Park Road Welsh Congregational Chapel 189–90
pastorality 93, 223–4, 233–5
patrilineal ties 21, 92–8, 127–8, 140, 153–7, 226–8
Payton, Philip 4–5, 21, 229–30
Peace Pledge Union 168–9, 207
Peers Memorial, Westminster 187–8
Pembrokeshire 53–6, 105, 154, 188–9, 202–3, 251–2

Peniston-Bird, Corinna 238–9
Pennell, Catriona 7–9
'performative' Welshness 13–14
personal narratives/biography 23–5
Petts, John 222–3, 228–30, 244, 277–8
philanthropy 36–7, 48, 53–5
Philipps, Colwyn 55–7
Philipps, John Wynford (Viscount St Davids) 53–6
Philipps, Leonora 53–5
Philipps, Roland 53–5
Pickles, Katie 147–8
Picton-Turbervill, Edith 47–9
Pill, Malcolm 65
Piper, Myfanwy 21–2, 97, 105, 229–30
place names 41–2
Plaid Cymru 12–13, 59, 66, 131, 170
Plas Brondanw 111–12, 130–1, 155, 158, 214
Plas Coed-y-Mwstwr 39, 84, 98, 107–11
Plas Dyffryn 158–61
Plas Newydd 220–1, 253–4, 257–8
Plas-y-Bryn 106
pluralist identities 123–4, 126, 130, 139, 147, 251, 271
Plymouth, Lord 119–21
poetry
    autobiographical writing 55–6, 68–9
    'claiming poets for Wales,' 276–7
    Colwyn Philipps 55–7
    David Jones 126–30
    Edward Thomas 76–8, 276–7
    Eliot Crawshay-Williams 41–2
    Evan Morgan 56–7
    John Betjeman 21–2, 229–30
    Margiad Evans 209–10
    'nightingales of Wales,' 56–7
    Robert Graves 222–3, 231–44
    soldier poets 56–7
Polezzi, Loredana 26–7, 68–9, 250–1, 274–5
Pontarddulais 74–5, 93, 111–12
Pooley, Colin 11–13
Porthmadog 106
Portmadoc Players 214
Powell, Anthony 2–3, 20, 153–5, 205, 209–10, 273
Powell, Dilys 19–20, 67, 86, 91–2, 95–9, 102, 106
Powell, Enoch 17–18
Powis, Earl of 52, 184–6
Powis Castle Estate 184–6
Powys, John Cowper 20
Poynter, Edward 195–6
Preston, Rebecca 60–1
Priestley, J. B. 22–3
Princes Road chapel, Liverpool 62–4

Pryce-Jones, Adrian 155–6
Prys-Williams, Barbara 208–11, 273–4
Pygmalion (Shaw, 1912) 87–8

Queen's Hall address (Lloyd George, 1914) 37–9, 119–21
Quennell, Peter 91, 258–60
Quinault, Ronald 34–5

racialized 'others,' 10, 17–18
racial prejudice 86, 88–9
Radding, Cynthia 15–16
Readman, Paul 15–16
Recording Angel 172–6, 184, 191
'Recording Britain,' 222
Rees, D Ben 11
refuge, Wales as 3, 29, 111–13, 166, 223–6, 233–5, 244, 277–8
regiments *see also* Royal Welch Fusiliers (RWF); Welsh Guards
    Artists' Rifles 76, 78–9, 136–7
    Leicestershire Royal Horse Artillery (TF) Battery 41–2
    King's Liverpool Regiment 133
    46th (Liverpool Welsh) RTR 9, 25, 140, 147–53, 275–6
    99th (London Welsh) HAA 9, 140–2, 147, 275–6
    Manchester Regiment 117–18
    South Wales Borderers 117–18, 133–4, 173–4, 223–4
    Welch Regiment 21, 153
'return' movement 3, 190
Rhondda 48, 226–8
Rhoscomyl, Owen (Lt. Col. Arthur Vaughan) 22, 218, 245–7, 270–1
Rhys, Ernest 60–1, 205–6, 219–20
Rhys, Keidrych 255–7
Richards, Jeffrey 260
Robbins, Keith 7–9, 14, 17–18, 208
Roberts, A. O. 214
Roberts, Ben 185–6
Roberts, Dennis 189–90
Roberts, Glyn 11, 62–3, 65, 88–9, 211–12, 217, 272
Roberts, Lynette 231
Roberts, O. E. 147–8
Roberts, Peggy (Margaret) 23–4, 67–8, 84–5, 88–9, 92–3, 105, 167–8
Roberts-Jones, Ivor 91–2, 202–5, 276–7
Roberts-Jones, Mervyn 91–2
romanticization of Wales 21–2, 47, 59, 108, 140, 233–4, 246–7, 277–8
Rose, Sonya O. 7–9

Ross-on-Wye 208–9
Royal Welch Fusiliers (RWF)
    5th Battalion 118–19
    15th (1st London Welsh) Battalion 9, 36–7, 117–30, 138–9, 275–6
    18th (2nd London Welsh) Battalion 121–2
    David Graves 236–40, 243–4
    James Venmore 117
    memorials 189–90
    Robert Graves 178, 222–3, 232–3, 236, 243–4
    Pyers George Joseph Mostyn 50–2, 118
    William Glynne Charles Gladstone 178–80, 182
Royde-Smith, Leslie 165–6, 248
Royde-Smith, Naomi 22, 68, 94–5, 100–1, 104, 208, 223–5, 245–8
Ruck, Berta 20
rugby 6, 65, 142–3, 145, 158–9
rural landscapes 59, 69, 73, 138, 210–11 *see also* mountains

Samuel, Raphael 17–18
Sassoon, Siegfried 51, 119, 135, 222–3, 232–4
Schwabe, Gwendolyn Rosamund 'Birdie,' 200–2
Schwabe, Randolph 200–2
Scots Guards 52, 186, 201
Scott, Giles Gilbert 182–3
Scottish National War Memorial 188–9
Scouting 53–5
Scully, Marc 15–16, 126, 250–1, 256–7, 270–1
second-generation identities
    alienation 86–7, 274–5
    chapel attendance 64–5
    definition of 14–17, 84–5
    difference, sense of 15, 20, 27, 40, 84–92
    functioning of dual identities 14–17
    naming practices 91–2
    Welsh language 64–5
Second World War 140–71, 275–6
    Anthony Powell 153–5
    Clement Davies family 158–65
    David Graves 236–40
    evacuation 111–13
    How Green Was My Valley (1939) 256–7
    identity construction 7–9
    memorials 189–91
    Richard Llewellyn 250–1, 258–9, 263, 270–1
    Robert Graves 236–43
    Welsh regiments 237–8
Senedd (National Assembly for Wales) 7
servants 36, 67–8, 107–8, 231
Seymour, Miranda 233–4, 241–2
Shakespeare, William 87–8

Shaw, George Bernard 87–8
Shaw, Phyllida 188–9
Shrewsbury 208, 223, 226–8
Shrewsbury House, Liverpool 148–52, 171
siblings 24, 67, 78–80, 85, 92, 98–9, 168, 171, 197–200, 218, 252–3
Silverstone, Roger 60
Simpson, Keith 119
Smith, Dai 250–1, 256
Snowdonia 105–6, 131, 144, 157, 229, 231
South Wales and Newport Argus 95–6
Spadaro, Barbara 26–7, 68–9, 250–1, 274–5
Spanish influenza 78–9
split identities 84–5, 90 *see also* dual identification; hybridity
St Basil's Church, Bassaleg 188–9
St David 119, 188, 195–6
St David's (city) 188, 251, 253, 263–5, 267–8
St David's Day 6, 36–7, 43, 62, 130, 144–5, 150–1, 157, 226–7, 236, 242
Stephens, Meic 250–1
stereotyping 27, 87–8, 96, 113, 151–2, 216, 258–9
Stevenson, Frances 120–1, 124–5
Streets, Heather 121–2
subjectivities, English Welsh 7, 17–23, 83, 113, 140, 272
suburbia 59–83, 165–6, 274–5
Summerfield, Penny 23–4, 166–7
surnames as carriers of identity 92
Swansea 134–5, 188, 203

Talacre, Flintshire 50–2
Taliesin 241–2
temperance 36–7, 63–4
Teng, Emma Jinhua 16–17, 25
Thomas, Bronwen 91–2, 95
Thomas, Dylan 229
Thomas, Edward 17–18, 22–3, 27, 37–9, 59, 64–5, 67–80, 87–8, 91–3, 95–7, 104, 217, 222–3, 273–7
Thomas, Elizabeth Townsend 70, 74, 93
Thomas, Ernest 78–9
Thomas, James Havard 195–6
Thomas, Julian 37–9, 72, 78–80
Thomas, Lucy 84–5, 234
Thomas, Mervyn 91–2, 104–5
Thomas, M. Wynn 15–16, 53–5, 57–8, 120–1, 208, 246–7
Thomas, Myfanwy 67–8, 73, 78–9, 91–2, 95
Thomas, Oscar 78–9
Thomas, Philip Henry 37, 70, 77–8
Thomas, Reggie 74, 78–80
Thomas, R. George 71–2, 75, 77–8, 96

Thomas, Theodore 72, 78–9, 96
Thompson, F. M. L. 60
Thomson, Alistair 23–4
Tomb of the Unknown Warrior 189–90
transcultural subjects 68–9, 80–1, 274–5
transnational landed families 33, 39–40, 49–57, 185, 274
Travers, Daniel 9
'Treason of the Blue Books (1847),' 5–6, 87–8
Tseëlon, Efrat 245–6
Tudor, Harold 61, 147–8

Undeb Cymru Fydd 147–8
University of Wales 5
upper class experience *see* aristocracy; transnational landed families

Vale of Glamorgan 42, 47–8
Valley of Bones, The (Powell, 1964) 21, 154
Vaughan, Hilda 211–12, 234–5
Venmore, James 117, 174–5
visits back to Wales 103–7 *see also* holidays in Wales
Von Rothkirch, Alyce 216–17, 220–1

Walham Green, London 60–1
Walter, Bronwen 2, 15–16, 84–5
Wandsworth, London 67–8, 70–2
Ward, Paul 6–9, 36–7
Ware, Fabian 181
war memorials 125–6, 172–91
Wasson, Sara 98–9
Watts, G. F. 195–6
Waugh, Evelyn 20
Webb, Andrew 70–1, 276–7
Welsh Army Corps (WAC) 117, 121–2, 246–7
Welsh Arts Council 203–5
Welsh Baptist Chapel, East Castle St, London 36–7
Welsh Calvinist Methodist Church, Bootle 189–90
Welsh Gazette 137
Welsh Gothic 98–9
Welsh Guards
  Allan Gwynne-Jones 131, 201–2
  Christopher Moelwyn Strachey Williams-Ellis 155, 274
  Clough Williams-Ellis 130–1
  Evan Morgan 56–7
  First World War 130–1
  Geraint Clement Davies 161–3
  Richard Llewellyn 258–9, 262–70
  Roland Philipps 53–5

Second World War 140, 155–8
Viscount Clive 52–3, 184–6
Welsh Half Hour (BBC) 144–5
Welsh language
  anti-Welsh prejudice 87–9
  BBC 144–5, 260
  border counties 208
  chapels 12–13, 16–17
  David Jones 127
  David Lloyd George 35
  depictions in literature 154–5
  Diana Wynne Jones 112–13
  diaspora 12–13, 89–90
  Eliot Crawshay-Williams 39–40, 276–7
  George Henry Borrow 222
  headstone inscriptions 117, 174–6
  Hedd Wyn as symbol of Welsh language identity 175–6
  How Green Was My Valley (1939) 255
  John Betjeman 229–30
  lessons in 131, 133, 136–7, 160, 166, 213
  Naomi Royde-Smith 248
  newspapers 12–14
  non-Welsh-speaking Welsh 12–13, 90
  Owen Rhoscomyl 246–7
  in English language plays 215–17
  Richard Llewellyn 266
  Saunders Lewis 132–5
  second-generation identities 12–13, 16–17
  secrets in 16–17, 87–91
  reluctance to use 89–90
  and Welsh nationalism 134–5
Welsh martiality 55, 121–2, 126, 140–1, 147–8, 262–3, 275–6
Welsh nationalism 18–19, 66, 123–4, 131, 134–5, 165–6, 170
Welsh National Opera 276–7
Welsh National Theatre 216–21, 253–4
Welsh Outlook 55–6, 195–6, 233
Welshpool 163, 185–6
Welsh Presbyterian Chapel, Clapham Junction 36–7
Welsh Review 256
Welsh Societies 12–13, 136, 144–5, 177
Welsh Troops' Service Club, London 36–7
West Baptist Chapel, Castle St 36, 125–6
West Derby, Liverpool 60–1, 117
Western Mail 216–17, 265–6
West Kirby 43, 97–8
Westminster, Palace of 4–6, 33–5, 57–8, 172–3, 187–8, 191, 196 *see also* MPs
Westminster Abbey 189–90
Whistler, Peggy *see* Evans, Margiad

Whistler, Rex 155–6
White Goddess, The (Graves, 1948) 222–3, 241–3
Williams, Arthur John 39–40
Williams, Chris 4–7, 12–13, 33–4, 123, 165–6
Williams, Daniel G. 5, 64, 256
Williams, Emlyn 87–8
Williams, Gertrude Alice 188–9, 191
Williams, Howell J. 65
Williams, Hugh 155–6
Williams, Ifanwy 64–5, 67, 97, 167–70
Williams, J. Mervyn 64–8, 88–9
Williams, Kyffin 202–5
Williams, Morris Meredith 188–9
Williams, Raymond 208, 273
Williams, William Emrys 18–20, 22, 245–6, 248–50
Williams-Ellis, Amabel 131, 214
Williams-Ellis, Christopher Moelwyn Strachey 155, 158

Williams-Ellis, Clough 111–12, 130–1, 155, 158, 202, 214, 218, 221, 274, 276–7
Wilson, A. N. 229–30
Wilson, Jean Moorcroft 70–1, 232–3
Wiltshire 71, 73, 75
Windsor-Clive, Archer 120–1
women
   gendered diasporic initiatives 36–7
   gendering dualities 47–9
   women's suffrage 53–5
Women's Royal Air Force (WRAF) 48–9
Women's Voluntary Service (WVS) 160
Woodward, Owen Leonard 189–90
working class experience 3, 25, 67–8, 148–51, 246, 256, 273, 278–9
Wrexham 37–9, 165–6, 178–9, 182, 219
Wyburn-Powell, Alun 158–9, 161

Y Brython 136, 189–90
Y Ddolen 36–7, 113, 141–2, 165–6